Alastair McIntosh is an independent writer, broadcaster, speaker and activist who is involved in a wide range of inter-connected issues, from land reform, globalization and nonviolence to psychology, spirituality and ecology. He is the author of the bestselling *Soil and Soul: People versus Corporate Power*, described by George Monbiot as 'a world-changing book' and *Hell and High Water: Climate Change, Hope and the Human Condition*, described by the former Archbishop of Canterbury, Rowan Williams, as 'inspiration'.

'*Poacher's Pilgrimage* is a book of beautifully compacted writing – clear, strong and constantly surprising – a fortnight's walk that contains a universe.'

Nick Hunt, *Dark Mountain*

'This is as much a journey into an unusual mind as it is about the Island.'

Madeleine Bunting, *Resurgence*

'A journey of people, history, geography and the deeper understanding of the connection between religion and nature.'

Lynne McNeil, *Life and Work*

'Much more than a nature book, he considers how religion, faeries and geology have shaped our history, politics, science, spirituality and imagination.'

Toby Clark, *John Muir Trust Journal*

'What engages him is a deep search – not unlike the vision quest of native Americans – that a whole culture has lost and needs to rediscover.'

Jim Griffin, *Beshara Magazine*

'The language is almost poetic, reflecting the writer's artistic gifts and his understanding of Celtic and pre-Celtic culture.'

David Thomson, *Press & Journal*

'*Poacher's Pilgrimage* is a book full of generosity, spry in its thinking and detailed in its observations. It will beguilingly give each reader a lot to think about, a lot to wish to see, and a lot to think about again.'

Stuart Kelly, *Scotland on Sunday*

'I've learned so much from it . . . warmth, humour, passion.'

Cameron McNeish, *Scots Magazine*

'Alastair McIntosh is already established as one of Scotland's greatest living authors . . . I read this book in the immediate aftermath of the Brexit vote and the Chilcot report into the UK's involvement in the Iraq war. Writing prior to these events, his reflections on a leader's "political paranoia", living out the myth of redemptive violence, seem prophetic. McIntosh, while immersed in the folk traditions and religious gravity of the Western Isles, simultaneously speaks to us about the most contemporary and pressing of issues.'

John Sturrock QC, *Progressive Voices*

'McIntosh uses a twelve-day walk across the length of Harris and Lewis, where he grew up, as the basis for an extended reflection on three things: violence, the theology which is complicit with it, and the way to deal with it; the ecology of the imagination; and the spirituality of place. All three are interconnected, and all bear on a world torn apart by rage . . . What the book challenges us to do is to find the locus of the holy inscribed in the places in which we live. This is a poetically imagined, politically engaged, narrative theology which illuminatingly tackles some of the deepest problems of our world.'

Professor Timothy Gorringe, *Theology*

'And here we come to what I mean about a good travel writer needing to have a mind worth following as well as an itinerary. McIntosh is good at this. For the last 19 years he's been a Quaker devil's advocate at the British Army's officer training college. Although we aren't given the names of the top brass, he is allowed to write about their discussions and does so in his book. They're fascinating.'

David Robinson, *Books from Scotland*

'This is a lovely book, a book to savour, a book to give – remarkable and unusual in its deep knowledge and its spiritual versatility.'

Bishop David Chillingworth, *Church Times*

'A quite wonderful book – a theology of justice and peace and love re-presented through human ecology. It's also wonderfully funny. I have friends and family who are keen walkers and pilgrims. Their journeys, by and large, are well-equipped, challenging and often very long. Mostly they don't get lost. I mean no disrespect to Alastair in saying that his is not one of these kind of walks. He takes twelve days to walk about sixty miles. He loses his way frequently. He fails to achieve one of his main stated objectives of poaching a fish from one of the island lochs. And he fights an epic battle with a Bog Monster.'

Rev. Kathy Galloway, *Iona Community Coracle*

'At times I found it a very frustrating work. He comes so close – and yet stays so far away – from the truth of the Bible. Nonetheless, this is a superb book from a fine and sensitive man.'

Rev. David Robertson, *Free Church Record*

'If this sounds more serious than a Presbyterian church service, there is great fun to be found in *Poacher's Pilgrimage*. McIntosh is an entertaining subversive.'

Nick Major, *The National*

'I am fascinated, if perhaps a little overwhelmed, by the depth of his philosophy. His honesty is humbling, punctuated with humour, laughter and a twinkle. He never skirts a question, is on a mission, and having been Scotland's first professor of human ecology, he seems at times prophetic.'

Polly Pullar, *Scottish Field*

'I read many of the chapters by the fire in the evening, occasionally with a glass of good whisky to hand.'

Dr David Lorimer,
Journal of the Scientific & Medical Network

Poacher's Pilgrimage

An Island Journey

Alastair McIntosh

BIRLINN

This edition first published in 2018 by
Birlinn Limited
West Newington House
10 Newington Road
Edinburgh
EH9 1QS

First published in hardback in 2016

www.birlinn.co.uk

ISBN 978 1 78027 468 3

British Library Cataloguing in Publication Data
A catalogue record for this book is
available from the British Library.

Designed and typeset by Hewer Text UK Ltd

Printed and bound by MBM Print SCS Ltd, Glasgow

MIX
Paper from
responsible sources
FSC® C117931
FSC
www.fsc.org

To the late Catherine MacKinven of
the Knapdale MacKinvens, Argyll,
tradition bearer, dear mentor:
le gach beannachd
mile taìng

And of the upcoming generation, to my dear
daughter, Catriona, with Kevin,
and to Finley, their
wee one:
bless

Contents

PART 3

Hare

List of Illustrations

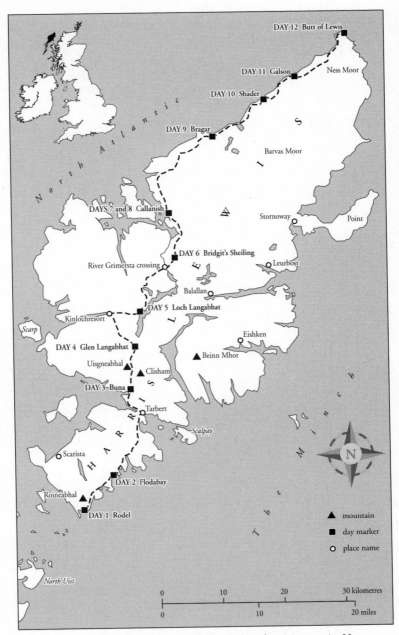

DAY 12 Butt of Lewis

Ness Moor

DAY 11 Galson

DAY 10 Shader

DAY 9 Bragar

Barvas Moor

North Atlantic

L E W I S

DAYS 7 and 8 Callanish

Stornoway

Point

DAY 6 Bridgit's Sheiling

River Grimersta crossing

Leurbost

Balallan

DAY 5 Loch Langabhat

Kinlochresort

Scarp

Eishken

DAY 4 Glen Langabhat

Beinn Mhor

Uisgneabhal

Clisham

DAY 3 Buna

Tarbert

H A R R I S

Scalpay

The Minch

Scarista

DAY 2 Flodabay

Roineabhal

DAY 1 Rodel

North Uist

N

▲ mountain

■ day marker

○ place name

0		10		20		30 kilometres
0			10			20 miles

The Isles of Lewis and Harris: Trail of the Blue Mountain Hare

An Tobar ('The Well')

Tha tobar beag am meadhon a' bhaile
's am feur ga fhalach . . .

Resting in the village there's a little well
and the grass hides it,
green grass in sap closely thatching it.
I heard of it from an old woman
But she said: 'The path is overgrown with bracken
where often I walked with my pail
and the pail itself is warped.'
When I looked in her lined face
I saw the bracken growing round the well of her eyes,
and hiding it from seeking and from desires,
and closing it, closing it.

'Nobody goes to that well now,'
said the old woman, 'as we once went,
when we were young,
though its water is lovely and white.'
And when I looked in her eyes through the bracken
I saw the sparkle of that water
that makes whole every hurt
till the hurt of the heart.

'And will you go there for me,'
said the old woman, 'even with a thimble,
and bring me a drop of that hard water
that will bring colour to my cheeks.'
I found the well at last,
and though her need was not the greatest
it was to her I brought the treasure.

It may be that the well
is something I saw in a dream,
for today when I went to seek it
I found only bracken and rushes,
and the old woman's eyes are closed
and a film has come over their merriment.

By kind permission of the island bard,
Professor Derick Thomson, granted
shortly before his passing in 2012.
His translation, Gaelic original.

BEGINNINGS

I have a pocket compass on my desk. It is the simple sort that many of us kept as children, the kind for which the natural play is not damped down by viscous liquid like you have today inside more fancy models. When laid upon a map the needle swings and dances, for up to a minute, as it slowly settles to the steady pull of north.

We human beings, likewise. We too need time and times in which to settle our souls' compass. We too are pulled by north, and at the deepest level, I suppose that's why I set out on this pilgrimage.

It was back in 2009 and I was in my mid fifties. For several years before embarking, I had felt the island's winnowing call. Felt it tugging, like an umbilical cord that ran beneath the sea. The journey was an answer to that call, but it didn't end there. Ever since, the walk has kept on walking in my mind, and this chronicle describes the action, but as deepened by seven years of subsequent reflection.

I say, and will continue to say, 'the island', as if this land that lies some thirty miles west from off the northern Scottish coast is a single entity. However, you'll get an insight into the psychology of the place, on learning that this is where they give you two islands for the price of one. Lewis, where I was raised and the most populous part, is the low-lying expanse of waterways and shallow hills that slip down to the north. Harris, that even as a child entranced me with its grandeur, soars up rugged to the south. The boundary between the two is not a watery strait, but the stately Harris Hills.

The Outer Hebrides are world famous for their Neolithic standing stones – especially those at *Calanais* or Callanish. What's virtually unknown, even to many in the archaeological world, is that these islands host an astonishing array of sacred natural sites. Their sheer concentration is almost without parallel elsewhere in Britain. They include 'beehive' dwellings of corbelled stone, nestled into hidden glens. Some will go back to the Celtic era, or even to an elder faith that lingers on in the abundance of stories, and place names, that witness to a worldview based on 'faerie'. These are fertile ground for the imagination and, in my experience, can open out reflection on the structure of the human mind with insights, even, into space and time and consciousness.

Then there are the ruins of 'temples', chapels built for veneration in a time before the Reformation shifted gear towards the Protestant faith. Most of these are tiny structures resting by the sea, their tumbled stonework bedding in, a little more with every passing year, to sheets of sand that drift in almost constant winds that blow along the shore. Often there are near-forgotten holy wells close by. Further afield, one might stumble upon Gaelic names that testify to sites of spiritual retreat, or to the elemental power of blessing – *beannachadh*. Most of these temples and the wells are consecrated to saints. Some remain familiar today. Others, half or long forgotten.

But 'religion is over', mused R.S. Thomas, in 'The Moon in Lleyn'. His poem was inspired by just such an abandoned chapel in North Wales, one that was being reclaimed by the sea. Impermanence is here to stay. Nature, in the end, humbles all the works of human hands. Yet which of us, the poet continues, can tell what might emerge 'from the body of the new moon'? As our city ways grow weary, 'people are becoming pilgrims again, if not to this place, then to the recreation of it in their own spirits'. We must remain kneeling. Hush!

Remember! 'These very seas are baptised. The parish has a saint's name time cannot unfrock.'[1]

As for my approach to such matters, my writing can be too pagan for the Christians, too Christian for the pagans. However, we're living in a time when many might feel drawn by the Welsh poet's sense of turning to be pilgrims once again. There's something stirring in a lot of us that feels the urge to place that compass on the map, to let its needle swing – the wider and the wilder, the better.

I suppose that, at the deepest level, that was the force that pulled me north to make this island pilgrimage.

The geographical distance that I planned to walk was not going to be great. Only sixty miles as the crow flies, maybe double that with all the meanders, and a generous twelve days for completion. I'd be navigating by map and compass through eight hundred square miles of mostly uninhabited territory, crossing the fifty-eighth parallel, and probably experiencing all the weather that's to be expected when you're halfway between London and the Arctic Circle.

If the spiritual search was one motivation, another, and a closely related driving force, was my work on war and peace. It happened that I'd spent the month before my departure delivering guest lectures at military training institutions across Europe. That might not be what you'd expect of one who's been put on trial for protesting against Trident nuclear submarines at the Faslane naval base. However, in 1997, I'd received a letter from General Timothy Granville-Chapman, Commandant at the Joint Services Command and Staff College of what is now the UK Defence Academy. He was refining the new Advanced Command & Staff Course at Shrivenham. It was designed for up to four hundred senior army, navy and air force officers each year, mainly British, but also drawn from sixty or seventy other countries with which the United Kingdom has military alliances.

Junior ranks in the military are trained to follow orders. At senior levels, they also have to think independently. This requires exposing officers to 'the alternative point of view'. As one of those alternatives entails the questioning of war itself, a discussion had ensued in Shrivenham, as to where they might find a speaker who might mount the challenge. One of the course design team, then a young lieutenant colonel, ventured to mention: 'I happen to have a brother-in-law. It's a high risk strategy that might backfire, but . . .' That was me, signed up for the Queen's shilling, at least, to her shilling minted to nonviolent mettle. It went on to become an annual fixture, with spin-off invitations to staff colleges or military think-tanks in Ireland, France and Switzerland. These days the Defence Academy also sets me loose on a higher course, one that trains the next generation of admirals, generals and air marshals. The deal is the Chatham House Rule – I'm at liberty to reveal what was said, but not who said it. Anybody who wonders what I get away with saying can find an outline published as a chapter in their textbook, *Ethics, Law and Military Operations*.[2]

My brief has been refined over the years and, frankly, I find the swing that it permits my compass quite remarkable. I get set loose to:

> . . . explore the moral implications of conflict that exceeds military capacity to deter or contain it; and the application of nonviolence, including its religious basis, to achieve security in a complex world where the net results of conflict are not easy to predict.

As I was making final preparations for the pilgrimage that May, I'd just got back from an assignment in Switzerland. I'd been asked to address soldiers and diplomats on the NATO programme, 'Partnership for Peace', that had grown out of the Balkan wars that had so sadly soured the falling of the Iron Curtain. It had been a day-long session. There'd been a range of speakers tackling the theme 'God, War and the State'. The mad thought did cross my mind that a fitting rubric for my pilgrimage (if anybody asked) could be 'God, War and the Faeries'. However, thankfully my compass quickly dampened down on that one. I mean, it's nice to get invited back.

The night before the lecture I'd sat up late, discussing conflict and religion with the course's academic dean. We were billeted in Geneva's Hôtel InterContinental. Normally I'd be more used to camping, but at least it wasn't on the budget of the peace movement. Our lodgings were rendered all the more surreal by being seated next to a large family of piteously rich Arabic brothers. I say piteously, for each one of them looked bored to death with all that money could buy. One young man had a box of matches. He struck them, one by one, until the box was empty. He watched each match flare up, let it burn down to his fingertips, then dropped it onto a growing pile that smouldered, like a burning ruin, on the polished mahogany table top.

The scene felt curiously like a metaphor. At the time, our wars were smouldering on in Iraq and Afghanistan. I couldn't help but watch the solemn dropping of each match. It felt like witnessing a countdown. The lighting of blue touchpaper. The final stage, before ignition, of my pilgrim journey's launch.

On getting back to Glasgow, I went to Tiso's store, which sells outdoor equipment. It had attached to it a specialist map-printing shop. I was planning to walk from Rodel, at the most southerly tip of Harris, right up to Ness, at the Butt of Lewis. I knew that if I made it over the Harris Hills without breaking a leg, I'd come down into the rump of central Lewis, bang into a quagmire of deep peat bogs and tortuously twisting lochs. These might be very good for fishing – I'd be taking a collapsible fly rod with me. But they'd also be very good for getting lost amongst. Hardly anybody ever goes to this most lonesome haunt. Even the Ordnance Survey almost gives up. Their large-scale maps, that can be bought off-the-shelf, select the region, devoid of all inhabitation, to overlap three neighbouring sheets. Trying to piece that lot together when it's blowing a hoolie would have left me in a right flap.

Hence why I was in the queue at Tiso's. I wanted them to print me a bespoke single sheet, one that would be centred on my intended route's most treacherous meanderings. My mind drifted off as I waited for my turn. Curiously, I was wondering how best to give account of myself to people I might meet along the way. To say 'I'm on a pilgrimage' might merely seem quaint to folks of a secular turn of mind. But many native islanders are Presbyterians, and that, of a 'strict' leaning. Such an interpretation of the Christian faith rests upon the teachings of John Calvin of Geneva. He, in turn, stood on the shoulders of Martin Luther – a tempestuous monk who, in 1517, reputedly pulled off the grand slam of nailing his ninety-five theses of the Protestant Reformation to the cathedral door of Wittenberg.

In 1520, Luther had issued an address to the German nobility. This decreed that 'all pilgrimages should be done away with'. These, he asserted, only served to keep the common people off their work. They encouraged 'a vagabond life' that lay at the root of 'countless causes of sin', and so, those 'country chapels and churches . . . to which the new pilgrimages have been set on foot . . . must be destroyed'.[3]

But there was a caveat. Luther had to win over the nobles and the bourgeoisie to his cause. Then, as now, such social classes liked their travelling. He therefore made an exception. Excursions were allowed, provided they were emptied of all spiritual intent such as might treat them as beneficial for salvation, which was the gift of faith alone. As such, travel could be sanctioned only when conducted, 'out of curiosity, to see cities and countries'. Unwittingly, with those words, Luther canonised himself the Patron Saint of Tourism.

I doubt that many islanders on Lewis or Harris would have read Luther's *Address to the Christian Nobility of the German Nation*. We were raised as Calvinists, not Lutherans. Nevertheless, as children even into the 1960s, we were warned of 'Papist superstitions' that harked back to this early Reformation mindset. That's why, as I slowly shuffled up to the head of Tiso's queue, I was pondering how best to give account of myself. Into what groove might I quickly fit my story, such as might lubricate a fleeting wayside encounter? Pilgrimage, I mused, could be a dodgy gambit. But tourism. And with early Reformation sanction. Well, that might be a different matter. So it was, that with my mind now itching for temptation, titillated at the prospect of 'countless causes of sin', a mischievous solution to my predicament thumped home. *Poaching!*

Let me explain, if I might be excused for taking a rough cut at history. The rising of the clans – the indigenous Highlanders – against the fledgling British state was crushed by sword and musket at Culloden in 1746. It was the last battle on mainland British soil. Ever since, the 'lairds' or lords – the landlords on a massive scale – have presumed to hold as private property the land that once was the tribal patrimony. They were of a breed that had been born to rule; others, they presumed, born to be ruled. Often absentee, perhaps coming up from London for just a few weeks every summer, they guarded zealously their claim of sporting rights to deer and salmon. Set against the game protection laws that they've created on the one hand, there's a raft of Gaelic proverbs on the other hand that give succour to the humble poacher's soul. Lines like: 'A salmon from the pool, a wand from the wood, and a deer from the hill are thefts which no man was ever ashamed to own.'

Even the island churches, otherwise so quick to damn transgression, have traditionally soft-pedalled on 'the poaching'. The Reverend Professor Donald Macleod of the Free Church of Scotland once gave a sermon on the matter in his column in the *West Highland Free Press*.[4] 'Until I have a lobotomy,' he proclaimed, 'I will never be persuaded that poaching is a crime or even a sin.' The advantage of living in the City of London is that the Good Lord ordained you to make money. The advantage of living in Balallan on the Isle of Lewis – with the lochs and rivers of the Grimersta system out the back – is that the Good Lord ordained you to catch salmon. But, concluded the professor, the British Establishment has nefariously decreed that London should have both the money and the fishing. Balallan would have neither.

By now, I'd made it to the head of Tiso's queue. I explained my Ordnance Survey needs to the technician. With a few clicks of his mouse, the familiar kite-shaped outline of the Outer Hebrides leapt up on a ginormous screen. We selected a rectangle that ran from the foot of the Harris Hills in the south, over to Kinlochresort in the west, straight down the eight miles of Loch Langabhat that straddles the centre of Lewis, and up to where the Grimersta meets the sea near Callanish. We set the scale at 1:25,000 – two-and-a-half inches to the mile. It was then that he insouciantly asked: 'And what title would you like printed on the cover of your map?'

Little do I think he suspected anything, but those words were the trigger for *the vision* that fell upon me. Here, dropped from Heaven, was the muse by which I was bestowed my ruse: a cover story, that would delight the ears of every true-blooded islander. In my mind's eye, I glimpsed myself a-huffing and a-puffing over the hills, peregrinating from loch to loch, with my collapsible fly-fishing rod sticking up like an aerial from out of the camouflage green of my rucksack. It looked, for all the world, like the walkie-talkie of some clandestine military operation.

I whispered my instructions back to the man in the white coat, hoping he'd not notice the manic gleam that had most surely filled my eyes. With what seemed to be a conspiratorial nod, he pressed the coloured buttons on his console. A humongous printer whooshed to life. All lights were a-flashing. Noises, quite unspeakable, wheezed and beeped and burped and blew. Dr Who had done his darndest. The Tardis was in take-off. Space and time themselves were on the brink of going AWOL.

Steadily, the island's graven image stuttered forth. There was, for me, no going back. The myth had now been resolutely activated. The blue touchpaper – lit at Hôtel InterContinental – had burnt down to ignition. The countdown, at ground zero, signalled *lift-off!*

The journey lay stretched out on parchment. It waited only to be walked. Printed boldly on the cover was the proclamation:

Alastair McIntosh
Central Lewis
Poacher's Pilgrimage

PART 1

BLUE

The Blue Trail: Days 1–2, South Harris

THE DEVIL'S DEBUT

An unseasonable hailstorm let loose as my wife Vérène and I set off from home in Govan, the part of Glasgow that had once built the ships of the Empire. It was Friday 8 May, and late afternoon. Winter had held a protracted grip that year. The distant peaks were icy dusted, flushed pink in the low-slung sun. We were stalked by rainbows of most startling iridescence, as we drove across the girth of Scotland, to what continues to be known as The Kingdom of Fife.

The philosopher and writer David Lorimer had asked me to give a talk in a series that he'd organised, called 'Café Spirituel'. These were held in the provincial town of Falkland, specifically at an organic farm called the Pillars of Hercules. The plan was for Vérène to take me thus far by car. We'd overnight with David and Jane. The next morning, I'd be dropped off at Ladybank railway station. I'd take the train to Inverness, then a bus for sixty miles, across the neck of the Highlands, to the fishing port of Ullapool. That's where I'd embark on the familiar three-hour ferry crossing of the Minch, this being the stretch of sea that separates the mainland from the Isle of Lewis.

In the port of Stornoway, I'd spend the weekend with my elderly mother. Then, on the Monday morning, I'd take a couple of bus rides down to the south of Harris. From there, at Rodel, I'd set out by foot on the long-awaited pilgrimage.

That's the plan, but right now, it's to Falkland, and as we drive across the rich flat farmlands of Kinross-shire, the sun dips down behind the Paps of Fife, and leaves the little town that we're approaching to settle into dusk.

David is the grandson of Sir Robert Lorimer, a noted architect of the Scots Baronial and Gothic Revival styles, also an exemplar of the British Arts and Crafts movement. I've come to know him through his leadership of The Scientific and Medical Network, a group of physicians and academics, along with the occasional artist and left-field aristocrat, who take an interest in the interactions between body, mind and spirit. 'The Pillars', as the Herculean farm is fondly known, is already packed with people as we arrive. All are finishing their meal and deep in conversation. I enjoy speaking to such provincial groups. In rural communities of place, there's usually not the same social stratification that you tend to get with communities of interest, such as academic groups. That's not to say there's not a social order. It's just that everybody's there.

There's Ninian, the local laird, descended from the Stuart kings and passionate about Falkland's sense of place: its wood, water and stone. There's my old friend Tess, who wrote *The Scots Herbal*, gorgeous in one of her homespun cardigans of browns, reds and purples as if to make an autumnal protest at the spring's late arrival. There's Bruce, a gnarled organic farmer in a set of dungarees, the epitome of fashion now the industry's decided that the in thing is 'distressed'. There are several hard-up hippie couples, the kind of folks who don't ask for much but bring a bit of sunshine to the community. There are the retired professionals, the caravan, yacht and golf club scene, who bring a bit of money and hard-boiled expertise. And there's Marianna Lines, a spirited American artist, who works her Pictish pictures from the thatched cottage studio of a nearby medieval village.

I can't resist, whenever I see her, from calling out: 'All hail, the Great White Witch of Collessie!' At which, on one occasion, wondering whether I might have overstepped the mark and be in peril of getting thwacked by her broomstick parked outside, I followed up, more discreetly: 'Er, I do hope you don't mind my acknowledging your professional status in public?'

'I'm glad *somebody* recognises it!' she exclaimed.

The whole room's buzzing and the plates are being cleared away. I prefer to do my eating after speaking, so David cuts to the quick, introduces, and we're off. I'm billed to give a blast about climate change: about the need to forge *resilience* in communities, how this entails the outer work of cutting carbon footprints, but also the inner work of learning to live more with less. After the allotted twenty minutes I sit down and await questions.

I'm expecting some of them to feel quite challenged. I'd talked about the quest for meaning, about the experience of emptiness and the false satisfier of consumerism that transiently fills the gaps, but drives the cutting edge of climate change. But they're not challenged. Most don't even want to talk about climate change, and it's David's fault. He'd told them I'd arrived with a backpack and a fishing rod. They don't want to hear about climate change. They want to hear about the poacher's pilgrimage. So it's *tally-ho* and off we go, with a stalwart young man in a singlet first off the mark. 'What training have you done?'

'None,' I confess. 'I've been so busy. Only time for a few walks within Glasgow. But as I keep reassuring my wife, *the pilgrimage will be the training.*'

I sense the raising of a few unconvinced eyebrows. Mine too.

'What are you going to eat?' asks one of the organic volunteers.

'Three boxes of oatcakes, muesli, a bag of bread mix, pudding rice, milk powder, honey, marmite, butter, cheese, sugar, seasonings, tea, hot chocolate, bags of nuts and raisins, a huge slab of Cadburys and a bumper pack of Mars bars.'

The wave of right-on kudos, generated by the muesli and bread mix, crashes as fast as the dough had risen.

'And, perhaps a wee nightcap too?' suggests a lady of librarian precision, in that kind of 'I've got *his* measure' tone.

'A wee dram along the way would have been nice, but I can't be fuddling the mind.'

'And for fresh food?' asks a douce Earth Mother type, probably suspicious of my ratio of oatcakes to chocolate. 'How are you going to stay . . . *healthy?*'

'I'll buy some more bits and pieces at the last minute on the island. But fresh food's too heavy. I need a week's supply of stuff to go across the moors, and my bag's already tipping twenty kilos. Hopefully I'll supplement by foraging.'

To which I add, hoping that she's not a born-again vegan: 'Edible plants, for sure, but also fish and shellfish. I'm hoping to catch part of my diet. You see, I'll be crossing . . . *the Grimersta.*'

'Ooh! You'd better watch out if you're near the Grimersta!' interjects a hale and hearty English woman. She's chuckling away, laying on an eeh-bah-gum accent as if that's the way it would be spoken by the crofters, the island's small-scale farmers and fishers.

'My son's been a watcher during his holidays on the Grimersta, catching poachers all the summer long. You know what they do with poachers up there? They string 'em up, you know, like grouse in the larder, till their maggot-ridden 'eads drop off!'

Well, those might not have been her precise words, but they were her gist and gusto. I should say, before proceeding further, that all conversations related here are necessarily paraphrased from memory, and that, I hope, in ways that would find my conversationalists' approval.

Now, it was true enough, that were all to go to plan, I'd be crossing several rivers. It rains on the island for two out of every three days, fifty inches annually at Stornoway airport, but much more heavily in the mountain regions where the wind, sweeping straight in off the Atlantic, regularly tops the ton-up in winter. The Grimersta – a boiling force of nature that drains the island's centre – is a legendary watercourse. They used to say it was the third best salmon river in Europe. In 1888, a certain Mr Naylor set the British record, landing fifty-four salmon on one rod. Such were the days of the great white hunters. Poaching the Grimersta was a rite of passage when we were boys. It was also a political education. How come *they* claimed *our* fish? It got folks asking questions – about social class, about landed power – and precisely who the British Empire thought it had the right to colonise, and how come so, so close to home? It was the audacity of having a bash at the poaching that counted. Even if you weren't a Mr Naylor, just the derring-do of daring to throw a line out from the Grimersta's hallowed banks was enough; the thrill of lying awake at night, with visions of the gamekeeper looming up from the heather – his dog and his big stick – the unspeakable in hot pursuit of the all-too-beatable.

Alas, such was an initiation from which my all too 'respectable' upbringing as the doctor's son had shielded me. In those days, incomers to the island came to provide professional services, and were granted privileges. The local estates gave Dad all the fishing he could desire. The only time I ever had to drop my rod and run was when in hot pursuit by vicious clouds of biting midges.

Most pilgrimages go to strange and distant lands. Mine was to my own land, therefore I should share something of our family's island connections. Moreover, my approach to telling people about this remarkable part of the world, and the arguable importance of its insights to wider burning issues of our times, is necessarily discursive. I might seem to wander off on a wild goose chase now and then, but *trust me* (said the doctor's son), there's method in the madness. Hopefully the goose comes home to roost in ways that help to build up layers of mood and information, gradually to knit together to a greater whole.

Dad had left Edinburgh, newly qualified after the war, to take up a post in the West Riding, Yorkshire, town of

Doncaster. There he met my mother, who was the nursing sister in the Royal Infirmary's children's ward. Her mother's people had Welsh roots, but all we knew was that 'they sung in choirs'. Her father ran the celebrated Ronnie Hancox Band for Dancers, and used to play *Come Dancing* in the early days of television. They were industrialists and squires, but he used to tell my mother, 'No-one teaches a Hancox how to ride a horse' – and it thrilled me when I found this out to be an old Gypsy name.

Dad had three parts Gaelic Highlands and one part Scottish Borders blood. Through these links, we have some very distant relations on Lewis. Moreover, his uncle, James Ewart Purves, was the superintendent of the Lewis Hospital in Stornoway in the 1920s.[1] To this day, an old woman, Mary Mackenzie, the widow of 'Sligo', lives in the village of Upper Bayble just a few miles outside of Stornoway. She has shown me the neat scar where 'Uncle Jim' had operated on a quinsy on her neck. It was on the kitchen table of her family's thatched house in Callanish, aided by a bottle of chloroform. She was just two years old at the time. 'I would be sorry for you if you'd left your child another night,' he'd told her parents as he headed off. Sometimes, the past seems very far away – yet there it is, just tissue-thin.

I was born in Doncaster in 1955, my sister in the following year, and my earliest memories are of the steam train that used to chug up from the Armthorpe coal mine to the slag heap. Dad, however, yearned to get back home to Scotland. He loved the outdoors, and especially yearned for a place that offered fishing. He said he wanted to be able to practice real medicine – 'medicine as both an art and a science' – but there had to be a salmon river. It was my mother who persuaded him to apply to an advertisement in the *British Medical Journal* for the North Lochs practice, midway between Stornoway and Harris. She, who was so into fashion and the modern life, and for whom the culture shock would be the greatest. She always had a feeling for the inner beat and ordering of things. So it was that we moved to the island in the summer of 1960. I was just four, but can still remember the excitement of that crossing on the old *Loch Seaforth*. At first, little Isobel and I were so urbanised that we called the Barvas hills 'the slag heaps'.

Being raised and educated on the island has shaped the person that I am today, yet I'll always think of Doncaster fondly, a place of holidays and grandparents. How easily my life could have configured differently. How easily, but for that winnowing compass call; the pull that Dad had felt on lifelines of the wild Atlantic salmon.

There was one last question at Café Spirituel that evening. 'Won't you get frightened, all alone, out in a tent at night in the middle of nowhere?'

'I don't see why,' I'd answered. 'I've camped out on my own, many times before.'

Yet there was a difference. Then it was just camping. This time it was pilgrimage; a conscious invitation to unconscious experience.

Once, when the Rev. Dr George MacLeod, later Lord MacLeod of Fuinary – a pacifist clergyman with double military decorations from the Great War – was praying in Iona Abbey, he was overcome with terror. It was his practice, like Jesus at the start of Mark's gospel, to rise and pray early in the morning. Before the world got going, he'd go alone amongst the Benedictine columns and arches that rest upon the probable site of the original Columban church. On this occasion, as he sat and opened inwardly, he was overcome by an overwhelming force of smothering malevolence. It was as if some quintessence of evil had risen up, perhaps to try and crush his work in setting up the Iona Community to recover Celtic spirituality.

'George was able to run out into the breaking daylight,' I had mused, lying in bed, pondering such matters in the wee small hours while planning my trip. But fear is an uncanny thing. We may not know it till the chasm opens.

'Where would you run to?' I'd thought to myself. 'Where, if it opened in the middle of a night, far out on the moors?'

Christ met the Devil in the wilderness. One doesn't, of course, believe in the Devil as such. But . . .

By now the hour was late and The Pillars of Hercules closing. Jane went off with Vérène in her vehicle. David put me into the passenger seat of his zippy little vintage sports car. It was very still outside. Both of us were quiet as we picked up speed. The country isn't like the town. The town maintains a never-ending buzz of normality that keeps reality stable. At least, a certain configuration of reality. That last question niggled slightly in my mind. It wasn't so much that it scared me. More, it intrigued me, like something to be picked up and examined.

David sped through darkening country lanes, lined with tousled hedgerow briars and the wilting pallid blossoms of the day's convolvulus.

'We'll just stop here – I'll show you something,' he announced unexpectedly, and pulled into a passing place.

Across the road was the pillared entrance to a grand estate. Beside it stood a Gothic gatehouse – a dumpy square residence, with a huge chimney rising from the centre. Seated astride the pot on top was a humanoid figure.

'Get out and take a better look,' he urged, turning off the headlights so that my eyes could get accustomed to the gloom.

'What . . . ?' I said. 'I can hardly make it out.'

'It is the Devil,' he replied, completely deadpan. Then, smiling to release the Peter Cushing tension: 'Rather splendid, don't you think?'

And there he was. A squat, cheeky-looking fellow, with cloven hooves, merrily tooting a bacchanalian pipe.

'It's called the Devil's Lodge. Designed for Balcarres House by my grandfather. He was into . . . many things mysterious.'

'Well!' said I, glad to have got off with making the acquaintance so lightly. 'I suppose that'll be me, now. Inoculated for the journey.'

2

A SACRED LANDSCAPE

There's a Calum Kennedy song that we all used to sing on bus trips: 'Make your way to Stornoway' where the town clock 'chimes its message every day.' This is where 'Heaven can't be far away'. Here, 'the folks are truly kind' and you 'leave the world behind'. Kitsch romanticism? And yet, there's something about a culture where such values are continually reinforced in patterns of song and story.

So here we are. I've arrived in Stornoway, and I've just spent the weekend with my mother. She's bright and well, but anxious at the prospect of my trying to traverse the island. At last, after all the preparations, it's Monday 11 May. Day one of my allotted twelve of pilgrimage. The bus is pulling away from its terminus on the pier, pulling away from Stjorn-Vagr as the Old Norse had it. Stornoway, as the Bay of Steering or Governing. Equally, it can be translated as the Bay of Stars. After all, steering is what stars were for in olden maritime cultures. They governed our passage and guarded our lives through cosmological connection. This sheltered inlet of the sea – this little port with its two-for-the-price-of-one inner and outer harbours, its fishing boats and its ferries – this is the centre of the island's governance, here in the Bay of Steering by the Stars.

The heart of Stornoway is a few criss-crossed streets of small-town shops, fix-anything garages and light industries. There's a library, a museum and a university college where you can study an enormous range of courses from marine engineering to Celtic languages, theology and hairdressing. There's the High Church on one hill. A castle on the other. Carry-out chip shops. Chinese, Thai, Indian and even Hebridean eateries. And bars. About ten of them. Nearly a pub for every church. No wonder Heaven can't be far away. No wonder, here's the place to 'leave the world behind', or perhaps to enter, with its lilting old-time motto, *God's Providence is Our Inheritance*.

These days, about nine thousand souls, a little less than half the island's population, live in or around the town. At this time of the morning, just at the back of ten on a gloriously sunny day, the bus is almost empty. Within minutes, we've reached the leafy outskirts, and at Willowglen slip past Uncle Jim's old house that stands, in faded glory, on the corner. Here pebble-dashed terraces of council houses yield to the prosperous villas of Stornoway's business and professional classes; their garages and their patios, their gardens and perhaps a boat outside. Next, we're into the crofting township of Marybank. Here it's rural but with signs of modest urban prosperity. The homes sit on several acres meant for the arable production of anybody who can be bothered these days, and out on the open moor, there's a much bigger share of common grazings for the sheep and cattle.

Another mile, we've sped past Tawse's quarry, and the road dips down to cross the River Creed. From here we come up into the moorland of a very different type of country. Now it's plain to see why a fond name for the island, popular in poetry and song, is Eilean Fraoich, the Isle of Heather. This is the road that leads to my home parish of Lochs, and from there, on down into Harris. All around, both visibly and dipped away in hollows, are shining lochs and smaller lochans. Each is threaded to a necklace by tiny burns that, according to their season's wont, trickle or churn a passage to the sea. And this is such a remarkably sunny day. Although I know the place so well, although I've crossed this Arnish moor so many times, I'm drinking it all in once more. Here, the rocky fortress of a *cnoc* or little hill. There, a puffed-out drifting sugar-candy cloud. Everywhere, these long and rusty heather ridges, that slouch to kiss their own reflections dipped in pools of liquid amethyst.

The change that's flipped since Marybank is geological. We shifted out of Stornoway's soft lime-rich and relatively fertile conglomerate, into the island's anchoring mass of hard, crystalline Lewisian gneiss. We're now bouncing over archaic beds of worn-down mountain stumps, these ground down to a low rumpled plateau over the aeons of the ice ages. Seen through the telescope of deepening time, glacial ice sheets are the default norm in these latitudes. Plant life is just a passing bloom of summer, one that flashes past in a blink, every hundred thousand years or so. In back-of-an-envelope terms, the last ice age ended ten thousand years ago. Since then, only thin peat soils have built up; these, from the remains of vegetation that wouldn't rot under such lime-impoverished acid-saturated conditions. These oozing beds of peat, resting on a spread of glacial boulder clay, are pretty much all that sustains the slender skin of life.

Pronounced 'nice', from an old German word that means sparkling, rocks of the Lewisian complex date to between two and three billion years, amongst the oldest in the world.[1] Known as metamorphic, which means 'changed form', they've been cask-conditioned deep within the Earth's crust, under enormous heat and pressure. This has caused their mineral composition to segregate into banded layers of dark and light, alternating every few inches. Add to this the fact that hot rocks bend as the Earth's crust slowly shifts over time, and it is common to see outcrops that have folded and contorted, like twisted bars of toffee.

Interpreting the island's place names is a further merry-go-round of Norse and Gaelic influences. Lewis, or Leòdhas, is thought to be cognate with the *Leod* of Macleod, and might suggest either *leodjus*, 'a place of lakes', or *ljóðhús*, 'the poet's home' or 'song house'. Harris – na Hearadh – probably comes from the Old Norse, *haerri*, meaning high ground, or possibly, 'the harries' where deer were hunted. Another Norse possibility is *hérad*, meaning a province ruled by a *hérsir*. The pioneering island historian W.C. Mackenzie said that such was 'not only the hereditary head of the community, but its "prophet, priest and king".'[2] The name Hebrides is a tougher nut to crack. The first written mention is in the *Natural History* of Pliny the Elder, a first-century Roman naturalist and geographer, who described the British coast. After mentioning Orkney, and what are probably the Shetlands, he moves south to 'the Haebudes, thirty in number'.[3] Quite what the name means is anybody's guess, but Mackenzie airs several suggestions, variously linked to Pictish kings, corn, habitation and Saint Bridgit.

The bus has just swooped up a hill. We're now on top of the Druim Dubh, the Black Ridge, and passing the little crofter's cottage where, for several years, we lived on first arriving in Lewis. Straight across the road from our garage there is a fallen stone circle. It was found by families cutting peat for fuel, and is visible partly excavated, just above the hollow where we had our rubbish dump. To think it was a sacred natural site, and that Isobel and I played there, never realising. To think that, even if we'd realised, we'd scarce have cared. To realise, moreover, that this whole chain of Outer Hebridean islands is so thickly freckled with places, stories and archaeological relics of sacred significance – both from the Celtic era and earlier – that it's quite extraordinary, and only superficially known about by most. What's more, it is documented that, from as early as the sixth century, people came from far and wide to these islands, specifically to pursue a spiritual life on the edge of the known world. Adomnán, the seventh-century biographer of Columba, speaks of one pilgrim, whose name wasn't Celtic, stopping at Iona, and asking 'the saint's blessing before setting out with others to seek a place of retreat in the sea'.[4] If there's such a thing as a spiritual gene, or even just a spiritual cultural meme, this is where it's been distilled. Furthermore, to use again that delectable term of maturity from the whisky industry – cask-conditioned.

It's not just what's above the ground or yet-concealed beneath the ever-growing depth of peat. It's also in the stories and the place names. A mile directly south across the moor from our house at Druim Dubh brings you to a loch, Àirigh an t-Sagairt, which translates as the Sheiling (or moorland hut) of the Priest. Go there, and in a sheltered cleft by its south-east end there are the foundation rings of several hut circles. My school friend, Rusty, took me to the spot. Next door is a huge ring of water with a large island in the middle, Loch Orisay. A patient told Dad that monks had once lived there, probably because the Arctic char, a mysterious fish that lurks in shoals deep in some of these waters, were (he thought) in good condition at Lent. The presence of a settlement like Àirigh an t-Sagairt lends credence to that theory. But there's another curious feature of this loch. Its name, *Orasaigh* in the modern Gaelic, suggests a causeway, probably one that once led out to the island. However, the name as printed in the first Ordnance Survey map conveys a very different sense. Completed for this part of Lewis in 1851, and based on local knowledge at the time, it renders it in large lettering as Loch Airidh Sìdeach. This suggests a green grove (or perhaps, a sheiling) of 'silkiness'. The word might be connected to the *sìdh* – meaning peace, or the faeries – thus linking, as we often see elsewhere, to the remnants of an elder faith with roots from times before the monks.[5]

The bus coasts down from the higher ground, passing a cluster of houses at the Leurbost road end. It swoops into a big dipper of a brae and runs past the house we moved to after living at Druim Dubh. Here, at Gleann Mòr, the Big Glen, is the parish doctor's surgery and what was, in our time, the doctor's official residence. In a flash, we career across the Abhainn Ghlas. Before the road was widened and the river straightened, there used to be two dry-stone tunnels carrying the flow underneath the bridge at this point. The one to the north was narrow; that to the south, very narrow indeed. We boys would dare one another to crawl through. It was scary, especially when it rumbled after a spate: dark in the middle, full of cobwebs, dripping moss and dangly things like a rural version of the Ghost Train. At the far end was a deep pool, where we'd spend hour upon hour with our bamboo rods, catching tasty little trout on dangled worms.

Some hold that Abhainn Ghlas means the Silver River. Others, the Grey, or Blue, or Green River. It depends who you ask and when. Why did I have to ask to try and clarify my confusion? The truth is, in those days we were told that Gaelic was a 'backward' and a dying language. An unintended consequence was that, apart from picking up a few words, I never learned the Gaelic when I could have done so. It's one of my few real regrets in life. The Abhainn Ghlas taught us many things as children. Today, I have found its very name to be a perfect illustration of what makes Gaelic such a difficult language to grasp. Or to be more accurate, a fascinatingly different language. To be told that one word can have several seemingly diverse meanings was scarcely an encouragement for a child used to the more prosaic rationale of English. It was only in adulthood that I came to appreciate that Gaelic is a poetic language, rippled through like metamorphic rock with metaphoric glides. A concept, or rather, a feeling like *ghlas* or *glas,* simply doesn't map directly onto Newton's spectrum of seven colours. Instead, the Gaelic reflects the shifting hues of a living and dynamic world. One definition of *Ghlas*, for example, might be: the colour of the moods of light from ever-changing skies, reflected on the surfaces of water.

Gaelic place names often derive from how a place might appear under certain distinctive conditions, or from a particular angle. From Dad's huge plate-glass surgery window, I would watch the upper reaches of the Abhainn Ghlas rise in the west and perhaps break its banks during a day of heavy rain. Later, if there was a ray of evening sun, I'd see the water shine like a mercurial rill from out of its raised position in the dark brown bosom of the moor. That, from my viewing angle, cements the name's translation as the Silver River. Silver-lined, too, after a spate, was my anticipation of a fresh run of little trout – up to quarter pounders – brought down from the stream's source in Loch Thobhta Brìdein. And there we go again. The Loch of Bridgit's Ruin. In the days when these moors were first baptised with names, the folklore tells that Bridgit was the guardian of the isles.[6] Whoever might have been the Bridgit of the ruin, the name points back towards an archetype. 'The parish has a saint's name . . .' – and if you pull in on the left, just before the Achmore road dips down to run along the waterside, you can still find traces of what look like hut circles, and the foundations of a rectangular stone building, on a little green ridge. We can but play a game of speculation if we so care to do, but looking back, the poet in me loves to think that Bridgit's fishes fed my fledgling bones.

Onwards rolls the bus, past the familiar villages of Dad's old practice – Keose, Laxay, Balallan and Airidhbhruaich – the latter meaning 'green grove on a bank', and too remote, in our day, to have been anglicised to something dreadful, like Ari-vrooak.

As Rusty, the red-headed Leurbost blacksmith, would call it, *stranglified*. My own use of these names is horribly inconsistent. I'm of that in-between generation, more immersed in how the English signposts used to be than in their new bilingual versions. Should I be saying Baile Ailein rather than Balallan, to show it means the Village of Allan? Probably, and yet, where to draw the line? It would feel pretentious for me, speaking English, to go round calling Stornoway, Steòrnabhagh, or to really play the trump, and take it back to Stjorn-Vagr.

Soon we're crossing the Aline or Ath Linne bridge that marks the Lewis–Harris border. It's not just the mountains looming up ahead that signal change. There's also a cultural shift, one that runs between two branches of a clan of dual ethnicity. Just over a millennium ago, the Norse came down from Scandinavia and melded with the Gaelic-speaking Celts, whose stock had much in common with the Irish. By the end of the ninth century, the resulting hybrid of the stranger and the heartland people caused them to become known as the *Gall-Gàidheil* (or 'GalGael'). To this day, one of the several names used for the Outer Hebrides, or Western Isles, is *Innse Gall* – the Island of Strangers, the irony being that these have now become the heartland people. Such is the power of fostership or adoption. The island's most common surname is *Macleod*. One branch, *Sìol Thorcaill* (the seed of Torcuil), inherited Lewis. The other, *Sìol Thormoid* (the Seed of Norman) was given Harris.

We've just sped past the head of Loch Seaforth. This huge fjord, gouged out by glaciers, runs like a tunnel for seven miles until it opens to the Minch. The water looks serene enough today, cradled by precipitous hills on either side; but out beyond the sea loch's mouth the Sound of Shiant is feared by mariners, as one of the most storm-stricken stretches of water of the British coast.

Now we're dropping gear, slowing as we grind a flagging way up Clisham, the island's highest mountain. Rising to just over 2,600 feet – some 800 metres – the Norse means Craggy. It commands the eastern flank of the dividing range that makes this island two-for-one. Here, we're into country where the land turns harsh and raw. I take a last glance backwards, out across the vast but soft expanse of Lewis, before we press into this yet more primal land that is the Isle of Harris. Gigantic boulders, ripped out from higher up during the Ice Age, squat like brooding trolls in lorry cabs. Gutters of shattered scree streak down from battered outcrops, into valleys that lie darkened by their depth. Landmarks have names like Creag na h-Iolaire – The Crag of the Eagle.

Along here there's a spot tradition calls the Leathad nan Clacha Mòra, the Slope of Big Stones. I can feel the churn of the story coming on, for these are places peopled through with legends. Here local folklore echoes universal themes that find a localised expression, whether as psychology that contours to the landscape, or landscape that contours the psychology. The tale that belongs to the Leathad nan Clacha Mòra was printed in 1900, by a renowned folklore collector, the Rev. John Gregorson Campbell of Tiree. He called it 'The Young Man in the Fairy Knoll':[7]

> Two young men, coming home after nightfall on Hallowe'en, each with a jar of whisky on his back, heard music by the roadside, and, seeing a dwelling open and illuminated, and dancing and merriment going on within, entered. One of them joined the dancers, without as much as waiting to lay down the burden he was carrying. The other, suspecting the place and company, stuck a needle in the door as he entered, and got away when he liked. That day twelve months he came back for his companion, and found him still dancing with the jar of whisky on his back. Though more than half-dead with fatigue, the enchanted dancer begged to be allowed to finish the reel. When brought to the open-air he was only skin and bone.

Here's far more than just a moral fable about alcoholism. What we're being shown is a portal to the unconscious and progressive depths of meaning. To tradition's ear, this discotheque beneath the ground was a *brugh*: the interior of a *sithean* ('she-han') – the hollow-hill that's home to the *sìth* or *sìdh*. These are the faeries, the gentry of the countryside. Iron constrains their power of enchantment, probably because, ever since the Iron Age with its axes that hacked down the groves, it's been an element that represents the modern way of things.

Such Rip van Winkle tales are common across the world. I've even spotted one in Surah XVIII of the Qur'an – *Kahf* – The Cave. There, a group of young companions fall asleep for three hundred years inside a cavern. On awakening, they think that but a day has passed, yet find themselves now purified and worthy of the Gardens of Eternity. The Qur'an describes it as a paradise of flowing rivers and clear springs. Here, the people dress in garments of green silk and brocade. They recline on couches in the gardens, wearing bracelets made of gold.[8] It sounds like Tìr nan Òg, the Celtic Otherworld, the land of the ever-young.

One can either brush aside such tales as child's play, fantasias that gave amusement in the age before TV – or one can seek to penetrate in ways that question the very structures of space and time, exploring consciousness and meaning in the deeper realms of life within the soul. This is what ethnographers call traditional cosmology, the study of the universe and worldviews. One person who would have loved the legend of the Leathad nan Clacha Mòra was the English anthropologist Gregory Bateson. In 1972 he wrote a book that continues to stir interest today, *Steps to an Ecology of Mind*.

Bateson had worked in New Guinea with his first wife, Margaret Mead, the celebrated anthropologist of child development. Their work suggested that to be psychologically healthy, children need to be supported by a rich web of loving relationships. That might not seem like rocket science today, but it was an eye-opener in the war-torn decades of the early to mid twentieth century, especially to the social classes of the stiff upper lip. Bateson's contribution was to suggest that diminished mental health – expressed in alcoholism and schizophrenia in particular – might have roots not just in the genetic make-up, but also in dysfunctional family relationships. The mechanism that he proposed to explain this was the 'double-bind' theory, those crazy situations where you're damned if you do, damned if you don't, and – here's the nub – with no prospect of escape from such damnation.

Although *Steps to an Ecology of Mind* had such a haunting title, Bateson never used the phrase between the covers. It appears as if it was an afterthought. The closest that he came to what might, with hindsight, be understood by way of definition, is in a single sentence where he wrote: '*Mind is immanent in the larger system – man plus environment.*'[9]

I had the opportunity to explore this gnomic statement with his youngest daughter, Nora Bateson, during a visit that she paid to Glasgow. She was previewing a film she'd made about her childhood and her father's life.[10] I was on the discussion panel, and took the chance to ask what she thought he had meant by 'ecology of mind'. She answered with a metaphor from biology. It draws on 'endosymbiotic theory'. *Endo* for within, and *symbiotic,* meaning life forms working together with other life forms. This is where certain cells are thought to have evolved by incorporating parts of other cells. If this is true, such cells are more than just the stand-alone building blocks of biological Lego. Rather, each could be said to be a composite living community within itself. The whole is greater than the sum of its parts. Nora suggested that her father had applied a similar principle to the structure of human consciousness. We're not just individuals, egos running about on legs of meat. We're part of something bigger. As she put it that night in her clinch phrase: 'I think perhaps my father was trying to say *that we don't know what we're inside of.'*

One of my questions to myself had been how to encapsulate what I hoped this walk would be. It helps to have a rubric to get started on. To be able to say to oneself: 'I'm off to try and find the lost Isle of . . .'

Like Bateson, I felt my quest was to explore the mind, but as an *immram* or *iorram* – a word that literally means a 'rowing'. It was used by the Irish monks to describe a pilgrim voyage, usually without a destination, and often with a tendency to slide towards the Otherworld. *Mind*, however, was not the nuance I was after. Mind, in today's mainstream culture, is too bound up with reason and cognition, too much a hall of mirrors that reflects its own consensus trance realities. I was yearning for something deeper. That night at Hôtel InterContinental had left me spooked. The matches burning down. The young man's stultifying boredom. The way that war becomes 'a force that gives us meaning',[11] and yet, when analysed by mind alone, can seem so very logical, all the way until you hit the double-bind of mutually assured destruction.

There must be more than mind alone in that so-very-reasoned sense of things, of Mr Spock's cold Vulcan logic. That was where Nora's words turned a key. That's what opened up a sithean on the hillside – a connection to a greater and creative sense of living being. *We don't know what we're inside of.* I'll take it for the rudder of my immram: a voyaging through, and voyaging towards, *an ecology of the imagination.*

The bus shifts up a couple of gears as the road levels out now to cruise the contours of the Clisham's middle flanks. What was once so slow and single track is now so fast. Soon, we're cruising on the west bank of a long dark loch, from which a near-sheer wall of mountain rises straight up from the shores. I remember stopping there, as a child, to sail my toy yacht. Dad said there was a story that the water was as deep as the hill was high.

'Really?'

'Well . . . Probably not really, but a way of saying that it's very deep.'

Deep water fascinated me as a child. I'd lie down in the heather, and gaze into a black peat pool that lay behind our old house at Druim Dubh. Often, at night, I'd have a recurrent dream. It would start beside the pool, but somehow this morphed into an underground cavern, with a stream running through. I didn't know where it went, except that it was heading deeper. There'd be just me and little Isobel, the two of us, sitting on the rocks alone. That would be all. Not a nightmare, but slightly ominous, and me aware of having to protect her.

No doubt Freud would have had much to say on womb symbolism. It also shows that our approach to nature was not idealised. But more than that, when I think back to those times, I still feel within my belly a deep draw to nature's depth. It's not just landscape features that are held by places. They also hold human, and more-than-human, embedded presences. I don't mean like 'energies' attached to the rocks. It's a much more subtle basis than such physics-envy New Age literalism.

It's something that just happens when space and time slip-slide. Something, more like Bateson's immanence of mind in nature, or Carl Jung's sense of the collective unconscious. I realise, now, that I was raised in a culture where such a reality was very real. Let me give an example that, for third party objectivity, I'll draw from the ethnographic literature:

> There were Gaels alive in the mid-twentieth century who . . . believed implicitly that the ancestral dead in the churchyard were in some sense all still alive there in another dimension of existence . . . I am thinking here of people I knew personally.

So wrote Dr John MacInnes, born on Lewis in 1930, now retired from Edinburgh University's School of Scottish Studies, and widely held to be the leading living authority on Scottish Gaelic culture. I shall be making frequent reference to him as I dip in and out of insights from traditional cosmology. But let me leave that hanging there for now. We've driven past the long dark mountain loch. We're now about to pace its tiny stream, and zoom back down to sea level and to everyday concerns.

Although I didn't know exactly what my walking route would be, I had thought through some options, and would decide according to the weather and my physical capacity. I had in mind to visit three special features of the cultural landscape. One was the island's stone *bothan* (singular, *both*), or 'beehive' sheiling huts. A few can still be found, intact, out in the remotest places. Second, the *teampaill* (singular, *teampall*) or 'temples', this being the name applied to the pre-Reformation chapels that dot the coastal villages, ruined and abandoned to the elements. And then, the *tobraichean* (singular, *tobar*), the drinking wells; and specifically, those reputed to have had associations with 'healing', or, before the Reformation, understood as 'holy' wells.

The bothan lend us, from the Scots and Irish Gaelic, the English words, booth and bothy. The oldest examples are domed, built up of inwardly circling stones. This 'corbelled' architecture led to their visual association with straw beehives. Nearly all such structures have long ago collapsed to tumbled rings amongst the grass and flowers. Be that as it may, their tales of sìth and sìthean echo down the generations, whether in story, poetry or song. Such sheilings sheltered the summer tenders of the cattle, but some would once have been permanent settlements. Others served as refuges for spiritual retreat. Often the place names give a clue, like as we saw with Àirigh an t-Sagairt between Druim Dubh and Leurbost – the Sheiling of the Priest. Tradition holds that some of these date back to the 'Druids'. Indeed, Martin Martin, a physician from the Isle of Skye with a reduplicated name, who wrote a key ethnographic account of the islands at the end of the seventeenth century, called them *Tigh nan Druineach* – Druids' Houses.[12]

A *drùidh* in the Gaelic context was a pre-Christian priest, an adherent of the 'Elder Faith' of our indigenous Old Testament. The Gaelic Bible variously translates the Wise Men of the East, in Matthew 2:1, as *Draoithe*, *Druidh* or *Druidhean*, and similarly, a fragment of poetry that is attributed to Saint Columba, speaks of Christ as 'my druid'. Many words in Gaelic take 'druid' as their stem. Again, and like with the colour *ghlas*, we see the metaphoric shape-shifting qualities of the language. MacLennan's dictionary links words like *drùdhadh* (pronounced *droo-u*) to qualities of essence, intimacy, influence and intimate penetration in the sense of moisture that seeps everywhere.[13] A wee dram of whisky is a *drùdhag*, the dew is *drùcht* and a teardrop, *drùchd*. The starling, a member of the crow family, is *druid-dubh* – the 'black druid'. There are also phrases like *cainnt drùidhbhteach* as the oratory of a bard or chieftain holding forth, with eloquence such as stirs the essence of a people's spirit, seeping through their bones, and binding them in spiritual, cultural and political cohesion.

My guide to bothan sites, with or without their Druids, was my old friend, the stonemason and antiquarian James Crawford. Seumas, as he prefers to be known. On the telephone before I left home, he'd given me the Ordnance Survey map references to a range of places that I might want to visit. These included The Major, a spectacular fallen standing stone at NB 27038:27875, and the site of a celebrated Last Battle at NB 15769:25169. I wasn't sure if I'd be going in those directions, but what most captured my imagination was a ruined both, one that he called Bridgit's Sheiling, at NB 21970:26890. This, as he described it, was a tumbled ring of stones in a lonely place of unadorned beauty. It was to be found at a rocky green ridge, the Rubha Leathann, that stood a mile north-east from the point at which he recommended that I try to ford the River Grimersta. It was right in the middle of the island.

Variously Bridgit, Brig, Brid, Bride, or most fulsomely *Brìghde* – with a breathed *bree-jah* sound, in the Gaelic – she was the patron saint of poetry, healing and the blacksmith's art of purifying metals.[14] She was – and depending who you speak to, still is – a Christian saint, the foster mother of Christ, and a daughter of the Elder Faith, the *Tuatha Dé Danan* or people of the Celtic mother goddess, who in turn became the *Aos Sìth*, the faeries.

'That's where I've got to go and spend a night,' I'd said to Seumas with an almost startling rush of conviction.

'I thought you'd like that one!' he said, and though his voice was coming down the wire, it sounded like he said it with a knowing smile.

If my notes from Seumas Crawford were to guide me to the bothan, his counterpart, my lantern to the temples and wells, was to be the Gaelic broadcaster, educationalist and cultural historian Dr Finlay MacLeod of the village of Shawbost on the West Side of Lewis.

'Doctor Finlay', as he's affectionately known, is the island's most outspoken atheist. Atheists are an endangered species, rare amongst indigenous Hebrideans. Whatever Finlay's version of the irreligionist's creed may or may not be, it hadn't held him back from writing a reverential little pocket guide, *The Chapels in the Western Isles.*[15] It underscores the sheer concentration of these relics of devotion from an age that is no more.

> These largely abandoned sites together build up a most intriguing network of locations throughout the length of the Western Isles; the fact that they still exist is surprising in itself, and the fact that they form such an unspoken part of the landscape and the history of the place contrasts with the more strident forms of belief which arrived in the islands during subsequent centuries.

In an equally exquisite companion volume, *The Healing Wells of the Western Isles,* Finlay's spirit again comes through, and that in a manner one might call *drùdhadh* – getting to the essence:

> Through the wells we are able to see vestiges of customs which were at one time widespread throughout the land. Water was seen as a live and powerful element, and people were drawn to it although they were also in awe of it. The knowledge they had was knowledge of how they could attain health and wholesomeness through the power associated with water and wells. Although the nature of people's information has changed since those times, there are still some remnants of ancient knowledge in existence, and some of the wells are still known, bearing witness to thought processes that are today not easy to penetrate.

When I was at school, the story went around that Doctor Finlay had done his PhD on Rorschach ink blot tests. I think his studies were actually in wider aspects of educational psychology, but for us the label stuck, as did its improvised methodology. We boys would huddle in the back seat of the bus. We'd spray our exercise books with fountain pens, and use the blots to scry into each other's souls. Strangely enough, our adolescent psyches were configured in remarkably similar ways: exactly as would please old Uncle Freud.

But now my bus is coming down the Clisham. We're coasting to the little town of Tarbert. Here, the first leg of my southbound journey terminates beside the pier.

I buy some fishing tackle from the ironmonger's. It's one of those remarkable olde worlde shops that has everything. Boxes are piled up to the roof and ordered either by their weight, or archaeologically. Anchor chains are on the lowest shelves. Nails, a little higher up. Pity help you if you want a feather duster, unless an Edwardian one lurks behind the stob hammers.

Mindful of Earth Mother back at Café Spirituel, I get some apples and visit the butcher's. I'm not sure if the latter's what she had in mind by 'fresh food', but we've all got our weaknesses, even if for her, perhaps, for tofu. I'm worried about coping with my rucksack's weight as I build up a semblance of fitness. Thankfully, when I present myself to explain this additional, if minor weakness, the kindly woman in the tourist office lets me offload the camping gear that won't be needed this first night, and park it in a black bin bag behind a promotional placard. I pledge to pick it up tomorrow afternoon when walking back this way.

Within an hour I'm on a lively little bus, romping at a giddy rate up and down and all around the switchbacks of the single-track east Harris road. It's a merry banter. The driver shouts back and forth between his passengers, cracking jokes, sharing news, and flipping interchangeably from Gaelic to English.

It sets me thinking of a letter from a tourist that was published in the *Stornoway Gazette*. On one of these buses, halfway to one of the ferry terminals, the poor man realised that he must have dropped his wallet. The driver pulled up to a halt. He got out of his seat, and asked the passengers if anybody would mind if he did the decent thing. Doubling back, there was the wallet, lying in the grass where its owner had embarked. Doubling back again, they made the ferry just in time.

'That would never have happened on the mainland!' blurted the grateful tourist.

'Ah well, you see,' replied the driver, 'You're in the islands now.'

Forty dizzy minutes after leaving Tarbert, my bus re-enters orbit. With a shuddering halt, the door hisses open. I spill out into a lay-by with my now-reduced rucksack, and look up woozily, feeling queasy. There stands Saint Clement's Church of Rodel, my first temple, and the starting point for the journey.

Of all the island's three dozen or so pre-Reformation chapels, only two have been restored: Saint Clement's, here in the far south of Harris, and Teampall Mholuidh, dedicated to Saint Moluag (as it is anglicised), in the far north of Lewis at my walk's intended destination. The church sits beneath the cloud-fringed summit of an iconic mountain, Roineabhal. It sits with its square lookout tower, tight-pressed into a rocky knoll with views down to the southern Hebrides. This, to my eye, in its setting on a rise above the sea, is quite the most exquisite little gem this side of Tuscany. It has been called the Westminster of the Isles, but blessed would be Westminster Abbey were it worthy to be nominated the Rodel of London. I enter by the roadside gate, and leave my rucksack by the lichen-bearded wall. A winding pathway, inset with seashells in the cement between the paving stones, leads up to a heavy-studded oak-wood door. With a lazy creak, it yawns open to my push, and I step through into the half-light.

Gradually my eyes accustom to the dappled shafts of fluted sunshine from the narrow windows. The scent of stone is dank, yet rich like woodland loam. I still can't quite believe that I've arrived. This is somewhere that I've always loved. The walls are lined with grave slabs scrolled with foliage and knotwork, the symbols of both life and life's eternity. The air is reverently still, and, resting underneath the floor, the MacCrimmons: the hereditary pipers to the Macleods of Harris and Dunvegan whose spiritual stronghold this was. It is said that their gift came straight from out the hollow hill, the gliding *siubhal sìth,* or 'faerie motion', of grace notes played in sheer quicksilver eloquence.

This might be embarrassing to contemporary secularism and to conventional religion alike, but you can't talk about the Sìol Thormoid Macleods without immersion from the outset into faerie lore. For generations, the 'Fairy Cradle Song' has been sung over the newborn sons of their clan chiefs. To this day, the Faerie Flag hangs, for visitors to see, in Dunvegan Castle on Skye, it having been the blanket with which the Otherworld wife of one of the first chiefs covered her little son on the day she was recalled to live amongst her own people. In 1922, the fabric was examined by a certain Mr Wace of the Victoria and Albert Museum in London. He offered his opinion that it was, in all probability, a relic brought back from the crusades.[16]

'Mr Wace,' said the clan chief of the time. 'You think that, but I know that it was given to my ancestor *by a fairy*.'

'Sir,' replied Mr Wace, in a masterstroke of English understatement: 'I bow to your superior knowledge.'

Built in its present form in the early sixteenth century, the church's centrepiece is an ornate sculptured tomb, completed in 1528 for the eighth chief, Alasdair Macleod. On account of battle wounds with the Macdonalds of Clanranald, he was nicknamed *Crotach* – Hunchback – but he eventually grew weary of war, and is thought to have lived out his days in spiritual reflection at Rodel.

Here is the finest piece of medieval sculpture in the Hebrides. A blazing heavenly sun shines out from just above the centre. Above that, stands Christ, crowned and crucified, with figures gathered at the foot of the cross. To the flanks are the four evangelists. Each is stylised with his totem mascot: Matthew's angel, Mark's lion, Luke's ox and the great eagle of Saint John. The scenes below include an exquisitely executed *birlinn*, a Hebridean longship, and a troop of deer, portrayed with all the natural poise of great cave paintings. Around the perimeter are effigies of the saints, with names or symbols to identify. James or *Jacobi* has two. One is probably James the brother of Jesus and first bishop of Jerusalem, to whom the Epistle of Saint James near the end of the Bible is attributed. The other is unquestionably Saint James the Greater. This is shown by the scallop in his halo. I'd noticed an abundance of the shells of the scallop's smaller siblings, the cockle, in the pathway that led up to Saint Clement's from the gate. *La Coquille St Jacques*, as the scallop is called in France, is the symbol of pilgrimage. Its radial ribs converge towards the hinge, like pilgrim paths all leading to the sacred place. Returning back by those same routes again, the pilgrim spreads out blessing, far into the world.

A flight of steps leads up into the tower. I climb, and from the top the island-stippled Sound of Harris and beyond reveals itself. This is a sacred landscape, a rosary in geography. Few if any of these places, each one of them a little world and mostly uninhabited, do not boast at least one temple, holy well, standing stone, set of prehistoric cup marks hollowed into rock, or a place name that bears witness to some distant saint, portentous happening, or antique tradition of blessedness. Forty miles out lies St Kilda, a part of the parish of Harris, with temples dedicated to Saint Brianan, Saint Columba and Christ. In 1758, the Rev. Kenneth MacAulay wrote that one of its four holy wells, Tobar nam Buadh – The Well of the Virtues – was believed to cure distempers, deafness and every nervous disease. It was, he said, the people's 'constant practice to address the Genius of the place with supplication and prayer', and to offer tokens of the lowest monetary value, such as 'very frequently the whole expense of sacrifice was no more than one of the little common stones that happened to be in the Pilgrim's way'.[17] In other words, what mattered was not the monetary value, but what the people carried in their hearts.

Closer in is Pabbay – Priest's Island – with temples consecrated to both the Virgin Mary and Saint Moluag, he having been a Celtic saint who died in 592 and left his mark all over the West Highlands. Pabbay's people were famed for their illicit whisky. There's at least one Hebridean storyteller who still entertains his visitors with the tales, such as how the doughty wives of Pabbay would get the better of the excise man.[18] The earthiness of everyday life interwove intimately with these people's spiritual lives; but it was not to last. In 1846, the entire population of Pabbay was cleared away by the landlord, turning their pastures over to a commercial sheep farm.

South of Pabbay are the isles of North and South Uist, and these, the home to many wells and several temples. The most notable of the latter is Teampall na Trianaid, Trinity Temple at Carnish. This was built in the thirteenth century by a woman, Beathag, the daughter of Somhairle, the Lord of the Isles. A century and a half later, it was substantially repaired by another woman of formidable ilk, Amie NicRuairidh. It was also a medieval university. A modest plaque, pinned to the ruins, marks the local tradition that it was here the acclaimed philosopher, Duns Scotus (c. 1270–1308), had studied.

The little islands all around are similarly saturated in the twilight of sanctity. The Monach Islands or Heisgeir, for example, are known as Heisgeir nan Cailleach on account of their nunnery. It had a long association with Iona, and right up until the Reformation the sisters continued to pray for the world by the light of their lamps, fuelled by seal-oil. Today, there are no longer any people; but there's a lighthouse that, in its own way, prays for shipping. Boreray was the burial ground of Celtic monks from north of Eigg. Once when I was being driven in the taxi of Alda Ferguson of Lochmaddy, he stopped and pointed out this double emerald hummock that lounges in the surf some three miles out into the ocean. 'That island,' the old man announced, drawing on a local tradition, 'is the birth place of the grandfather of Neil Armstrong, the first man on the moon.'[19] I just thought to myself – if that's true, then these people know a thing or two about pilgrimage.

Coming back up into the Sound of Harris, four miles off Rodel sit a pair of islands, fringed with ivory sand, called Ensay and Killegray. The latter means the place of the monastic 'cell' or church. Again, place names bear enduring witness to sheer spiritual intensity. Teampall na h-Annaid – the Temple of the Monastery or Mother Church. Tobair na h-Annaid – the Well of the Mother Church. When I was a teenager, the South Harris doctor Angus MacKinnon took me out there in his boat. Some time later, he showed me a child's skull that he'd found washed out from the wave-encroached cemetery on Killegray. He placed the white sphere in my hands. I felt the sadness surging. For the first time in my life, I was looking into tragic death, straight through the eyes. 'It's all right,' Angus said. The shadow side of life was there, but also its absorption in some greater whole of being.

Tradition holds that the Druids were the first here at Saint Clement's, then the Columban monks from Ireland and Iona, and in their footsteps, the Culdees or *Céli Dé* – the Servants of God – who were noted for their simple lifestyles, their pastoral dedication to the poor and sick, their Sabbath observance, and for their love of sacred chant and hallowed song.[20] Then came change. The brutal Norman invasion of England in 1066 caused the Hungarian-born Margaret of Wessex to flee to Scotland. There she married the king, Malcolm Canmore, and this either made for, or coincided with, a turning point for the Scottish church. Gaelic liturgies started to be replaced with Latin ones. The localised basis of authority that had character-ised the Celtic Church, with its nod to Ireland, began to bow distinctively to Rome. This wasn't all down to Margaret's personal influence. Similar changes were also happening in Ireland, the driving force being the Gregorian Reforms that strengthened the hand of Rome.

In 1093, Malcolm was killed in battle. According to the Irish annals, Margaret died a few days later from her sorrow. A pious woman, she was later canonised. Their youngest son, David, was sent away, at the age of nine, to be raised in the Norman court of England. When his brother, Alexander I, died in 1124, the adult David returned and, in a bloody power struggle, seized the kingdom with the backing of Henry I of England, a son of William the Conqueror. David went on to introduce feudalism into Scotland. Land was given to Anglo-Norman friends who had helped him. These became the rootstock of many of 'Our Scots Noble Families'.[21] Their sense of underlying Christian cohesion as brothers in arms, notwithstanding all the internecine feuding, had been strengthened by the practice of 'taking up the cross' during the First Crusade of 1096–99.

So began the long erosion of Scotland's customary system of tenure, where the land, especially in Gaelic-speaking areas, was held by the chief on behalf of the clan as a whole. While he was consolidating his power and rendering Scotland a coherent nation, David radically accelerated his mother's innovation of introducing the European religious orders. While the facts are limited and much debated, this probably subsumed the Céli Dé and remnants of the original Celtic Church. David set up (in the course of making land grants to various European orders) some two dozen Augustinian priories. According to the Old (or First) Statistical Account of 1792, Rodel was handed to the Canons Regular of Saint Augustine in 1128.[22]

It would seem that this settlement settled down, and held sway until the Protestant Reformation took grip in Scotland in 1560. It was to the Reformation that Doctor Finlay had referred, when he dropped a mention, in his little book of chapels, to 'the more strident forms of belief which arrived in the islands during subsequent centuries'.[23]

Scotland's pioneering reformer, John Knox, had taken his lead from John Calvin's Geneva in implanting the Presbyterian version of Reformed religion. It was, at least until relatively recently in Scotland, a harsh approach. Calvin, for example, had denounced religious art as 'brutish stupidity'.[24] His best friend, the iconoclast William Farel, went around Geneva stirring up mobs that persecuted priests, harangued the nuns to marry, enforced attendance at their interminable sermons, robbed religious houses, smashed the statues of the saints and icons, whitewashed over the murals, and tossed the bells out of their belfries. The latter, according to the detailed chronicle of a Poor Clare nun, included melting down the fragments to make them into weapons.[25]

It is no longer possible to be sure what may or may not have happened to echo all of this in the Outer Hebrides. There is, I've heard it said, 'a black hole' in the post-Reformation oral memory. What is beyond dispute is that every one of the *team-paill*, the pre-Reformation churches, fell into ruin. Whether some of these were also racked – that is to say, wilfully destroyed – is a more variegated question.[26] But for now, I must take leave from this sacred place. I can hear voices, and as I alight from the tower's flight of steps, I nod a silent acknowledgement to a group of visitors who are wandering around with cameras flashing.

Turning towards the oaken door to take my exit, I glance up at a large white marble tablet that is set at head height into the wall. Its iron fastening studs have corroded, tarnishing the surface with a rusty stain. The inscription, discreetly couched in Latin, signalling only to the few, bears ominous testimony:[27]

> This sacred edifice, the very walls of which had been scarcely spared through the fury attendant upon religious change, which in its universal pillage devastated everything, and levelling the adjoining convent of friars and nuns to the ground, consecrate to the piety of his ancestors in former times, to God and St Clement, after having been for now over two hundred years roofless and neglected, was repaired and adorned . . . by Alexander Macleod of Harris in 1787 AD.

On the one hand, the eighth chief's tomb was left intact. At least that wasn't desecrated. But looking at the wider history of that era, what was such Reformation fury all about? What kind of problems in theology leave it vulnerable to associations with violence, and therefore, to ongoing problems within some religions? These are questions that I want to muse on as I walk. Questions that are not just historical, but also, and for our own times too, 'attendant upon religious change'.

I take a final glance down the length of Saint Clement's, then step outside to face the brightness of the daylight. The door draws slowly closed behind me. Its iron latch drops into place, a farewell clunk resounding to the ear.

3

BLUE MOUNTAIN HARE

I have a couple of respects to pay before leaving the churchyard, and a cemetery is a place of such unlikely bedfellows. Set half-way up the south face of the tower is one: an astonishing stone-crafted figure, the Sheila-na-Gig of Rodel. The lady crouches there, as if she's giving birth. Her womanhood is unconcealed in all its fullness. She nurses in her arms a heavily eroded figure that looks more like an animal, a lamb or seal, than the babe one might expect.

Only speculation surrounds the meaning of these peculiar features of medieval church architecture. They are found mainly in Ireland and the West of Scotland, including the isles of Eigg and Iona, and one suggestion is that they're like gargoyles, intended to frighten away the faithful from the allures of sexual love. If that's the case, then for me the Rodel 'Sheila' doesn't cut the bromide. Another suggestion is that they're fertility symbols. To me, she's just beautiful. Her presence tunes me to the note of mystical religion; to the way erotic love becomes a metaphor of Heaven. It's there in Hinduism, with the union of Shiva and Parvati, the Daughter of the Mountains. There, too, in Tantra, with Sky Dancer, Yeshe Tsogyel, whose consort, Padma Sambhava, carried Buddhism from the Swat Valley to Tibet. And although it is a matter about which few sermons are preached, it's in the Bible too. Voluptuously so, in the Song of Solomon. There's even a chapter in the Book of Job that, twice, pictures aspects of the Creation as breaking forth from out God's cosmic 'womb'.[1] Quite where that leaves the gendering of the deity, might well be pondered.

An inscription found above the entrance to some churches, reads: *This is the house of God and the gate of Heaven.*[2] Perhaps I'd better leave my speculations there. Suffice to say that the mystics, like the poets, have always been a risqué bunch, which brings me to my next stop. Underneath the south transept window rests the Rodel-born seventeenth-century bard, Mary Macleod, or Màiri Nighean Alasdair Ruaidh. It's said that Màiri was remembered into the early twentieth century as if she'd ambled through the village only yesterday, tap-tap-tapping along the road with her trademark silver-topped walking stick.

It was she who was chosen to sing the 'Fairy Cradle Song', or 'Cradle Spell', for a newborn infant son of Chief MacLeod. She rests in the church vaults, but lying face down. Why so, is much debated. The simple version is that she was a witch. However, that would be hard to square with such a sanctified place of burial. Locally, I've heard it suggested that she'd told too many lies in her poetry praising the chief of Macleod. She asked to be buried face down, 'so that her lying tongue would not be pointing to heaven'.[3] There are other views. Was it that her feisty nature had caused offence? The Gaelic scholar and singer Dr Anne Lorne Gillies points out that Mary was a powerful figure, a charismatic poet, but she was not a member of the elite bardic order. Indeed, 'she was not even a man'.[4]

Another, and a very lovely perspective on her, comes from the Rev. Dr Kenneth Macleod of the Isle of Eigg. His father's people had been from the north of Skye and were steeped in all the olden lore of clan Macleod. The Reverend Kenneth would have enjoyed some of today's scholars, who point out that Gaelic had no native word for a 'witch', and that women of such bearing as Màiri might better be understood as powerful shamans.[5] Indeed, Kenneth seized 'witch' from out of the mouths of churlish patriarchs, and gently cast it back, writing in 1927:[6]

> Such as wish to understand the Scottish Gael, what he is and what he is not, should study our witches as well as our saints. The responsible witches of Gaeldom were not the weaklings who are merely bad-hearted, or are tricksters in self-defence. They were rather highly-gifted women who loved being alive, and who won their place by force of character, and by right of service . . . The only vice in them which would, perhaps, have shocked the saints was their keen sense of humour.

His book, *The Road to the Isles*, was an anthem to the old Hebridean ways. In taking special care to laud the spiritual élan of women, it devotes a full chapter to Màiri, this Daughter of Red Alastair. Kenneth concurs that the bard was buried face down, but not from any excess need for penance. Neither does he mince his words in what he goes on to say about her. Already, he would have been feeling the challenges to his style of 'romantic' Celtic 'twilightism' that set in following the disillusion of the First World War.[7] This accelerated through the century, often in a sceptical alliance between secular figures and the conservatively religious, who either hadn't experienced his world, or if they had, suspected it of being backward, pagan, and even Catholic, as are the southern Hebrides. This might explain the urgent tone of Kenneth's rallying call to hold the faith.[8]

> There is a bidding to which the Gael is never false, the bidding which puts him under the spells. An Islesman is under spells both to his heart and to his head to give love to Mary Macleod, the most fascinating figure in Gaelic poetry from the beginning of the seventeenth century to a century on which fate has not yet put a name. A woman not of the schools but of herself, and fond of taking her own way when her own way seemed the best . . .

Mairi, Daughter of Alastair Rua, sleeps face downward, by the Church of Saint Clement, in Rodel of Harris, the Iona of her clan. 'Not on the clouds would my eyes be, O kinsfolk,' said she in the parting, 'but on Rodel of Harris.' Her thought was, perhaps, the thought of St Bride, the Foster-mother [of Christ], even as her blood was the blood: *Beautiful the cloud on high, my children, but more beautiful still the shower which falleth, giving growth to the corn and milk to the cattle, for little children.*

If this version is correct, it seems to me that Màiri is reminding us that Rodel is a place where Heaven grounds itself on Earth. 'Thy kingdom come . . . on Earth as it is in Heaven' – and those petitions of the Lord's Prayer, so cogent in these times of ecological predicament, preached by the post-mortem yogic posture of a so-called witch.

I'd like to feel that Kenneth will be one of my unseen companions on this walk. In the first half of the twentieth century he was considered to have been the greatest living authority on Gaelic traditions.[9] He was born on Eigg, and during the 1990s this island became the focus of my work with land reform, the residents eventually succeeding in bringing it into community ownership after a six-year-long battle with landed power.[10]

Kenneth ended his ministry at the Church of Scotland on the Isle of Gigha, and died in 1955. Both that island's parish church and Iona Abbey have stained glass windows to commemorate his life. When Vérène and I first visited Gigha, we marvelled at the wonder of this memorial, crafted in the manner of the Celtic Revival. Threaded in with knotwork symbols and a prominent white seagull, are the troika of Irish and Scots Gaelic saints: Patrick, the one-time slave, conferring blessing; Columba, in a birlinn on his immram voyage to Iona; and Brìghde, Shepherdess of the Flocks, cherishing a lamb. The infant Christ has arms outstretched upon a cross ablaze

with golden flames of love. The same rare portrayal of an
infant crucified, yet glorified, also hallows the altar of the
Catholic church on Eigg. An English inscription hails Kenneth
as a 'preacher, pastor, poet'. Alongside, there is a treasured
Gaelic saying:[11]

> *Thig crìoch air an t-saoghal*
> *Ach mairidh gaol is ceòl*
> (The world will come to an end
> But love and music will endure)

As we both soaked in the window's beauty that day, a beam of
sunshine burst in through the glass. The colours quickened
into vibrant life, and to Vérène's astonishment, and my
embarrassment, I just burst into tears. It felt as if I'd seen a
glimpse of all that has been lost from the deepest spiritual
culture of the Hebrides. And yet – this was the strangest
thing – those very tears were rippled through with joy. It was
as if a silver pool had spilled and overwhelmed my disconso-
lation, lifting it to rapture.

I later learned of what tradition calls 'the carrying stream'.
Not for the first time had I felt propelled along by its unending
current.[12] John Lorne Campbell of Canna often said that that
whereas the modern mind exists on a horizontal plane, 'domi-
nated by scientific materialism and a concern with purely
contemporary happenings', the consciousness of the Gaelic
mind may be described as existing in a vertical plane, 'possess-
ing historical continuity and religious sense . . . an ever-present
sense of the reality and existence of the other world of spiritual
and psychic experience'.[13] That was how it felt that day. The
experience left me with a sense of calling to unspecified work
ahead, an Otherworld path to walk and share into the world.

Well! Better be getting walking after all this talking. I'm going
to spend tonight with my old friend John MacAulay of
Flodabay or Fhleoideabhaigh, a boatbuilder and tradition

bearer. His several books include a study of the birlinn as indigenous ship craft, not to be confused, he says, with Roman galleys; and *Silent Tower*, which is the definitive history of Saint Clement's. I'd said to him and Jane that I'd be there around six. I don't carry a watch, and my phone is off to save the battery, but judging by the sun it must by now have clocked three.

I lift 'Osprey', as I'm calling my rucksack, onto my back. That's the brand I'd purchased for the trip, not that I'd gone after sponsorship or anything. Thank goodness all my heavy stuff got left behind at Tarbert. This next twenty-four hours can be a gentle wooing of our new relationship.

The galvanised churchyard gate clanks closed – and finally I am walking.

'Just feel it,' I'm saying to myself. 'Just feel these footsteps. On the road. Actually walking.'

Rodel glen is rich and green, thanks to a seam of crystalline limestone that moderates the acidity of the peat. The road runs east, then sharply to the north, before narrowing to single-track with passing places. Spring is late this year. The heather's still in browns and greys and rattled from the winter gales. Today, it's breezing from the south-east. That's great. It cools the sunshine on my back and gives a gladness to my stride. That's also why I'm walking from the south to north. The position of the sun, and the prevailing southerly winds.

Across the Minch I can see the Isle of Skye, and, now and then, I maybe glimpse the Shiant Islands. Na h-Eileanan Seunta in the Gaelic – the Enchanted or the Sacred Isles. What a name – and where, you have to ask, would it have come from? And then, that crazy stretch of water. The Sound of Shiant in English, but in Gaelic, Sruth nam Fear Gorma. The Straits of the Blue Men – and they the oceanic faerie lads that dance to every storm.

One of these volcanic outcrops that comprise the Shiants is called Eilean Mhoire (or Mhuire). A late seventeenth-century traveller recorded that it had a chapel, 'dedicated to the Virgin

Mary', and an early eighteenth-century map shows it as 'St Maries Isle'. [14] Mhoire (pronouned 'Vor-u') is the honorary equivalent of Màiri, used specifically for Mary as the mother of Christ. It makes me think of lines from Eliot's *Four Quartets*, to me the greatest mystical poem in the English language, though Hugh MacDiarmid's *On a Raised Beach* comes a very close second. [15]

> Lady, whose shrine stands on the promontory,
> Pray for all those who are in ships, those
> Whose business has to do with fish . . .

Good start, for a poacher's pilgrimage. I'll just leave out the verse that follows: '. . . and those concerned with every lawful traffic'.

There is such a lazy feel to this road. Only the occasional car slips by and even these go slowly. My pace is settling to a rhythm. My eyes are resting mainly on road. A road is such a physical thing. It flows towards me like a tarry river set with flotsam shards. The ubiquitous greys of Lewisian gneiss. The orange glints of feldspar and dirty-yellow stains of iron. The gemlike sparkle of black hornblende chips and snowy flecks of quartz.

MacDiarmid was supposedly an atheist. Whether or not that was so, I worship at his church.

> Let men find the faith that builds mountains
> Before they seek the faith that moves them . . .
> These stones go through Man, straight to God, if there
>   is one . . .
> What happens to us
> Is irrelevant to the world's geology
> But what happens to the world's geology
> Is not irrelevant to us.

Climbing higher now, and the heather and the red deergrass yield to bare grey rocky beds, gnarled and wrinkled like pegged-out sheets of rhinoceros hide. I'm on the flanks of Roineabhal. The slope rises sharply upwards as a moonscape to my left. This peak, reclining out of view, has meant so much to me. We'd fought a battle in the 1990s. It stopped the mountain from being turned into the biggest roadstone quarry in the world. For sixty years, its belly would have been ripped out by thirty-six tons of explosive a week. Ten million tons of rock a year, crushed for paving motorways in the already over-developed south.

John MacAulay was the island's representative in the matter. He'd been elected to chair the Quarry Benefit Group, set up to look at the upsides – and the downsides – that the proposal might have brought to Harris. My part had been to bring the Mi'Kmaq War Chief of the time from Canada. He had stopped a similar superquarry on Kluscap, his people's sacred mountain in Nova Scotia. Stone Eagle was his name, and he told the government planning inquiry that we had to call a halt to such trashing of the planet. 'If we fail to do so, Mother Earth will cleanse herself of the offending organism that is killing her. This is our teaching.'

A leading environmental educator, Dr Robbie Nicol, who heads up the Institute for Education, Teaching & Leadership at Edinburgh University, emailed me out of the blue recently. He's one of a growing number that I hear from who'd been drawn, he said, to make 'a pilgrimage' to the summit.

> I say, *pilgrimage,* because I know how hard so many people worked to avoid the development of this mountain. It is achingly beautiful. The view down into the *coire* is unlike any other I've experienced, and I felt compelled to write.

Suddenly I freeze. A grassy gully runs up the side of Roineabhal, just past a solitary modern bungalow at the turnoff down to Lingerabay.

That looks like a *hare* amongst the rocks. Either that, or a huge rabbit.

The only island species is the Blue Mountain Hare, *Lepus timidus*. The habitat is right, but I've never previously seen one. 'Blue', they call it – said to be the tint the coat can take at certain times of year. Reminds me how the naturalist Frank Fraser Darling observed that mountains, too, 'become Highland blue, a deep ineffable shade.' Oh my! What a contribution to the artist's palette. Highland blue. Ineffable. That's how the mountains are today, the compass of the oceans too.

While brown hares came to Britain with the Romans, only the blue is truly native. Julius Caesar said the Celtic Britons held them to be sacred. *She* – as gendered in the folklore – is a witch disguised. She, true nature wild and free. She, the shape-shifting shaman – Is she human? Is she animal? Does it matter? – whose nest is called a 'form', and whose spiritual form is the walker between the worlds.

The quickest way for an amateur like me to tell a hare from a rabbit is by the long, black-tipped ears. I slowly reach to Osprey for my binoculars. But I'm spotted. She louches off, and disappears amongst a pile of boulders. But she's given me a metaphor. I've been thinking about the stages of this walk. Blue Mountain Hare. Here's *blue* along this smoky azure south-east Harris coast. Tomorrow night, into the *mountain* passes for several days. And if I get to next week, I'll play the mad March *hare* – well, maybe stretching it to May in these boreal parts – coursing through the villages of north-west Lewis.

I stand and peer through the glasses for several minutes. Not a movement. Nothing. Only Màiri Nighean Alasdair Ruaidh, a parting nod from hefted haunts on Roineabhal, nestling down into the crevices of my mind.

Here you'd hardly think that the Ice Age ended ten thousand years ago. The rocks are scored by great striations, etched like chalks on screeching blackboards trapped beneath the glacier's long-sliding gait. Hardy alpines – blue, white and yellow come the summer – have made their homes in soil-filled chinks that give their roots a stony toe grip from the gales. Everywhere are rills that seep from crumpled folds, deepen into pools, and, when the year warms up, will teem with water beetles, dragon-flies and long-legged water skimmers.

I'm well into my stride now, and the road traipses down a long curved dip to pass across a bridge. I step aside and slip down beneath the hand-wrought layers of stone. Fast flowing water is my friend, and I lie down to sup my fill from Abhainn a' Choire – the Stream of the Cauldron. I love wild water's peaty taste – it's what we always drank as kids. Up and off again, climbing the hill, replaying all the switchbacks of the little bus in elegant slow motion. Goodness! How that seems like days ago, but scarce an hour or two's slipped past.

Now, I'm heading down from Roineabhal, slipping off the north end, and it leads into a very different scene. Coming up, I sight the staggered crossroads of the village of Àird Mhighe. Here, it's all change. Instead of the plant life struggling to hold on, the land is fertile. Either there's been a shift of underlying strata that's changed the soil type, or, more likely, it's the seaweed, blown up from the bay, and rotting to yield nutrients. The bare mountain, too, has fallen into relief behind me. A gentleness has settled into place. Instead of sheets of flayed rhinoceros, the ice down here has rounded off and polished the bedrock into strange humps. The French call them *roches moutonnées* – mutton or sheep rocks. In some parts of the world, the bigger ones would be called whalebacks. That's what I'm seeing as my mind, in playful mode, morphs the geol-ogy into animals of stone. I'm in amongst a pod of whales, fresh swum from out the studio of Henry Moore. They breach, and lounge, and lunge in sumptuous curves upon the surface of a bright green sea of short-cropped meadow grass.

I step aside from off the road again, and rest my back against one of these behemoths. It's been harpooned! A metal pin, staining the stone with rusty blood, anchors an iron ring. Of course. This is a crossroads from before the days of cars. This is where the youth would meet to dance away the evenings, maybe with a pony tethered. This is where you'd tie your cow while asking of a passer-by the perennial question: 'What's fresh?' And if there's nothing fresh, then there might be some sharing of the tales brought back from whaling fleets, or from the herding in the hills. And if the work is done, and leisure offers time to loaf at ease awhile, then maybe there'll be hoary tales of long ago. And if, instead of going north today, you went west. If you went not in a car, but by foot, or ever so gently on a bicycle. If you headed inland for a mile or two, past little lochs that shimmer in the summer's sun with water lilies, and the hoary dance of interstellar filigree of the bitter bog bean blossom, then you'd reach a loch called Langabhat. The Norse means 'lang-vat' or 'long water', but don't be confusing this Loch Langabhat with the other, even longer one, that stretches up through southern central Lewis. This is the Langabhat of Harris, more economical in scale, yet still quite long enough to span, from east to west, the middle half of southern central Harris.

A dearer little road that carries you there could scarce be found, and it was in *Crotal and White,* his homage to a crofting childhood, that the late BBC journalist Finlay J. MacDonald described a boyhood excursion to that very loch.[16] He speaks of the Isle of Harris as a place that 'wove a spiritual and physical magic as I grew up with it'. He adds, lest any latter-day churl be listening in: 'If it all sounds idyllic, it's because it was to the boy who I was.' And he tells of a tiny island on Langabhat called Eilean na Caillich.[17] Now, the *cailleach* – *caillich* being the possessive case – is an old woman. However, there's an older and more particular usage of the word that implies a *holy* old woman, and, according to tradition, there had been a nunnery attached to Saint Clement's. For whatever reason – some say she'd been banished, but maybe she just wanted peace from the priests – one of the sisters had built her hermitage on this wee island in Loch Langabhat. She'd get to it by a semi-submerged causeway. It's still there to this day, even shown on the oldest maps.

All through Finlay's childhood, he had been 'absolutely and firmly forbidden' to go to Eilean na Caillich. However, when boys reach a certain age – at least, the crofter boys in these parts – they get fired up with a kind of derring-do. So off he went one day, setting out two miles across the moor from his home at Scarista, supposedly on a fishing trip. Always be suspicious of a man you meet out in the wilds, who says he's 'only' on a fishing trip.

So, out he goes, gingerly edging his way across the causeway's rocking stepping stones, using his fishing rod as a steadying staff – and halfway over, what does he hear, but this long, slow, eerie whine . . .

Aaawwwoooooo. . . .

And he's looking back, and it's his dog! The hairs of his tail and ruff are standing on end like the bristles of brush, and he's baying like a beast demented. *Demented,* I'll tell you, as if he's been touched by the Hound of the Baskervilles itself.

Well, Finlay can't turn back at this stage. If he did, he knew he'd only have to do it another time, or else he'd lose something in himself. So he presses on, and he gets to the island, and sure enough, there are the outlines of a hermit's cell, a doorway and its long lintel stone.

'And then I heard a voice,' wrote Finlay in his book. 'Or rather, felt a voice. It came from my ears but at the same time it came from within my head. It said, *Put off thy shoes from off thy feet for the place whereon thou standest is holy ground.*'

The boy dropped his fishing rod and bolted. He splashed back across the causeway, tore up the hills with his dog close to heel, and ran, non-stop, all the way home to Scarista.

Of course, everybody knew everything in those days. They didn't watch the television, they watched the sea and hills. They watched each other like they'd watch the weather, both on the outside and the inside.

That night at the dinner table, his father asked what he'd done with the day. But it wasn't anger that flashed in those eyes when he learned that his son had been to Langabhat. It was a twinkle.

'Did you go to Eilean na Caillich, by any chance?'

'Yes.'

'Well, you had to – some day!' said the old man. 'I suppose the surest way of making you go, was by telling you not to.'

As Finlay grew up, he learned that other villagers had also made their secret pilgrimages. Each tale of derring-do had its own circumstances, but:

What was interesting – and why I wouldn't go back – was that one sentence was common to all the stories. *Put off thy shoes from off thy feet for the place whereon thou standest is holy ground.*

Beyond Àird Mhighe, leaving Roineabhal and the whales behind, I come into a genial and well-lived-in land. The road meanders over rocky bluffs. It skirts around the curves of little bays with causeways and box-girder bridges that span the frequent inlets of the sea. There are houses here, or rather, homes. Fields and gardens, old tractors kept for spares, boats pulled up and lobster pots, pastures grazed by sheep and pecked by flocks of hens and ducks, and sometimes a gaggle of hissing geese.

I pass a family couple, sitting on their veranda, a hundred or two hundred yards away. Their children all come running out and stare. I wave, and they return the gesture, giggling now. Oh yes, I know their game! I'll be the first of this new season's crop. We used to call it 'Spot the Tourist'.

Over the brow of a rise and a great gaunt shape looms up, another of those breaching whales, but just the whitened ribs and spine. Alongside stands a barrel-shaped shed. It's made from those curved sheets of corrugated iron, like the kind you see left over from the war, when Rodel was a pioneering early-warning radar base. And you know, I like that. My mind could play games with that one! Rodel still is an early-warning radar base; the spiritual life of Celtic times, not just a relic from the past, but missile incoming.

A Saltire, Scotland's flag, the cross of Saint Andrew – a fisherman, feminist and pacifist who convinced Roman soldiers to disarm – flutters idly from a pole above the shed.[18] A wooden sign over the arched doorway, reads 'Boatbuilder'. I have arrived at John MacAulay's workshop. And the roadside skeleton? That's his latest venture. An ocean-going sailing boat, set to an ancient design, taking shape in ribs of larch tongued into spine of oak.

It has taken me nearly four hours to go a mere seven miles. But so what? I'm here! John had seen me coming and, from his house across the other side of the road, stands beaming at an open door.

4

THE ELDER OF ROINEABHAL

Were there such a home as that of a seafaring Amish farmer, this stone cottage would be it. Built by his father, shared with his wife Jane and her teenage daughter, Ella, a blazing fire is the focal point, with armchairs and a sofa curled around its hearth, and not a television in sight to steal away attention. A fiddle hangs from the wood V-lining of one wall, a navigation chart of local waters on another, and, perched on a shelf, sits an old brass sextant. If it sounds set for *National Geographic* – too late – they've already been here.

He's a wiry, late sixty-something, my friend, arms like the hawsers of an ocean-going tug, blizzard-whipped white curls and a slight moustache. His piercing blue eyes convey a capacity to enchant that, according to Vérène, must have melted many a heart down the years.

'I've a bit of news for you, John,' I say, as we settle down to a massive pan of butter-fried scallops, dived for off the bottom of a local sea loch. 'I've been speaking at a conference of Lafarge, and I've got the inside story. From the horse's mouth!'

Lafarge is the biggest cement and roadstone company in the world. Based in France, they had swallowed up Redland, the smaller English company that had originally devised the scheme for blowing up Roineabhal. My having called Chief Stone Eagle over from Canada, inviting him to bring his sacred pipe (but to leave the AK-47 behind), had lent a bit of oomph to the campaign. But there'd been many hands to the pumps. Between the lot of us, we managed to stall the granting of planning permission to the point that Redland's share price had dived into decline. That was when the French swooped in with their predatory takeover. It felt like a masterstroke of karmic retribution. Redland lost all control of its ship. Through the intervention of a French banking executive, Thierry Groussin, I went to Paris and negotiated what we called the 'dignified exit strategy' – of withdrawing from the project.[1]

But there was a *quid pro quo*. Lafarge pointed out that we all use quarry products, even me, and therefore asked me to serve on their Sustainability Stakeholder Panel, 'to help us understand how to run our business better'. In consultation with my campaigning colleagues I'd agreed, but on an unpaid basis so as not to risk misunderstanding. So began a remarkable experience – I watched them radically cut their carbon emissions per ton of cement produced, build up expertise in conservation ecology for old quarry sites, recognise the UN Declaration on the Rights of Indigenous Peoples, and shift the axis of their business from an emphasis on resource extraction to what they called 'sustainable building solutions', based on developing efficient new materials and processes.[2]

'So what did you learn?' John asks, as we sit around the fire, and he pours us each a glass of wine. It was our first chance to talk in depth about it all.

'Well!' I say, with an almost boyish enthusiasm towards the older man. 'You know how our weakest link in the whole saga was all those unemployed guys who'd hoped to get a job for life on Harris?'

He stops me in my tracks. He says stiffly: 'I never saw that as a weak link.'

'I never, ever, trusted Redland's claims,' he continues, poking the fire.

'You know, Alastair. Those modern plants are so highly mechanised that they employ very few people. They'd have brought in their own specialists. All that Harris would have got is a few low-paid jobs for digger drivers and cleaners. The place itself – the place that our fathers and our mothers handed down to us in trust for the future – that would have been shipped away, from beneath our very feet.'

He pauses, visioning the scene.

'Shipped away . . . like the people themselves were shipped off in the Clearances.'

It hadn't been just the illicit distillers of Pabbay who were dispatched on emigrant ships, sent to feed the industrial revolution in emerging cities, or lined up as imperial cannon fodder. The Highland Clearances of the eighteenth and nineteenth centuries had had a very much wider geographical spread.

'I know,' I say. 'Lafarge's executives confirmed all that. Mostly low-grade jobs for the locals. But what's more, they never intended to open up a quarry in the foreseeable future anyway. They just wanted to get the planning consent *in principle*, so that they'd have it as a land bank on their balance sheet.'

'Just as we'd always suspected!' he said. 'But why did you say you thought the jobs argument had been our weakest link?'

'It was just . . . the thought of all the hopes and expectations of out-of-work folk being dashed by our campaigning. Such high unemployment in Harris. Their perception – and I agree that it was only ever a perception – was of economic salvation, forsaken at our doing.'

'Ah!' says John, broodingly. 'And that was the problem all along. You've put your finger right on the problem there, you have, my boy.

'Most of those who were pushing for the quarry were seeking precisely that. *Salvation*, as they called it.

'Salvation of the kind that went no deeper than their own hip pockets.'

There is a postscript. In my book *Soil and Soul* I'd referred to John MacAulay, anonymously, as 'the Elder'. It was he who had removed the summit rock of Roineabhal during the public inquiry in 1994, asking me to give it to Stone Eagle for symbolic safe-keeping. Under article seven of their 1752 treaty with the British, the Mi'Kmaq nation of Nova Scotia had agreed to 'use their best endeavours to save the lives and goods of any people shipwrecked on this coast'. Often, this was extended to helping distraught Scottish immigrants through the winters. Many of these were folk of crofting stock, forcibly cleared from their lands as part of the process that had released rapacious landlordism in the aftermath of the Highlanders' last stand at the Battle of Culloden.

As John saw it, having cleared the people, similar forces of greed, under the modern corporate guise, had attempted to clear even the very rocks themselves. This was what made such a powerful gesture of having Stone Eagle carry Roineabhal's sugar-bag-sized pinnacle of rock back to Nova Scotia.

In June of 2004, I went to Nova Scotia to retrieve our rock. There was a hand-over ceremony in the town hall at Pictou organised by Ishbel Munro, followed by a Mi'Kmaq sweat lodge ceremony for purification. Later that summer, a small procession of us climbed up Roineabhal. With immense dignity, John restored the summit rock – with the help of a small bag of Lafarge cement. Some of my old school friends from Leurbost had come with us. As we headed back down the slope, Alex George Morrison let out a whoop of surprise. From a cleft between some rocks, he pulled out a golden eagle's primary and, that night, gave the precious feather to John, the Elder of the Mountain.

At one point in the campaign, I'd been asked by the United Nations Environment Programme to write a contribution for their landmark volume, *The Cultural and Spiritual Values of Biodiversity*. I penned a piece that drew a parallel between the shooting of Scotland's 'last wolf' in 1743 and Culloden three years later. As part of this I'd needed to ask John's permission to quote from his closing submission to the public inquiry. I'd described him as *the community's* principal spokesperson on the superquarry issue. His reply, however, recast my framing to a wider perspective: to one that set things not in terms of a community of interests, but as community of place.

> I willingly endorse the inclusion of material from our submission to the public inquiry, with one proviso; that is, to alter your description of me as 'the *community's* principal spokesperson,' to that of 'the *island's* principal spokesperson.' This powerful sense of belonging goes infinitely deeper than that of the inhabitants of a built environment. The wolf and the mountain are one.

But by now, by this late hour in the evening, the living room fire has died down. John and Jane have gone upstairs. I've unrolled my sleeping bag. As we'd lingered with the embers, finishing off the wine, I'd asked Jane about her nursing work, in which her speciality was heart disease. She's originally from Yorkshire. She brings to the island an inside-outsider's eye. I'd asked why she thought our incidence of coronary illness is so high. Is it all down to our fatty mutton chops, salt herring, and frying scallops in the way Saint James intended, in butter?

'That's part of it,' she'd mused, 'but I can't help thinking there's something emotional as well,' and she went on to describe new research into the cardiovascular implications of anxiety and grief, the health consequences of raised cortisol levels in the bloodstream. 'And when you think about it, there's so much suffering here that's carried forward from the past.'

'Like? What kind of suffering?' I wanted to hear how she'd put it in her own words.

'Like . . . just so much . . . emotional burden. Look at their history. They had the Clearances. Then the Great War and the *Iolaire* going down . . .' that, having been the ship that hit the rocks just outside Stornoway harbour in January 1919, with more than two hundred of the surviving sailors coming home from the war going down with her. Then in the twenties and thirties there was the TB epidemic, hard times on hard times, and nearly three hundred of the young men, average age twenty-two, sailing off on the *Metagama* light-heartedly to seek a new life in Canada, not realising the all-round emotional consequences. Ironically, as the ship pulled away on 21 April 1923, the pipe band played *The Road to the Isles*, a tune that had been renamed thus after having been set to words by the Rev. Kenneth Macleod of Eigg and Gigha. It was a road that few would ever tread again.[3]

'It's like the life never stopped bleeding out of the place,' Jane continued. The Second World War followed. Many of the boys were on Atlantic convoys. Now the fishing's been all but wiped out, and crofting can no longer compete with industrial agriculture. 'It's just been the constant loss and battering of an ancient culture.'

'And do you really think they carry that inside?'

Her soft face grapples for expression.

'People just have such deep memories here. That's what I see when I go from house to house. If you're a fully feeling human being, you can't just grin and bear such burdens of the past and carry on unfazed.

'Not when the emotional currents run deep, so very deep, and run on between the generations.'

'So . . . you're suggesting,' I concluded, with a little too much of my own interpretation, 'that the weight of history *breaks the heart*, as it were?'

'Well don't get me wrong,' she'd said, with a slight jerk. 'It's not like everybody's miserable! There's plenty people living very fulfilled lives. But in terms of health, there's some pretty staggering statistics. It does make you wonder.'[4]

The night had drawn far in. We'd sat and gazed, all three of us, at the opalescent shimmer of the fading coals. Watching them shudder, one by one, like ruined castles that collapse and rattle down to ashes in the grate.

'And it's not just heart disease,' she'd concluded, getting up to straighten the sofa. 'You also see it in the Highland rate of suicide. The alcoholism too.'

The alcohol-related death rate is five times the national average, and everybody wonders why.

'It's a very west of Scotland thing,' she resumed. 'I really feel for some of the young men. They hardly know what their role is anymore.

'So I don't know. Is it the weather? The religion? Or something in the genes?

'Or is it just what happens when the ground's been pulled from underneath your feet, and you're stranded high and dry, cast up on rocks on which the past has left you?'

I awaken to the aroma of a heart-whacking fry-up in the kitchen.

'I thought you'd be needing something that would keep you going on the road,' John calls out cheerily, 'and it's another lovely sunny day.'

Day two it is, Tuesday, and Jane's going off to work. She's taking Osprey on ahead to dump him at the Tarbert doctor's surgery. This is the life! I'll be even lighter now. It means I'll only need to carry my skimpy day pack with a few essentials.

I chat with Ella as she's getting ready for school. She loves drawing. As I doubt I'll need both notebooks that I'd brought, and as they're of Moleskine art-grade paper, I take the opportunity to do the decent thing and lighten up my load a little further. She says she wants to be a vet. I say that, when I was her age, we all wanted to get off the island. Sow wild oats, get out of 'the dump' as we called it. *Familiarity breeds contempt* and all that. It sounds sacrilegious to say it, but me and many of my pals, we'd have been the adventurous ones, standing on the *Metagama*, waving goodbye forever. Until you lose that conviviality, you just don't realise, as an exile song has it, that 'there's no ceilidh on the prairie'. Ella concludes, however, that these things are changing. Many of today's teenagers have been there, done that. They've seen what's on offer elsewhere and, if they can, would rather spend the greater part of their lives at home.[5]

Over breakfast, I pick John's brains about my route and pilgrim stopping stations on the way. With no load to carry, I should be able to crack along at three miles an hour to make Tarbert by lunchtime. I'll then take the road back out towards Clisham, but cut up into the mountains at Bun Abhainn Eadarr – the River at the Foot of the Narrows – the glen and pass that runs between Clisham and surrounding hills.

Seumas Crawford, the stonemason who knows all about the bothan, had put me up to this route when we'd spoken on the phone. There were easier options, served by fishing tracks from Amhuinnsuidhe Castle further west along the B886. 'But you'd love going up from Bun Abhainn Eadarr,' he'd chuckled. 'The path withers out a mile or two beyond the village, then you're into wild land. If anything happens to you there, it'll take them long enough to find you!' It sounded like a very empty place, and, in my mind, I came to call it the 'Lost Glen'.

This east side of Harris, my route for this morning, had been sparsely populated until the early nineteenth century. The whole of Harris was inherited around 1818 by a thoroughly anglicised gentleman, one Alexander Norman (Hume) Macleod. The poor man – he'd probably been sent to one of those frigid boarding schools, where the sons of Highland aristocrats received the privilege of being cleansed of their cultural bearings, and 'educated' into modern mores. That's what happened to so many of them.

On acquiring the 'property', Alexander came back to Harris with his lady wife, hoping to create a huge sheep farm along the fertile south and western coasts. How else could the family maintain its new-found social standing in *polite* society? The Harris people had no idea what such 'politeness' might cost. They rejoiced, when they learned of their laird's return. In their trusting eyes, he was a long-lost son. This was like the return of a chief; perhaps the hope of bringing back the good old days that Culloden's social repercussions had diminished.

It is said that a group of village maidens met the couple on the road and danced an impromptu reel of welcome. But within a year, as testimony to the Napier Commission on the crofters' plight would record, 'these twenty women were weeping and wailing; their houses being unroofed and their fires quenched by the orders of the estate'.[6] In Rodel alone, one hundred and fifty hearths were swept bare. Seven hundred and fifty souls were evicted from the green glen where once the bells of monks and nuns had sounded. One old woman was dumped in the ditch while her home was physically dismantled, to ensure that she could never return. A young wife had just given birth, but her pleas for a few days' stay of execution were heartlessly rejected. These were no longer a people, a community with sense of place and dignity. These were now unwanted tenants, 'the surplus population' to be disposed of.

Many families were forced to flee to summer pasture sheilings in the hills until they came to terms with what had come to pass. An unknown number left Harris forever. Others squeezed in with relatives along this rocky east coast where John lives. When I asked him why there are so few sacred sites along this stretch, in comparison with the south and west of Harris, he said that it was probably due to the relative recency with which the people had concentrated there.

On my route this morning there is, however, one significant point of attention, noted in Doctor Finlay's guidebook. A well in the village of Leac a Lì called Tobar a' Ghobha – the Well of the Blacksmith – said to be named after Iain Gobha na Hearadh. This John Morrison (or Morison), the Blacksmith of Harris, had lived from 1790 to 1852. As I'd left Saint Clement's churchyard yesterday, I'd made a note of the inscription on his headstone.

> A great poet
> a saintly Christian
> an eminent evangelist.
> Erected by the people of Harris
> and other admirers of his genius
> at home and abroad.

The well named after him was said to cure stomach cramps and headaches. Its waters reputedly had their greatest efficacy at liminal times – either dawn or dusk – on the thresholds between day and night. But John is puzzled. According to Doctor Finlay, the Ordnance Survey grid reference is NG 134916.

'That can't be right,' he mutters, shaking his head as we push aside the breakfast plates and pore over the map together. 'Those coordinates would put it away up in the moor, near the old Mission Hall. The *Gobha* would never have had his well so far away from his house.'

'So where would it have been, then?'

'His croft was at the start of the village. Unless there's more than one tradition, or more than one well, that's where I'd start looking.'

5

ON THE GOLDEN ROAD

I head out the door, light of step, and onto the Golden Road. Strictly speaking, the name applies to a stretch that's further to the north. However, in these touristic days, it's often applied to the whole length of single-track carriageway that threads through the Bays of Harris. The tourists like to think it's so named for spectacular sunrises that set the Minch ablaze. Local humour is less romantic. The only gold involved was the construction cost of hacking through the adamantine folds of metamorphic rock and bridging numerous little inlets.

I've not even warmed up, but straight away I feel just so light and happy to be here. Not even any aches and pains from yesterday's endeavours. As I move slowly through the fields and scattered houses, I'm kind of watching myself, and observing that my senses are wired in to every detail. Especially the details. In this terrain, the older homes squat tightly on the bedrock. There's no need to have foundations, when the Earth itself is your foundation. The problem for building on Harris, is finding a patch that's flat enough. You can own a bit of land, but try developing it, and you'll need to call the boys with dynamite.

Most of the homes are traditional two-up two-down cottages, with chimneys built onto the sides. Always seems to me a waste of heat, but I suppose that, in the days before modern linings, it made for greater safety. Grander residences, that were built between the wars, stand gaunt and shivering in their declining majesty. Most of these have roofs of Ballachulish slate. You can spot it from the little cubes of fool's gold that, as boys, we'd chip out and play tricks on the unwary. A range of red-tiled bungalows and pre-fab kit houses give a nod to improved recent living standards. Here and there, the strangeness of some architect designs hint at either gold dug from elsewhere or, perhaps, a hippie with an inheritance.

Snaking down most of the hillsides are the wrinkled parallel curves of *feannagan* – the old raised beds, or 'lazybeds' – but lazy only in their languor of appearance. Thin soil had to be scraped together, literally made with sand, animal dung and creels of seaweed, hand-hauled from the shore, to eke out a meagre livelihood. Today, these ridge and furrow patterns on the land, like the dry-stone walls that perhaps enclose them, are settling slowly back into the ground. The same attrition of the past is true of much of rural Europe. The very features that lift a traveller's heart are turning into fossil landscapes. It takes a whole community to sustain an embedded way of life, but when your neighbours have forgotten how to milk a cow; or worse, if your neighbours have become a crowd of fleeting holiday-makers, who come and go as waving ghosts in revving 4x4s, it's you, and not the cow, that ends up feeling tethered to the rusty iron ring of antiquity. It's you, that in a short wave world is hefted to the long wave, with few remaining listeners to share your bandwidth – crackling and cackling for what's fresh.

In the early 1960s, at this time of year, I'd watch the feannagan in our part of the island being ploughed and harrowed by a proud white horse called Tommy. Some of us learned to ride him bareback, and to slide off down his side when he'd break into a canter. He'd overwinter in a field beside our house, and I'd scythe grass to pay him for the rides. We all made hay then, but when a company called Transatlantic Plastics started advertising its sacks in the *Exchange & Mart*, I switched to bagging it as silage. That way you weren't dependent on good weather for the drying. Tommy loved its sweet and musty richness. I can feel it in my nostrils now. On Berneray, which is off North Uist but counted as part of Harris, there's a crofter, Seonaidh Mòr, who used to do the ploughing as a boy. Today, he's the plague of mainland white van men, as he trundles round the island at twenty miles an hour in his car. 'Don't be blaming me, Alastair!' he called out one day. 'Remember – I learned to drive on a horse.'

The crofters planted potatoes, turnips, oats and *bere* – a native strain of barley, that had been bred to suit the harsh climatic conditions. Along with fish and shellfish, meat, eggs and dairy products, these were the staples of our diet. In my time I've enjoyed a feed of what, these days, would be classed as oddities, if not downright illegal. Dare I say it, roasted curlew, dried salted gannet (if 'enjoyed' was the right word), and regularly around this time of year, a boiled seagull's egg for breakfast, gathered from the nesting grounds on Loch Orisay island by one of Dad's patients.

Work was gendered in its braided rhythms. Women to milk the cow or treadle the spinning wheel. Men to plough the soil and set the long-lines to catch cod and haddock from the village boat. Grandmothers and children to bait the hooks with mussels gathered at low tide. And the old men? They told stories, tapped their pipes, and puffed out clouds of Virginia twist. From time to time they'd shuffle around the closer hills with walking sticks, keeping an eye on their wiry Blackface sheep and on the lads out at sea. You'd hear them go '*uaich, uaich, uaich*' as they'd come home and sit down, tired. They'd say it with that long guttural 'ch' that doubles up for clearing phlegm, and that only Gaels with words like *loch*, and Jews with names like *Chaim*, are properly qualified to pronounce: and even then, only with sufficient weariness of age.

A true peasant is of a nobility invisible to the urban effete. An old Catholic man from South Uist confided to me – I say confided, because he wanted to pass on the story, but did not want attention to be drawn to his person:

We did not have fences on the fields until the Second World War, when timber came off the convoy ships that had been sunk. Before that, we boys had to constantly herd the cows, to keep them from eating our neighbours' crops. We grew up always with the cattle, and always with the old people, and we learned to be alive; to be humanity.

He gave me this example from his childhood, anxious to illuminate the dignity of that humanity.

One day, an old woman caught a bee and drew from it a tiny drop of golden liquid.

'What is that?' I asked her.

'Taste it,' she said. And I tasted. It was a wondrous taste.

'That,' she said, 'is nectar. Only kings and royal people get to taste that. But we taste that; but we don't talk about it.'

Everybody says the same. They say, in contradiction of their own nostalgia: 'The old ways were so hard. We'd none of us be wanting to go back.' And yet, that very refrain heaves with strains of lamentation, and their eyes take on a near but distant look, as if they're seeing into something just behind. 'In the old days', they'll say, at the start of so many sentences, the fields and hills rang out with song. Working rhythms and laughter eased the weary aches of communal labour. Today, for all the gains – the television and the refrigerator; central heating and the incontinence tablets – they fear a loss of real education that comes from bonding into place and one another, a sorry pruning of the roots of character.

My father's retired practice manager, Agnus Maclennan from Achmore, must be round about eighty, but she goes every week to visit even older folks in a care home. 'How do they see the changes?' I asked, and did so, mindful that it is change, and not just loss. There are so many bright new openings – in renewable energies and high technology, in ecotourism and the arts, in fish and shellfish farming, and in agricultural products aimed at niche food markets, like the fabled Stornoway black pudding. It's not all gloom, just in case I'm sounding a tad . . . retro.

And yet: 'They feel confused,' was this dear woman's rueful answer. 'They cannot understand why nobody's keeping cows anymore. And why they're not planting the potatoes. And not putting out to sea together in their fishing boats.'

But what is this? O ho? Just look at this! Here I am, walking on the Golden Road, and I'm greeted by a Golden Stag. Where two fences meet at an acute angle, some joking artist has wedged a stag's skull with its antlers painted gold. A tad pantheistic, if you ask me.

I take a close look at the strainer in the corner – the post that takes the tension of the wires. It's cut from off a pine log in the round, and has rotted hollow at the top. Into this has grown an ecosystem of green mosses, creamy branching lichens, and blobs of weird transparent jelly, plus, when I give a poke, all manner of wee critters that creep and burrow, that linger and slither. The aroma is of autumn mushrooms in a Languedoc glade. Hmm. Maybe, Vérène would think I've gone a bit OTT there. The French do get rather fussy with their *appellations*, if less so with their husbands. How about: the aroma of a bubbling batch of botched home brew?

To most *normal* people this would be a picture of hell, an image from Hieronymus Bosch. But to an ecologist, it's heaven in a fencepost. My mind's mostly just been mellowing as I've walked, yet somewhere in the background, I've been mulling over what was said around the fire with John and Jane last night. We got on to Heaven and Hell and all that; indeed, I've yet to find the native Hebridean home where, late at night, the conversation doesn't turn to religion. We'd been talking, as one inevitably does in the islands, about John Calvin. About the straight line back from him, pivoting on Saint Augustine's interpretations, to some of the hard-line positions attributed to Saint Paul. John had said you get a very different impression from the New Testament if you read the gospels of Jesus first, than if you start with some of the epistles of Paul. 'It's as if,' he'd mused, 'Paul steps in and reinvents the very legalism that Jesus had thrown out.'

Augustine of Hippo – today, Annaba, a small city in Algeria – has been on my radar since leaving Saint Clement's yesterday. Augustinian houses, such as Rodel and the nunnery on Iona, may have settled into places of deep peace. However, it was he, more than any of the Church Fathers, who disrupted early Christian pacifism and substituted in its place what is now drawn together as 'just war' theory. In so doing, the original Christian message is abused and discredited.

For the first few hundred years, most Christians had tried to follow Christ in accepting suffering, but not fighting fire with fire. One example is in a second-century manuscript, *The Acts of [Saint] Andrew*, which portrays a Roman legionnaire telling his colleagues: 'You fools, do you not see what sort of man this is? There is no sword in his hand nor any instrument of war, yet these great acts of power issue from his hand.'[1] However, by the fourth century, Constantine had taken over the show, declaring Christianity to be the new state religion of the Roman Empire. This stopped its persecution but neutered its vision of nonviolent revolution and, by the year 418, Augustine was writing to Count Boniface – later the Roman Tribune of Africa – offering these words of comfort:[2]

We do not seek peace in order to be at war, but we go to war that we may have peace. Be peaceful, therefore, in warring, so that you may vanquish those whom you war against, and bring them to the prosperity of peace.

Calvin's leaning on Augustine's interpretation of Paul provides the basis for the Westminster Confession of Faith. This remains a central influence on the Church of Scotland and, in variations of its themes, on many Presbyterian offshoots across the former British colonies. Drawn up in 1643, the Confession sets out the principle of predestination. God ordained the future of the universe in advance. Human beings are therefore powerless in the question of their own salvation. It's all been prearranged, 'before the foundation of the world was laid'. We are, as the Confession has it in the doctrine known as *total depravity*, 'utterly indisposed, disabled, and made opposite to all good, and wholly inclined to all evil'.[3] As a consequence, said Calvin, God is 'armed for vengeance',[4] and Hell, our default destiny.

However, it's not all doom and gloom. Thanks to God's 'good pleasure', some will be saved. The Elect will go upstairs to Heaven. The Damned, downstairs to Hell, and this is the doctrine of *double predestination* – the idea that God elects (or chooses) who will either be *saved,* on the one hand, or *damned,* on the other.

However, in this cosmic schema, only the preordained Elect can be saved – through God having sent himself, in the form of Christ his Son, to take their punishment for them on the cross. According to the Calvinist doctrine of *limited atonement*, this benefit of Christ's sacrifice is 'limited' to the Elect alone. The Damned are, quite literally, the godforsaken. As America's 'Godmother of Punk', the singer Patti Smith, summed up such dogmas in her lyric, *Gloria*: 'Jesus died for somebody's sins, but not mine.'

On the Scottish Borders side of our family, a supposed ancestor is the preacher, Thomas Boston of Duns and Ettrick. I'm sure that had I mentioned him last night, John would have known all about Boston. There won't be many pious homes in Harris that don't have, somewhere, one of his books in either English or a translation into Gaelic. Here lies a tale that draws together my interests in ecology, the imagination, hard-line religion and its links to war.

Born in 1676, Boston became a foremost interpreter of Presbyterian thought in Scotland and beyond. His books have remained continuously in print to this day. Robert Burns described them as 'damned trash', lampooning him in a poem to a 'brother sinner' as cause to 'grunt a real Gospel-groan'.[5] To evangelical traditionalists, however, his writings were, and remain, sweet music to the soul.

To start with the best foot forward, it is a little known aspect of early Scots Calvinism that the emphasis on divine providence, illuminated by a vibrantly extant rural life, lead to some sublime reflections on nature. This was not *pantheism* – the idea that God *is* nature – and with it, very easily, a denial of the transcendent. Rather, it was *panentheism* – the sense of God being present *in* the material world of nature but not limited to it. These are some of Boston's words upon the matter:[6]

> Here the goodness of God shines with a glorious lustre. All the varieties of the creatures which he hath made are so many beams and apparitions of his goodness . . . Every creature hath a character of Divine goodness upon it. The whole world is a map to represent, and a herald to proclaim, this amiable perfection of God . . . See how the Earth is kindly furnished with vegetables by providence, not only for men's necessity, but their conveniency and delight (Psalm 104) . . . Every pile of grass is a preacher of the loving-kindness of the Lord.

So far so good. Heaven in a fencepost, and I can imagine the Golden Stag quite perking up at such a sermon. But have a listen to this, extracts from a section of his writings with the subheading, 'The wicked shall lie for ever under the weight of the curse in Hell'. Here, spread-eagled over four pages, Boston relentlessly details the plight of *reprobates* – those poor souls who, out of God's 'good pleasure' (and not even for any particular sins of their own), have been irrevocably damned from before their birth:[7]

> They shall be cast into the lake of fire, as death and Hell are, to be shut up there without coming forth again any more . . . Yea, and to bind them in bundles for the fire of God's wrath, that companions in sin may be companions in punishment . . . and there shall be weeping, wailing, and gnashing of teeth. The curse shall enter into their souls, and melt them like wax before the fire; it shall sink into their flesh and bones, like boiling lead, and torment them in every part . . . No pity, no compassion to be shown any more, but fireballs . . . *Lastly*, the curse shall lengthen out their misery to all eternity.

Jeepers! You'd wonder what's the difference between God and the Devil with such shuddersome dread from out the Hammer Church of Horror. When I first encountered such passages I found myself asking: Was my ancestor suffering from a condition, hopefully not inheritable? Then I remembered something that my grandfather, with his mercifully merry Ronnie Hancox Band for Dancers, used to tell my mother. He'd say: 'You know, Jean, *I don't like that man*. I must get to know him better.' It occurred to me that, just as psychologists have pondered Luther's harsh parenting, and Calvin's loss of his mother at a tender age, so, too, I should inquire into Thomas Boston's circumstances before being too harsh in my judgement.

What gradually pieced together was that the young Thomas had gone through his most tender years in the Killing Times of the 1680s – the religious civil wars of Charles II and his successor, James VII & II. Both of the boy's parents were Covenanters. These were folk of a mostly southern Scottish peasant stock. They had valiantly hunkered down and dug in their heels for the right to practise their chosen religion – Presbyterianism. Why would they have chosen the legacy of Calvin and John

Knox? One reason was that it answered to their need for religious freedom. The Reformation had advocated a 'priesthood of all believers' – the right to read the Bible by oneself, to have a hotline up to God without the need for priests as intermediaries. Calvin saw no need for hierarchies of bishops. However, royal and other aristocratic power liked bishops as a medium through which to exercise their political control. 'No Bishop, no King,' James VI & I had said, meaning that a king needed bishops to sustain his divine right to rule.

In contrast, Presbyterianism meant church government by *presbyters*, from the Greek for elders. It was democratic insofar as these were drawn from the congregation, and Presbyterian congregations claimed the right to 'call' a minister of their own election rather than to have one imposed from above by church authorities, usually in league with the patronage of feudal landed power. As such, Calvin's epic *Institutes of the Christian Religion* has been described as 'the seedbed of democracy'. Like most religious radicals, the Covenanters paid the price of challenging the power structures of their age in suffering. Throughout the Killing Times they were tortured, rendered fugitive, and slaughtered in their thousands by the Episcopalian (or bishop-based) Royalist regime.

There are stories of how, when Thomas was a small boy, he voluntarily passed the nights in Duns prison to comfort his father, John, who had been jailed for his Covenanter preaching. Could it be, I wondered, that Thomas' theology took its excoriating vim-and-vigour from real-life trauma, that was always just around the corner? For example: in 1685, when he was nine years old, two Covenanter women, who had refused to renounce their faith, were tied to stakes in the Solway Firth and left to drown on the rising tide. The youngest, Margaret Wilson, was only eighteen. Later she was immortalised as *The Martyr of Solway* in a heart-rending painting by the Pre-Raphaelite artist Sir John Everett Millais. No less woebegone would have been the first- and second-hand accounts of such sufferings, moving from hearth to hearth in every Covenanter home.

In any war, each side amplifies the cruelty of the other, the better to energise and legitimise its own reciprocal atrocities. God – the deepest sense of inner sanction – must be co-opted to the cause. If not, it comes undone. That's why, across most faiths (and even nonviolent Buddhism), narratorial control is so vulnerable to capture by the violent religions of violent men of violent times. It leaves me pondering how far Thomas' lurid sense of Hell might have been linked to such exposure. I can imagine real-life images, that must have stormed the vaults of his unconscious, whirring in demonic flight through the magic lantern of his psyche; and then, in adulthood, beamed out to monstrous proportions on the silver screen of his theology.

I'm just wond'rin', that's all. And that silver screen, ministering both to those who knew the suffering from first hand, and those touched by its cold finger from afar. I am suggesting that it left them tinder-primed to believe in a system of cosmic apartheid. One that separated out the Damned (*them*) from the Elect (*us*). One that gave succour by the prospect of comeuppance for the reprobates.

Was such a system God-given? Or a plant from the other chap's department? Whatever, it would certainly have been an all-too-human response. It might have helped the people to process bitter experience. And who knows. For all that we, today, might think ourselves so clever, and so classless, and so free, might some of us still carry such psychohistories of bygone persecution within? And if so, how wide, and with what unconscious effects, their remit?

I have parted from the Golden Stag, gone through the villages of Beacrabhaic and Geocrab, and happen now upon a rocky bay. There are islets just a stone's throw off the shore. A colony of seals, maybe eight or ten of them, are lounging in the sun. But they're playing 'Spot the Tourist', and have seen me. They're flopping down into the sea on chutes between the rocks, festooned with dark green bladderwrack.

That's the kind of seaweed that pops. As kids, we used to chew it for the iodine. We'd be told that 'iodine's good for you'. Folk wisdom, with a dash of chemistry. We'd ruminate on a pod or two, especially when we'd take our buckets down to the head of Loch Leurbost to gather mussels. The right place – the furthest away from village septic tank outlets – was at the abandoned village of Crothairgearaidh. Goodness, that name looks pretty far out when you see it on old maps. We'd just say it something that sounds like 'Croi-gary'.

Alex George said that it was safe to pick the shellfish from one side of a particular fence, but not from the other. We'd be most punctilious about the matter. That was the 'done thing'. He was six months older than me, so he knew everything. Also, you were only supposed to take them in months with an 'r'. That way, with a dash of biochemistry, I suppose that we avoided any toxic summer algal blooms. It also meant this food source was conserved for winter. The best place for picking them is a little bay, right beneath the blackhouse ruins. There's a half-moon row of boulders, strategically laid out in the days of long ago. They're placed at just the right spot in the tidal range for mussels to prosper – not too high and not too low – and they grow huge, with shells that have the most lovely blue-green striations when held up to the light. When you lightly steam them, the tasty flesh falls out like golden egg yolks. Just mind you don't crack a tooth on the pinhead pearls that often lurk inside.

We'd yank them off in handfuls, and in no time we'd each get a haul to feed our families. Afterwards, we'd usually play awhile in the ruins. We'd be digging, turning over stones, looking to see if we'd find anything worth keeping. It might be me, Alex George himself, Derick, Calum Ian, Donald, Duncan Norman, John Neil, Murdie 'Plum'– that sort of crew, the boys from up the New Holdings and Cameron Terrace end of Leurbost. Our locus, mostly, was no further than a mile away from home. Before heading back, we'd scoop a wee *deoch*, a few slurps, from the little stream that comes down off the long low hill

called Cailleach Crothairgearaidh. There she goes again! The
feminine embodied in the landscape. This time, the old woman
of the hills. You can even see her in recline from the roadside,
though I only recently became aware of the fact.[8]

When done – when hungry, midge-bitten or seeing the rain
threatening – we'd head back up to the road. We'd usually lift
a few stones, looking for eels, as we'd wade across the estuary
of the Abhainn Ghlas. We'd get onto our bikes, those of us
who had them, and wobble home with the heavy buckets
swinging from the handlebars. We'd say to one another that
feats like this were 'good for the practice'. Quite what we were
practising for, or who put that idea into our heads, nobody ever
asked. There was just a sense in many of the things we did, that
we were 'practising' for something. I suppose it was that kind
of random readiness that fitted us to our surroundings.

The seals are through with playing 'Spot the Tourist' now.
They've humphed back up onto their rocks, having figured out
I'm just another bit of wildlife, not in predatory mode, so not
enough to keep them off their sunbathing.

That's a sharp glare that's coming off the water. Time to don
my Polaroids. A smear of sun cream too. Hmm – I've only
brought a smidgeon. To save space and weight I'd decanted it
from a bottle into one of those old black 35mm film canisters.
One doesn't really come to this part of the world expecting
good weather. However, if I've judged it right, there should be
just enough to give precisely *half* protection, and that, enough
to build up a protective tan. How so? Because, to really skimp
on what I'm carrying, I only need sufficient to cover my east
side in the mornings, and I'll swing round to the west in
afternoons.

At this dawdle, I've only done two miles, but a good hour
has slipped by. I've met absolutely no-one on the road. Cars
and nine-to-five routines have killed off so much village life.
I've not even seen a field planted with potatoes. Mind you,
there'd be no point laying them out with this *rotach donn,* this
dry and biting easterly wind. It leaves the seed lying cold and

dormant in the ground, a meal for crows and mice before it gets a chance to germinate.

Round a bend, and now the road's rising steeply up a hill. On the right, and bounded tight by cliffs and ridges, lies a vale that spreads down towards a pair of lochs. In July, one of these fills up with water lilies, white with golden hearts, the lotus of the Hebrides. This glen would once have fed several families. The ridges of feannagan still freshly runnel its floor, each bed some six or eight feet wide, with a yard or so for drainage in-between. I love the way they vector down like herring bones, to meet the tiny burn that glimmers as a silver backbone through the middle.

A footpath slopes off through a field, a looping remnant from before the road was built. I follow, for I can hear the splash of running water. I'm thirsty. I've never made it my habit to carry a water bottle on this island. It's usually 'water, water, every-where' and barrel-loads to drink. A tiny stream is falling over cliffs. I come to a kind of platform where the path crosses it amongst rocks. The stones are smooth from centuries of village use. It feels so good and right to join this ancient ritual. I kneel down and pout my lips, to draw directly from the flow.

The anxiously wary say: *But there might be a dead sheep upstream!*

My blasé thoughts reply: *At least you'll know it's been well washed.*

Yet, even as the devil speaks, the brakes slam on. Something's not right! Something's not quite . . . dancing with this water. There's not the sparkling scent I know of pristine purity.

I shudder to a jarring halt, ramming my motions into reverse. All senses raise to danger revs, as every instinct in me demands in outrage and repulse: *What is going on around here?* And there's the culprit! Tiny white flecks of *something* are caught up in the weedy margins of the stream. I shake my head, bewildered like a flummoxed sheep, and scurry on along the path to where it rejoins further up the road. And there's the explanation: A sign in blue and green that says 'UBC'. The burn runs right beside a heavy haulage parking bay of Uist Builders Construction. Dead sheep may be of nature's making, but I've just dodged a bellyful of lorry-washing suds.

Another half mile further on, and here's another stream. This time I take my fill, familiar and wholesome, whisky-tinted from its peat-infusing journey through the moors. I sit awhile and listen to its tinkling over shallow stones, its rumbling as it drops down into thunderous hollows. Marsh marigolds are blooming in the bank. I've always loved marsh marigolds. They're usually the first out in the spring; but still no sign of dainty blushing lady's smock, or raffish ragged robin flirting pink from boggy dips. Neither have I heard the out-of-nowhere chimes of cuckoo call: here today, gone tomorrow, coming back another day.

The road keeps lilting gently up, and it undulates again across an open moor. It winds past long dark narrow lochs, so tight between the cliffs that the verge drops, straight off, into deep water. A mountain lies ahead that's famous for its contours as a haggard woman's face. The guys just don't seem to get the same look in round here. It's getting very warm now, and I'm coming up to a bus shelter of all things, parked right out here in the middle of nowhere. I'll stop, take a layer off, and have a bag of fruit and nuts.

I sit down on the shelter's outer lip, and even as I do so, find myself interrogating myself: Why here? I mean, I've got the whole of nature, but without so much as thinking, I've chosen a concrete slab. Lafarge got me after all! I think it must be something in me seeking company, but company doesn't disappoint. Company comes, in the form of a colony of small black ants that stream like daubs of spilling ink from out the shelter's cracked foundations.

I chew a single raisin to a paste, spit the humble offering out, and push myself – just for the laugh – to shout aloud: *To the faeries!* Like Pharaoh's masons off they go, transporting massive chunks, from quarry to their den. I chuckle out aloud – *One more ant that believes in God!* – and I wonder if it's only me, or are they conscious too?

If we're conscious in our way, why not they in theirs? Could it be that our brains are radio receivers? Tuned to wavelengths we can handle? Ant to ant. Human to human. And *go, go, go!* said Eliot's bird, amongst the unheard music in the shrubbery. 'Human kind cannot bear very much reality.'

Or maybe, pace Thomas Boston, cannot bear the thought of loving-kindness preached from every pile of grass.

At Flodabay last night, we'd also discussed the Calvinist insistence on humanity's total depravity. It's not just Calvin who plays this tune. It's found wherever Augustine's teachings on original sin are emphasised including, some scholars argue, in versions of Irish Catholicism that got carried to America.[9]

As we sat round the fire, Jane was agreeing that none of our flames burn clean. We're all a bit of a mixed bag. 'But *total* depravity?' she'd asked, douce eyes agape. 'It just doesn't square with my experience. I see so much human goodness on this island as I go about my work.'

When the woman came to Jesus with her pot of precious oil, when she'd kissed his feet, massaging them with running tears and flowing hair, he didn't turn and tell the Pharisees what they'd have liked to have heard. He didn't say: 'She's done a *totally depraved* thing to me.' He said, 'She's done a beautiful thing to me' – or as the King James Version has it – 'She hath wrought a good work on me.'[10] Likewise, he never told a parable that posterity might have called: *The Totally Depraved Samaritan.*

What is it in us, we'd all three wondered, that disposes some of us, at least some of the time, to wallow in the pits of human nature, and maybe have our eyes dimmed? Could there be some sense in which, as my theologian friend Walter Wink put it: 'You get the Jesus you need'? Like Thomas Boston maybe got the vision of Hell he needed; and I mean that not pejoratively, but in seeking to understand.

The unyielding version of total depravity might be the currency of a Hebridean dinner party, but it also plays out, albeit in more unconscious ways, within wider society. Once, when I was debating on a military panel at a school of war, we hit on why it is that tiny Britain felt the need to have a level of military expenditure that, at the time, was fourth only to the United States, China and Russia.[11]

The analyst sitting next to me said: 'We must not forget that human beings are born to fear.'

'Born, or taught?' I replied. 'It makes a difference.'

One way invests in arms; the other way invests in trust.

One shoots from a presumption of depravity; the other hopes for the atomic power of love.

In Calvinism, to emphasise the point again, the doctrine of total depravity sits alongside that of predestination. As the Westminster Confession of Faith puts it: 'God from all eternity did . . . of His own will, freely, and unchangeably ordain whatsoever comes to pass.'[12] Everything that happens is fore-ordained. We therefore have no free will, no human agency in life, no real ability to change the way we're born. Why? Because God's sovereignty – omnipotent, omniscient and omnipresent – trumps everything.

The trouble with such logic, so trapped within the head, is that human reason tries to trump the divine mystery. I've noticed, however, that the island has its ways of coming to terms with these unyielding aspects of its religious status quo. There's a book called *Lewis in the Passing* by Calum Ferguson. Some of his interviews with the older generation of islanders show these ways at play. One approach is to not confront things head on, but just to quietly let them fall away to the sidelines. For example, John MacDonald of Port nan Giùran, born in 1911, told Ferguson:[13]

Today, Lewis has many religious denominations – even in the Christian Church. Some theologians argue about this and that. Is there a Hell? Is there a Heaven, even? Well, I never considered whether or not there is Hell. To me, my awareness is of the existence of God . . . [the] absolute certainty that there is God . . . because of things that have happened in my own life.

Another approach is through the telling of spiritual teaching stories that reframe a given situation to a bigger picture. Such a technique reminds me of the Sufi mystics of Islam. They'd gently trounce the heavy-handed clerics with their anecdotes, just like Jesus trounced the Pharisees with parables. An example that Ferguson recorded came from a crofter born in 1917, John the Miller of Habost.[14]

In his youth, John had known a woman living on the peninsula of Point, which runs east of Stornoway. It was during the poverty-racked 1930s. The woman was desperately poor, and her daughter lay dying in the house from *a' chaitheamh* – the 'wasting' or 'consumption' – as the tuberculosis was known. There was an epidemic at that time. Indeed, my father, who saw its tail end, suspected that it had been caused by strains of the bacillus, brought back by soldiers from the Great War, to which our insular population had piteously little resistance.

'Some of the most beautiful girls that I ever saw,' John said, suffered from *a' chaitheamh*. 'There was a certain kind of luminance in their countenances.'

And this woman on Point – her daughter was weakening by the day – and her mother heard her calling out for food.

'My *darling* girl,' she was forced to reply, using one of seventy or so terms in Gaelic to express endearment. 'There is nothing inside this house that I can offer you to eat.'

The mother then went and stood at her doorstep. She gazed out, across the moor and to the sky, and wept. After a while, she saw a man coming along the road. She stepped back inside so as not to let him see her tears. The man walked past the house, but turned round, retraced his footsteps, and came up the path and knocked.

'I wish you to have this,' he said, passing her a pound note. 'The Lord directed me to give it to you.'

And that's it. That's all there is to this deceptively simple tale. At least that's all there is on the rational plane. However, I've come to think of it in my own mind as 'The Parable of the Lord's Pound'. Only very slowly do such armour-piercing stories explode into the layers of the heart.

One can read it at a surface level. The man had simply found a ruse for helping. He had freed the woman from the burden of an obligation – one that she might have never been able to repay. It was no longer *he* to whom she owed gratitude. It was to *the Lord*.

But at a deeper level, who might be this *Lord?* Who, this ground of sovereign being?

It takes us to the heart of agency, to the question of free will, to the question: *who acts?*

On one side of the coin, it was, of course, the man who acted. On the other, it is the Lord.

Logically, it can't be both. But human logic stalls at celestial elevations. For me, this story points – as the apostle Peter put it – to our being 'partakers in the divine nature.'[15] To the level of mystical union.

Who said we can't transcend dichotomies? Who said *it can't be both*?

After I leave the bus stop of the swarming ants, another stretch of faded path leads me off-piste. Another of the olden ways dives sharply down a grassy brae. It allows me to short-cut the road's meanders. I rejoin the tarmac by the bridge at Liceasto, go wandering on around a corner, and there awaits an old friend.

I'd been looking forward to renewing this acquaintance. Normally, one whizzes past too fast. It is a small ruin, built of stone toed in to stone, without a touch of cement. Now, only these walls remain of what was once an outhouse byre, or shed, the larger blackhouse ruins themselves being higher up the slope. My memories are from its glory days of more than forty years ago. Then, it had a roof made from an upturned fishing boat. Whenever we'd come down this way on a family outing, I'd marvel at its striking ingenuity. I loved its frugal functionality, and though I didn't know the term for overlapping planks back then, I loved its curving lines of clinker elegance.

I peer in through the vacant doorway, and then turn to take a closer look at something lying to the side. You know what? There it is. The very boat that was the roof.

A twisted length of planks, criss-crossed with in-stepped ribs, is lying rotting on the ground. She's slowly growing back into the grass. Dust to dust. Wood to soil. The ministry of laying down. And copper nails that held her fast unto the last – *Hold fast!* – the boys would shout, as she rocked and rollicked to the pitch of nature's moods.

It's quite emotional, just being at this ruin, the lantern thoughts that flicker through my mind. Who built her? Who sailed her? Who worked beneath the upturned harbour of her shelter in this shed? Aye, the pang of long-lost secrets brought to mind. To think that I still know what these grey-brindled timbers once had been. Trivial knowledge, yes, and yet a vessel laden full with memory.

See those black splashes? They're her caulking tar. It was Archangel tar we always used. Distilled from roots of pine in Russia or Sweden. Aye, its thick aroma that would hang along the shoreline in the spring, before the boats went in. The kipper-scented wisps of smoke, that drifted from the pot that brooded over Finlay's small peat fire. The way the brush dripped hot black runs of treacle tears against the larch – and I'm feeling it quite viscerally – this cloying sense of presence now, so guttural and heavy in my chest.

Oh yes, it's 'just' nostalgia. But curiously I'm also feeling happy that it's come upon me. It opens up a deeper way of seeing. It reminds me that partaking is the fabric of experience, what sets the sail for seeing so much else. And that for all the hurly-burly of the world, I still have sentient capacity. And that nostalgia is *nostos-algos*, Greek words that mean 'returning home' and 'grief'. And that this great longing is what's called me here; this sailing home, this pilgrimage of slowly walking home.

From this point onwards, the road twists narrowly between the sea and landward cliffs. The cliffs press right up to the road, a reminder here that people fitted in to nature, not the other way around; yet this is what makes Harris such a very human scale of place.

I'm coming up towards another crossroads. One branch is a footpath that leads off to the left into the moors. The other turns right into the village of Leac a Lì. Here, if can I find it, is Tobar a' Ghobha, the well that John MacAulay and I had pondered over. The well of John Morrison, blacksmith, poet and healer – for they say the preacher gave out medicines as he went from settlement to settlement.

When understood as more than just a grocery chain, Morrison is a very great name. The Gaelic original is either *Moireasdan,* or *Mac Gille Mhoire,* the latter being anglicised as Gilmore. It means the Son of the Servant of the Blessed Virgin Mary. Such designations carry a packed payload in the old lore of the Hebrides. The relationships of who served whom, and how such service all went round in circles, is wonderfully interlaced by bonds of spiritual kinship.

The National Galleries of Scotland have a much-loved painting by John Duncan, an artist of the Celtic Revival. Called *Saint Bride* and completed in 1913, just on the eve of the First World War, it shows a sleeping, praying, island lass being carried by angels on the night of the nativity from Iona to Bethlehem. There she served as nurse to Mary. Out of this tradition, recorded the great nineteenth-century folklore collector Alexander Carmichael, Bride, Bridgit or Brìghde became *Banchuideachaidh Mhoire*, Mary's aid-woman. Also *Muime Chrìosda,* the Fostermother of Christ, and even *Bana-ghoistidh Mhic De,* the God-mother of the Son of God.[16]

Christ himself is therfore *Dalta Bride,* the Foster-son of Brìghde, and more fulsomely, *Dalta Bride bith nam beannachd*, the Foster-son of Bride of the Blessings, or *Mac Moire min, Dalta Bride nam buar*, Son of Mary fair, Foster Son of Bride of the Cattle.[17] As is often the case, even the animals get woven in. As Carmichael explains, the significance of fostership is that here was a culture where adoption counted for even more than blood lineage. Fostership chooses and is chosen, its conscious action lending it great spiritual significance. Brìghde thus becomes 'the Mary of the Gaels', and in this way, a remote culture on the furthest fringes of Europe managed, most profoundly, to localise the nativity. This is not to marginalise the Bridgit of Kildare, the keeper of the sacred fire, with whom traditions overlap. It's just to say that, in the Hebrides, we've even trumped the Irish: and Duncan's painting is the living proof.

Alexander Carmichael also held *Eileana Bride* to have been an old name for the Hebrides. Whether or not 'Hebrides' itself pertains to Brìghde is unproven and probably unprovable. What can be said with certainty – both from the oral tradition, and because I've found it written in an old legal title – is that the whole of pre-Reformation Harris was the Parish of *Kilbride*.[18] That is to say, this was the parish of Bridgit's *cille*, her hermit cell, or church; or at least, of ones named after her. In those words of the Welsh poet that keep on coming back to me: 'The parish has a saint's name time cannot unfrock.'

Brìghde was a preacher and the patron saint of blacksmiths, poets and healers. I cannot help but notice that those qualities, too, were the attributes of John Morrison of Leac a Lì. It was she who, according to the Irish tradition, 'turned back the streams of war'.

Both she and John were passionate about salvation – the 'salving' of the human soul.

And why? To heal our *nostos-algos*, at an armour-piercing depth.

6

THE BLACKSMITH'S WELL

At the crossroads, a handmade sign points off in the direction of Leac a Lì. It proclaims 'The Bays Café', and in my mind on this bright day, it's California dreamin'. Who'd have thought such luck would chance my way, a coffee just in time to fix the old elevenses itch.

Inside the community hall, two women stand behind a counter. They're hard at work, preparing lunches. It's like I've walked back fifty years ago. They could be period actresses, dropped in from a more stately age. Actually, they're just the timeless island matrons that I've always known: the kind you'd always see, in flowery pinafores and knee-length dresses, starched blouses and ever-so sensible shoes, and mellowing locks bunched neatly back – what I always think of as a 'Presbyterian bun'.

These are a kind of people whom I almost feel I know without so much as knowing. There'll be a whole culture to them, and that, braided to distinctive individuality. In the villages of Harris, such wealth of what it means to be a person can still be very strong. The isles' poet, Iain Crichton Smith, wrote of what he called 'real people in a real place'.[1] That's my gut sense of who this pair will prove to be. Mind you, Smith's words leave some folks slightly edgy. So many have succumbed to the things that try to turn so many of us into plastic people. Happily, there's nothing plastic in what's spread out before me here. It's all home made. Their apple crumbles, and their sponge cakes packed with jam and cream. Their bulging sandwiches, and pies that ooze dark gravy out of earthquake fissures darting through the glazed brown pastry. Why, there's even quiche for those who don't eat meat – something that's still hard to fathom in a crofting culture where we caught or reared so much of it ourselves, as near organic as it comes.

'I can see *somebody's* been hard at work over the stove last night,' I say, as I request a slice of shortbread with my coffee. I'm signalling that I sense they're probably not just employees. It's most likely something that they're doing also, as they'd say, 'for the community'.

'And where will you be coming from today?' asks Jessie, introducing herself.

'From John MacAulay's at Flodabay, and Rodel yesterday.'

Not the usual tourist.

'Ohhh,' says Anne, searchingly. 'And where would your accent be from?'

'Leurbost, but with an English mother. You see, my father was Dr McIntosh. You might have heard of him?'

She thinks awhile. 'Oh yes, *a ghràidh*,' she says, with the familiar 'my dear', 'my love'. 'I think that I might remember the name, right enough. And where will you be walking to?'

'To Ness, but not all the way today. Today, I'm only heading for the hills above . . . urr . . . Bun-Avahhh-Eaddd . . .'

'*Oh yes*, a ghràidh. *Buna!*' she says, rallying to my rescue. '*Bun Abhainn Eadarra*. But we just call it Buna for short. You'll be wanting to see the old whaling station, are you?'

'I'll pass by that way, I'll see it from the road, but I'm hoping to spend tonight in the hills above *Buna*.' This time I thrust out the name with renewed confidence. 'Then tomorrow I'll go on to Kinlochresort, and from there, another nine days if I take it easy, up to Ness.'

'Oh well!' chips in Jessie, at the mention of Kinlochresort – *Ceann Loch Reasort* – the Head of Loch Resort. 'That will be some journey,' and she's looking at my pack. She'll be wondering how its slightness squares up to the story.

I explain that my stuff's straddled between the surgery and tourist office in Tarbert. As they ask more questions, I crack a joke about the poaching pilgrimage and a 'wee cast' on the Grimersta – at which they warn me, in a pretendy-finger-wagging sort of way, not to get caught.

'And your tent?' muses Anne, bemused. 'I suppose that it will have . . . *a flysheet*?'

'Oh yes, nothing but the best!' I laugh. She's obviously picked up the name and knows that it will keep the banter going. 'But at this time of year, more for keeping off the rain than flies.'

From there, it's down to business. I reach into my bag and take out the map and both of Doctor Finlay's books. The impending tourist influx will have to wait. The lunchtime preparations have been put on hold. All three of us gather round a table, and I point to the area that's up beside the mission hall. One half of me is musing that such halls were just a normal part of village life, especially for the mid-week meetings in the days when people lacked the cars with which to take their elderly a few miles to the nearest church. The other half of me thinks how very interesting that such a title throws back to a time when missionaries would come, just as they did in 'darkest Africa'.

I explain to them that, according to Doctor Finlay, there's a famous well '. . . that's called . . . now, how would you say it? Tobar a' Gughhh . . .'

Anne rallies to me again. 'We would say it *Toh-par-a-goh-a*, a ghràidh. That's how we would say it.'

Softly she repeats the phrase – *toh-par-a-goh-a* – and I mark her old-world politeness, the emphasis on *we would say it*, as if to bow to the possibility of 'superior knowledge'.

A possibility, but not this time. 'Toe-bera Go-er,' I repeat, in stranglified self-conscious clumsiness. Even as a child my hearing was poor. I struggle to catch the soft consonants. That's partly why I never picked up Gaelic. But only partly. Mainly, it's just the way it was in those days. I even remember feeling superior that I didn't speak Gaelic when visitors would ask. In the 1960s, the others were told to learn 'the English' from me and the only other two who had it in our class of nineteen. It was something that we all had 'to get' – as if it was a type of vaccination – a 'must' in order to 'get on' in life, and not 'fall by the wayside'. More like, 'get on and get out', for that's what happened in the fast lane. The island was no place 'to succeed'. And today? I feel as if it's left me almost with a psychological blockage. I can scrape my way along in French. Even in Papua New Guinea pidgin. But for some reason, or some complex constellation of reasons, not so in Gaelic. Even with the most basic greetings I feel a collapse of confidence, often under-scored at the crucial moment by a frustrating inability to remember the words.

But this is not the time to go there. I just point to my hearing aids to show I've got a problem. Sometimes it helps to blame the hardware for the software.

'*Toh-par-a-goh-a*,' says Jessie, with painstaking slowness. 'You see, it is the well of Iain Gobha na Hearadh, John Morrison the Blacksmith of Harris,' and, between the three of us, we settle for something that sounds to me like *Tobar-a-go-er*.

'Oh, a ghràidh,' resumes Anne. 'That is a wonderful thing, that you have come here to find the well of the Gobha. You see, he was a very great Christian. *Very great*, my dear,' and she starts describing him, as if it was just the other day that he'd been spotted, going about his preaching in the village.

'You see, he brought so many people here to Christ.'

He cuts an enigmatic figure, this largely self-educated Iain or John Morrison. You'd wonder how a name like Ian maps onto John, but think of Jan, and you'll get a sense of how the sounds migrate. They say that he was descended from Roderick Morrison, *an Clàsair Dall* – the Blind Harpist – who died in the early eighteenth century and has been called the 'last minstrel' of Gaelic Scotland. On the one hand, the Gobha was a party to all the usual Puritanical put-downs on secular music and dance, such as Calvin and his followers in Geneva had tried to squash. So much of the culture has been lost in this way.[2] On the other hand, he saw himself as dancing to a higher tune. Literally so. In 1830, when he heard that John Macdonald of Ferintosh, 'the Apostle of the North', had arrived with missionary fervour to preach on Harris, he wrote:[3]

> Some one came one evening to the smithy where I was hard at work at the anvil and mentioned that Dr Macdonald was come. I tried to subdue my emotion; and I longed for the absence of the messenger; and whenever the messenger had gone I ran to the smithy door and bolted it. I could then, when alone, give scope to my emotions. I danced for joy – danced round the smithy floor; for I felt a load taken from off my spirit suddenly. I danced till I felt fatigued; and I knelt down and prayed and gave thanks.

An anvil from his workshop still exists. It sits outside the house of his great-great-grandson, Alastair 'Alda' Ferguson, the Lochmaddy taxi driver who told me of the tradition that links Neil Armstrong to Boreray. Another time, Alda told me that his wife was looking out the window, when she shouted to him: 'Come and see this. There's five ministers in our garden, standing round the anvil.' To which I couldn't resist the quip: 'And were they dancing?'

The Gobha's poetry heaves with old-style evangelical effervescence. It's mostly not to my taste, at least, not as it comes through in English with its heavy, born-again theology. But that's me speaking, what they'd probably call an unreconstituted reprobate. That said, it has a spiritual integrity that can be moving. *An Nuadh Bhreith* – The New Birth – is said to be his greatest work. It depicts the 'old man', the Old Adam of the Gobha's unregenerate self, battling it out with the 'new man', the New Adam of Christ, struggling to be born from within.[4]

> *Tha mi bàtht' an cuan an t-seann duin',*
> *Fo gheur fhuar-dhealt 's fuachd a' gheamhraidh;*
> *Thig an t-òg na ghlòir gu theampall*
> *Chuireas mis' a dhanns' lem chasaibh.*

> I am drowned in the old man's ocean,
> under the sharp, chill dew and cold of winter;
> the young man will come in glory to his temple,
> which will set my feet to dancing.

The well that I was looking for, the women told me, would not be found up by the old mission house. They didn't know of any well up that hill. The well that I was looking for is right across the next fence. It's on what used to be the Gobha's croft.

What's more, 'You'll have to go and look for it!' they kept insisting – as if I needed any encouragement. When they were young, the village girls all used to go and take a drink. 'It was for the health, you see, for the health.' Not just the girls, but everybody in the village would go there, 'just to take a deoch' – a wee drink – 'for the health.'

'It had the sweetest water in all of Harris.' The spring that fed it rose from deep within the rocks. 'Rising water, we would always call it,' and no matter what the weather, it always came out very cold. These days, however, the well is all closed over. It hadn't been seen for easily thirty years. When not in use these little wells fill in, or grass over, so very quickly. About ten years ago somebody had come to the village on a search. Nothing was found. And yet, 'It must be over there, hiding somewhere in those boulders. Just you go and look! Go take a look.'

At that moment, a car came down the hill from the direction of Tarbert.

'Look!' says Jessie, pointing out the window. 'It's Morag. If anybody still knows where to look it will be herself. You sit down and finish your coffee. I'll give her a ring.'

Ten minutes later, and I'm off. Morag lives across the road and up a driveway. It's a long, modern house with three white dormer windows. Built, I'd guess, in that period of relative prosperity in the sixties and seventies.

Morag is a Free Presbyterian, these often being thought of as the islands' 'strictest' denomination. Their community on Harris has been described by a historian of religion as retaining 'that abiding, faintly Edwardian dignity'.[5] If that's the case, then she's the perfect picture. As erect in posture as, no doubt, in mind, she conveys the analytical, no-nonsense air of a woman who is well educated, but who takes her distance from the greater part of that which passes for the norms of worldly mores. Her pleated skirt itself speaks volumes, hanging almost to her ankles; and she's sizing me up, like I'm before the headmistress and have to give respectable account.

'So, that's why I'm here . . .' I conclude, daring to mention neither poaching nor pilgrimage. 'Doctor Finlay shows the well at one location. John MacAulay suggests another. Jessie and Anne said if anyone would know, it might be yourself.'

Her hand rests holding to the door, making up her mind, and with no slippage, prematurely, to *a ghràidh*. It's rare to feel so seen right through, and yet refreshing in its penetrating honesty. Her Westminster confessional worldview might not be mine, but still I feel a warmth for these, the type of folks who raised me. There's a kinship that goes deeper than the outer schisms of belief. These are, quite plain and simply, *good people*. And if she sends me packing, it'll only be because they've had enough of visitors who turn up – journalists from the south in the silly season, or the writers of flippant travel books – to find some aspect of their piety at which it can be easy to poke fun.

The hand drops slowly from the door.

'The Gobha's well . . .' she announces solemnly – and then speeds up her words, as if to get them out before a change of mind – '. . . is right over that fence.'

The gatekeeper has let me through

'It is on the croft of Dr Anthony Latham. That's where the well used to be when we were girls. But nobody has drunk from it for years and years. I don't know if it will ever be found again.'

'Do you think that Dr Latham would let me have a look?'

'Oh, I'm sure that he'd be very happy. Now, you climb over that fence. See if can find anything there. The well you're looking for used to be amongst those boulders. Go and see if you can find it.

'And if anybody passing by on the road asks what you're doing, just tell them that *Morag Macleod* gave you permission. And if you need a spade, you'll find one in that shed.'

I can't believe it. Not just permission, but aiding and abetting too. The fence is low, and with a hop, I'm over.

My mind's a-race. I have to still myself, and think about it logically. What signs might give away a hidden well? Old stonework, or the vestige of a path? Soak-ways, or rusty staining on the rocks? Plants like sundew and bog violet – the sorts that grow in boggy ground – compensating for the lack of nitrogen by trapping living insects on their sticky hairs. Oh! What a way to go!

I mosey through the boulder field, taking in every detail. There are maybe twenty rocks protruding from the sward. Each are the size of Fred Flintstone wheelbarrows, left over from the Ice Age. Only two of these have any sign of seepage from below. One has a massive wodge of sphagnum moss at its base. The other, a long depression running from it, perhaps a dug-out channel that's now partly filled. I take a photograph of both and, realising that I'll need the spade, take my camera back across the fence and knock on Morag's door.

'I think *that* will be the one,' she says, peering at the digital display and pointing to the channel. 'Have you tried digging?'

'Not yet. Are you quite sure it's alright?'

'Oh yes! Dr Anthony Latham will be *very* pleased if you can find water on his land.'

Apparently, the physician and his family came to Harris not just for work, but for its strong religion. I notice how she always speaks his name in full, and with respect, to say the least. My stark use of 'Dr Latham' sounds clinical in comparison.

'That well,' she adds, 'used to be about eighteen inches deep. It had stone walls, about eighteen inches square. Now, go and take the spade, and see if you can find it.'

I cross back over and begin to dig around the channel.

But nothing. Just dampness, and a slight trickle that comes to nothing. Maybe, I think to myself, the channel was cut by the person who searched ten years ago. It looks about that vintage. Maybe it's a red herring. I'll try the rock with the sphagnum moss instead. Come to think of it, that only grows in saturated ground.

I punch the spade down, but it bounces right back up. I try pressing with all of my weight, but it simply refuses to slice through. I even try bouncing on the spade, jumping up and down like one gone crazy on a pogo stick. Let's hope no passer-by calls Dr Latham on the 999! But still no joy.

Maybe it needs a little more intelligence. I probe in with my fingers to feel what's there. The moss is threaded through with toughly stringy roots of grass. It's got the texture of a sponge cake reinforced with wire.

Ah – there's a small hole going in by the side of the boulder. It's too narrow for rabbits, but maybe made by mink. Mink like water, but their razor teeth, like an overgrown shrew, are vicious if they're cornered.

Needs must, and so I lie down and slowly stretch my arm into the dark.

Oh wow! We have water. This must be a drinking hole for little creatures, right enough. What I can feel is not a depth of eighteen inches, but maybe three or four. I'm also feeling something long and smooth, a jar of some sort. It's an old Tennants' screw-top. So this'll be the well, right enough. They'd usually leave a cup or some container so that passers by could take their fill. It must be thirty years at least since beer was sold in these pint-sized brown bottles.

I try to yank at handfuls of the sponge, but the mass is just too tightly knit together. I'm puzzled, for sphagnum moss will usually pull out easily in tufts. As kids, we used yank out huge dripping clumps, and hurl them at each other in a prototype of playing paintball. During the First World War, vast quantities were gathered, dried, and sent off to the trenches for the soldiers' dressings. The plant can absorb as much as twenty times its own dry weight in liquid. Its chemistry creates an acid bog environment which gives it antiseptic properties. We used to use it for packing salmon, filling the gutted belly and surrounding spaces, but that's also why it worked for wounds. As a certain Mrs A.M. Smith rhymed in 1917:[6]

> The doctors and the nurses
> Look North with eager eyes,
> And call on us to send them
> The dressing that they prize
> No other is its equal -
> In modest bulk it goes,
> Until it meets the gaping wound
> Where the red life blood flows,
> Then spreading, swelling in its might
> It checks the fatal loss,
> And kills the germ, and heals the hurt
> The kindly Sphagnum Moss

Well! At least if Dr Latham intercepts me, I've got a talking point. *The Poacher's Contribution to Medical History*. But I'm mindful that I've got to get to Tarbert before five. Brain is failing in the task. It's time to try that Flintsone brawn.

Crouching down into a lifting position, I get both hands around the mossy plug. I'm hulking-up, Sumo style, locking into mythic battle with what morphs into the *Bog Monster*.

Leaning back with all my weight, I push as hard as I can with my legs, and pull with bulging arms.

No damned luck! I'm winded, and my finger nails are ripped and running red.

'So the Bog Monster demands *blood sacrifice*, does he?'

I've got to get cracking up the road, so it's the last chance. *Ahhrrggh!* I expire, in a long, wild, guttural growl. Here's hoping Morag's got her windows shut. Some pilgrim.

Come on! I'm saying to myself. *It's all or nothing. One more go at it. Heave! Heave! Heave boys, heave ho!* And it's like we're hauling out the boat before a storm, and it's *Come on boys! Put your bloody backs into it. Give it something. Go on, GIVE – IT – SOMETHING!*

My clothes are dripping with the green-jellied goo that squeezes out of sphagnum. But slowly, with a mighty sucking *Gloooooch* from out his lair, the monster pulls away. Back he comes, upwards, outwards, a slobbering mass of moss and roots all stitched together like a fothered sail. And there's the explanation. By growing down into the moss, the grass could trail its roots into a constant source of water. For there my beauty stands. There stands a rippling pool of icy water. All eighteen inches depth of it, the four-square stone surrounds – of Tobar a' Ghobha.

I climb back over the fence and knock again on Morag's door. There's no reply, then I hear she's talking on the phone. Probably the whole village has been ringing up, wondering what's going on.

I stand and wait, pondering what a well might mean in her worldview: the poetry of Psalm 104 that Thomas Boston leaned on for his sense of providence, where God 'sendeth the springs into the valleys, which run among the hills' and 'watereth the hills from his chambers' until 'the Earth is satisfied'.

But now she's coming to the door.

The woman looks me up and down. I'm dripping gobs of monster goo onto her step. Her face is deadpan. Words are hardly necessary.

'You've found it,' she says. 'You've opened Tobar a' Ghobha.
'Come on in.'

I reach down to untie my laces. 'Oh, don't worry about
that! Come on in. You can take a wash at the kitchen sink
over there.'

'Are you quite sure that Dr Latham's not going to mind?'

'Not at all! I'll tell him what has happened when he gets
home.'

She passes me a towel. I mop my hands and eyes. Her eyes
have softened to their kindness now.

'Did you take the water?'

'Yes, but only three wee sips. It's still stirred up and
muddy.'

She slowly nods.

'We're very grateful to you,' she says.

It is written that Gobha na Hearadh was 'an aristocrat of
nature's creation'. He would share 'with the needy and starving around him' his last morsel of the kail – the poor-man's
cabbage.[7]

As such, he stood the test of the Gaelic proverb, *'Se càl a
dhearbhas an creideamh* – 'It is the kail that tests the creed' –
and I feel that, mainly by her bearing, Morag too has nourished
me on such a creed.

I step back out of her doorway. She catches my eye across the
threshold.

'I haven't gone over that fence for several years,' she says. 'I'll
give the water a couple of days to settle, and then I'll maybe
put on my Wellington boots, and go and take a drink myself.'
After all, it is written that even 'David longed, and said, Oh
that one would give me drink of the water of the well of
Bethlehem, which is by the gate!'[8]

'God bless,' I say, as I turn to part.

I surprise myself at such an utterance. Her face flickers too.
Perhaps we're both surprised at just how deeply run the chambers of those stone surrounds.[9]

'And will you go there for me,'
said the old woman, 'even with a thimble,
and bring me a drop of that hard water
that will bring colour to my cheeks.'
I found the well at last,
and though her need was not the greatest
it was to her I brought the treasure.

Lunch was over by the time I got back down to the Bays Café. Here the tourist season measures more in hours than months. The guests had been and gone, and Jessie and Anne were wiping down the tables.

Unable to contain myself, I yelled out: 'I found it!

'Got it all dug out. Brimming to the top. Lovely!'

They could hardly believe me. I had to show them the pictures on the camera.

'Ohhh! We are very pleased,' Anne effused. 'So you are now *the discoverer* of Tobar a' Ghobha!' She looked at me and shook her head, as if I was a wonder to behold. And so I was, given the state of my clothing. Had there been an anvil on the floor to circumnavigate, we'd have danced a little jig.

One of them suggested there should be a plaque erected at the roadside to mark the rediscovered spot. People would come to take a drink. They'd want to remember 'what he did for us'. Repeated Anne: '*Oh . . . to remember what the Gobha did for us!*' as if he'd been a figure of their childhood days, and not the century before.

'And did you leave the ground all neat and tidy?' Jessie asked, tilting her head with a coquettish tweak, as if about to launch another of her pretend reprimands.

'Tidy as your kitchen!' I assured her. 'I spread the mud down the feannagan, and covered it with a skin of turf.'

They both glanced at each other. A key had turned, a penny dropped.

'Oh, *ma tha . . .*' said Anne, her voice fading as she spoke, to a wistful remnant. 'So you spread it down . . . *the feannagan*.

'So . . . you know about . . . *the feannagan* . . .' and her words are lost in reverie. Those bygone days. Those days of laughter and togetherness when working on the land.

Her mind was rolling back through time to lifelines.

My mind was racing forward with the clock to deadlines.

It's now twenty to three. I've been in the village for a good three hours. Tarbert remains a full six miles away. I say I'd better dash. Jessie, realising the urgency, offers to run me there in her car. I could very gladly take up her kindness, but wish neither to consume her time nor short-change the walking. If I crack along at near three miles an hour, I should just make the 5 p.m. curfew at the tourist office. Three miles an hour, over hills, sustained! That'll be a pace, indeed, to test the kail.

We make farewells, and I hotfoot off and up the long and winding hill. Behind me, to the south, the silhouette of Roineabhal is fading in the haze, the grace of 'fair maid Harris' as I have it written by an old crofter living in her lee.[10] From here, her tresses sweep back to the west. They say you shouldn't 'anthropomorphise' nature. You shouldn't project human qualities onto the non-human. That's what I've heard some academics say. But others say that the mountains of the Hebrides were once a race of giant women who laid down to rest. I just give my scholarly colleagues a pretendy rattled look, and ask: 'But who are we to disregard such voices from the margins?'

Soon, my beloved Roineabhal is lost amidst a plethora of intervening hills. I'm high up on the level now, rejoining the main road, beating it along a winding way that runs amidst more beds of boulders interspersed with rank dark heather growing from the peat. To the north, a new horizon opens up. It spurs me on to see the tops of mountains that I'm heading for. Clisham's in the background, straight ahead. Big and Little Uisgneabhal, slightly to the left. Somewhere in-between them is the pass through which I hope to wend my way this evening and tomorrow.

I'm really pushing it hard, grinding in low gear up the steeper braes, then coasting down the far sides, sometimes breaking to a half apology for a trot. My radiator's overheating. Like this, I'll get to Tarbert looking like, and smelling like, a pig that's spent its day in muck. I come upon a stream, drop my bag, wade right in, and vigorously wash both body and my clothes. I wring them out as best I can and put them straight back on again. That'll cool the engine as they dry.

At last, I round the corner high above the Tarbert pier. I stampede full throttle down the precipitous hill, quite forgetting to mark any observance that, somewhere underneath the tarmac of this widened modern road, was once the Well of Mary – 'Tobar Màiri' – as a place sign on a corner house gently reminds me, as I breathlessly rush past.[11]

I hit the tourist office at precisely five past five. The notice on the door says: CLOSED.

Luckily, the lass is still inside and making up her till. Sometimes it's best to pull the tourist rather than the local card. The Joker justifies the eccentricity, for a crazed bog warrior is waving at her window. Unfazed, she lets me in. And I have to say it. You'd go unto the ends of the Earth before you'd find more kindly people than on Harris; and Harris – at least, the part for which I'm headed – is pretty much at such an end.

I get my bags, recover Osprey from the nearby surgery, and prompted by the screw-top bottle that I found at Leac a Lì, make for where I know I'll find salvation for the day's long drawn-out thirst.

7

MY OWN LOCHS NOW

The Harris Hotel in Tarbert is a wonder of the old world, a venerable fisherman's rest that is run to new world standards. The elderly proprietor, John Murdo Morrison, one of the last of a breed of Highland gentry, was not around. It's mostly his children, Sarah and Andrew, who run the place. When I told Andrew that I hoped to make it by tomorrow night to the abandoned village of Kinlochresort – the Head of the Red Fjord, possibly so-named because of sunsets, as it stretches out to the west – he answered with a longing smile: 'That is one of the most beautiful places in the world.'[1]

With a pint of ale in hand, I went out into the garden and the languid evening sun. I spread out all my gear on the lawn, arranged it into strata, and with not a nook or cranny to spare, repacked Osprey. An English lady, a tourist in her later years, came over to watch what I was doing. We struck up a conversation. It was one of those quite intimate exchanges that you sometimes get when both parties know they'll probably never meet again. She had come to the islands seeking something – she didn't know quite what – and was taken by my story of the well. It seemed to mean a lot to her, and telling it was also like telling it to myself. I suppose her listening ear and warmth helped me to process the day's experience. We both were pilgrims on respective paths. I told her where to find the writing on the hotel window: the swirled initials,

etched in with a diamond ring – *JMB*. And there lies quite a
story.

With books and plays like *Peter Pan,* Sir James Matthew
Barrie probably did more than any other writer to bring alive the
faerie genre to the British imagination of the early decades of the
twentieth century. He was born in 1860 at Kirriemuir, a country
town north of Dundee, that was seeped in *sìthichean* – the faerie
tales that the Scots and Irish 'Tinkers' or Traveller folks brought
back each summer when they came to pick soft fruit. The son of
a weaver, both of his parents were active members of the Free
Church of Scotland, the doctrinally strict but very grassroots
movement that broke away from the establishment Church of
Scotland in a schism called 'the Disruption' in 1843.

Barrie had voyaged to Harris in the summer of 1912. He
grandly rented Amhuinnsuidhe Castle for a fishing holiday
with his friends. These included the orphaned Llewelyn Davies
boys, as were depicted in the 2004 movie, *Finding Neverland,*
where Johnny Depp played the tender if enigmatic Barrie.

At the height of his fame at the time, the writer had stayed
at the Harris Hotel on the way to the castle, signing both the
visitors' book and the window.[2] It was while fishing in the
Harris Hills that he seems to have encountered local tales that
contributed to a play that was at least fifteen years germinating
in his mind – *Mary Rose*. His notebook for 1912 contains lines
typical of Hebridean stories, one of which – 'the island that
likes to be visited' – takes centre stage. Inspired by a tiny island
on a salmon loch called Voshimid – Bhoisimid in the Gaelic –
Barrie later wrote to the orphaned boys, in a dedication to the
published version of *Peter Pan*, that this was *'where we caught
Mary Rose'*.[3]

Although the work is rarely staged today, it was a massive
box-office success when it first opened in April 1920. The initial
staging in the Haymarket Theatre ran to almost four hundred
performances, making it Barrie's longest-running play.[4] Behind
what could be misread as a whimsical plot, the playwright
masterfully explored the in-between states of life, death and

consciousness. The emotions evoked would have spoken powerfully to his audience, recently afflicted as so many of them would have been by the traumas and the losses of the Great War. It would seem that the work also drew on a well-known ballad from the Scottish Borders, *Bonnie Kilmeny*. He had described it in a 1905 notebook as 'a sort of Rip Van Winkle'.[5] Young Kilmeny, in her bloom of innocence, had wandered up a wooded glen, where a faerie led her to 'a land of love and a land of light'. Her abductor from the Otherworld considered it a work of mercy, set against a harsh world for which she was too good. He had 'brought her away frae the snares of men/ that sin or death she never may ken'.[6]

Mary Rose is about a sensitive, pure-hearted little English girl, whose parents bring her on their holiday to the Hebrides. 'There's a whaling station,' said Mr Morland, her emotionally stuck, upright and uptight, upper-middle class father. 'We went because I was fond of fishing.' While sketching on an island while her father was in the boat, Mary Rose was spirited away by the faeries. Twenty days later she came back. Her distraught parents found her sitting, sketching, on the selfsame rowan branch from which she'd disappeared. The child was blithely unaware of any untoward happening or lapse of time.

She went on to grow up almost normally, but come her engagement to a young naval lieutenant, Simon Blake, nick-named Simon Sobersides, her mother felt it necessary to explain why the little island in the loch 'became the most dreaded place in the world to us':

> I have sometimes thought that our girl is curiously young for her age – as if – you know how just a touch of frost may stop the growth of a plant and yet leave it bloom-ing – it has sometimes seemed to me as if a cold finger had once touched my Mary Rose.

Three years after marrying, with a baby boy left back in England, where does Mary Rose choose to go for a delayed honeymoon, but back to the Isle of Harris, which held for her dim memories of some childhood paradise. Their boat on the loch is rowed by Cameron, a gawky youth from the village. Barrie's stage instructions pitch him 'in the poor but honourable garb of the gillie'. We're told that he is 'not specially impressive until you question him about the universe'.

The threesome land on the Island that Likes to Be Visited to have a picnic lunch. There, Mary Rose presses Cameron for a creepy story. Uneasily, he tells one about a little English girl. She had come to Harris ten years previously, and there she 'heard *the call* of the island'. It was a true story. Cameron's father had gone out looking when she'd vanished, they'd even dragged the loch. 'They searched, ma'am, long after there was no sense in searching,' and then she reappeared.

'I am glad,' Mary Rose responds, 'but it rather spoils the mystery.'

Simon, however, makes the connections and is now completely spooked. He tries to force a change of subject. 'You and your bogies and wraiths, you man of the mists,' he tells Cameron, patronisingly. He speaks disparagingly to Mary Rose in French, only to have Cameron reply in like tongue. It turns out that for all his humble appearance, the ghillie when not home for summer is studying for the ministry at university.

'It is not good to disbelieve the stories when you are in these parts,' he tells his social superior. 'I believe them all when I am here, though I turn the cold light of remorseless Reason on them when I am in Aberdeen.'

'Beware, Mr Cameron,' chides Simon, 'lest some day when you are preaching far from here the call plucks you out of the very pulpit and brings you back to the island like a trout on a long cast.'

At this, Cameron takes umbrage, and retires to bail the boat. Mary Rose seizes the opportunity of privacy to beg Simon to make love to her. He, however, in his sober emotional frigidity, has forgotten how. He takes his eyes off her to tend the fire on which they've cooked their trout, and as he does so, Mary Rose hears *the call* again, the unearthly music and the soft and furtive whisperings, as if from holes in the ground.

'How cold and grey it has become,' says Simon, and then sees she's gone.

Mary Rose, where have you got to? Please don't hide. Dearest, don't. Cameron, where is my wife?

Cameron, I can't find her. Mary Rose! Mary Rose! Mary Rose!

The scenes that follow swirl in and out of psychic twilight zones of the Great War. Bereft of his wife, Simon stoically worked his way up through the Royal Navy's ranks. In a second war that takes place twenty-five years later – prophetically anticipated by Barrie – he attains command of HMS *Bellerophon*. The allusion to this vessel would have pinged the sonar depths of Barrie's audience in 1920. Just four years previously, the dreadnought was one of the very few vessels to have sailed, like a ghost, unscathed through the Battle of Jutland. Within a few hours of maritime fury, six thousand British hands had been lost beneath the waves to the firepower of the Kaiser's fleet.

The play closes, as it had opened, in an English country mansion at the end of the second war. The house had long been lying empty, stuck on the market because of its haunted reputation. Hardly any of the neighbours could now remember the long-departed inhabitants, a certain Mr and Mrs Morland. A young Australian soldier, demobbed in London and with time on his hands, has turned up, posing as a prospective buyer. The housekeeper is suspicious, but he manages to fob her off to go and make a cup of tea. While she's away, he enters a forbidden room.

That young soldier turns out to be Harry Blake, Simon's estranged son. Semi-orphaned on his mother's loss, the boy had run away to sea, and in a deeply moving closing scene, he lays to rest his mother's ghost – the soul of Mary Rose.

It was my mother who first told me about *Mary Rose*. Even today, in her eighties, she vividly remembers watching it at the Birmingham Rep when she was a student nurse. It was in the late 1940s, just before she met my father. All that she can still recall is that it was about an island on a Hebridean loch, or maybe Lewis and Harris itself – an island that *liked to be visited*. When I think about it, that must have been her first encounter with the Outer Hebrides. It had then been she who had pushed Dad to apply for the vacancy for the North Lochs practice when it was advertised in the *British Medical Journal* in 1959. She'd pushed and pushed him, she told me, pushing to an almost irrational degree. He'd otherwise have thought the place too remote. I've therefore wondered whether Barrie's *Mary Rose* had played a role in us coming to the island, and to me being on this walk now. A little opening of the way, perhaps? A home-call from a place that welcomes visitors, and has something to say.

My mother was by no means on her own in having experienced such a sense of enchantment. Sir Walter Langdon-Brown was a regius professor of medicine at Cambridge in the 1930s. In a public lecture on the subject of 'Myth, Phantasy and Mary Rose', he offered the opinion:[7]

> I think in some respects *Mary Rose* is Barrie's greatest work. To deal with it fully is impossible . . . for it seems to me one of the completest expositions of the working of the unconscious mind to be found in contemporary literature.

But you could get carried away with such things! It has just clocked seven. The English woman has gone back inside for dinner, I've downed the last of my pint, and now must needs 'hard nose the highway'. This time, and for the first time, I'm as a fully laden pack-horse. I heave Osprey up over my shoulders and pull tight the straps. Wow! It's now going to be a four-and-a-half mile tramp along the road to Buna, then a further couple of miles up the 'Lost Glen' – the one that Seumas Crawford said would take them 'long enough to find you'. That's where I want to camp, beside a mountain lake called Loch a' Sgàil.

If the conditions underfoot are good, there's still a chance to catch the 'evening rise'. That's the witching hour when fish come on the take, just at the cusp of day and night. At these latitudes, and at this time of the year, the sun comes up around five o'clock in the morning, and it sets just short of ten. You've then another hour of decent twilight before night wins the day. But frankly, the odds on a sizzling trout supper are lengthening with the shadows.

It can be a sombre stretch, this length of road along the northern rim of West Loch Tarbert. A leaden flank of hills looms tightly to the south. They rob the ocean inlet of its due illumination. Further out, the sea loch brightens as it widens, until you get to Taransay. This four-mile stretch of island had its day on reality TV, when a group of strangers came and lived together for a year in space-age eco-pods – the so-called *Castaway 2000* 'experiment'.

More lastingly, as such residential experiments go, the island hosts two chapels side by side. These are Teampall Chè, dedicated to Saint Keith, and Eaglais Tharain, to Saint Tarran.[8] If *eaglais*, meaning 'church', sounds French, it's because Gaelic often drew from Latin. Indeed, the Celtic monks were bilingual. I've not been able to find out anything about Keith, but Tarran, Ternan or Torranan as he's variously named, may have been a missionary visionary who set up churches in the Hebrides. The truth is that no-one any longer really knows. The Celtic Church, like the early Christian church more widely, seems not to have made a great song and dance about canonisation. Even into medieval times in Scotland, saintly sorts were so declared by their communities – by 'popular acclamation'. I suspect the practice didn't entirely stop there, or with the Reformation. I'm thinking of the houses in our village that were especially pious. There'd be not a Catholic halo, or a statue to the Virgin in sight. But often, there'd be a table, or a mantelpiece, given over to framed photographs of black-suited ministers in their white dog collars. And then there was this morning. Our musings on the saint-like Gobha.

'Ah – *Saint Torranan of Taransay*', I'm saying to myself as I walk, picking the version of his name that packs the most poetic punch.

'Ah – *Saint Chè of Taransay*'; the only one this side of Cuba.

'I invoke you, patron saints of all we'd love to believe about the Celtic Church – but lack a shred of evidence to back it up.'

Vroom. Vroom. Vroom. The cars go jetting by, and I am truly famished. All day long I've thought of catching worms. Worms for catching fish. I've kept a weather eye out for turves along the verge, the sort that I could overturn and have a rake through. But there were no such useful spoil heaps. Time was, when men would clean the ditches out by hand with spades and shovels. Worms thrived amongst the rotting vegetation in the clods. But now, it's all gung-ho machinery. Good for neat-and-tidy. Bad for worms and fishing.

Wish I'd gone for fish and chips while still in Tarbert. Here I am, stalking the ocean, but not a fish to hand. It gets me think-ing of something that I saw back at the Lorimers' house, after Café Spirituel. There was a print on their wall, a map that had been made in 1714 by the London-based cartographer, Herman Moll, showing: *The North Part of Great Britain called Scotland.*

For West Loch Tarbert, the legend reads: *Here is plenty of Cod, Ling and large Eels.* For the stretch of the Minch that I walked up yesterday, that which runs between Harris and Skye: *Abundance of herrings taken here.* For St Kilda, where the inhabitants live '. . . in their little Stone Houses, of which there are some hundreds': *Plenty of Cod, and Ling of a great size all Round these Ifles.* And for central Lewis, bang over the headwaters of the Grimersta system: *Here are many Frifhwater Lakes.*

The map was made just seven years after the 'parcel of rogues' – a bankrupt squad of aristocrats – acceded to the shotgun marriage between Scotland and England. So began a new joint venture, the 'British' rather than the English empire. Scotland had been too poor, and too preoccupied with its own struggles, to have had anything but a failed attempt to establish a trading colony in what is now a part of Panama. This, the Darien Scheme, had bankrupted her feudal overlords who, under such straitened circumstances, turned to their Anglo-Norman cousins for a helping hand and with it, the prospect of reaching new markets through England's grip on sea power and shipping lanes. The intent of Moll's map appears to have been to promote the natural resource wealth of 'North Britain' to a southern client group. Scotland had not come empty-handed to the marriage – it only needed investment. The script immediately beneath the title tells 'how easy it would be to settle the most advantageous Fishery in the World here', as well as to modify rivers for bringing timber down to the sea. 'If things were rightly managed' – whatever that means – there'd be no need any more to go to Norway for wood, or to Newfoundland for fish, 'seeing North Britain can plentifully furnish us with both'.

What we see here, then, is an exercise in political cartography; even, from the point of view of the isles, a coloniser's, or at least an adventurer's, charter.[9] To push the point, and only slightly tongue in cheek – *Here be the archaeology of poaching as a crime.*

Moll's inscription for the Hebrides' largest port touches on the backdrop of violence. It says: *Stornoway Castle was destroy'd by the English Garrison, kept there by Oliver Cromwell.* Within those words lies quite a story. Not content with having devastated Ireland, Cromwell's New Model Army invaded Scotland in 1650. The plan was to consolidate Great Britain as a specifically Protestant state. His Roundhead troops met stiff resistance on invading Stornoway. The clansmen eventually sent them packing, but not before a loss of life that was said, on both sides, to have been 'severe'.

In a reflection on the name of Stornoway's Cromwell Street and its links to a religious legacy, the historian, Dr Macdonald of Gisla, mused:[10]

> We behaved well under his stern Puritans, and must have picked up some good habits from them. We still retain a grim Calvinism, and a main shopping boulevard, called after the stern Protector.

As for Dr Johnson, who toured the Highlands and Islands with Mr Boswell in 1773, for him the stern Protector's colonising rationale was cut and dry.[11]

> What the Romans did to other nations was in a great degree done by Cromwell to the Scots; he civilized them by conquest, and introduced by useful violence the arts of peace.

I'm walking, on and on, and the road climbs gently up towards the strung-out settlement of Ardhasaig. Osprey sits comfortably across my back and shoulders – a growing heaviness – but the belt drawn tight around my hips is helping to spread the weight.

Everything around me here, and all the terrain that I'll be passing through tomorrow, is land that has been owned since 2003 by a community land initiative, the North Harris Trust. The people here – some seven hundred of them – now run the place. They manage its sixty thousand acres for such priorities as affordable housing, tackling fuel poverty, low-impact renewable energy generation, job creation and eco-tourism.[12] Their hope is to reverse the sharp population decline that, in the previous half century alone, had caused Harris to lose half of its people. The very thought of such a change of fortunes puts a spring into my step.

Coming into view, a mile ahead, is Buna. I can see the river threading through the pass that climbs between the Clisham and the other peaks. Shadows are creeping up the glen. Only the upper slopes remain bronzed, while out to sea the settling sun rakes down the embers of the day.

Below a line of houses sits the whaling station. I can just make out a slipway and a tall industrial chimney stack. They're all that's left. Once, I went into a Tarbert shoe shop that was run by a frail old man. He had only a few boxes on his shelves, none with contents that were in fashion, but it was his residual contribution to the community. He told me that he remembered the way Bun Abhainn Eadarra was back in the 1920s. Steam-powered whalers heaved into the bay with up to three carcases at a time being towed behind. They'd winch them up the slipway, flense the blubber off in strips, boil out the oil in vats and, lastly, grind the bones to fertiliser. The smell, he said, was like the Devil's kitchen; yet nothing could make leather softer, nothing burn a lamp's flame brighter, than pure sperm oil.

All of a sudden, a head pops out the side of a shed door, and hollers: 'Nice evening!'

I am about to be granted a very great pleasure: the acquaintance of Mr Samuel Macleod of The Anchorage.

'Where are you off to?'

'Camping at Loch a' Sgàil tonight,' I shout back, optimistically, given where the sun had got to, 'and then over to Kinlochresort.

'I don't suppose you'd know the best way up the glen?'

'Keep to the right, up from the village, and you'll be alright. They usually go by Miabhaig or Amhuinnsuidhe, but by the time you've walked along the road you'll be just as quick setting out from here.'

'Would you have any other *recommendations*?'

'Well, don't go along the river. It's full of bogs and gullies. Above the village, you'll come to what's left of a stalker's path. That'll take you on a mile, and after that, keep tight to the side of the glen. You'll find the ground's better drained on the slope.'

He's reading me, trying to put together the pieces and figure out the story.

'But why are you wanting to go there?'

'I'm on my way to Ness,' I say, throwing my thumb back at the walkie-talkie-like protrusion from the side of Osprey. 'Taking a few wee casts along the way.'

'Ahh! So you're a *poacher* are you?' His head tosses up and to the side, as if welcoming an old friend. 'I was wondering, when I saw you coming down the road with that rod. Well, you won't get much in Loch a' Sgàil. It's only full of tiddlers.'

'And yourself? A poacher too?'

'Poaching!' he spits it out in mock disdain.

'Well, I'll tell you something. My poaching days are over. Over and out! We don't need to be poachers anymore round here. You see, we've got the land. Anyone who lives here fishes for free.'

'And the rest?'

'They can buy a permit' – and he takes a breath, filling his lungs with pride – 'because, *these are my lochs now.*'

'Thanks to *the buyout?*'

'The buyout! *You said it*, my boy. The *best thing* that has ever happened round here.'

He emerges from the shed and comes down to the fence.

'You see, ever since I was ten years old I've wanted to control my own lochs. And now I do. We all do! How about that?'

'Since you were ten? Why ten?'

'Because . . .' and he points to a stream that runs down the side of the Clisham road: 'You know that chain of wee lochs up past the quarry?' He means where the water's as deep as the mountain's high.

'When I was a boy, the estate couldn't be bothered with those lochs. So we used to go there. We thought of them as our lochs. One day, I caught six little sea trout. *Lovely* little sea trout. But the keeper came and caught me. Red-handed, with my rod, and the fish. They were all dead, of course, but would you believe it? Wait till you hear this! He said to me, this keeper said to me: *Just put those back from where you took them out!*

'And I had to throw them all away. Every one of the six of them! Had to watch them swept down by the river to the sea.'

He shakes his head in dawning disbelief. 'That's how it used to be on these estates. From that day on, I just knew it. One day, I wanted to control our own lochs.'

'But who are you, anyway?' he asks, in an unexpected bark. The old Scots challenge. The demand to *Stand and give account!*

'My father was Dr McIntosh of Leurbost.

'I was involved in the buyout on Eigg.

'I write books.'

He looks at me, unsure what to make of it.

'What kind of books?'

'Best known is *Soil and Soul*. About the land reform.'

He shakes his head.

'Never heard of it. Never heard of it at all.'

I might as well bite the bullet.

'It wouldn't be so popular with everyone in these parts. It's also about the superquarry at Lingerabay.'

He jerks himself erect.

'*For . . .* or *against?*' as if enquiring: *Damned . . .* or *Elect?*

I gulp, sealing my fate.

'Against!'

He just stares at me. Dungarees and braces, chequered shirt, a big round balding bronzed head with reddish blotches bitten deep from years and years of working in the sun and rain. And he's got a gold chain hanging round his neck.

Might as well be for a sheep as for a lamb.

'I was the one who brought the Red Indian chief to the inquiry.'

He's shaking his head again, connecting streams of memory.

'Well, well, well . . .' he says, with slow-releasing relish.

'Just imagine that.

'You! Just you come on over this fence. Leave your bag beside the road. Nobody's going to touch it. Just step over at that post. I want to show you something.'

I follow him back into his shed. It's a workshop, stuffed with spare parts of this and that, and lobster pots and nets. He rummages through some shelves at the back, and pulls out a large cobweb-trailing picture frame. With a few rubs of his cuff it smears clean.

Pressed beneath the glass is a double-page article from the *Sunday Mail*. The date is 27 March 1994. It's about a Harris superquarry, but not the one that I'd been involved with. At the same time as Redland had been strutting around South Harris, another corporation had been eyeing up the cliffs of Loch Seaforth in North Harris, just a couple of miles over the hills from where the sea trout incident had taken place.

'You see *that*?' he says, as he jabs a fencepost of a calloused finger at the glass.

'That Ready-Mix quarry . . . that concrete mixing lot . . . that was very nearly our Lingerabay.'

'If they'd pushed Lingerabay through, then *she* – that *aristocrat*, who acted like *she* owned *us* . . .'

'Er – Mrs Panchaud, the heiress?'

'*That's* the very one. You named her. *She* was going to . . . well . . . you just read all about it here.'

And he stands to attention. Like a soldier waiting to be decorated.

'You just read what I told them.'

My eye falls on a yellowed quote ascribed to the 'local fisherman', Mr Samuel Macleod.

I've been here all my life. And there's something wrong when she dictates what is going on from Switzerland. It's not right that a hole can be blasted in the landscape without the people being consulted. The scheme was sprung from out of the blue. She's not the most popular person on the island.

'But we saw her off!' he resumes. 'We saw the lady off, and now we've got the land. We've got the Trust, the North Harris Trust, and with the Trust, we're the ones who call the shots.'

And he's off into stories that could run until the dawn.

'You see, one day she calls me up. *Herself* it is. She calls me up, and she's speaking to me in a *very nice* tone of voice. Very polite, indeed.

'*Sammy*, she says sweetly. *Sammy, I would like you to come down and talk to me at the Castle – please.*

'So I'm thinking to myself, *O ho! What's cooking here? This will be interesting* . . . and off I go in my van, down to see her there at Amhuinnsuidhe.

'Well, she takes me into the office, and she starts hunting around all over the place, opening drawers and cupboards, *f'ing* and *b'ing* like you'd never have believed the language that was coming out of the woman. And all just to find a pen!

'*You need a pen?* I say.

'*Why do you need a pen?* I ask her, because, you see, Alastair, I'm suspicious of her mind.

'*Oh*, she says, as if I was only there to do her bidding, *For you to sign something, Sammy* – and she finds a pen and brings it over to me with a sheet of paper.

'*I am not here to sign anything, Madam*,' I say to her. But she ignores me, the way she'd ignore anyone when it suited her.

'*Now Sammy*, she says in that grand tone of hers. *We have been noticing that you go backwards and forwards every day in your little boat, checking your lobster pots. And we have been thinking that while you're out there, you must see the poachers' nets. So we've been wondering whether, the next time you see one, you might lift it? Or at least, tell us where it is so that we can send in the estate boat.*

'Well, she nearly blew me out of the water, she darned well did!

'What was I expected to say? Did she really think I was going to shop the boys?

'So I said to her: *It's not for me, Madam, to be telling what I might be seeing, or what I might be not seeing, when I'm at the lobsters.*

'*Ohhh, Sammy!* she says, sounding so let down. *We thought you might say that, Sammy!*

'I mean, can you imagine? The cheek of it.

'*But Sammy*, she says, as if she was putting cream out for the cat to dip his whiskers. *There might be MONEY in it for you . . .*

'Now, I can tell you, Alastair,' and he draws in very close, dropping to a whisper. 'As soon as I heard that little word – MONEY – little wheels started spinning in my head. So I said: *So what do you have in mind, Madam?*

'And this is what she says to me. She says: *We have been thinking, Sammy* – meaning herself and the old *bodach*, of course; though he was all right, he and me got on alright when he'd want to buy lobsters. I'd give him the best, and he'd know it.

'She says: *We have been thinking, Sammy, that if you'd only like to sign this little agreement that my husband and I have drawn up, then we will pay you seventy-five pounds for every salmon net delivered to the Castle.*

He grins, draws back, and stares at me, as if glazed by astonishment at his own story. My eyes, too, are bulging like a cod's caught in a lobster pot.

'So I say to her, *Madam, you are making a man an offer that he cannot refuse* – and I took the pen, and signed the agreement, right there and then, bang on the dotted line.'

'And then?' I ask. And though I'm mindful that the Buna glen has dropped down into half-light, this is just too good to hurry.

'And then, I get back home,' he says. 'And I get on the blower. And I say to the lot of them. *Boys! Guess what? See all those old nets you've got sitting up the back of the byre? All full of holes and good for nothing but the haystack? Well, just you bring them right round here to Sammy at The Anchorage.*'

'And she paid up?'

'Well, no.

'Because she went and told the factor. And the factor phoned me up.'

He shakes his head in sore disdain.

'He phoned me up, *on a Sunday afternoon*, I tell you. *On the Sabbath Day!*

'He was wanting to make his point, you see. And he said to me, he said: *Samuel Macleod. You may think that you can pull the wool over the old woman's eyes. But never over mine.*'

In a small community like this, even the factor, the estate legal agent, gets given his due for a bit of wit. Even so the old *bodach*, as with another tale that Sammy threw in about a nice connection in the course of trading lobsters. If I'd hung around for long enough, even Mrs Panchaud would probably have been left a redeeming chink through the eye of Sammy's needle. He'd have had some little story secreted away of an unexpected kindness, or an endearing touch. Such counterpointing doesn't stop the hard truths from being spoken, but it does help to lubricate wheels for the times when people have to pull together, as well as rubbing sperm oil into the leather of one's own humanity.

As I made moves to continue on my way, Sammy apologised for not having invited me into the house. He was having to go out shortly. However, seeing as I was a writer, and he too, a writer of poetry, would I just come over, so that he could read me something that would be, as they used to say, 'one for the road'?

He led me into a boxroom office, and pulled a folder from the desk. From it he recited a tale, set to verse, about a crofter who was coming home drunk one day on a bicycle. While crossing the Clisham, and stopping to do a little business, he parked his bike amongst a cluster of boulders, perhaps somewhere on the Leathad nan Clacha Mòra. When he was ready to set off again, he couldn't for the life of him remember which cluster.

Eventually he found a bike. He grabbed it by the handlebars, swung into the saddle, and helter-skeltered down the mountain side – only to be paraded through the village on an angry Highland cow.

With the permission of the Bard of Ardhasaig, I copied down a couple of his lines into my notebook:

> *And you heard the fairies' laughter,*
> *When you were looking for your bike.*

And that was it. Time to hard nose the highway again. Osprey's waited safely by the roadside. The foot of Clisham lies at the bottom of the hill. There, I take my leave from retracing the bus route by which I came down this way from Stornoway yesterday, and take the turning to the west and into Bun Abhainn Eadarra.

I trot off into the settling mire of dusk, chuckling to myself. What poetic justice! For all their powers of capital, persuasion and modernity. For all their double-barrelled whammy, trying to take pot shots at both ends of Harris. For all that, neither Redland, nor Ready-Mix, had managed to blast out those whisky-reeling residents of hollow hills – the timeless gentry of the sìthean.

There's not a cat's chance of reaching Loch a' Sgàil tonight. By now, it must be after ten, so over to Plan B. While there's still an inkling of twilight, I'll try to get up through the maze of fences that criss-cross the in-bye crofting lands. I'll pitch my tent just far enough into the glen to lose sight of the village lights, and get a touch of proper darkness and of wildness. I've come into Buna, over the cattle grid and just beyond the whaling station, but the day's already so far gone that I simply can't make out where best to cut into the hills.

From up ahead, my ears pick up a rapid scuttling sound. I strain my eyes, and through the gloom three panting shadows surge towards me. They're collie dogs, and following on behind them looms a big man, paradoxically wearing a baggy pair of khaki cotton shorts and a body warmer on top. His animals look pretty local, but not his gait or dress code. Turns out that he's an incomer from England, one of a team of professional trappers that's employed by the Hebridean Mink Project.

The American mink had established and become a blight in the late 1960s. There had been a short-lived fur farm on the island, some of them escaped and went feral. Like many translocated species, they found plenty of prey but had very few predators. Their penchant for eggs and chicks wreaks wildlife havoc in the nesting season. To try and curb their numbers, even with the hope of eventual elimination, my new-found acquaintance tells me that there's a network of some seven thousand traps laid out in lines around the island. He works the Harris Hills. He goes out nearly every day, and his dogs help by sniffing out the minks' musky trials. He baits each cage, sets the trap door, and logs the exact position by GPS for regular checking. When he makes a catch, the animal's dispatched humanely with a powerful airgun pellet through the head.

A lonely road, a chance but warm encounter, can launch an avalanche of memories. I, too, once shot a mink with an airgun. It was back in Leurbost, around 1970, the first time we'd known such an animal to turn up at our end of the village. George and Kate Allen had spotted it a few days earlier while at work in their weaving shed. At first they didn't know what this strange creature was, skulking round their henhouse, casing out the joint. But soon word got around like wildfire.

'Have you anything fresh?' people would say, always on the hunt for news.

'Yes. George and Ceiteag *saw the Minx!*'

At first, that's how we thought it was called. We had in our minds a holy terror, Minnie the Minx from *The Beano*. It was a comic that we passed from hand to hand, until it fell apart and would be used to light the fire. In those days there weren't any Gaelic radio stations. People often picked up new terminology by listening with a Gaelic ear to English local news bulletins. Sometimes they'd hear it slightly wrong, and so the Minx hit number one in village chitter chatter. Dad had patients stopping him by the roadside to report sightings. One man even managed to catch it under a bucket, but when he came back later, it had managed to escape.

Dad, no doubt, would have discussed the matter with Ken Walker at the seaweed factory. He knew everything about wildlife. Quite likely, it would also have come up at the weekly meetings with John Murdo at the school, along with both the Church of Scotland and the Free Church ministers. Such was how social services operated in those days. The outcome of such counsel and deliberation was resolute. This mink, or Minx, or whatever it was, had to be executed. If it wasn't, and if it found a mate to breed, that would be the end of all our free-range hens.[13]

It was one afternoon in the thick of this, when us boys were all eyes and ears for anything untoward, that I heard a most terrible shrieking from Ceiteag, matched by an equally horrendous squawking from her henhouse a hundred yards away.

I grabbed my airgun off its holster on the wall. It was a *Diana* .177 with an engraving of the huntress by the rear sight. That would have been the only look-in that a goddess had in my upbringing. With Wink, my mongrel terrier, yapping rabidly at my heels, I ran across the road and leapt the fence.

Ceiteag had always been like a second mother to me and Isobel. In Africa, they say it takes a whole community to raise a child. This time, it was my part to comfort her. There she was – in her blue pinafore, arms held out wide, and everything a terrible *bùrach*. Before me was a murder scene, a mass killing, blood and feathers everywhere, and poor Ceiteag trying to shoo away this sleek black demon. The size of a large kitten, it hopped about between the clumps of heather. If anything, it seemed to resent more than fear her intrusion on a process of industrial killing that had just ripped out the living throats of half her flock.

Wink and I closed in. It was the kind of moment that is normally only dreamed about by boys and dogs alike. As we got within ten feet, it reared up on its hind legs and bared a spread of snarling needle teeth. I not so much as aimed, as pointed down a firing line of lethal instinct, and pulled the trigger. The creature half crumpled to the ground, but before it dropped completely, Wink had followed through in rearguard action. She got it by the neck, shook like crazy, and that was that. All before the astonished eyes of Ceiteag, who thereafter spent the remainder of the afternoon plucking for the stewing pot what had been six good laying hens.

Such could be the gory realities of a semi-subsistence rural way of life. It's called 'back to nature', except that, for us, there was nothing 'back' about it. Most of us were very close to our animals. Cows especially would be almost a part of people's families and genuinely loved. But when their time was up, we'd kill and eat without compunction. We understood that we were all part of a cycle that rotates the wheel of life and death.

The question for us was not whether it was right or wrong to kill living creatures for our staple diet. That would have seemed a stupid question. Rather, the question, one that was often discussed, was doing so in right relationship. We knew that managing the grazings, going at the fishing, gathering shellfish and so on had to be carried out in ways that would sustain the stocks. It surprised me when, in my late teens, I learned that 'ecology' was considered to be a subject. It was what we lived and talked about for much of the time. It was, quite simply, the balance of a nature in which, we too, had our place. I later learned that academics called this 'Human Ecology'.

The problem with mink lay in their disruption of that balance. These are beautiful, intelligent, playful and even very affectionate creatures in their proper place. But – location, location, location! Translocation, and the competitive advantage over native species that it provided, had turned the lithe

American mink into the Greater Hebridean Minx. This was what had led to the government-funded Mink Project. A sad necessity, though even then, some people argue that we should just get used to translocation. It's just a part of nature's future. I've also heard it said that, without the mink, the rats come back more, and they're also hard on ground-nesting birds like arctic terns and waders.

There comes a point in such debates that I just know my knowledge has run out. Also, it has to be conceded that we could be harsh without intending so, or in a manner that was inured in rural life. Not for nothing did the little van of the 'cruelty man' – the animal protection society – drive around to check on problems like sheep being left without sufficient feeding in the winter. Suffice, however, to say that I've enjoyed this short encounter with my trapper friend. We may have overlooked exchanging names, but our shared interest in the mink gave a common handle to connect. I tell him where I'm trying to make for. He points me to a track running up between two houses. Go in there, he says, and go on through the field. Go this way, turn that way, across the reseeded grazing and out through the village gate. That'll land me in the unfenced wilds.

By now it's very dark. Much too much so for sensible adventure. Fear is for safety on the moorlands too, and not just for the sea. 'If you don't have your wits about you . . .' as they'd say. But I'm determined, and within another quarter hour, I'm scouting round the perimeter fence of the reseeding.

It proves impossible to pick out any gate. I've only brought a tiny flashlight, and that's too deep inside my pack to bother. I'm forced, instead, to clutch at fenceposts, wobbling a few until I find one good to take my weight. Precariously, I clamber over the barbed wire, managing not to get snagged.

And that's it. I've broken loose! I've crossed a threshold through both land and mind. I'm outwith the village bounds, and into what I've built up in my imagination as the 'Lost Glen'. Mind you, if the good folks of these parts ever get wind of that particular romanticisation – especially, pray, not Samuel Macleod – then it'll be me who'll hear the faeries' laughter.

Out here, it's mainly dark beds of heather interspersed with little greens of tough and spiky grass. Pools of water, mostly shallow some profound, lurk amongst the bare rock sheets.

It's now so dark you have to second guess each step. You have to walk with toes upturned to reduce the chance of stumbling. They used to say in Inverness that city dwellers could tell the country folk by their *ceum a' mhonaidh* – their 'heather loup'. Test every footfall with your heel before committing weight. Watch for hidden trips and dead man's drops. Watch, too, for wider patterns in the land – the flow of shadows that distinguish different types of vegetation, or the raised ground from the dips, or the dry from the wet. Let the eyes accustom to these mottled shades of grey and black, for here is 'relief and drainage' abstracted from the abstract school geography books. Here it is, all set out in the raw.

I remind myself (as if to give a pinch) that if I hear a sudden shriek, it'll just be some poor critter, startled from its slumbers, and more alarmed than me. But all is still. I haven't even heard the drumming of the snipe. The night has claimed the day, and cold itself stands watch and takes the helm. The moon is on the wane this week and won't be out 'til after midnight, but when she rises, there she'll ride. *Banrigh na h-oidhche* – the Queen of the Night. *Lòchran àigh nam bochd* – the Joyful Lamp of the Poor.

It's written that, in both the Catholic and the Protestant districts of these parts, when folks would first catch sight of the new moon they'd greet her with the invocation:[14]

> *Siud agaibh a' ghealach ùr – Rìgh nan Dùl 'ga beannachadh!*
> 'There is the new moon – the King of the Elements bless it!'

And I have to say, that kind of peasants' Christ attracts me more than the arid version of urban theologians. Give me any day the one who'd go and pray alone up mountains, who'd wander with the angels and wild beasts.

The village has dropped out of sight. I come up to a flattish spot of moss and grass. This will do to pitch my tent. Up it goes, more by a sense of touch than by the light of dithering torch. It looks a little kinked, but no-one will be looking. It's good enough to do the night, especially as the trapper said the forecast was for cold but calm. I feel my fingers numbing as I blow into a valve and roll out my mattress, fluffing up my sleeping bag to lay it down. At last, I crawl inside with a cosy sense of relief, zipping shut the flaps as if to roll a boulder across the entrance of my cave. Only then does it occur to me: I clean forgot to eat! Oh well – I'll just have to take recourse to childhood reading on survival training. *The Famous Five*, with their chocolate bars beneath the stars.

I'm lying here, aware the stars are out above the flysheet. When we were young, the old folks used say that on a moonless night, they'd move from house to house by just the light of a glowing peat taken from the fire. You could make a biography from those peats. Their great migration paths from hearth to hearth. Their kindling, dying and rekindling. The stories that they'd hear along the way.

Truly, so much has happened since I left John's place this morning. It's been a day without redundancy, a day when every tiny thing came filled replete with meaning, right through to the worms and even ants. Maybe that's what flysheets do – and, you know, that would have been a good laugh! To have said to Anne at the Bays Café: 'Oh yes, it's got a flysheet, sure enough. A magic sheet, on which to fly.' She'd have liked that one.

It would be fun to walk at night by just the moon. Not even with a compass, just going by the Pole Star. And no way, GPS. But satellites – now, they're a strange addition to the constellations.

I remember the first time I ever saw a satellite, transiting across a Hebridean sky. In those days, when the nights were mild, Dad and I would go out fishing once he'd finished with the evening surgery at seven. It would be just him and me, out on a moorland loch. He'd be on the rod. Me, at the oars. We'd talk, and catch the evening rise. We'd usually land a few, then drive back home. He was kept so busy with his burden of responsibilities. It was probably the closest that I ever got to him, just a boy and a man, together in a boat.

I think it must have been September or October. Which, exactly, doesn't matter; but it must have been late in the season, for although the nights had not yet chilled, twilight had fallen fast. We were out on Loch na Craoibhe – the Loch of the Trees. It lay at the end of the peat cutters' road, up from the council houses at Balallan. It had an island full of rowans, safe where the sheep couldn't get at them. Dad and his good friend, Dan Smith of Sildinis, had stocked the water with a golden-coloured strain of hybrid trout, called Sunbeam. They'd been given the fry by the Highlands Board. This was in the experimental days of fish farming and restocking.

Dad was single-handed at the time, on call 24/7, with eighteen hundred patients for whom he had to be available. He held his patients like a hen would mind her chicks. The loch was up behind the police station. If needed, they would come and fetch him for emergencies. For a time, the Balallan folks called it 'the Doctor's Loch'. That's how places get or change their names. They knew he couldn't go and fish just anywhere out on the distant moors. Poachers, though some were, it's said they did the decent thing, and left the fish on Loch na Craoibhe to him and Dan alone – there is a poacher's honour.

That night, the evening rise had run far on into the dusk. Dad was reeling them in, and me, scooping them up with the landing net in virtual darkness. Nice half-pounders mostly. I asked how they could see his three tiny flies in such poor light. He said they felt vibrations in the water down the lateral line. That's why the twitching motion of the rod must be just right.

We filled the wicker basket with a hefty haul. Then the wind dropped. It went flat calm, and that was them, gone off the take. Usually we'd have packed in there and then. But this was such a 'glorious night', as Dad would say. That was his favoured turn of phrase. He laid his rod across the stern, lit a cigarette, and passed me back a chocolate bar.

I shipped the oars and crossed their butts beneath my knees. We drifted, pensively, out from the island of the berry-laden trees, off the headland where the water lay the deepest. The world had settled to a hush untroubled by the slightest ripple. The sky was settling down to midnight blue on charcoal.

Then we saw the fires come out. Odd embers blown ablaze at first but gradually, the speckled sheen of shimmered starlight right across the Milky Way. And we were there. Inside of all of this. Just the two of us.

A shooting star streaked by, and then another. You glimpse your life as held in cosmic splendour on such a night as this. Dad pointed out a satellite, a sight still rare back then. We watched the tiny speck of light, as if a distant carriage that was lantern-lit and pulled by pounding horses through the freckled constellations.

Such depths of silence let you feel another person's spirit. In ways I hadn't known before, I felt Dad's layers of being. His qualities of presence. His standing, in the sense of all he stood for. I was growing up, and he, it must be said, was growing older.

The satellite crept ceaselessly across the sky, and both of us were rapt, transfixed. Each knew it meant our world was changing. Such signs had not been seen before in Heaven or on Earth. We followed, wordlessly, like shepherds watching flocks by night.

For me, I have to say, I felt the surge of youth's excitement. It was Apollo's age when men from NASA reached out to the moon. We were in the space age, right here, right now; and there'd never been a thrill before quite like it – or, for that matter – since.

Dad sat straddled across the wooden thwart. His thick Harris Tweed jacket. His conspicuously Victorian plus fours and gartered socks. Back then, his white or chequered shirts would last a week. Their cuffs and collars were the olden sort, that could detach for daily washing and a dash of starch.

He was conservative in politics, as many country doctors those days were. That said, he was an ecologist of both planet and the body. A man who planted trees, who kept a tank of tropical fish for patients in the waiting room, who delivered a whole generation of babies with the district nurses, and who prided himself on having one of the lowest prescribing rates in the north.

He didn't believe in a pill for every ill. Instead, he'd make the time to sit with failing patients, to hold their trembling hands, to share about life's meaning and the future of the world.

That night, we watched the satellite go down on the horizon. I wondered when it would come round again. I wonder, now, what went round in his mind?

PART 2

MOUNTAIN

The Mountain Trail: Days 3–6, North Harris into South Lewis

8

THE RISING OF THE SÌTH

The sun is breaking over the peaks and already, as I peer from out my shakily-erected tent, the sky is radiant. It must be nearly eight o'clock. This is Wednesday, day three, and I've had a deep and dreamless sleep. Apart from fingernails that sting from the tussle with the old Bog Monster – to whom I feel a slight remorse for such a rude dislodgement – my feet feel none the worse for wear, and Osprey has been kind, indeed, to my back.

I draw the zip back fully along the flaps and shuffle out, like a slowly stretching cat. I fetch some water from the stream and, within a few minutes, have it bubbling on the hissing little gas stove. While my tea infuses, I overturn the tent and face it east to catch what gathering warmth there is, and dry the underside.

Some powdered milk made up with another splash of Adam's Ale does for the muesli, and I squat on top of Osprey, munching meditatively, scrying all around for the promised path built for the deer stalkers. There's not a sign of any trail in sight. Only the blue and silver glimmer of the river spilling down the slope. Only the tufts of purple moor grass speckled at random through the heather. And everywhere, a landscape strewn with boulders that ice once ripped from the towering mountains that surround me.

Down at this level, the valley is still broad, but higher up it tightens to a pass. That's what gives the meaning to the fully expanded name of Buna: the River at the Foot of the Narrows. Rising sharply up to my left are the slopes of Brùnabhal. Across, on the other side, loom the foothills of craggy Clisham. Beyond, and only just coming into sight, his horseshoe ring of sisters run with slides of jagged scree like laddered stockings dappled pink and grey.

I check my bearings with the compass, wanting to make sure that what I'm seeing squares up with the map. To reach Loch Langabhat, it looks like six miles up this glen then down the other side. I'd better allow four hours. When I get there, I'll maybe have a quick cast with the rod to see if I can land a trout, before heading west up a stalker's path that appears to run between the peaks of Stuabhal and Rapaire. From there, I'll probably head down a pathless glen along the Harris–Lewis border to Kinlochresort and come into a land of wide-spaced contours and a peppering with tiny lochs – a sign of boggy ground – before pitching camp for the night. Hopefully, I'll be there in time to gather a meal of mussels from the sea loch's Atlantic shore. I'd checked the tidal predictions before leaving Glasgow. The water will be low at around two o'clock. The shellfish – assuming that I find them there – should still be within reach for another couple of hours.

But it's going to be a slow start. I hadn't factored in that having packed Osprey so tight means that until I've eaten my way through some food, every time I repack will be a slow job. By the time I've got everything squeezed in and balanced just so, a full half hour has gone. Eventually, I swing him onto my shoulders. With a little shuffling jump, I pull the waist belt tight, and that's it. I'm off! Walking again. And it seems incredibly simple that all I have to do now, after all these weeks of thinking about it, is to walk, walk and walk – and this, with a rising sun on one side of my face and a chill wind like a helping hand on my back.

Very quickly, however, Osprey assumes the upper hand. I'm moving amongst gravelly beds of stone, weathered hunks of turf that have turned to mud, and innumerable little pools. The weight starts to feel like I'm walking in a deep-sea diver's leaded boots. Normally, you go across the moor in little leaps and bounds, a kind of ballet of the bog hop. Not so today. I'm much too heavy to jump, and whenever there's a patch of mire, I just have to clodhop through. This is going to slow me up a lot. Even the most modest slopes are forcing me to chug down into low gear. What's more, I keep on turning round every five or ten minutes to see how far I've gone. After a while, I get a grip, and tease myself by saying: 'You won't go forwards looking backwards!'

Gradually, I come more into the swing of things. It's as if my body was behaving like a stubborn nag. At first it kicked up a fuss, making out it was no longer up to the task at hand. Now it's knuckling down and getting moving, albeit surging with all manner of rare sensations. What's more, these twinges in my bones and muscles are, as it were, clicking hyperlinks within my brain. They're loaded with associations from other times like this of long ago, other times that I've carried heavy loads across the moor.

There was the time that we teenage boys were helping our dads to build dams on a stream above a trout loch. For several weeks running, we'd go out on Saturdays in one of those communal work projects that village groups would organise. This was the Loch Keose Angling Association, and our task was to make low weirs which were to catch the gravel and provide improved spawning beds for the fish.

It was nearly forty years ago, that must have been, and we'd be struggling with our sacks of cement – scarcely able to bear the weight that we'd insisted on taking on – when someone else's dad would ease alongside, like a gently docking ship, and without a word, drop his shoulder with a nudge to relieve you of your burden. There'd be the sheer relief to the neck, shoulders, biceps and even the gripping finger joints and nails as you'd roll your load off onto the broader set of shoulders. Then there'd be that half minute to follow, when you'd feel like you were floating – kind of walking on the air – as your muscle toning and deportment readjusted to the ease of relative weightlessness.

There was no humiliation in that yielding as you struggled to test your limits. Neither any hyped-up praise. At most, there'd be a passing comment, within earshot, from one man to another – 'The boy did good' – or some such other way of passing on between the generations what I've come to think of as the touch of blessing. The ethos wasn't one of competition. Like with gathering in the sheep or peats, or heaving stuff between the boat and shore, there was just a sense of common cause as everyone gave of their best and helped each other, likewise, to give of theirs. I've known men who'd take a sack across each shoulder blade. It sounds astonishing these days, but I emailed 'Jock' or Iain Mackenzie, an old school friend from Keose, to cross-check my memory with him.

'Were those really fifty kilo bags of cement – twenty of them to the ton?' I asked.

'Yes, indeed,' he replied, though email felt like such an incongruous technology by which to complete that circle of experience.

'A full hundredweight. One hundred and twelve pounds. Phew!'

Aye – those were the days, before the fuss of Health & Safety enforced the twenty-five kilo limit for a sack of building materials. The days we boys were raised with not a doubt of what it meant to be a man. The days we rippled through with fledgling brawn – though often, as we eased into our middle ages, a fledgling hernia too.

The ground is getting worse and worse, more heaved and churned by elemental forces as I climb up higher. I inch across a boulder field that's fissured through with break-leg crevices. What would it be like to slip, and twist, and with an inner crack of tensile shock, sustain a fracture? To have to crawl back to the village on my elbows – the pain and the disgrace – dragging the useless limb behind, like a maimed fox that's sprung the jaws of the gin, and praying to spot the mink trapper on his rounds, to summon his attention with blasts on my whistle, and an airgun shot of morphine to the veins to be put out of the misery?

God! You'd never go anywhere if you thought too much like that. We were always mindful when heading out alone, but we never let it worry us too much. 'Fear the sea' – for sure – but not enough to freeze it over.

It's taken maybe one and a half hours to get to the top of a ridge that's only half a mile from where I camped. But what a scene now opens out! Close by are two large pools, small lochans, rippling topaz in the strengthening sun. To the north-east are the Clisham's cliffs above Mò Buidhe – the Yellow Moss. North-west, the twin pyramids of Uisgneabhal. The name means either Ox Mountain by Norse derivation, or Water Mountain by the Gaelic. Either could be fitting, but John MacAulay thinks the Norse is more probable. The suffix *Bhal* or 'val', as he points out, is Nordic. It means a summit or 'abode of gods', as in the heavens of Valhalla.

But where's my Loch a' Sgàil? Where, my hoped-for destination of last night? Still hiding in the folds of rumpled hills, it seems. A mile or two is such a dawdle on the map when thought about from far away, with a coffee mug in one hand and a magnifying glass in the other, but it's not so much a dawdle out here. The notion that I'll be at Langabhat for lunchtime looks already like the pipe dream that the hope of a fried trout had proved to be. But here's the good news – I've actually hit on Sammy's stalker's path. Looking back, I can see now that I've been on it for a while, but such were the severity of the wash-outs lower down that I hadn't realised until in this better position to get perspective. Without its help unwittingly, I'd have been even more minced in the mash.

These Victorian trails are artefacts, for sure, of blood sport. And yet – if I might put in a special plea that might surprise – conducted well, the pursuit is of a character that binds the people to the land and to the deer themselves. Not everybody

will agree, but to me it's like the Native American approach to
hunting, the interlace of predator and the predated. But you
don't have to be a carnivore to enjoy the stalker's paths. Many
aren't marked on the Ordnance Survey maps, at least not on
the older and most interesting ones. The estates didn't want to
encourage walkers who'd unsettle the herds, especially in the
shooting season – July to October for the stags, October to
February for hinds. I've heard it said the estates would sometimes get their Ordnance Survey pals to forget to mark the
tracks, as if they were military secrets. When you're in the
know, however, or with a modern map, they're a joy to tread;
though in the season I'd not go without first checking locally,
not least by way of rural courtesy.

These thoughts set off another row of hyperlinks, clicked and
popping open in my brain – windows on my teenage summers as
a ghillie on the lochs and a stalker's pony boy amongst the hills.
It surprises some folks when I say that I'm all for land reform
and for responsible stalking. I even think that, if it's not lording
it over the local people, or depriving them of a needed resource,
a well-run private deer estate can be a service to environmental
management. It's about maintaining the balance of nature, for
the hard truth is that the stag has yet to be found that carries a
condom. When deer exceed the carrying capacity of their environment – and that can happen in just a few short years of
breeding – then it's quite the saddest thing to see them staggering
around, on incredibly skinny legs, scraping at the seaweed along
the shore to seek a bite worth eating. Better, a clean shot through
the brains, or into the 'engine room' (as stalkers call the chest
compartment with all its vital organs). From that quick ending,
to be carried down from off the hill and to the larder; and from
there, wild venison. Like the drop of nectar from the honeybee,
such is food that 'only kings and royal people get to taste'.
What's more, miserable indeed would be the larder from which
there were no offcuts to the crofter's pot.

The men I've worked with kill the deer, but not by way of
brutal slaughter. They also love them as a part of symbiosis

between species, a fitting and well-fitted relationship. Sometimes it touches on the spiritual, even what might edge towards the psychic. Recently, I received a letter about something I'd written about relationship to the land from a Highland stalker, Iain Thomson of Loch Monar. His words turned my attention to his elegiac book, *Isolation Shepherd*, and there, to his tales – so common in the Highlands and Islands – of personal encounters with the seemingly paranormal. Why do such things interest me? Because of the light that they might shed, in Nora Bateson's sense, on what it is that we might be inside of. He correctly states: 'No Highlander has any doubt about the existence of *the second sight* or indeed simple prognostication.'[1]

That's quite a sweeping statement – 'No Highlander' – but it struck me because, in my experience, speaking of my own locale and formative era, it would be substantially true. These are parts of the world where the indigenous people have lived with one another, and their place, for a very long time indeed. I know families that can still trace their history back to Culloden, and, John Lorne Campbell maintains, even back to the Norse of a thousand years ago. This immense continuity creates a different set of relationships to space and time, and its implications for full human being, than is found in mainstream modernity, with its more shallow sense of temporality and its commodification of space. Campbell, one of the pre-eminent Hebridean folklorists and historians of the twentieth century, was well aware of the possible insights this might shed into the further reaches of human nature, for he rued: 'The scholar has not yet arisen who can apply Jung's ideas on the archetypes of the collective unconscious to Highland second sight or to Gaelic folklore: it would be well worth making the attempt.'[2]

Another stalking correspondent who reaches to this metaphysical hunting ground is Iain Thornber of Morvern, an old-school Highland gentleman, who doubles as an honorary sheriff and the deputy Lord Lieutenant of Inverness. He described to me the funeral, in the 1940s, of Rory MacLeod, who had been a head keeper on the Isle of Jura – 'a well known character, and a first class stalker, who had a great love of the deer'. As the mourners gathered in the cemetery, a hind came over the brow of a nearby hill. She moved in, so close, that everyone (being well aware of the timid habits of the deer) was quite astonished. The animal stood, and watched, until the coffin was lowered into the ground. At this point, and with a loud bark, she turned and ran back to the wilds.

In another of his letters, Iain told me how, in the days when he was never off the hill, 'I used to be able to sense where deer were; I could physically *feel* them in much the same way as a water-diviner does.' He described the *gralloching* – the shedding of the entrails that are usually left out on the heather for the birds of prey – and how:[3]

> It is a fine thing, after the gralloch, and the knife has been washed in the nearest burn and dried among sphagnum moss, to sit for a while with the stag. Usually not much is said among professional stalkers. To me, it is honouring the soul of that animal. I never shot, or have been involved with the killing of a beast, without coming away thinking I'd been at a funeral.

The same ethic was also very present in Tommy Macrae of Eishken, who kept the hills of south-east Lewis. Such men as these are *keepers* of the herd in more than any narrow understanding of a gamekeeper's profession. Such men, in my experience, are integral to the ecology and welfare of the deer. With skills honed sometimes from generations of handed-down experience, they will select and stalk the older, weaker, or diseased beasts; and when the kill is made, see that the deed is done in such a way as to try and avoid scattering the herds, or breaking up their family groups.

Tommy taught me how to handle a pony with a stag strapped to its saddle. We'd work a route home that would take us over bogs, through rivers, and sometimes up and down what seemed like terrifying gradients for a beast lumbered with such a load. On getting back to the larder, usually quite late in the evening, we'd hoist the carcase on a pulley to the rafters. From that eye-level working angle, I'd take my knife and flay the bristled hide, trying not to nick and thereby spoil the meat.

Since those days, I've been back once to my old job for a week-long sojourn at Eishken. This time it was with Christopher, who follows his late father's footsteps as the fourth in the Macrae lineage of keepers. When we'd finished for the day, Chris would pour out drams all round in the larder. Half jokingly, lest any think it quaint, but only half jokingly, he'd raise his favourite toast: 'To the Soul of the Stag'.

While on the matter of toasts, I am coming up to a gully, and hear the rushing of a stream. It's narrow and is partly hidden under heavy fronds of heather. The track dips sharply down and stops abruptly at its bank. This is Abhainn Thorabraidh – the Burn of the Wide Mound. I crouch amongst the stones, cup my hands, and sup.

In the lore of chemistry there is a silver-white metal that can emit beta radiation, called strontium. It counts as number thirty-eight in the Periodic Table of the Elements, and it takes its name from Strontian, a tiny West Highland village, where the ore was first discovered. It happens to lie in the vicinity of Iain Thornber's stamping grounds. I doubt that many chemists will be aware of this fact. It might sit uneasily with the nuclear age. But the name, Strontian, is stranglified from Sròn an t-Sìthean – The Nose of the Faerie Hillock. As such, the lead mines that first yielded up this strange element – now used in power supplies for space stations, and in radiotherapy for bone tumours – were tunnelled deep inside a place where only those safeguarded with an iron needle jammed into the door hinge were safe to venture to and fro.

One glorious morning, as he recounts it, Iain was out in the nearby hills. It was the season for the culling of the herds of hinds. As he made his stalk, his ears picked up the sound of what, he believes, may have been the *oiteag shluaigh*. This phenomenon is also known as the *gaoth nan sìth*, for in the science of Gaelic, as in chemistry, there are often several isotopes, or subtle variations, of much the same thing. These terms pertain to the 'faerie wind', the 'hosting of the sìth' – the rallying and riding, mostly almost silent, sometimes raucous rollicking – of the Otherworld folk. In his journal entry for Monday, 4 December 1995, he wrote, as follows, of that glorious morning of the stalk:[4]

> At some stage as I was watching the deer, I can't recall exactly when, I became aware of the silence being broken by a sound which I initially took to be a little breeze picking up among the rocks above me. I paid little attention to it to begin with, but then it seemed to expand across the face of the hill. Although it grew in intensity, I found it impossible to say with any certainty where it was coming from, largely because I could not physically feel it on my face and neck. At times it seemed to start in Coire a' Chùil Mhaim to my left, and then move over to Coire an Dubh-alltan and Coire nam Muc ahead of me. Much like the end of a rainbow, it was everywhere but nowhere.
>
> It is difficult to describe the sound. If one can 'feel' or 'see' a noise, it seemed cold, almost metallic and grey-blue in colour, like Payne's grey. Coming as it did on an otherwise fine winter's day, it felt strange, almost ominous. I was not aware that the deer reacted to it though. I don't know why, but I thought of the young USAF pilot (Capt Morris Reed, 28) who was killed in 1964 when the F101 Voodoo Jet Fighter he was flying crashed into the north side of Meall Odhar, a little way above. It was that sort of atmosphere.

There could, of course, be many interpretations of such an experience. What interests me is how Iain felt that something 'inner' was going on, and set it within a traditional framework of interpretation. His journal goes on to describe the callous commercial stalking practices that new foreign owners subsequently introduced to the area. Gaelic place names replete with meaning were mechanistically renamed as Corrie 1, Corrie 2, Corrie 3, and so on. Family groups of deer would be blown apart, the calves left with their 'pathetic human-like crying noise' as they searched in vain for their mothers, and wounded beasts left to wander, starving, with their lower jaws hanging off. He concluded, 'If the sound I heard was an *aisling* or a vision of something to come, especially concerning the deer, it could not have been more accurate . . . These people . . . should be dead themselves . . . but soon it will catch up with them.'

What interests me is how – at least in Iain's mind – the uncanny rising of the faerie wind spoke within his psyche to upheaval in his outer world. And that, in full Voodoo drama. Whatever he might have experienced in Payne's grey, the old lore of the place – faerie lore or *sìthichean* – provided a framework of interpretation, together with assurance of comeuppance for the reprobates.

Suffice, for now, to say that each of these four stalkers – the Macrae father and son, Thomson and Thornber – are men whose proven skill involves spending prolonged periods of time on the cusps of the human and non-human worlds. As Christopher once told me, his work means 'thinking like the deer thinks' – and that requires a seasoned empathy. Each of these people is bound in with a sense of being grounded, homed, and belonging to a greater whole. This, at levels where the physical flows into the psychic. I want to reflect more on this as I go, but here we have started to glimpse a deep and very natural ecology.

Onwards from the Abhainn Thorabraidh, but no longer on any stalker's path, as I go up and over the shoulder of Mò Buidhe. A fresh panorama now stretches out and, at last, I see the shining of the fabled Loch a' Sgàil in a hollow half a mile away. To reach it means shifting diagonally back across the valley, while still gaining altitude. I'm getting more into my stride now. The ground up here is firm. That's probably why the path stopped. It's hardly needed, and I'm starting to enjoy swinging with my load. It's now the beauty more than the struggle that makes me keep stopping every few minutes. That blue haze still on the mountains, their wisps of irides-cent clouds, the grandeur of this tapered amphitheatre – and to be here all by myself.

I'm making fun of myself. 'The Juggernaut of the Moors' I'm thinking, each time the gradient makes me chug and puff. 'The bog hop' I've already called it it, when I make what little jumps I can across the lurking lengths of morass. I'm creeping crab-like up the valley, traversing the neural networks of its watercourse way where seepages drain in to little rills, and these build up to burns that dash down to the river. I'm now onto a flat stretch of land that edges towards the lip of Loch a' Sgàil. In half an hour you could write a coffee table book out here called *Bogs that I have Known and Loved*. Here's one that shimmers with a rainbow iridescence that is caused, not by oil pollution, but by a molecule-thin layer of iron minerals that float on the surface and refract the light. Another, fed from an underground spring that issues from a pair of boot-sized holes that plummet down too deep to find the bottom. Pity help the one who might tread there when walking in thin winter ice. Next, a muddy moat around an island tuft of mosses, red and green, and bristled through with stems of last year's blossoms, resembling tiny flagpoles.

Give this moor just one more month, and the rusty swards of winter will dimple through with polka dots of colour. There'll be spiky quills of bog asphodel, bristling yellow to attention. Orchids, in every hue of pink and blue, white and sometimes yellow. There's even a subspecies of the common spotted orchid that's endemic to the isles – *Hebridensis* – with confetti petals etched in dainty loops that drape as if dropped down from out of dreamland. Along the river banks, there'll be starry paws of midge-devouring butterwort, its nodding pendant blossom winged and spurred, the dainty violet dancer on the breeze. And everywhere, in dryer parts, the foursome heart-shaped petals of the tormentil; sometimes as a single tiny plant, elsewhere raked in balls of tangled tumble.

My friend, the island artist Alice Starmore, was born a *Nic Mhathainn* – Matheson in English – the Daughter of the Bear. Even in the early 1960s, the family used to walk their cattle from east of Stornoway, through the town, and out to their summer sheiling that was situated just half a mile across the road from our place at Druim Dubh.[5] For her, the magic of the moor weaves memory, ecology and the imagination. She called one of her exhibitions *MAMBA – Miles And Miles of Beauty Astounding*. Its catalogue explained:[6]

The moor is bound up in my very first memories, and that must be the reason why I associate it with my mother. The springtime smell, when everything is just starting to grow, particularly reminds me of her, and I cannot help but think of her whenever I leave the road and take a first step onto the moss and heather; the softness beneath my feet is somehow maternal and life-affirming.

One of her pictures in the exhibition that explored the infinite depths of green in sphagnum moss, was called *Eye of Creation*. That's the literal translation of *sùil-chruthaich*, the Gaelic for a quaking bog. Another, in a maelstrom of greens and blues, drew on local tales of worlds beneath the waves. It was called *The Water-Horse of Loch Mhisteam*. A wooden door portrayed *The Sheiling Remembered*, and while the door has lost its knob, it begs the question if it ever needed one.

And then there was *The Witch of Roineabhal*. Aye, there she was. My friend, the Blue Mountain Hare, seated in her winter coat upon a lichen-crusted rocky ledge. Woman wisdom in the sage astuteness of this spirit creature's haunting eyes. Nature fleeting free and wild, and love; oh yes, I saw the love that day in Alice Starmore's mountain hare of Roineabhal.

Above the sharp sides of a deep kettle pool, my eye catches a wispy haze. A freshly hatched-out swarm of mayflies dance a frenzied eightsome reel. A puff of wind, and off they flurry, back beneath the safety of the bank. Half a minute later, out they come again, whirling to some hidden bagpipe skirl until the next gust of *gaoth nan sìth* that shoos them back into their sìthean underfoot.

The *sì* or *sìth*: that twinkling sense of living laughing spirit danced through nature. I mouth the word and practice breathing out the 'h' – *shee-h* – drifting it off ineffably; playing too with the variations – *sìdh, sìd, sidhe* – that have, or so I am instructed, more of a y-glide, making a *shee-y-e* sound that works the tongue and mouth, like the syncopated rhythms – the lilting and 'Scotch snap'– so characteristic of Celtic music.[7]

Such are the *daoine sìth*, the 'people of peace', the 'silently moving ones', the gentry or gentle folk of Scots, Irish and, I believe, the English tradition as well. But to be scientific about the matter, it is the male mayflies that dance while waiting for their lovers to hatch out. Waiting for their *ban-shithichean,* their 'banshee' faerie wives. Moving with that gliding grace that classical pipers know so well, and speak of in their pibrochs as the *siubhal sìth*, the 'faerie motion'.

They're also called *daoine còir* – the 'honest folk'. Some have suggested that such honorifics were accorded only out fear, a kind of whistling in the dark, as if to ward off unwanted attentions. One who held this view was the late Dr Alan Bruford, a renowned archivist at the School of Scottish Studies at Edinburgh University. In the early 1990s, I was co-supervising a PhD student with Alan, and we met for lunch to discuss her progress and for me to pick his brains about the sìth. Unfortunately, I'd forgotten my wallet, I had only a pocketful of small change, and had to ask him for the loan of a couple of pounds. It was slightly embarrassing, not to mention the impending inconvenience of having to arrange repayment.

As we sat down to eat, we found that our tomato juice was sour, as if it had been diluted with vinegar. I got up and complained. The cashier was most apologetic. She didn't know what could have happened in the kitchen, but gave us back sufficient of a refund that allowed me, on the spot, to repay my debt.

As we settled down again to eat, I made a flippant comment about traditions of the faeries souring milk. Flippancy was compounded by folly in my conclusion: 'Whoever would have thought that the staff club of the University of Edinburgh is actually a *sìthean!*'

The elder scholar arrested his wayward understudy with a sharp and anxious gaze. 'Be careful of the faeries,' he said, grimly, and with every seriousness, as if something about what had just happened had left him slightly spooked. 'They can be *capricious,* you know.'

That said, there is a mitigating point of view. An eminent nineteenth-century authority on their behavioural sociology, the Rev. J.G. Campbell of Tiree, wrote down from an informant: 'They never took anything without making up for it in some other way.' W.B. Yeats recorded much the same from a woman in County Mayo: 'If you do good to them they will do good to you . . . They are always good to the poor.'[8] And then there is the way this genre of experience will often seem to pull down a notch those for whom, as W.Y. Evans-Wentz put it in his classic study, 'the outer is reality, the inner non-existent'.[9] As peasant informants told him, 'One does not have to be educated in order to see fairies' – the implication being that too much learnedness can get in the way. I could have patted such a statement on the head, were it not for a personal experience one night that still leaves me scratching my head.

During the six years that I taught at Edinburgh, I would usually take my human ecology master's degree students up to Lewis for field trips. We were in the Faculty of Science and

Engineering. It was important that we should be empirical, or experimentally based, about matters that our colleagues in the humanities approached in a more relaxed manner. On the island we'd stay at Gearrannan (or Garenin), a conserved blackhouse village near Carloway on the West Side. It was 1995, and the further north we drove the more we felt a loosening of the faculty's constraints.

One of our number was Patrick LaViolette, now a respected professor of social anthropology. He was doing his thesis on the biodiversity of faerie hills in the Trossachs, the hills north of Glasgow. He combined a series of ecological surveys with interviews of local people. The conclusion was that old taboos about not removing anything from a sìthean – allowing dead trees naturally to rot away, and treating it as a haven – were still alive. This led to a richer variety of flowers, fungi, bird life and all the rest of it. In short, the sìthean are our residual indigenous equivalent of sacred groves, scattered little ecological islands, that sustain a wealth of biodiversity. Just to prove that such work was *scientific*, we jointly published his findings in *ECOS* – the Journal of the British Association of Nature Conservationists.[10]

Anyway, there we all were, a minibus of fourteen of us, happily heading north and playing the game of 'Spot the Sìthean'. 'There's another one, Patrick!' somebody would shout, as we'd pass a typical tree-fringed mound that mushroomed up from a farmer's field. It was dusk as we came upon a particularly fine example. I stopped the bus, wanting the students to experience the stillness that is often in such places, the softness of the uncultivated earth underfoot and, sometimes, such features as standing stones in the middle.

However, not all our crew were happy. That year we had an Irish lass in the class, a marine biologist from County Clare. She'd grown up with a sìthean out the back where she and her sisters played – except at dawn or dusk. Why that limitation? 'Because that's *their* time,' she told me forcefully, the threshold time of day, and I should be knowing better than to lead a study tour into a sìthean at the witching hour.

At this point, mindful of the faculty of which I was the representative, I stood in my superior knowledge, and proclaimed: 'Faerie is an imaginal world. It's more a metaphor than reality.'

'No!' she retorted sharply. The 'folk' to her were in no sense imaginary – and this was scarcely the right moment for me to introduce Henry Corbin, a French philosopher of Islamic mysticism, and his notion of *'le monde imaginal'* as the 'suprasensible' grounding of the soul, where prayer itself – interestingly – becomes 'the supreme act of the Creative Imagination'.[11]

'They're a different order of reality,' she insisted. Their world runs in parallel to ours, and quite frankly, she thought that my high-brow claptrap was disrespectful. If I carried on like that, she said, they'd withhold their revelations from me. So there! It was a strange rebuke. I confess it left me simultaneously bemused and slightly addled.

By the time we'd rolled off the Stornoway ferry the following day and had driven over to Gearrannan, it was dark. Some of our number were staying in the hostel. The rest pitched our tents. I placed mine on a little green promontory, just above the well at the end of the terrace of thatched dry-stone houses.

It had been to Gearrannan that my mother would come and do her oil painting in the 1970s. Three old women lived in the houses then, the last to do so. One of them led her to a well and dropped a pebble down. My mother heard its bell-like plop, and the old woman said: 'That is the finest water in the land.'

I got into my sleeping bag and lay awake, letting the busy-ness of the day settle down to sediment. Gradually, I became aware of a very strange sound. It was a like a sheet of tinfoil being shaken. Something high-pitched, tinkling and bright.

Viscerally startled, I shot bolt upright in the tent and found that I could see straight through its fabric walls. The land outside lay still and silver, clad by moonlight in unearthly beauty. Then I saw from what the sound was coming. It was a luminous disk, shimmering in lightening blue, moving down the winding path from higher up the hill. It was maybe two or three feet wide, a couple of inches in depth, and it gently rose and fell to the bumps and dips as it glided, just above the ground, at a slow walking speed.

What most alarmed me was a sense that this was something utterly other. As it approached my tent, I felt myself fill up with fear. But the fear was needless. The light went past, slipping between me and the well. As it did so, the thought came into my head from a place that was beyond intellectual censure: *That is their possé going down to the sea for the night. They'll head back up at dawn.*

Years later, when the island's first Ordnance Survey maps from the 1850s became available online, I discovered that a prominent hillock in the fields below which I had camped is marked – and in especially bold lettering – *Sìthean*. I made enquires. It turned out that such had been the old village name.

Now, at last, I've reached the edge of Loch a' Sgàil, and it's created quite a stir. Little trout are darting V-lines through the sandy-bottomed shallows as they beeline for the middle, out of harm's way. I find a peaty bank on which to rest my back, get out a pack of oatcakes to eat for lunch, and feel as if I've reached a Himalayan holy lake. Its mirrored calms reflect the mountains that have closed in tightly all around.

Sgàil could mean a sheiling, covering, shade, shadow or a ghost. Rising precipitously above the west bank is Uisgneabhal Mòr. As seen from here, my mind elaborates the name to either Great Ox Mountain, or the Abode of Great Waters. No elaboration is required, however, to report that this is the very spot where Noah's Ark briefly ran aground, forcing its captain to unload some of the cargo, before refloating at high tide, and carrying on to Mount Ararat. That explains why Harris has blue mountain hares and red deer, while the Middle East got lions and camels. At least, so goes one of the many legends that were collected in the first half of the twentieth century by Otta Swire, a direct descendent of the South Uist-born Jacobite heroine, Flora MacDonald of 'Over the Sea to Skye' fame. Otta's granddaughter, Flora MacDonald Margaret Swire, was a medical student whose life was taken in the 1988 Lockerbie bombing of Pan Am flight 103. Her father, Dr Jim Swire, went on, with a valiant sense of justice, to lead the campaign to exonerate the convicted Libyan, Abdelbaset al-Megrahi.

According to Otta's sources, Noah's mishap here on Uisgneabhal took place during the second of the Three Great Floods. The first flood was God's creation of the world's primordial oceans. The second was that of Noah, caused, we're told in the Book of Genesis, because 'the wickedness of man was great in the Earth . . . and the Earth was filled with violence'. The last, they say, has yet to come, yet:[12]

> Before the end of the world a great flood will sweep over and drown all the islands . . . but Iona will rise on the waters and float there like a crown; and the dead who are buried in her will arise dry and so be easily recognised at the Last Day.

There were so many stories like this. They conveyed a folk worldview and mindset, ones often folded in the twists of comedy or tragedy. Consider the golden hue to Loch a' Sgàil's sandy bottom. The effect of peaty water – or so you might think? Perhaps. But last night, after leaving Sammy's house, I glimpsed back in the direction of Luskentyre – *lys-kyn-tyre* – the Headland of Light. So it was that, once upon a time, according to Otta's sources, its miles and miles of sands were made of grains of solid gold. But a greedy man filled up his boat and sailed away to sell it in the markets of that source of sin, the mainland. A storm rose up around the Shiants. It did what storms are prone to do to overloaded boats. Why? Because *They* do not like greed. And *They* then changed the golden beach to sand. But once a year at sunset, *They* change it back again – so that we will not forget the truth of nature.[13]

I am noticing that the sand along this shoreline is banded dark and pale. Heavy grains of magnetite have been graded out from the lighter grains of quartz by the lapping action of the waves. And in this moment, I see my 'traces on the Rhodian shore' – for when the shipwrecked philosopher Aristippus was cast upon the sands of Rhodes, he saw some geometric drawings; and he comforted his crew, saying: 'We can hope for the best: for I see signs of men.'[14] But these are no signs of men. These are the signs that *They* have passed by, a-shepherding their herds. *They* with their *crodh-sìth* – the 'cattle of the faeries' – for what I see are footprints, the cloven hooves of deer.

I get down on my knees to take a closer look. The casts remain sharp-edged, and all the tiny scuffs and sprays still hold their pristine definition: dried, but not yet crumbled in the breeze. Probably the creatures watered here at dawn. And then I notice something else. The lake is fringed with brush strokes all around the water's rim. Or more precisely, a tide mark, scarce a finger's length, made up entirely out of bristles.

Ah! The washing of *Their* brushes after painting flowers all night. Such, it is said, throws light upon the striking hues of many a Highland loch. And spring is when the red deer shed their winter coats. And soon the buds of summer herbs will swell and burst to blossom.

I move on and upwards, and as the valley narrows and the gradient sharpens further, the stream begins to purr a tumbling song. I stop beside a pool to watch some bobbing water plants that weave from side to side, hypnotic in the current. There is a trout! It hasn't seen me. Must be getting on for several ounces, I'd say – and even as I say it, I note with a slight dismay the calculating measure of the angler's eye.

I drop down on my knees and edge close in. He's stalking round the stones, chasing after beetles, worms and all those May-time larvae – the naiads and the nymphs. Do fish have souls, have feelings? To watch this individual – this creature of intelligence, of loveliness and even personality – it scarce can be denied. If I have soul and feelings, the fish has too, as Schubert's quintet, *The Trout*, suggests with its portrayal of its purposeful movements through the water.

Should it be caught and eaten?

Well, should it catch and eat?

That symmetry noted, I think I'll leave my rod unpacked, this time.

I climb another fifty metres, and am standing now at around eight hundred feet. It's amusing if confusing how my generation muddles up the measures. All around the peaks exceed six hundred metres. But to say two thousand feet seems to proffer up a more munificent sense of justice. I'm nearly at the top, nearly reached the saddle of the pass. The valley has constricted to a funnel. The stream is petering out now. Its dulcet sighs have long since raised to xylophonic cadences, and now to quivering bells.

Here and there the water vanishes beneath some hollow ground. I seek the source, but, more and more, it eludes me. There is no single point of source. I'm on the watershed now.

And now is such a very thin place. Such a faraway place.

No planes or cars or fire engines. No fingers tapping texts on little screens, or kettles rumbling for another cup of tea. Not even moaning wind or birdsong. Only silence. Sheer silence.

The soil beneath my feet is firm but curiously soft. A short-cropped emerald fairway winds on through a cleft, past ghostly boulders strewn on either side. A few more paces, and behold. Beyond!

Far below, a faltering stream builds up momentum and then hurtles down a stair of cataracts en route to Loch Langabhat, and from there, the eight miles through to the Grimersta. Down I jaunt, and down and down and down, until within an hour the hillside flattens to a grassy plain, another country here, of crescent pools and gravel beds, the autumn spawning grounds of salmon and the sea trout.

Suddenly I see a movement, and now I spot the stalker's path that zigzags down from Stuabhal and Rapaire. Close on a mile away, an ant-like speck of camouflage brown is shifting rapidly from west to east. A hiker, or mink trapper? A crofter, minding sheep or cows?

And – oh, ohh! I am taken by surprise. A lunge from out my belly. A realisation that, for all my self-containment, a part of me is already pining for human company.

The figure goes as quickly as it came. I'm left with a yearning rawness within. A hand near-touched, but now withdrawn. Contact without connection. The crackle of the static when the radio has gone off-air at night.

I knew that this would be a lonely place, and . . .

Are . . . you . . . there?

Is . . . anyone . . . listening?

Does anybody remember that novel, *On the Beach,* by Nevil Shute? A thriller of the Cold War, just after I was born?

There was a movie. Created quite a stir at the time.

There'd been a massive nuclear exchange. When the submariners surfaced, they thought they'd picked up Morse code.

Took the bearings. Triangulated the source. Motored to a coastguard station on a cliff. But only a loose wire – tap, tap, tapping in the wind.

'They shall grow not old, as we that are left grow old.'

Only the loneliness.

The river passes through a lochan on its way to Langabhat. Its name shows on the map as Loch an Teine – the Loch of Fire.

Teine sìth. The faerie fire of in-between places. In-between states of being.

War leaves behind a very lonely sort of in-between world.

Few traces left upon that stark, Rhodian shore.

Lay down your hopes of making Loch Resort today.

Lay down your hopes of poaching Langabhat.

It's getting late, and cold, and as they say: *When the wind's in the east, the fishing is least.*

The famous 'they' who always have so much to say!

Know what? I'm going to give myself a break. Pitch camp and make a fire.

I've reached the stalker's path down which that walker came. Beside it runs a burn lined with ruined sheilings, just falling walls of stone, some four feet high at most. None has dimensions larger than a garden shed, but here's one with the remnants of a chimney and a fireplace. Time, I think, for me to warm it through again.

Further back, I'd found some fencepost offcuts. They had a greenish hue from being 'tanalised' with copper – an impregnation that prevents the rot. I set myself to work, gathering up an armful of dead heather stems to serve as kindling. I pile them into a pyramid, set up a chimney effect, and light a match at the base. Now we're in business! I've got three lamb chops from the Tarbert butcher's shop, plus a packet of Wright's ciabatta bread mix.

The wave of loneliness is lifting. The sheiling's coming back to life, as the heather crackles in the smoke. I watch the stems explode alight, the fenceposts slowly catch and then to pop and spit. They're blazing out in lovely blue-green *teine sìth* copper flames. Luckily, they don't add arsenic like they used to for the treatment.

I'll let the posts burn down to charcoal before I start the cooking. That'll drive off any toxic volatiles. You'd not want to be doing this every day, but as a once-off – *well* – there are clinics in California where you could pay a lot of money for such tonics of trace elements.

The flour contains its yeast already added to make the bread rise. I add sufficient water from the stream, and knead it into two small pats. The air is turning cold, but the stones that face south-west are still warm from the day's long sunshine. I should have warmed that water first to speed the yeast. Trouble is, when it comes to baking, as the prophet said, 'He that believeth shall not make haste.'[15]

My mixture's only puffed up slightly. Too bad. I'm too hungry to hang around. Within an hour I'm tucking in to

Blackface chops and flattened if blackened bannocks. Were it in season, I'd have sprinkled the meat with wild mountain thyme. As it is, I'll just have to tell Vérène that I had to make do with an old Hebridean standby – the one we have to use when we can't get any better – *Herbes de Provence*.

So here I am. Dining out on Tanalised Lamb, seasoned with bitter herbs, and filling up with near-unleavened bread. An unwitting Passover meal. The evening is well advanced. Now is the time for reverence, and in the testimony that he gave to the Napier Commission in 1883, Alexander Carmichael spoke about the way of life that was followed by the people who came to such summer sheilings with their herds.

> When the grazing-ground has been reached and the burdens are laid down, the huts are repaired outwardly and inwardly, the fires are rekindled, and food is prepared.

He described their songs and prayers as: 'singularly chaste, beautiful, and elevated'. Many of them stretched back, he suggested, from evidence collected over several decades, 'to the time of bows and arrows'.

Never have I spent a night in a more solitary spot. And yet, I'm at this ancient people's hearth. The hearth that is the heart of home. What better a valediction? Nay, what better a *benediction* than what I have here? As Carmichael translates the Gaelic lines from an evening prayer of days that are no more, but which run on like a warp to which the future weaves its weft:[16]

> *Mhoire ghràdhach! Mhàthair Uain ghil,*
> *Cobhair oirnne ghlan Òigh na h-uaisleachd . . .*
> Mary beloved! Mother of the White Lamb,
> Shield, oh shield us, pure Virgin of nobleness.
> And Bride the beauteous, shepherdess of the flocks.
> Safeguard thou our cattle, surround us together.
> *Safeguard thou our cattle, surround us together.*

And Columba, beneficent, benign.
In name of Father, and of Son, and of Spirit Holy,
Through the Three-in-One, through the Trinity,
Encompass thou ourselves, shield our procession.
Encompass thou ourselves, shield our procession.

O Father! O Son! O Spirit Holy!
Be thou Three-One with us day and night,
And on the back of the wave as on the mountain side
Thou our Mother art there with thine arm under our
head.

And on the back of the wave as on the mountain side
Thou our Mother art there with thine arm under our
    head.
. . . 'S air chùl nan tonn no air thaobh nam beann
Bidh ar Màthair leinn 's bidh a làmh fo 'r ceann!

9

TWO AIRMEN

Day four, Thursday, and another clear cold morning. The temperature during the wee small hours had sunk to around freezing point. As I peer out from the tent, my breath joins volleyed banks of hanging mist that fill this silent mountain amphitheatre. The heather is weighed down with dew, as if with tiny fruits, and every stem of grass stoops pregnant with a beady sheen. The mountains to the east remain in heavy shade, but the sky behind them has assumed a tungsten glow. West, the twin pinnacles of Stuabhal and Rapaire are soaking up the sun-line's warmth that's creeping down the slopes and causing them to steam.

I clamber out, take a token glacial splash in the burn, and fill the cooking pot with water for my muesli's milk and brewing tea. If it had been necessary, the condensation on my flysheet could have yielded up a cup of drips. It sags, dejected, like an old nag's back after a hard day's night. I spread it out to dry where it will catch the soon-arriving sun, and choose a mossy cnocan – a soft little hummock – on which to take my ease and write some notes.

The back pages of this Moleskine 'cahier' have a row of perforations, close to the spine, which makes it easy to pull pages out. That was what had clinched my choice at the stationery shop. But I'm disappointed by the cover. I'd thought it would be waterproof, but not so, I see, with this version.

The quality of the paper, however, is lovely – smooth to the touch and creamy to the eye. Each day, I've been tearing out a sheet and folding it in four to fit into one of the pockets of Osprey's hip belt. These loose folios have become my daybooks, as I'm calling them; my place for scribbling notes while on the trot, or even just odd keywords that will later kindle memory. Right now, while the tent's drying, I want to write them up before their meaning sinks forever into jumbled bogs of tattered scrawls.

I have brought with me for the purpose, of all things, my fountain pen. Just for the ceremony! Back in the days of Leurbost School, our teachers – Miss Montgomery, Miss Graham, Miss Mackinnon – insisted that fountain pens were better for our writing. They hadn't bargained on a class that had a doctor's son. Yes, it seems to be hereditary, and in years to come a lecturer at Aberdeen University would write on my examination script – when lecturers could still have fun without being had up for traumatising their charges – 'Your writing, young man, is moronic. Your geology, it seems, is little better.'

The need to fill the pen, however, presented me with a problem. I had no wish to lug around a chunky ink bottle, and to have used cartridges, wouldn't quite have carried the pomp to match the ceremony. I'd therefore decanted just sufficient ink for the journey into one of those individual-sized jam pots that they give you in posh hotels. If it's jam-tight, I reasoned, it should be ink-tight – and what a splendid little jar this is! 'Baxters of Scotland, by Royal Appointment' it says, in gold lettering on the cap. I squint at it more closely. There's a royal coat of arms. The lion rampant. The unicorn in chains. And there's the motto of the British royal family. *Dieu et mon droit.*

'God and my right.' The heraldry buffs argue what it means. Some hold that *mon droit* signifies the right hand, the one that bears the sword. With spiritual power in the one hand, and secular in the other, you've got it made both ways. Others suggest that it refers to the 'divine right' by which medieval kings legitimised their rule of subjects they had conquered. Between the two interpretations, same difference, if you ask me. The truth is that *mon droit* has always tried to co-opt poor old *Dieu*. The world is oh so 'bright and beautiful' – both today, and in that dear old hymn – until you hit the verse that goes:[1]

> The rich man in his castle,
> The poor man at his gate,
> He made them, high or lowly,
> And ordered their estate.

I've now got a second cup of tea steaming beside me, and I'm slowly drawing back the plunger, filling up with ink from *Dieu et mon droit*. The moss goes turquoise as I dab the surplus off. That'll be fun for any earnest botanist that happens past this way.

Freed of the usual pressures of a day, I notice that I'm bestowing every act and observation with miniscule attention. My world is expanding to fill the space available in consciousness. Even such a tiny thing, as touching pen to paper, carries with it magic as I watch the flowing lines take shape in royal blue. In medieval monasteries, the scriptorium lay close to the sanctuary. Iona's monks, the ones who made the *Book of Kells*, knew about ink's alchemy as prayer. And now the sun has reached the valley floor. In its blaze, I watch the way my writing glistens on the paper – each letter as a mayfly, dancing in its momentary glory – before settling down into the pores and drying to a melanoid maturity.

Dieu et mon droit! God and war. All along, these past three days, I've dragged it in my mind. It's like a dream I had when the struggle with the superquarry was going tough. I was crawling along the side of the road at Roineabhal on all fours, dragging my satchel briefcase behind, at risk of being struck by passing cars, hypothermic and exhausted.

I've dragged war with me because I'd had it so much in my face before I left, just back from speaking to the soldiers and the diplomats. *Dieu* either gets the credit or the blame for wars. Nobody really wants to know that poor old *Dieu* got co-opted to the cause. 'Don't have a king,' said God to the Israelites, through the prophet Samuel. 'He'll only take your daughters to be perfumers and bakers, and your sons to run before his chariots of war, and levy on you all manner of tithes and oppressions.' But no. The Israelites replied: 'We want a king to be over us, like all the other nations. A king who'll go out before us, and fight our battles.' And God shrugged God's heavy shoulders. It's just so hard to be God sometimes. And God said, 'OK. I'll not stand in your way. You go and do it your way.'[2]

While the early followers of Christ were pacifist, the Roman Empire under Constantine became nominally Christian in the fourth century, and went on to crush the heathen with its battle cry *Nobiscum Deus* – 'God with us'. When colonisation is spiritual, as well as corporeal, the vanquished find it hard to process what has happened to them. They were meant to be grateful. They'd been 'given' God, after all. As such, the oppressed so often meld to join the next wave of oppressors. Pillage, rape and the scars of banal brutality run through the ancestral veins of everyone.

Warlords like William the Conqueror went on to dignify their act, paying their spiritual fire insurance by bestowing abbeys with the spoils of rack, ruin and serfdom. The Nazis didn't miss the trick either. For all their supposed paganism, German soldiers had the Roman motto stamped onto the buckles of their trouser belts: *Gott mit uns*. Goebbels read the New Testament with a jaundiced eye, concluding: 'Christ is harsh and relentless.' Erich Koch, the commissar of East Prussia who sent hundreds of thousands of Ukrainian Jews and Gypsies to the death camps, held that National Socialism was nothing less than 'Luther's unfinished Reformation'.

Why Luther's? Because in 1543 the reformer had said of the Jews that, as a deed of kindness, rulers 'must act like a good physician who, when gangrene has set proceeds without mercy to cut, saw, and burn flesh, veins, bone, and marrow'. Accordingly, German Protestants must 'burn down their synagogues [and] force them to work, and deal harshly with them'. Of such measures, Himmler remarked: 'No judgement could be sharper,' and asked that, after the war, his own contributions to such a Reformation cause should be remembered at the Luther Archive in Wittenberg. In the view of the historian, Richard Steigmann-Gall, the Third Reich developed a war theology that understood itself to be a 'favoured nation' where 'most Christian clergy condemned Germany's adversaries in harsh moral terms, elevating the war into a type of crusade in which God had chosen Germany to punish his enemies'.[3]

From such roots, Hitler's 'spiritual struggle' found inner cohesion and, therefore, outer legitimacy. The problem is not unique to Protestantism. Roman Catholicism and Orthodoxy have also been riddled through with violence and authoritarian religion. So, too, are some facets of other faiths, including the supposedly peaceful Buddhism of Burma or Sri Lanka. But those aspects of the Protestant tradition that entertain a binary division of the Damned and the Elect, and the ongoing God-sanctioned legitimacy of violence, arguably have a special problem at mission control. As Erich Fromm surmised: 'Calvin's theory of predestination has one implication which should be explicitly mentioned here, since it has found its most vigorous revival in Nazi ideology: the principle of *the basic inequality of men*.' That said, we should not make the mistake of imagining that this Nazi hijacking of the cause was true to the fullness of the faith. 'Hitler's ideology,' Fromm took care to point out, 'lacks the emphasis on freedom and moral principles which was inherent in Protestantism.'[4]

These issues surface in the military staff colleges whenever we debate the 'just war' theory of Saint Augustine: 'we go to

war that we may have peace.' Why should the military entertain such theology? Why should such theory hold a central
place in their curriculum and many of their debates? Quite
simply, they understand that their values are their value.
They have seen how otherwise decent people can, under
compelling circumstances of social psychology, do the most
terrible things to one another. They know how easily the
moral anchor can drag if not well toed-in. They also know
that we are living in a world where old certainties are gone.
A world where, as my speaking brief from the UK Defence
Academy puts it, 'the net results of conflict are not easy to
predict'. Where the very 'utility of force', as they call it, is
undergoing reappraisal.

In 1898, Winston Churchill rode into the Battle of
Omdurman (in present-day central Sudan) on horseback, with
a sabre by his side. By the end of his political career, it was
Hiroshima and Nagasaki. Today the cutting edge of conflict
has become 'asymmetric warfare' – the military's name for
terrorism – the little guy's ability to paralyse the big, because
technology has democratised violence. As General Sir Rupert
Smith writes: 'Our opponents are formless, and . . . even if
military action is on a big scale, and even if it is successful the
confrontation will remain, to be resolved by other means and
levers of power.'[5]

When I speak at staff colleges, I'll be in an auditorium
with anything from thirty to four hundred serving officers.
I'll pose questions like: *What might be those other means
and levers?* To use a Quaker turn of phrase, *How might we
seek to live in the virtue of that life and power that takes
away the occasion of all wars?*[6] I'll maybe start by acknowledging that, so far, nobody has managed to rid the world of
war with nonviolence. But neither so, with violence. We can
proceed from the basis of such mutual deficiency, and nonviolent approaches have now built up an extensive track record
of success worldwide – the revolutions in India, Portugal, the
Philippines, Eastern Europe, to name but a handful. I find

that there's a very thin line between the principled soldier
and the principled pacifist. Both see peace as the end, but
differ in the means. Both, in their own ways, are imperfect in
an imperfect world. Said Martin Luther King: 'I came to see
the pacifist position not as sinless but as the lesser evil in the
circumstances.'[7]

'All life entails violence,' said Gandhi. 'Our duty can only be
to minimise it.' As he taught it, nonviolence as *ahimsa* (literally
'not striking') is driven by *satyagraha* – a Sanskrit word that
means 'truth force', 'soul force' or 'God force'. As such, 'The
badge of the violent is his weapon, spear, sword or rifle. God is
the shield of the nonviolent.'[8] Jesus never taught 'just war'
theory. Jesus taught full-on *nonviolence*. 'Put away your sword,'
he told Peter. 'We shall have no more of this.' And to Pilate at
his trial: 'My kingdom is not of this world. If it was, my followers would fight to save me.'[9]

Killing is a very ultimate thing to do. Many are the occasions
that I've heard fighting men privately express their ethical
disquiet. It can be very humbling. One time, an RAF man came
forward in the coffee break, just as I was about to go up on the
podium. He had hovered in the background amongst all the
buzz of activity until we could be momentarily alone, then
closed in and announced, with an air of burning urgency: 'I
just want to say that I'm just back from Afghanistan . . . and I
feel . . . *defiled*.'

That was all. Those are the only words by which that
airman etched himself upon my memory. But something in
me shot into action. I told him that, whatever it was that he
might have done or seen, it was forgiven. Point blank.
Forgiven. 'Now, move on, and live the rest of your
life – undefiled.'

The energy with which I said these words felt outlandish
even as I spoke. I thought afterwards, 'What right have I . . . ?'
But sometimes it's like that. The military have a good understanding of these moments. You only get one shot. If you

pussyfoot around, the magic of the 'activist moment', as I call it, has moved on. We speak of 'baring the soul', and to experience it in such a way always feels a specially tender sort of intimacy.

I've not always caught such moments elegantly. Another time, a Brigadier at the Joint Services Command & Staff College, laterally a Lieutenant General, a man well-known for his bluntness but much loved by his colleagues for his fairness, came up to me the evening after my talk. He looked me square on, and said: 'Quite frankly, I think that you are mad.'

'Have you ever killed?' I retorted.

It took him aback visibly. He was one of the Pilgrims, as the SAS special forces call themselves, and he'd seen full-spectrum action, from Northern Ireland to Iraq.

'That's not a fair question!' he snorted, throwing back a thick set of martial eyebrows.

'Yes it is!' I said acerbically, throwing up a wall between the two of us. 'I am a taxpayer. You are a public servant. We are a democracy.

'Now: have you ever killed?'

'Yes,' he said, in a deflated air, and we parted, loose ends left hanging like raw flesh.

At first I felt quite proud of myself. Later, it came to me that all I'd done was play Smart Alex. It wasn't the validity or otherwise of the point I'd made that was the problem. It was how I'd made it. I'd gone on the attack rather than sitting down to listen. There'd have been a story, and bridgeheads, within that man if I'd understood the opportunity. As it was, I'd only fed the spiral of violence.[10] I'd flunked the Quaker test of 'seeking that of God in everyone'.

Another day, another lecture, and we're all relaxing in the officers' mess the night beforehand. We've had a couple of beers, and are thoroughly enjoying the challenges of one another's company. Tornado airman is on one side of me.

Harrier airman, on the other. We're laughing, because they've noticed that my security pass indicates my status as *Unescorted*. How come such likes get set loose here? I must be part of the woodwork now. What's more, my mugshot on the pass has me saluting. A double-fingered V for peace.

'Lest we forget!' I tease them, adding that I'm still waiting for the index-linked pension and the medal.

Another round of ammunition has been ordered from the bar. Jolly good. Tally ho. We all three know its time for battle to commence.

'Gentlemen,' I say. 'You'll be aware that they only let me out of my box here to test your resolve under fire. And you'll observe that I'm not house-trained. Not even wearing a tie.

'So tell me,' and I turn to Tornado, and pop to him the question that I'd popped the brigadier, albeit in a more convivial spirit. 'Have you ever killed?'

These days, so many of them have seen death, or been its direct cause.

'I have,' he says, and starts to tell of dropping thousand-pound bombs on an Iraqi airfield in the First Gulf War. They'd been trained to fly low, but on this occasion were told to stay high. Lights off. Tight formation. Following each other's burners by the naked eye in the darkness to keep radio and radar silence.

The bombs were dropped on targets set entirely by their programmed instruments. Tornado had been troubled that he couldn't first eyeball what was down below. He couldn't double-check on manual control. When the payload hit the ground, 'it was like Armageddon lighting up'. Thankfully, when the recce pictures came back the next day, the strike had been spot on. Everything was fried. The runways would never run again. He was glad the raid had taken place in the middle of the night. Not so many people to be killed as there would have been in daytime.

'How did it make you feel?' I ask.

'Gut-wrenching.'

Long silence.

Over to Harrier.

'And you?'

He's a much younger man. He'd dropped cluster bombs on an Iraqi barracks.

'We wiped it flat.'

Longer silence.

'How did it make you feel?'

'Satisfied!'

And he's in for the kill. Newly back from Afghanistan, but smiling. I'm the one now in his sights, finger poised to zap the pickle button.

'Alastair – let me put this to you.

'Consider the reality in Afghanistan. You're at a checkpoint, and a civvy car drives up. A man gets out with two small children – arms blown off. They're dripping blood, too shocked to cry, just whimpering.

'Whatever's happened has only just happened, and in spite of all your training, you're completely thrown.

'All right!' the man shouts. 'I surrender! I confess. I am Taliban.'

They'd been making IEDs. Roadside bombs. One went off in the kids' hands.

'I give myself up,' he says. 'I renounce the Taliban! But please, please, help my children. Do what you want with me, but in the name of Allah, get my children to a hospital.'

The coalition's mission was to win hearts and minds. So what were the boys to do? They did what every decent instinct told them to do. They called in a medevac helicopter. Luckily, one was passing close by.

Just as it was lifting off, Daddy Taliban dives back into his car. He pulls out an RPG – a rocket-propelled grenade – and fires it at the chopper, with his own children inside.

'Now, *what do you say to that*, Alastair?' concludes Harrier. '*With his own little children inside.*'

Utter silence.

'You see,' he resumes, 'That's why! That's why – when they've got our boys pinned down in a fire fight. That's why – when I'm called in to take out a nest of Taliban. That's why I find the sound of cannon fire . . . *so satisfying*.

'What do you say to that? Alastair?'

And like an eagle, he circled around, climbing higher and higher in the silence. And when he was sure, he zeroed back in with one long thunderous blast on the pickle button.

'What does *pacifism* have to say to that?'

And, trapped in the crosshairs, it came to me the way that, once every few years, I'll have a recurrent nightmare. I'll be caught up in a savagely violent situation. Acting on instinct – before even having chance to think about 'my principles' – I'll have grabbed and used a weapon. It's as if the dream is to remind me not to be too self-assured.

'So?' Harrier asked, permitting no quarter.

Solemn pause.

'*Brutalisation*,' I replied. 'I would say that is what's happened to your Taliban man. That Taliban's whole culture has been brutalised.

'And guess who did the brutalising? Hardly cricket, was it? All the way back to 1839 – the first British occupation of Afghanistan – our power struggle with the Russian Empire, what we cheerfully called "The Great Game".'

'Hardly cricket, is it?'

And my mind was running in parallel with the presentation that I'd be giving in the morning. The images that I'd put up on the screen that spans the huge front wall of the auditorium of the Joint Services Command and Staff College.

A clipping from the *Daily Telegraph*. It had angered many readers at the time. Dr Muhammad Abdul Bari, the Secretary General of the Muslim Council of Britain, explaining the psychology of the making of a suicide bomber.

'I deal with emotionally damaged children. Children come to hate when they don't get enough care and love . . . It makes a young person angry and vulnerable.'[11]

And then the terrible images that I've gathered from the web that make even seasoned soldiers flinch.

'We don't get to see these in our media,' I say, 'but the Arab world sees them. In fact, this is how they've seen us for a very long time.'

The first is from *Al Jazeera*. A child's head exploded, his little face flowing in the dirt as if it has become a plastic mask that's melting in the fire.

'This is somebody's son.'

And then a man sitting in a truck, gone from the neck upwards, brain remnants dripping down his leather jacket; and in the final indignity, he has visibly wet his trousers.

'Somebody's daddy.'

Followed by an Iraqi woman. Her thighs are beautiful, her vulva neatly shaved, and hanging from below one knee are blackened drapes of tangled flesh and sinew.

'And this is what happened when Mummy went to the market.'

And now is such a very thin place. Such a faraway place.

Such a faraway place – where Harrier still circles – somewhere among the clouds above.

'Those Iraqis . . .' I say.

'We had to stop Saddam!' he interjects, throwing out distracting chaff.

'They chose to be there in those barracks. They chose to fight for his regime.'

'And the conscripts? Did your cluster bombs distinguish?'

His face twitches. Tornado watches like an old owl. I've made my point sufficiently. Time now to climb down from the tumult.

'But I invite you, gentlemen, to ask the same question of me. *Have I killed?*'

Both looked puzzled.

'You see, I'm a killer too. Every time I get into the car or on a plane, burning oil that's been fought for, poisoning the planet. Who can really tell?

'Goddamnit! Maybe even every time I don't do what you do.

'We're all complicit. All in this together. All so very human.'

10

RULE, BRITANNIA!

The morning dew has almost gone. It lingers only in the shady nooks, but even there it quickens to a rainbow sheen of pinprick diamonds for a while, then yields its iridescence to the climbing sun. My tent has now dried, my daybooks going back to Monday are written up, and I have lingered here for long enough. It's been a precious couple of hours. A time for settling into place, its utter stillness; and for taking stock, recalling all the reasons that have brought me here.

I tighten Osprey's straps, nod a ceremonial farewell to the sheiling's presences from which I am divided only by the veneer of time, and head off up the stalker's path. Compared with the one I touched on yesterday, this trail is in a reasonable condition. Perhaps it comes from having worked with stone, but I always love to walk on stonework that's been laid to last. What's right beneath my feet right now was made to take the pummelling of a pony with two hundred pounds of stag strapped to its saddle. You can see the quality of construction in the culverts and the cambered angles, as well as in the tightly packed mosaics of cobbles that are toed in deep to one another's heels, thus to give sure footing even on the steepest reaches. Those stones back on the road at Rodel – they'd been crushed by force to chips of standard size and grading. But these stones, uncut, range from a fist-sized pound in weight up to a hundred-weight and more. Of these, each lives out its service at a stone-paced rate of life – if such a thought is meaningful. Said MacDiarmid: 'I lift a stone; it is the meaning of life I clasp.'[1]

Here and there, every hundred yards or so, I pass the mossy pitted faces of tiny quarries. These were gouged out more than a century ago, for building up the foundations of much more ancient footpaths. I picture them being grafted at by men with picks and spades, and muscles knotted like Scots pine. Crofter men, in homespun tweeds and jerseys, an oilskin for the rain, who carted grit in baskets or on barrows while bantering in the Gaelic. The whereabouts of cattle, sheep or deer. The price per cran of herring landed on the Tarbert pier last week. The latest scrape of the Scalpay boys drift netting off the Shiants. The strength or weakness of the new minister's sermons. The who's who of shooting parties due up to the Castle next month. The furtive sharing of who got tipped by whom, fishing which loch, on what flies, and with what weight of catch. And from newspapers and letters read out by the literate, or from word of mouth from ships and those returning home: what's fresh from the shipyards of the Clyde. Or the whalers of the Arctic. Or the sheep ranches of the Falklands and Patagonia. Or the prairies of Canada. Or India and the Cape. Or whatever other fighting fronts were open in the name of God and Empire with the Cameron or the Seaforth Highlanders, who'd be recruiting, respectively, in Tarbert and in Stornoway.

There'd be the studied contemplation, too, as they'd sit and pare at liquorice slabs of plug tobacco, tapping ash from out the bowls of briar pipes, tamping down the aromatic flakes. The never-ending ritual of lighting up, expiry in the damp, asking round to see who's got another light, dispelling clouds of midges with the satisfying puffs, and smelling like the tar and tallow-seasoned toilers of the soil that they were.

Here the gradient sways and twists, in an easy-going switchback sort of way. It means you only get to see a little way ahead. The shorter lengths seem to shorten time. I scribble in my daybook: 'On the winding path no stretch is long'. There's a spring in my step. Even Osprey's lighter than yesterday. I feel so happy, and an hour soon idles by as last night's campsite slowly shrinks from sight.

I've come up to the pass, and another watershed. Rapaire is over on the right. On my left, the sheer black cliffs and chutes of scree of Stuabhal – the Abode of Staves, or of the Rocky Columns. You could trim that down to one word, metaphorically speaking. Fortress.

Just visible behind me, in the east, appears the summit tip of Beinn Mhòr. With it comes back Eishken, and those stalking days with Tommy. Ahead of me lounge the hills of Uig, and beyond, the two-toned Plimsoll line from where the pale blue of the horizon's sky meets richer hues from fathoms of the Atlantic's bounteous depth.

There is a headland somewhere over there that's called Am Beannachadh – The Blessing – and by it Taigh a' Bheannaich – the House of Blessing. It's part of Gallan Head, one of those old temple or related sites, a low stone ruin of some unknown antiquity. There used to be a spring, now just a muddy squelch, but you can still see rings amongst the grass of the foundations of their bothan dwellings, their little cells of prayer and spiritual retreat.

Right next to it, on the neighbouring promontory, is the Àird Uig NATO base. Some of the bunker-like buildings are still there, but the huge sweeping radar scanner and the six-hundred-foot-high mast with strobes that stabbed the Hebridean night have now been taken down. Rumours come and go as to whether less obtrusive structures have been set up elsewhere on the island to fight, they say, the War on Terror. Well, I've never quite seen Bin Laden getting this far north and west. But you never know. You just never know where the Devil's going to creep in next.

You just never know – and part of what I've been wanting to think about on this walk is the way that 'just war' theory locks religion in to an endless identification with violence. Christ, if we give him credence, was very clear. His world was not one to be fought for with the sword in any outward sense.[2] Paul, however, took a more pragmatic view, and with Augustine's influence, Calvin further ramped it up:[3]

> Hence we infer that empires did not spring up at random, nor by the mistakes of men, but that they were appointed by the will of God, because he wishes that political order should exist among men, and that we should be governed by usages and laws. For this reason Paul says, that all who resist the power are rebels against God, because there is no power but what is ordained by God (Romans 13:1, 2).

Such a theology of 'might is right' lies behind notions like 'American exceptionalism', 'favoured nation' status, the sense of being the 'chosen people', and the presumption of holding a 'manifest destiny' to order and command the world.[4]

In his book about predestination, the leading Reformed church theologian, Loraine Boettner, claimed that America represented 'one of the brightest pages of all Calvinistic history . . . Our forefathers believed in it and were controlled by it'. He quoted the renowned historian and US Navy Secretary, George Bancroft, that the Founding Fathers had been, 'Calvinists . . . according to the straightest system'.[5] The United States may proclaim a separation between church and state, but the underlying ideology, proclaimed in *The Star-Spangled Banner,* the national anthem, has these closing lines:

> Then conquer we must, when our cause it is just,
> And this be our motto: 'In God is our trust.'
> And the star-spangled banner in triumph shall wave
> O'er the land of the free and the home of the brave!

For some of those who draw depth and richness from Calvin's theology, it was a tragedy that the McCarthyite persecution of intellectuals in the 1950s inhibited America from evolving a liberal, mellowed-out mainstream Protestantism, such as came about in European countries like Scotland and Holland. Instead, the field was cleared for the business-friendly neocon-servative gospel of evangelicals like the Reverend Billy Graham, with an obsessive focus on the privatised spirituality of personal salvation, and little by way of social witness.

Raised of Scots Presbyterian stock, Graham was ordained as a minister in the Southern Baptist Convention, a church that is, itself, of a substantially Calvinist disposition.[6] Every recent American president, right through to Obama, has found it expedient to sit in prayer with the preacher. Most strikingly, in January 1991, on the eve of launching Operation Desert Storm to initiate the First Gulf War, George Bush Sr called Graham in to pray with him at the White House. The evangelist later disclosed: 'Our prayers were for a short war and one that would be followed by a long period of peace in the Mideast.'[7] It was a short war, but war nonetheless, and with lasting ramifications.

As father, as son; and come the year 2000, George W. Bush drew on the ideology of American exceptionalism in his elec-tion campaign. 'Our nation,' he said, 'is *chosen by God* and commissioned by history to be a model to the world of justice and inclusion and diversity without division.' Bush had found his way to conservative evangelical Christianity. As he later put it, 'Reverend Graham planted a mustard seed in my soul.' With it came a heightened and very personal sense of manifest destiny.[8]

I feel like God wants me to run for president. I can't explain it, but I sense my country is going to need me. Something is going to happen, and, at that time, my country is going to need me.

Something did indeed happen the following year, on 9/11. Within a month of the Twin Towers attack, America's neocon-servative politicians had seized the chance to invade Afghanistan, albeit having promptly to rename 'Operation

Infinite Justice' as 'Operation Enduring Freedom' to avoid seeming to appropriate an attribute of Allah.[9] The 'special relationship' between Britain and America fell into place and, starting from day one of these asymmetric hostilities, Tony Blair ordered British submarines to strike the poverty-racked landlocked country with Tomahawk cruise missiles.

Blair had been eased into power in 1997 as the UK prime minister with the godfatherly help of Rupert Murdoch, the Australian media magnate, whose grandfather and great-grandfather had both been Presbyterian clergy of the Free Church of Scotland.[10] His lead British newspaper, then with a circulation of nearly four million, had run a full-front-page headline before the May general election that announced: *The Sun Backs Blair: Give change a chance.* It was a sorry perversion of John Lennon's peace anthem. The following year, as ethnic conflict blew up in Kosovo, Murdoch's *Sun* ran another full frontal: *War in Europe: BOMB BOMB BOMB.* Not since the tabloid newspaper's famous *GOTCHA* when, in 1982, a British submarine sank the Argentinean *General Belgrano,* had the British nation been stirred up with such jingoism.

Come the Second Gulf War and the invasion of Iraq in 2003, George W. Bush's defence secretary was the arch-neoconservative Donald Rumsfeld. His Christian name is the anglicised form of *Dòmhnall,* Gaelic for The Ruler of the World. That perhaps befits one credited with the one-liner: 'Death has a tendency to encourage a depressing view of war.' Very little has been written about his religion, but in a 1962 campaign leaflet that is replicated in his memoirs, he described himself as attending a Presbyterian church.[11] In the early days of the second Iraq War, Rumsfeld allowed his military advisors to put jokes on the covers of his daily intelligence bulletins that were given to Bush. However, as American lives started to be lost, the jokes transmogrified into belligerent Bible verses. Alongside photographs of tanks and US soldiers at prayer, the chosen passages included:[12]

Put on the full armour of God (Ephesians 6:11)

Their arrows are sharp . . . their chariot wheels are like a whirlwind (Isaiah 5:28)

It is God's will that by doing good you should silence the ignorant talk of foolish men (1 Peter 2:15)

Ironically, it was the apostle Peter whom Jesus had explicitly disarmed.[13] Whether war was the kind of 'doing good' that Peter later had in mind with his epistle, is a moot point. The apologists for war repeatedly told the media: *this is not a crusade.* Such rhetoric was all very well. However, if anyone from al-Qaeda happened to switch on their television, and watched the crowd's annual rapture as they swayed to the chorus of 'Rule! Britannia' in London at The Last Night of the Proms, they might well have been forgiven for being fooled.

When Britain fi-i-irst, at heav-en's command,
Aro-o-o-ose from out the a-a-a-zure main,
Arose, arose, arose from out the a-azure main,
This was the charter, the charter of the land,
And guardian a-a-angels sang this strain:

Rule, Britannia! Britannia rule the waves
Britons never, never, never shall be slaves.

The nations, no-o-o-o-ot so blest as thee,
Must i-i-i-i-in their turn, to ty-y-yrants fall,
Must in their turn, to ty-y-rants fall,
While thou shalt flourish, shalt flourish great and free,
The dread and e-e-e-e-nvy of them all.

On the day after the session in the officers' mess with Tornado and Harrier, I was escorted down from the rostrum by a briga-dier. He had that rather sweet, concerned manner, that is characteristic of a certain vintage of English gentleman, and he cleared his throat and asked me, almost shyly: 'Er, tell me, do the politicians ever have you come and say these things?'

'Never!' I said.

'The trouble is, I get the feeling that they can't believe they've made it until they've been blooded in a war.'

I had in my mind the way that a certain kind of guest at the sporting lodges will dip their finger into the entry wound of a freshly slaughtered beast, and daub a patch of blood on their foreheads. I had in mind, too, an article that had been in the *Daily Telegraph* about Lance Price, one of Tony Blair's spin doctors. Price said that he had felt the Prime Minister 'was relishing his first blooding' when he authorised air strikes on Iraq in 1998. Despite all the public hand-wringing about having had to act 'with a heavy heart', it was his sense that Blair had felt that dropping bombs was 'part of his coming of age as a leader'.[14]

The brigadier harrumphed. 'Yes,' he said. 'I feared that might be the case.

'Such a pity.'

We retired into an anteroom for a quick round of refreshments, then back into the auditorium for questions.

'So, what would you have done about inspecting Saddam's weapons?' asked a military policeman.

'Set a good example,' said I, cheekily. 'First send them up to Scotland to inspect our own weapons of mass destruction – Trident at Faslane.'

'And Saddam himself ?' yapped an army major, as the tempo hotted up. I'm the fox, they're the hunt, and its *tally-ho* for the chase.

'A monster of our own making,' I retorted: 'But where were *you* when the West was arming him as he gassed his own people? What were *you* doing while the rest of us were writing our Amnesty International letters, getting fobbed off with Xeroxed replies from the Ministry of Defence who were in cahoots with the arms companies?'

'Pardon me, sir, but what would you do if somebody broke into your home?' inquired a punctilious Kuwaiti naval captain.

'I've been there,' I was able to say. 'They cleaned out the house while one of them held a knife to the throat of our friend who had been sleeping downstairs. If we'd had a revolver, like some expatriates kept under their pillows, she'd have got her throat slit.'

'And rape?' asked a USAF pilot, with that languid faraway air of having seen and heard it all before. 'Suppose they came for one of yours?'

So I told a real-life story.

It was in 1985, and I was working in appropriate technology in the capital of Papua New Guinea. One night, a young woman in our tiny Quaker Meeting – she was just seventeen – was dragged out of her car by fourteen disaffected young men, a so-called 'rascal' gang. Her boyfriend was beaten up. She was taken to a nearby hillside, where they took it in turns to rape her.

Normally the police would have gone in to their squatter settlement and administered indiscriminate rough justice. However, from her hospital bed, she said that she wanted no more perpetuation of the violence. Instead, she wanted something that might 'touch their hearts', that might have a chance of opening paths to empathy.

Her father, a university teacher, was friendly with the chief of police and sent a message to request restraint. A few days later, he asked me to accompany him to the settlement, so that we could talk with its leaders.

We walked in, unannounced, and sat down with the 'old' men underneath a tree. None of them would have been over forty. They told us straight out that they knew why we had come, and that they were deeply sorry about what had happened. They very much appreciated the police restraint, for they, themselves, had lost control of their youth. The old ways were in chaos. The bewildering new ways of rapid social change had broken down the customs and constraints. Their poverty contrasted painfully with the 'fruits of the white man's garden' and this generated frustration and alienation. Most of the boys in the gang had come from rural parts, hoping they might 'make it', but with not a hope. They'd fallen to a subculture of violent crime with all its brutalising rites of passage. The old men knew. They'd been there, done that, too.

We asked them a question. What, in their culture, would make for a fitting reconciliation with our community? They said that they would have to hold a compensation ceremony.

On the appointed day, the girl's father and I stood in ceremony, facing one another at the university gates. About a dozen of our companions witnessed in silent Quaker worship in the background. Processing down the main street, amidst much beating of drums and with all the bravado of a carnival, walked the entire squatter settlement. There were perhaps two hundred of them and of all ages.

We had said that we did not want any material compensation, that it was not our people's way. However, it was their way. The compromise was that the food would be sent up to the patients at the hospital afterwards. There they all were – a whole community – and pushing a cavalcade of six or eight wheelbarrows piled high with pumpkins, tapioca, yams, sweet potato, sago sticks, coconuts, pawpaw, chickens, tinned fish and betel nuts. Goodness knows where it all came from. One prefers not to ask. And right at the head of the procession, was a column of fourteen young men.

They had never expected to be treated in this way. Many were in tears. One by one, the lads filed between us. Each briefly looked us in the eyes, and said: *Mipela sori tru.*

'I'm truly sorry.'

That was it – and that was the end of that particular session with Harrier, Tornado and their colleagues. However, not all of the military with whom I have shared that story have been touched by it. Once, I was invited to speak to non-commissioned officers. These are the connecting link between the officers and other ranks. They're the spanners who use clout to make the army work at ground level. It was at the Army Training Regiment in Colchester.

I could feel their energy darken with a pensive hostility as I gave my lecture. Afterwards, in the mess, a wiry, moustached and fiery-eyed NCO came up to me.

'What you did,' he said, 'was to *prostitute* that girl! All you did was put a price on a white woman's rape.'

The mainstream expatriates in Papua New Guinea had said the same thing. There had been letters in the press saying that castration was the only answer: in Pidgin, *rausim bol bilong ol!*

'Then, what would you have done?' I asked the NCO.

'I'd have . . . *I'd have gone down to the market*,' he said, blurting out the words. 'And I'd have bought an AK47 . . . *and shot the bastards to Hell!*'

'And would that have made for a safer future?'

He held fire, fazed by the question. It seemed like for a long time. Then he shrugged his shoulders with a warming smile – and goodness, there is something that I love about the honesty and decency of these hard-bitten fighting men – 'Probably not. But what can I get you to drink?'

From here, the land dips downwards, and the view towards Àird Uig starts to slip from off my radar. The path winds on beneath a volley of looming cliffs. These rise so high and sharply that, for the most part, their lower faces hide inside deep shadows. At their foot lies a heart-shaped lake, Loch Chleistir. It means the Loch of the Cascading Rock. I stand awhile, and watch its surface billow with the gusts of breeze to sheets of rippling sapphire. I half think of getting out my rod to fish, but there's no point. The wind is still sat resolutely in the south-east. In any case, there is a sacrosanct feeling to this place. It should perhaps be left in peace.

The temperature can't be more than ten degrees, but that's been absolutely perfect for the walking. I've made it all the way up here, laden as I am, but shedding not a drop of sweat. Now, there's a choice of two route options down to

Kinlochresort. Either I can keep to this path for another couple of miles, then strike directly north from the tail end of Loch Voshimid. Or I can turn off here and follow the stream that leaves Loch Chleistir and which defines the border between Harris and Lewis. Its name is Abhainn a' Chlàir Bhig – the River of the Little Plain – and it meets up with the river that flows out of Voshimid at a junction past the said small plain, shown on the map as Clàr Beag. To go too close to Voshimid looks terribly boggy, even on the small scale map that I'm using at the moment to get more of a panoramic perspective. You can tell by all the tiny lochans and the spread-out contours. The Clàr Beag route looks like it's on a steady gradient, and drier. Hopefully, I'll dodge the marshes until much nearer to my destination.

Thus far, the ease of the path has made the day genteel, but very soon after leaving it I'm into rough and tumble. The ground comprises beds of peat incised by frequent flood path waterways. These chop it into little plateaus, rarely bigger than a tennis court. I have to keep on scrambling up the one side, and then skidding down the other with my boot heels on the slippery bare black 'hag'.

There is hardly any wind now, as I fall below the skyline. The silence ruptures only from the croak of ravens. I can make out three or four of them, somersaulting as black kites, playing in the thermals from the upper and now sun-soaked reaches of the cliffs behind. The deer have left their footprints in patches of the mud. Some, freshly flecked; others gone to mush. And although this is golden eagle country, I've seen but one so far, and that, far off on the horizon.

The lower down I get, the more the ground cuts up. Another half an hour on, and the tennis courts have shrunk to ping-pong tables – these, heaped up with clay and boulders that are the host to rank and thigh-high heather shrubs. This is where the retreating glacier forgot to tidy up. I'm in amongst the so-called 'hummocky moraine' of crushed rock debris. Its rugged chaos was laid down amongst blocks of ice, caught up within to melt away and leave behind the pits that are now kettle holes and sloshy bogs.

You could hardly say I'm walking; only a slow meander. I've given up on time, and just accept I'm near enough a day behind schedule. Ahead, I see Clàr Beag, a grassy clearing as it were, about the size of a football pitch. It looks as if a flattening of the slope has caused the stream to braid, and spread out levelled beds of fertile sediment. I'm just ambling towards it, musing on nothing much, Osprey swaying this way and that way, up here and down there, maybe better go that way, when – as if whisked off by a gust of *gaoth nan sith* – I'm into faerie land.

A miniature village! For such is what has come into my focus. Had I more carefully studied my bespoke map earlier, the large-scale one, I'd have been forewarned. They're marked clearly enough. Three times, at that: 'Old Sheilings'; 'Beehive Huts'; and 'Both a' Chlàir Bhig'.

In all my days out on the moors, I've never seen such likes before. It's a vision straight from Middle Earth. What I've stumbled on is a beehive sheiling settlement. Squatting on a grassy hump with the stream meandering around both sides, is a double both, in fact, two bothan, joined together like a castle with twin turrets. Each is conical, about a full-grown person's height, and wide enough at the base to be able to lie down outstretched inside. Each has its little doorway, an opening, square-set, with a lintel stone above, but only a couple of feet in height. The smaller structure is completely intact. The roof of the larger one stands open to the sky as if it is a cratered volcano, about to puff and blow.

I drop Osprey, kneel at the entrance, and pause for a moment. Then, lying down with my belly pressed flush to the ground, I wriggle through and slip backwards in time.

The ground inside is firm but filthy. Sheep have overwintered here, seeking shelter from the storms. Leaning back against the wall, a dappled splendour fills my eyes. Light is breaking through the cracks between the stones. The elements have stripped away much of the weatherproofing layer of turf outside. It's like I'm in a Stone Age planetarium. Pinprick stars are twinkling through the nooks and crannies. The dust raised by my entry is dancing in the hollow stillness. It makes the tapered shafts of sunlight seem to rotate, as if they're spiral galaxies at the birthing of creation.

The stones of which it is built are variable in size. They range from sacks of coal to bags of sugar. Each row steps in above the one below, spiralling to a cupola with the smoke hole at the top. There are several little recesses, 'cupboards' where they would have kept their things. This is an original eco-house. It was grown from out the moor, and now it settles slowly back from whence it came.

I crawl back out, back into a world that feels at first to be an overweening brightness. My stomach clock is chiming, and I settle down against one of the big foundation stones. Osprey gives soft padding for my back. I'm on standard lunchtime fare again. Oatcakes and cheese, freshly drawn stream water, and a bag of fruit and nuts. I'd thought they'd tasted slightly fusty back when I shared a pack with the ants on the Golden Road. Only now do I read what's written on the packet. *'Snack lovers rejoice. You are what you eat.'* And then the small print: 'Best before the end June 2006.' Oh well. Only three years gone.

Before I'd left home, Seumas Crawford had directed me to the writings of a certain Captain Thomas of the Royal Navy. In 1859 he'd made a formal notification of the existence of beehive structures on the island, sending it to the Society of Antiquaries of Scotland.[15]

> The general opinion is that they are very ancient. Martin, in his account of Skye, mentions them as *Tigh nan Druineach*, or Druids' houses . . . I consider the relation between the *bothan* and the Picts' houses of the Orkneys (and else-where) to be evident . . . All the natives agree that no-one knows who built them, and that they were not made by the fathers nor grandfathers of persons now living.

In 1863 the captain returned to the island, this time with Sir Arthur Mitchell, who was the Professor of Ancient History at the Royal Scottish Academy. It was another double both structure that they'd found, one that (from the drawing) is nearly identical to mine, but located four miles north from here, at Làrach Tigh Dhubhstail. In 1880 the professor published an account of the experience in his remarkable book, *The Past in the Present: What is Civilisation?*[16]

> I confess, however, to having shown, as well as felt, the effects of *the Wine of Astonishment*. I do not think I ever came upon a scene which more surprised me, and I scarcely know where or how to begin my description of it . . . We were in a dwelling in the construction of which neither wood, nor iron, nor cement had been used. Stone and turf, and nothing else had gone to make it. No tool had been used; scarcely even a wooden spade, and not a hammer of any kind . . . We felt that we had been almost introduced to the stone period without going either to far-off lands or far-off times to find it.

His astonishment was further amplified when he discovered nearby freshly broken fragments of what looked to be ancient pottery. Shortly afterwards, he made the acquaintance of the bothan's occupants. These were three sheiling girls who he found sitting on a cnoc. During the day, they minded and milked their cattle. At night, they slept inside the ancient shelter, just as their sisters before them had always done. The pottery was theirs. It had come from a seam of clay at Barvas, thirty miles away, worked by practices that had gone unchanged since Neolithic times. The women cut a touching pastoral picture:

> It was Sunday, and they had made their toilet with care at the burn, and had put on their printed calico gowns. None of them could speak English: but they were not

illiterate, for one of them was reading a Gaelic Bible. They showed no alarm at our coming, but invited us into the *bo'h*, and hospitably treated us to milk. They were courteously dignified, neither feeling nor affecting to feel embarrassment. There was no evidence of any understanding on their part that we should experience surprise at their surroundings.

Sir Arthur speculated that some twenty or thirty such bothan remained in seasonal occupation on Harris and Lewis. However, 'it is not likely that a new one will ever again be built,' and he concluded: 'I leave this subject with the remark that the beehive-house certainly belongs to the man without a story, though the man without a story is still found clinging to it.'

11

VENISON AND HONEY

Perhaps Sir Arthur had to watch how deeply he drank of his Wine of Astonishment. Wearing another cap, he was also the Commissioner of Lunacy for Scotland. Captain Thomas had a more relaxed understanding that you cannot scratch beneath this landscape – into its place names and its people – without the stories stirring from their slumbers. He had enticingly entitled his 1859 missive to the Society of Antiquaries –

Notice of Beehive Houses in Harris and Lewis;
with Traditions of the 'Each-Uisge', or
Water-Horse, Connected Therewith

These are tales, like the one about the night a young man came to the sheiling door and asked if he might rest awhile from his weary travels. Of course, the lassie, being hospitable, offered him her lap to lay his head. As she stroked the sleeping man's hair, she realised that it was riddled through with waterweeds and gravel. He was the dread *each-uisge* in disguise, and when he awoke, he would change back into his true form, and hurl her onto his back, and gallop off into the depths of the loch – there to serve forever as his wife beneath dark waves. Picking up her sewing scissors, she carefully cut a circle in the fabric of her clothing around his head, and lifted it aside so that she could take her exit without causing disturbance. She ran non-stop all the way back to the village, and when she got there, the proof of the truth of the tale was the hole in her dress.

Stories like these continue to be handed down into the present generation. At one level they encode customary warnings. *Be careful of unwanted pregnancy* with the young man, or *be careful of the water's edge* if you're a child living by a loch.[1] At a deeper level, they open out into the old indigenous sense of Otherworld, into the realm of *sìthichean*, the *imaginal* realm, that overlaps with but should be distinguished from the merely *imaginary*. The imaginary is make-believe. The imaginal pertains to that which is in some sense 'there', because it arises out of the mythopoetic (or mythopoeic) realm.[2] This *Mythos,* as the Greeks called it, is the underlying ground of deep story or metanarrative. It is the realm from which the meaning-structures of our world arises; that which gives meaning to the meaning of meaning. The poetic 'making' of reality – that is what *poesis* means – and that as coming from beyond our conscious ken. Creation as the breaking forth from out the cosmic womb.

As Yeats described it, such is 'the soil where all great art is rooted [whether] spoken by the fireside, or sung by the road-side, or carved upon the lintel'. It is something, he goes on to say in *The Celtic Twilight*, that the western world has nearly lost 'in a society that has cast out imaginative tradition'. That is to say, in a society that, for the most part, no longer knows what it is that we might be a part of. One that has relegated the big picture – the frameworks of story, the values, the premises, the feelings and in a word, the spiritual – to a twilight world, for sure; but a far cry from the one of 'dew ever shining' of Yeats' poem, 'Into the Twilight', where 'God stands winding his lonely horn'.[3]

The Mythos pertains to the inner life, the soul and its imaginative intelligence.Its counterpart, the *Logos,* which frames the rational mind with its organising intelligence, pertains to the outer life of creation manifest. It is when it is uprooted from its grounding in the Mythos, that the Logos wallows in the monotonous materialism of its ever-so-logical positivism. This is the closed spirit that underpins Mark Twain's dire maxim: 'familiarity breeds contempt'. The only antidote to such life-retarding nihilism is mythopoetic reconnection. The reactivation of our creative spirits. It is why imaginal realities like faerie tales, miraculous Bible stories and epic legends, such as in the Hindu *Mahabarata* or Homer's *Iliad*, might seem like make-believe at one level, but reveal uttermost truths at another. Without such modes of knowing and being, the well-springs of the soul run dry. We start to live a life that becomes, quite literally, soulless.[4]

The Angus and Aberdeenshire poet of the Scottish Revival, Marion Angus, was the English-born daughter of a Presbyterian minister. The latter qualification is almost *de rigueur* for writing in this metaphysical genre, and getting away with it. In 1928, she expressed the cultural and geographical significance of the imaginal realm in these terms:[5]

> I myself would like to be the one (unfortunately I am not) to write a great poem on the spirit of place, *producing something born of myself and of the place*, which would be neither one or the other, but something very strange and beautiful. I should like to write of fairies, not the identical fairies of the old days, but the elusive glamour of the universe; and above all I would fain give voice to Scotland's great adventure of the soul. I never shall; some one may, perhaps.

Similarly, a decade earlier, in his book *Scottish Literature*, Professor G. Gregory Smith coined the corkscrew term, 'Caledonian antisyzygy', to capture what he saw as the quality of a culture that can entertain two seemingly contradictory worldviews, held together in creative tension. Like a battery with a high 'potential difference' or voltage between the terminals, this produces cultural energy. The antisyzygy, Smith said, is 'a strange union of opposites' in which rational reality on the one hand, and outrageous fantasy on the other – the realms of Logos and of Mythos as we might have it – become the 'two moods', the 'warp and woof', or the 'polar twins of the Scottish Muse'. On the one hand, you have the down-to-earth practicality of humble homesteads such as produced engineers, politicians and a breed of clergy who, in their more hidebound moments, could treat even theology as a dry rational pursuit. On the other hand, within the selfsame psyche there exists a counterpoint capacity for such sobriety to be, as Smith put it, 'thrown topsy-turvy, in the horns of elf land and the voices of the mountains'.[6]

The function of the prophetic artist, a shaman of our times, is to sip the Wine of Astonishment: to be tossed high on the horns and wander amongst the voices. Provided that the good Commissioner of Lunacy is safely out of range, then that bardic function is to go a little crazy on behalf of others; on behalf of those who either lack the time, or whose 'sober wishes never learn'd to stray' far from the madding crowd, and yet whose lives would stultify without the winding horn of spiritual infusion, not least as received through the arts.

But stop! Practicality has come to claim me back. It's time to withdraw my iron needle from the door of Both a' Chlàir Bhig lest I wallow here for aeons, and to move on and hasten down to catch what's left of the low tide at Kinlochresort. Anything much past mid-water will be too late for the mussels. These can be found beneath the seaweed on the rocks of almost any sheltered bay in these parts, where a stream comes in. A touch of fresh water is said to deter their chief predator, the starfish. 'A good feed of the mussels' – that's how they used to say it back in Leurbost – and that's what's rumbling in my belly for this evening.

Down here, getting close to sea level, the ground collapses more and more to rough and tumble. The slope has slipped away. Everywhere is bog except for piles of rocks, dropped as if by parachute. The remnants of abandoned habitations? I don't know. My eyes are not informed enough to judge, and who knows what more might hide beneath the peat.

Now's the time for large-scale, and I check my bearings on my bespoke Poacher's map. Looks like all I need to do is keep on inching down until I meet the big river that flows out from Loch Voshimid. The wind has dropped right off, and Abhainn a' Chlàir Bhig has almost ceased the playful tinkling of its splashes as it starts to coil in a series of switchback meanders. I have to keep on leaping over squelchy soaks that mark out remnants of a former course. Even without Osprey on my back, this would be hard going, and I'm moving so very slowly that it feels like forever. Words like 'drudgery' and 'trudgery' dance mockingly around my head. 'God made the back for burden' – and I wonder where that one came from? The tiredness, oh a heavy tiredness, is coming over me. If it wasn't for the push to catch the tide, I'd curl up in the heather for a nap.

I stop to take stock, and stare up to the skyline. And there they are! Profiled on the shoulder of the hill. A herd of *their* cattle.

They're standing in a line, not yet seeing me, craning their stocky bristled necks and sniffing at the air. They're talking to each other with the twitching of their ears. This following wind has been why I've seen so little wildlife thus far. Up until this point, at which the valley base is broadening out, they'd have easily picked my scent up as it wafted tightly through the narrow glens. They'd have slinked away, before I ever had the chance to notice them.

Old stories suggest the existence of a deer-goddess cult in early Scotland. The herds were shepherded by the Cailleach as the wise old woman, the crone or hag, a seasonal face of the Celtic Goddess. The word for venison, the flesh of the deer, is in Gaelic *sithionn* or *sitheann* – almost the same as the sìthean. There are ancient songs and poetry about the 'darling deer', the 'beast of my love', and a lullaby called *Bainne nam Fiadh* – The Milk of the Deer:[7]

> On milk of deer I was reared,
> On milk of deer I was nurtured,
> On milk of deer beneath the ridge of storms,
> On crest of hill and mountain

Iain Thornber told me of an old stalker, with very little English, who used to say: 'I never once went to the hill but the deer didn't send me to university.' The Gaelic for the deer is *fiadh*, and I'm struck that one of the names in the old dictionaries for my friend, the Blue Mountain Hare, is *gearr-fiadh*, which means the 'short deer'. Fiadh is another of those words of a magnificently gliding semantic range, for it also means 'the wild'. John MacInnes of the School of Scottish Studies was born in Uig, the south-west parish of Lewis, onto which I'm presently bordering. Right now, I've probably got my left foot in North Harris and the right in Uig. He is – no surprises for such a preacher of the *sìthichean* – the son of a Church of Scotland minister. He explains:[8]

> Wilderness is a fundamental concept in Gaelic tradi-
> tion . . . the distinction between humanised land and
> non-humanised land . . . The wilderness, being outside
> the normal boundaries of convention and order, was asso-
> ciated with the supernatural. The deer was the creature
> most strongly associated with the wilderness, as is
> suggested by its common name in Gaelic *fiadh* 'wild'. The
> deer were believed to be the livestock of the fairies, and the
> fairies themselves represent in many ways the powers and
> dangers of the wilderness.

John ends a pivotal essay, 'Looking at Legends of the Supernatural', with a personal memory that conveys a feeling for the depth and even the everydayness of the mythopoetic as it survived into his lifetime in traditional Gaelic communities:[9]

I remember very vividly, when I was a little boy, seeing a wild hind grazing within the confines of the *baile* [the village]. Those who could read the signs realised that the natural order was being overturned and said: '*Se comharra cogaidh a tha seo* – 'This is an omen of war.' Not very long after the Second World War began. That sighting, that metaphor of order invaded by the wild, helped those who witnessed it to arrange their experience. The metaphor has a very long history behind it.

Similarly, John's colleague at Edinburgh University, Ronald Black, has described how the each-uisge, that lurked in every self-respecting Highland loch, also codified the invasion of order by the wild. In psychological terms, its sighting might be understood as an intrusion into consciousness of the archetypal contents of the collective unconscious; a superimposition, as it were, of inner vision onto the outer perception of reality. Like with John's wild hind as an 'omen of war', the tradition held that sightings of the water horse were harbingers of doom. That, in the full sense of destiny unfolding; of massive transformation, usually a disaster, impending on the clan. It is therefore no surprise, Black has argued, that reports amongst the indigenous population of the Loch Ness Monster attained epidemic levels in the 1930s. It was just as Hitler was rising to power, with consequences that would decimate many a Highland village.[10]

In John's opinion and life experience, 'Gaelic tradition implies that the distinction between wilderness and humanised space is mirrored in the human psyche.'[11] The sìthean – the encapsulation of wildness personified – is, he suggests, 'a metaphor of the imagination'.[12] It was (or is) an indigenous expression of the Jungian unconscious and not to be confused with the merely imaginary.

Such is why village bards whom he has known in person might, after composing their poetry or music, come out with such expressions as: *Bha mi 's a' Chnoc o chunnaic mi thu* – 'I was in the [fairy] Hill since I saw you'.

And the conclusion of this, from the greatest living Scottish Gaelic scholar, as if for any who might miss the full significance?

'From this shadowy realm comes the creative power of mankind.'

In his same essay on the supernatural, John MacInnes remarks that while Kenneth Macleod of Eigg and Gigha – the clergyman who wrote so warmly about Màiri, Daughter of Red Alastair, buried face-down at Rodel – has sometimes been taken for a romantic, the truth is that 'all the essential beliefs he draws upon are still talked about by bearers of Gaelic tradition'.

Once, Lord MacLeod of Fuinary was having dinner on Iona, with Kenneth as his guest, and it was old George's son, Sir Maxwell MacLeod, who gave me this story. Apparently, the two men had a terse relationship. There they were, sitting around the dining table, talking probably in that clipped manner of Presbyterian gentlemen whose prime fell in the first half of the twentieth century, but were truly of a much more ancient vintage. As the Winchester-schooled and metropolitan George struggled to make conversation with the Eigg-schooled and rustic Kenneth, he recalled a titillating sliver of local folklore that, he hoped, might make a suitably polite talking point.

'Er . . . we still have old Mrs So-and-So on Iona, and she *feeds the faeries*.'

'Oh? Really?' replied Kenneth, slowly. 'And tell me, at what time of the day does she feed the faeries?'

'I don't know!' said George, perfunctorily. 'Breakfast time? Dinner time?'

'Wrong time; wrong time,' said the Reverend Kenneth with a grave shake of his head.

'Then, what is the right time?'

'The right time to feed the faeries . . . is when the rain is still raining, and the sun is beginning to shine.'

Awkward silence.

'And tell me, on *what* does Mrs So-and-So feed the faeries?'

'Oh, I don't know!' said George, by now visibly irked that his olive branch of conversation had been taken up so seriously.

'Bread and butter, perhaps?'

'Ohhh!' exclaimed a pained Kenneth.

'Wrong food; wrong food!'

'Then what is the *right* food?' snapped George.

'The correct food on which to feed the faeries . . . *is venison and honey*.'

With a bounding turn, propelled as by a single motive force, the herd are off. Over the skyline I watch them go, bobbing their white rump patches as they run, back into the fiadh that is the sìthean of my mind. And when Gregory Bateson said, 'Mind is immanent in the larger system – man plus environment', he touched on a cultural carrying stream that is both human, and much more than just the human on its own. What the modern world calls the *supernatural*, says John MacInnes, is in Gaelic culture 'regarded by members of that society as part of the order of nature itself'. The 'super' is quite 'natural', a deeper ordering of reality that is made known through the second sight – *an dà shealladh* – literally, 'the two sights'. This, a stepping back of consciousness into what is normally unconscious, and with it, a corresponding loosening of the bounds of space and time.

The Gaelic term usually translated as the 'supernatural' is *anaghnàthaichte*. My friend the American scholar Michael Newton, who takes a special interest in Gaelic metaphysics, tells me that it is pronounced like *ana-GRAAAA-eech-ah* – except with sounds that scarcely exist in English. It means the unusual, the uncanny, but these in a sense that is not completely of another world. Rarely do I come home to the island without receiving first-hand accounts of anaghnàthaichte. If I seem unusually open to such a contested reality, it is in part because I have experienced a dramatic case myself. When I was eighteen, I had the experience of watching helplessly as my father's beloved whippet crossed the road and was killed outright. My mother had left for Stornoway, seven miles away, just ten minutes previously. She went there nearly every day, but, on this occasion, she was just on the outskirts of the town when she was hit by an overwhelming compulsion to turn back. As I set about digging the dog's grave in the practical way one does in a rural society, I saw her car speeding down the hill. She skidded to a halt in the gravel of the driveway, jumped out, and looking racked with dread, demanded to know what was wrong. My answer was a relief. She said, 'I thought it might have been a child.'

In the island's traditions such experiences usually surround emotionally charged events like marriages, deaths and collective calamities. For example, in 2002, a retired policeman and lobster fisherman on Harris, Norman Macleod of Bridge House, wrote me a letter after reading *All in the Mind: Farewell to God* by Ludovic Kennedy. The broadcaster had pooh-poohed the idea of prophecy, to which Norman responded:[13]

Even if I had never heard of a Bible or God, anyone as afflicted or gifted with the second sight as I am, to put it mildly, could not accept that. To give one tiny example, I could have written an account of the Falklands War and every stage of it, weeks or days before it happened, including being transported the 8,000 miles there in a split second and seeing . . . things that were to appear on TV afterwards, such as the warship HMS Sheffield with the metal superstructure going up in white incandescent flames.

It actually happened. I could go on at great length, but as you are unlikely to believe a word of it, I will leave it at that. *My God*, Alastair, is the high and lofty one who inhabiteth *eternity*; whose name is *Holy* – not subject to any laws of man, mathematics, time or motion, and certainly not to be catalogued within the tiny mind of Ludovic Kennedy or any other mere mortal.

Dad's practice manager, Agnus MacLennan of Achmore, told me of an old man amongst her people on Great Bernera, who could locate the bodies of drowned fishermen — because he 'heard' the scream as they fell overboard.[14] 'Make sure you keep thinking about the stories I'm telling you,' she said at the end of one of my visits. I wrote her words of advice down in my notebook. They signified an importance that ran deeper than just superficial curiosity. Another time I asked her: 'Do you think that people experience the second sight these days as much as they used to?'

'No!' she harrumphed. 'Because these days, everybody is *too busy* and *too noisy*.'

In his record of the faerie faith amongst his seventeenth-century parishioners in Highland Perthshire, the Rev. Robert Kirk quotes at length from correspondence between his contemporaries, Lord Tarbett and Sir Robert Boyle. The former was a Highland judge of the Mackenzie landowning dynasty. The latter was the physicist who gave us Boyle's Law about the expansion of gases. Tarbett told Boyle of an observation made by a gentleman of his acquaintance, who had gone to Barbados. 'Several of those that did see with the Second Sight when in the Highlands or Isles, when transported to live in other countries, especially in America, they quite lost this quality.' Tarbett also noted: 'There were more of these seers in the Isles of Lewis, Harris, and Uist than in any other place.'[15]

Margaret Bennett is another of the School of Scottish Studies folklorists. She has observed that stories of the second sight have remained strong, to this day, wherever community and tradition remains strong in Hebridean diaspora outposts — including pockets in Newfoundland, Quebec, North Carolina and New South Wales.[16] Why, then, might it have been lost so quickly to those of Tarbett's near-acquaintance? Tarbett took a business interest in the 'African trade' — which is to say, slavery.[17] Barbados was a slave colony in his time; the Deep South that would one day become the stronghold of the KKK and the Bible Belt, much the same.

Could it be that violence to one's fellow humankind inflicts internal injuries upon oneself ? That it violates a deeper psychic cohesion, the very basis of our interconnection through mind's immanence 'in the larger system'? And that the effects of war, its 'moral hazard', can therefore linger on, long after the outward guns have fallen silent?

I have tottered on, lurching and swaying through a deepening morass. My movements are ludicrous compared to the grace of the wild things I've just seen. This terrain is mired and jumbled, almost to the point of impassability. Thank God it's been dry weather. I am holding to the burn that winds like an Ariadne's woollen thread through the labyrinth. Again and again, I stop to check the map, wishing its large scale were even larger. There's got to be a better way through than this. I should have stayed up high, but if I'd done so, I'd have missed the Clàr Beag bothan.

If I cut directly west for a quarter mile, I'll come to the Voshimid river. The map names it as the Abhainn Mhòr – the Big River of Loch Reasort. Perhaps it has carved out deeper banks that might make for better drainage and a firmer footing. I veer off on a compass bearing of 270° and this, surely, can't get any worse. But it does. The Bog Monster, my Minotaur, seeks vengeance.

I'm moving in amongst a vast expanse of black peat ooze. It is a surface that would, in more normal rainy weather, be mostly under water. Here and there on higher parts are polka dots of tufts of wiry grass. This may or may not present me with a problem to cross. Usually, when it's relatively dry like this, you can tread with care. You'll mostly sink in only halfway up your boots, more if burdened with a load, like Archimedes' Principle, but without the bathtub. But you never know. People do, rarely, fall through and flounder.

I advance, hopping from one patch of firm ground to the next. An eye for vegetation types is crucial. A tuft of grass – not to be confused with water plants – will have a safety net of roots that can support some weight. But clumps of rushes are the best. You'll never sink if you land your foot on one of them – and I'm just about to step into a stretch of stiff black porridge, that runs pretty much as far as I can see at this low angle – when I freeze.

It's like when the music stops in a statue dance, and your foot's left dangling in the air. Or in the jungle, when you spot the raised head of a snake. But here's no dance, no snake. Here's Ariadne's ball of woollen thread. Unravelled. Splayed out. Dissipating back into raw fleece.

Uh-uh, I'm thinking to myself. *I see the wool, but not the sheep.*

What has happened to the sheep?

I press my heel onto the gingerbread-like surface of the partly dried-out peat. It bounces up and down. Sùil-chruthaich! The Eye of Creation! The crust is just a couple of inches thick, and this, a quaking bog.

I pump my foot, but not too hard, and the whole surface wobbles like a waterbed. There must be a stream or spring running underneath. These things are death traps to the sheep, who spy a juicy tuft of grass, plough right in, and never quite manage to wallow out. It's as if the Bog Monster, like one of those insect-eating plants, can feed itself. Sometimes you'll see a patch that's grown bright green from where a sheep has been devoured. Plants thrive on the released nutrients, and their foliage attracts the next unwary grazing victim in a system of ecology that is, to say the least, dastardly.

'To be born is to be wrecked on an island,' wrote J.M. Barrie in 1913, always playing with the nexus of life and death. And when Peter Pan thought he'd met his end, stranded on Marooner's Rock, he only felt a single shudder, telling Wendy: 'To die will be an awfully big adventure.'[18] Not so, for the poor sheep. Sunk up to their bellies, thin legs churning in the mire, they starve and slowly weaken in their struggle over many days. Perhaps it's almost merciful when the eagles gather, and the ravens, hooded crows and greater black-backed gulls; and like

Prometheus, punished for his theft of fire, they peck out the living eyes and tongue, and at the last, the liver.

There are other meanings, too, for *fiadh*. It also means 'barbarity' and 'cruelty'. The islander knows full well the beauty of their *dùthchas* – their heritage in the land. But like most other rural folks, they also feel disdain for urban myths of Bambi. Not for nothing did our forbears reject a direct pantheism – the worship of God as nature. They chose, instead, panentheism: that double sense of God as immanent in nature, but also out beyond, transcendent. That way holds the prospect of release from tortured suffering.

There is a famous passage near the start of *Missionary Travels,* where David Livingstone was seized by the shoulder and mauled by the lion.[19]

'It caused a sort of dreaminess,' the explorer wrote:

> . . . in which there was no sense of pain nor feeling of terror . . . like what patients partially under the influence of chloroform describe, who see all the operation, but feel not the knife . . . The shake annihilated fear, and allowed no sense of horror in looking round at the beast. This peculiar state is probably produced in all animals killed by the *carnivora*; and if so, is a merciful provision by our benevolent Creator for lessening the pain of death.

In other words, it caused a sort of transcendence. A contraction from this world of pain, into the realm of soul. A drift from incarnation, towards disincarnation, and it makes me wonder, too, about some of the knock-on effects of war.

From where I've reached, it looks as if this sucking bog has arms that go in all directions. The weariness weighs heavily upon me, a bank of fog that's put a flannel on my senses. This place is leaching my morale, making me dismayed and disarrayed. I could retrace my footsteps, but then which way through such a soggy maze?

I suppose it comes from having grown to know terrain like this so well, that the eye is always tuned in to small signs. *What are those marks?* I'm wondering, as I peer to take a closer look at something in the mud.

It's *their* cattle. Right where I most need them! The *lorg nam fiadh*. The cloven footprints of the deer.

Where they can safely pass, then so can I.

Scarcely even bothering to test the sureness underfoot, I bound ahead and crunch across the crispy surface crust.

I follow their winding line of tracks, and pass from out the clutches of Bog Monster's arms. What's more, I think I hear the sound of waterfalls. It must be the Abhainn Mhòr, fresh flowed down from Loch Voshimid, where Barrie 'caught Mary Rose'. The weariness just washes from my eyes. A fresh excitement turns back on my senses. Higher up, and just before a long ravine, I catch a glint of dashing blue; and I have just spied . . . poaching!

It's like my fishing rod is twitching like a dowser's fork. For sure, there's still the underlying chill upon the breeze. But this is mid-afternoon. The water's temperature will be near its highest. Now's the day and now's the hour!

Sammy's face peers in. He's giving me a bright *aye-aye* with a cheery sideways nod. That the only permit I'll require for this once-off 'wee cast'. The community would never grudge the prospect of a fish to fill a pilgrim's pot.

I clamber down into the gully, carved out by the river's bed. The whisky-tinted water heaves and pitches down the chasm. I begin to shuffle cautiously along the sides. Now it narrows, then it widens, spreading gently like a sail, murmuring around the stones and tinkling over gentle weirs. The flow has slackened, backed up and held within a baggy lagoon that is too shallow for the fishing, but doubtless once a paddler's paradise for sheiling boys and girls.

A river of this nature, however, possesses fiadh as well as more bucolic properties. Lethargy soon irks its restive kelpie spirit. Fed up with going round and round in aimless eddies of recirculation, it pulls its act together, and with a martial roar, takes off in flight. A thousand elven hooves go cantering down an incline, thundering through the glen. They hammer at unwavering walls of solid rock until, at last, they burst into a boulder bed, and dissipate their laughter into blasts of spray that mist the air with dancing sheens of rainbow.

This time, the river draws into a spiralled coil. Shelving rocks have put a twist into a pool's bag end. It launches, hissing, on and through a lengthy worm-screw channel that reminds me of the confines of a bobsleigh run. It gathers speed until it hits a line of jagged fangs that guard the head of a most lovely, pear-shaped pool. Through the water comes, and through and through, churned into a spume of witches' spittle that skids onwards, reaching outwards, in streaks of marbled fingers. I watch them fizz, and dissipate; and halfway down the pool's blue length I find a spot where sunlight fails to penetrate the olive depths. Here a flight of rocky ledges reaches down into a darkening underworld, and who knows the size of the fish that will have rested there.

The fiadh is on me, and with a slip of my shoulders I shrug off Osprey, and unpack my fishing rod. Suitably, for a pilgrimage, the brand name is *Bob Church*. Given my failure to find worms – the best lure – I'll have to act the proper sportsman and use a fly, but only one given the high risk of snagging on the rocks. Which one, I'm wondering, for these bright conditions? Perhaps the Teal Blue & Silver? No. It's an awfully tidy, suit-and-tie sort of a fly. I'll save it for more civilised conditions. For such a place as this, perhaps more of a Celto-hippie feel? I'll try a shaggy looking Blue Zulu with its punkish Afro-haircut, spiky beetle body, a twist of silver bling and a classy tail of Scarlet Ibis; only that the latter, in my budget edition, is a bit of red fluff.

I tie it on with a clinch knot and, with a few brisk flicks of the wrist to get the line out and flowing gracefully, I cast across the pool. It crumples with a splashy flop onto the water.

Too much line!

Salmon 1: Poacher 0.

I've spoiled my chances here, so I use the pool to practice casting, and then move on down. This leads me through a battlefield of vicious rocks, with water coursing fast and deep between their clefts. Another pool, this time a long deep stretch of perfect width. My knack with casting has come back. The fly lands perfectly, within a foot of the opposite bank. The current curves it gracefully downstream, and my eyes are keened for the swirl of a tail or the roll of a dorsal fin. Again, and again, I flick the fly out – and just as I'm about to move on, my line goes taut.

'Rod up and take in slack! Drop rod if he jumps! *Drop the rod,* before he smacks his tail down on the line and breaks you!'

But this isn't me, back as the ghillie, master of my boat, issuing instructions to a guest in need of help. This is me, right here. And it's only a tiddler, with rainbow fingerprints down either side; a cheeky little salmon parr that caught me by surprise. I wet my hands so as not to hurt his scales, let him off the hook, and away he goes with a quick tail wag.

By now I'm deep down in the gorge. These pools are such a thrill, so inaccessible I bet they're hardly ever fished. I'm just rock-hopping along, quite the dancer of the chasm, and this is such a gig. The sides are looming high above me, cutting off the sunlight, and it's getting to a tumult in a bottleneck down here. Looks like there's no way through ahead. I'll need to climb up higher. Spiderman along an edge. Rod gripped in one hand, rocks and tufts of heather in the other. And I again freeze.

For God's sake, look at yourself!

Here I am. In the middle of MAMBA. Miles and miles of bugger all, and bugger all of a mobile signal this side of the nearest mountain top. And I'm swinging about like Tarzan with twenty kilos on my back.

A chill overcomes me. My movements jam. Can't see my footholds to get back down. Too vertiginous to carry on up. Knuckles locked and whitened onto what is now a crumbling rock face, with only loosely rooted heather.

If I stay like this, I'll just become exhausted. I'll further lose my nerve. I'd have to drop Osprey into the river, everything would get lost or soaked, and I'd have to end the trip.

Needs must, so, very slowly, I edge upwards, upwards, until I grapple sheepishly over the top.

Salmon 2: Poacher 0.

'Poacher's pilgrimage?'

Sammy shakes his head, another poem coming on. 'More like poacher's comeuppance.'

The end, however, is in sight. A further half a mile of easy going down the bank, and I reach my destination: Kinlochresort.

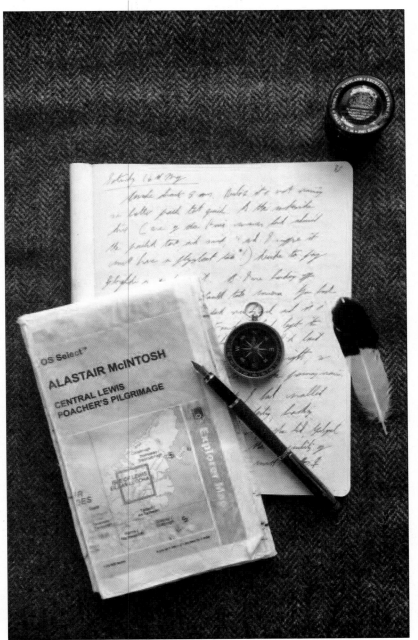

Artefacts from the journey, on Harris Tweed by Norman Mackenzie, weaver of Carloway.

RIGHT. Christ of St Clement's Church, Isle of Harris, carved in the sparkling hornblende schist found locally. It was dug up in the churchyard during renovation works.

BELOW. Detail from the tomb in St Clement's of Alasdair 'Crotach', 8th chief of the Macleods of Harris and Dunvegan, completed 1528.

'The Sun of Righteousness', as St Clement of Alexandria called this symbol of perpetual resurrection.

The red deer, at once both the *fiadh* – 'the wild' – and 'the cattle of the faeries'.

Perched in the bright green glen of Rodel in south Harris, Tùr Mòr Chliamain – the Great Tower of St Clement – was my pilgrimage starting point. The site is linked to the Celtic monastic heart of Iona.

St Clement's Church is said to sit upon a Druid site on the lower slopes of Roineabhal. Shown here, obscured by clouds, the mountain narrowly escaped destruction for a roadstone 'superquarry'.

Day 2, on the Golden Road through the Bays of Harris. Originally the name belonged to the section north of Leac a Lì. Today the term is often applied to the whole of the east-coast route.

This byre (or crofter's cow shed) was roofed with an upturned boat when I was a boy. The relics of such memory now rest in the grass against the starboard wall.

The rediscovery of Tobar a' Ghobha – the Well of the Blacksmith – in the village of Leac a Lì. The remnants of my 'Bog Monster' with its bleaching of the boulder reveal the depth of moss that had caused the well's loss for 30 years.

The ecosystem of a rotting fencepost and the Golden Stag. But remember, it's pan*en*theism, not pantheism!

JMB – the initials of James Matthew Barrie – etched on a window of the Harris Hotel in 1912. Barrie drew on island faerie lore to explore the cultural psychology of war and its trauma.

Sundown at Ardhasaig. The chimney of the old whaling station down at Bun Abhainn Eadarra has lapsed to dusk. Higher up, my apocryphal 'Lost Glen' tracks north between the twin peaks of Uisgneabhal and the Clisham horseshoe.

Day 3, entering the glen on my way to Loch a' Sgàil, using fragments of Sammy's stalker's path. This whole 'country' is now community owned in a partnership for people and conservation with the John Muir Trust.

It was a lonely place, here on the watershed of the 'Lost Glen', as I passed over into Glen Langabhat. The Isle of Lewis and the start of the 8-mile long Loch Langabhat is in the distance, Loch an Teine – the Lake of Fire – is on the river.

ABOVE. I pitched my tent beside a ruined sheiling and dined on tanalised lamb with bitter herbs.

LEFT. My semi-leavened bannocks cooking on the charcoal of the fencepost embers.

ABOVE. Day 4, heading over to Kinlochresort, down through the glen below Loch Chleistir, the Loch of the Cascading Rock. On the horizon, the Atlantic surfs with whales at Gallan Head with its old NATO base, and older still, the Blessing Place.

RIGHT AND BELOW. From the previous day, red deer traces on the shores of Loch a' Sgàil, and one of thousands of 'bogs that I have known and loved'.

Both a' Chlàir Bhig, after following the stream down from Stuabhal and Loch Chleistir.

The planetarium-effect inside this double-chambered *both* or 'beehive' sheiling is exaggerated by the limited settings on my cheap camera. Originally, I had not intended to take photographs; I didn't want to filter the world through a digital lens. My wife Vérène persuaded me otherwise, but with just a single battery charge to constrain its use.

Ceann Loch Reasort (or Kinlochresort). The river with the watcher's cottage on the Harris side is the Abhainn Mhòr Ceann Reasort – the Big River of Kinlochresort – where I nearly came a cropper when fishing. It flows down from Loch Voshimid, where J.M. Barrie 'caught Mary Rose'.

Taken from the hill where I feasted on mussels, the 5-mile length of Loch Reasort, looking towards the Atlantic and the Isle of Scarp. The bank opposite shows traces of the *feannagan* raised beds. These shores were emptied of their people in the 19th-century Clearances.

St Bridgit's Sheiling at the Rubha Leathann, looking back across south central Lewis. There are two ruins – the main ring of stones is the one slightly further away. The mists have almost lifted from the distant Eishken hills that I love so much – one of the last wildernesses of the West.

A fern grows by the fallen lintel, here where Brighde's (or Bridgit's) memory is set in place. 'The parish has a saint's name time cannot unfrock.'

From earlier in Day 5 at my lunch stop, the little *both* of Loch a' Sguair. Brighde's would have stood like this, made wind-tight with a coat of living turf.

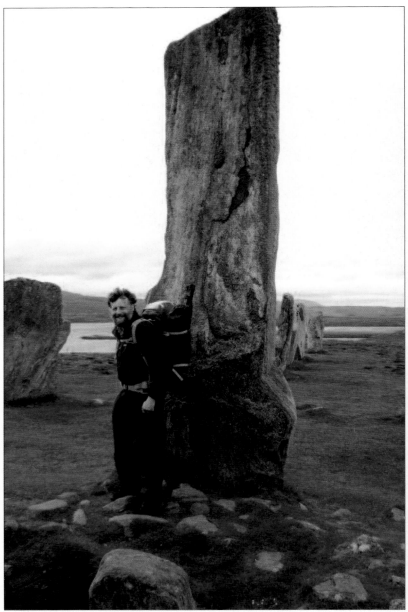

Day 6, Saturday, at the 5,000-year-old standing stones of Calanais (or Callanish). This, taken by my fleeting friend, the 'dead' American tourist lassie. My waterproofs were variously constricted by belts and puffed out by the brisk breeze.

This picture is from the previous summer when we'd walked out to the Campbell family's sheiling on the Barvas moor. Vérène (left), is with the sisters Catriona (who met me at Teampall Eòin), and artist-archaeologist Anne. Little Peigi Ann is hidden behind her dog.

Tobar Mhoire, St Mary's Well at Siadar (or Shader). Tobar Brìghde, St Bridgit's Well at Melbost Borve. These were visited over Days 9 and 10.

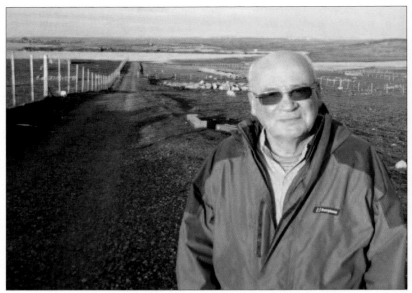

Dr Finlay Macleod of Siabost (or Shawbost) – the beloved 'Doctor Finlay' – sending me on my way to meet Catriona and Peigi Ann Campbell at Teampall Eòin, on the other side of the bay.

The close of Day 8 at Teampall Eòin, St John's Temple (or chapel), dedicated probably to John the Baptist and surrounded by the 'plainsong' headstones of a humble people, whose God 'is the high and lofty one who inhabiteth *eternity*: whose name is *Holy*'.

Day 10, at Teampall nan Crò Naomh at Ghabhsainn (or Galson), looking up past a series of headlands to my destination at the Butt of Lewis. The chapel lies mostly under windblown sand. Does its name mean simply 'Holy Cross', or is it more nuanced? Does it also mean 'the kernel of life', 'the pulsing heart of the holy'?

Day 11, Teampall Pheadair at Suainebost (or Swainbost). Most of the headstones in its ancient cemetery are 'plainsong'. As the modern fancy for more privatised memorials took hold, the community of the dead ran out of space and had to relocate over the hill.

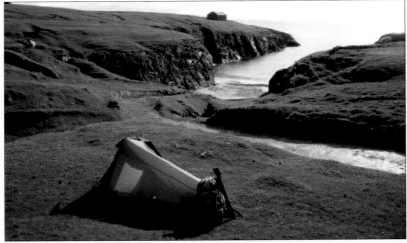

Day 12, Friday morning, my final camping pitch at Stoth Bay, Butt of Lewis.

Cameos of wild food and other nourishment along the way. The mussels found at Kinlochresort. The sorrel that went into Doctor Finlay's sandwiches. The bread I made at Galson hostel, photo taken by Graham. As for the can amongst the seaweed, the less said the better.

12

CATCHING MARY ROSE

Andrew Morrison was right about the beauty of this place, and the mussels were waiting here, sure enough. I made it just in time to grab some handfuls from amongst the greens, reds and browns of seaweeds growing on a rock, before they slipped beneath the whelming tide.

From my vantage point on top of this hill, the Abhainn Mhòr spreads gracefully out into the head of Loch Reasort, the Red Fjord. From there the brackish mix of waters curl their way five miles between low hills to the Atlantic. All that now remains of what was once a thriving village are a few stone walls, some blackhouse ruins, and everywhere, the ripples of feannagan that slumber back into the bog.

There are two boarded-up cottages. One is on the Harris side of the river, the other in Lewis, and an old map also reveals a shooting lodge. These days, only watchers stay in these to combat commercial poaching in July. That's when the shoals of salmon come into the bay, waiting for a spate to take them upstream to their spawning grounds amongst the hills.

My little gas stove is hissing in the early evening breeze. I've already boiled a cup of water for a pack of chicken soup, and now I've got another half cup on, just enough to raise a rapid head of steam to cook my mussels. They open within minutes, translucent shells of navy blue, some striped with dashing rays of green, and delicious is the creamy orange flesh inside.

I always try to cook them very quickly, aware that even bivalves will feel pain in their own ways, and then there's all the little critters hanging on as collateral damage – the barnacles and the tube worms, the tiny sponges, snails and shrimps. I'm just another predator, and it could have been worse. The steady hack, hack, hacking of a seabird's bill until a fatal crack appears. The starfish arms wrapped round in death's embrace, secreting digestive juices slowly to suck out the goodness. Such is the fate of all wild things. Predation, pestilence or privation always get you in the end. I hope that David Livingstone was right about his anaesthesia. William Blake too, with 'The cut worm forgives the plough.' Even vegans have to deal with the maggot in the apple, the weevil in the flour.

I'm chewing on these mussels, softening my oatcakes in the cup of soup, and soaking up the splendour of this splendid isolation. And yet, I also feel great sadness in this place. It's coming over me in waves. The *nostos-algos* of that home pain. There is a Gaelic word, so onomatopoeic, that describes this soul-felt wearisomeness: *Cianalas* – 'Key-ann-a-lass' – and that, exhaled in anguished cadence.[1]

Truth is, that pretty much this whole western coastline of North Harris and South Lewis cries out, laconic in its emptiness. There are no longer any villages between Hushnish and Kinlochresort on the Harris side, and from here to Mealasta on the Lewis side. As an elderly historian who was born on the Isle of Scarp at the mouth of Loch Reasort wrote to me: 'Some of the most brutal evictions were in Harris, but little is known about the brutality as vast swathes of the population were evicted and they took their history with them overseas.'[2]

The Harris clearances hadn't stopped with Rodel glen. There were other waves during the nineteenth century. For example, in 1839, the Earl of Dunmore cleared some fifty crofting families, estimated to have been about 700 people. When these resisted his orders, he brought in from Fort George on the mainland the 78th Regiment of Foot – the Ross-Shire Buffs, also known as the Seaforth Highlanders.³ It was imperial divide and rule. Many of these soldiers would have been recruited, or press-ganged, from neighbouring Lewis. The measures were reported to have been 'very severe'. According to *The Times,* the troops terrorised the local population, who thought that the Crown was about to re-enact upon them the Massacre of Glencoe. However, to be dispatched from such a 'rugged land' to live elsewhere, the newspaper suavely concluded, was surely a blessing.⁴

If the Crown was feared, it had form in its historic subjugation of the Hebrides. In 1599, Lewis was wrested from traditional clan control. King James VI of Scotland, four years later to become James I of the United Kingdom, granted a band of venture capitalists from Fife a colonial charter for 'the conquering of the Lewis . . . by rooting out of the barbarous inhabitants . . . void of all religion and humanity'. This, he hoped, would raise rents for the Lowland-based state authorities, and generate commerce from both land and sea. To such effect, the 'Fife Adventurers' were granted a Commission of Fire and Sword; namely, the authority to perpetrate 'slaughter, mutilation, fire-raising and other inconveniences'.⁵

When that endeavour failed due to clan guerrilla resistance, the Crown, in a further act of sowing division, gave the island to the Mackenzies of Kintail. Next came Cromwell's men. Then Deaf Mackenzie – Colonel Francis Humberston Mackenzie – who used it as a breeding ground for soldiers for the Empire. He is of considerable consequence to my story. 'The lads of this regiment will live and die together,' said his recruitment posters of 1793. 'Now for a stroke at the Monsieurs, my boys! King George for ever! Huzza!' It was Deaf Mackenzie who sent in the press gangs where volunteers were not sufficiently forthcoming. Whole villages saw their men scattered to the hills. Mothers and sweethearts were held with bayonets to their breasts as their sons and lovers were marched off to colonial wars across the globe and, in the case of one village that was perhaps not untypical, only one ever came back. Mackenzie was rewarded with the governorship of Barbados which, at that point, was still very much a slave colony. Living the Caribbean high life, he ratcheted up gambling debts. These required him to have the villages of south-east Lewis cleared of their native populations, and to be leased as a vast commercial sheep farm.[6]

That, in very general terms, is the kind of history that's laid before me here at Kinlochresort as I finish off my meal. I can't help wondering how much we carry of these things in our psyches; how much they might rub off and knock on down the generations. In my own case, I wonder if it influences my work in being so drawn to the confluence between landed power, militarism and religion? My twice-great-grandfather on my paternal grandmother's side was Murdo MacLennan, belonging to the Strathconon area of Ross-shire. He was a famous 'precentor' in the Free Church, a leader of the old 'long tunes', the drawn-out haunting way of singing Gaelic Psalms. Some of his tunes were set to pen and paper by Joseph Mainzer, the German ethnomusicologist. Murdo's grandparents had been cleared from elsewhere in the glen by the Balfour family. In his 1929 study of the making of the Scottish working classes, Tom Johnston mentions these evictions and, in so doing, touches on the spiritual depth of bonding between people and their places that the Highland Clearances violated:[7]

> The evictions of the Clan M'Lennan from Strathconon by the Balfour trustees were carried out in a most barbarous manner, and to this day the spot is shewn where the dispossessed men and women crouched together, praying rather for a merciful death than that they should be driven farther from the strath of their birth. When the father of the late leader [Arthur Balfour, prime minister] of the Conservative party fell heir to the estates 'the gallows had succeeded the fever,' for he directed prompt eviction of another twenty-seven families, and today a parish, which

in 1831 had a population of 2,023, carries only 445 people, mostly ghillies and their dependants on a London brewer's hundred square-mile deer forest.

The same had also happened in the making of the English working classes, but further back in history, leaving the English with less understanding of their relatively untaught social history, and more in the grip of its resultant social class system. I just feel saddened to survey the richness of community that has been lost. The resulting poverty, these days more psychological than material. That's the sense of cianalas, the melancholy that touches me now, as I gaze down the full length of this sea loch, thinking of its empty – cruelly emptied – little bays.

It touches me in just so many ways. Out there on the horizon, cradled on either side by the sea loch's widening hilly arms as it enters the Atlantic, I can see Scarp. As late as 1881, this island still supported more than two hundred souls. They had their own 'parliament' that was similar to that of St Kilda. When the estate told the people that they were to be deprived of their vital summer grazings along the southern shores of Loch Reasort, their abject appeals for clemency were met with the stark response. 'Go to America!'[8]

These estates were run by, and for, an alien class of people who had a very limited idea of what it meant to be a connected human being. They behaved as if they neither knew nor cared that the sheiling way of life meant so much more than just the economics of a pastoral way of life. For the Scarp people, these grazings would have been their *geàrraidh* or 'garry', their pastoral garden of storied places soaked with time-enamoured familiarity. No wonder, that Carmichael had described the songs and prayers that emanated from such a way of life as: 'singularly chaste, beautiful, and elevated'. No surprise, that Sir Arthur Mitchell had encountered the sheiling girls from near here engaged in spiritual reflection. From such haunts as where I'd camped last night, or chanced upon with the Clàr Beag bothan earlier today, the teenage girls, when done with their milking, made cheese and butter to take home at weekends. Sometimes they'd be quietly joined at night by village lads, home from the fishing. Marriages were known to follow. They'd become the mothers of the village, then the matrons, and that, in every soil- and soul-soaked richness of the word.

By 1971, isolated and with such a constricted resource base, there were only twelve people left on Scarp. They took the hard decision to evacuate to the 'mainland' of Lewis and Harris. Again, these things can rub off on one in such evoca- tive ways. I was at school in Stornoway at the time. My passion was for geology. I'd read that Scarp was known for an outcrop of green-tinted rocks of an asbestos mineral. When I heard that a girl from Scarp had joined the school, I eagerly asked around. Helped by my female classmates, a meeting was arranged.

Funny how she's coming to me now. I haven't thought of her for years and years. It was such a small thing. We met in no-man's-land between the boys' and the girls' cloakrooms. She was maybe thirteen. Me, perhaps a year older. She said her father was a lighthouse keeper.

Funny how I'm seeing it so clear again, in my mind's eye. Seeing that way of life beyond the memory of words. Seeing her father, far away from home, on aching spells of duty. High above the churning surf of some half-sunken, devil-stricken skerry. And she, back home, brave smiling with him in her fret- ful dreams through nights of storm-tossed wakefulness.

These thoughts have grown in my imagination, but not as figments of imagination. They're from a very real meme in the culture. An old woman from Scalpay, an island on the other side of Harris, has told me how it was in her mother's time in the 1920s, when the father – my correspondent's grandfather – was at the herring fishing:[9]

When it was a stormy night her mother, Peggy, could not settle in the house for worrying about him – there was no radio contact in those days. She used to wrap her shawl around her and take my mother, her eldest daughter, with her and go up the hill behind the house to pray for his safe return. Somehow being out in the elements she felt closer to God and returned home feeling calmer.

I asked my school friend of such fleeting acquaintance how she felt about having just left Scarp. She shrugged, and pursed an unrequited smile. As I see it in my mind now, it said more than she could ever have known nor I could then have understood. God! I never thought that lass had touched me so. Fair wispy hair that straggled to the shoulders of a standard issue blazer. A boyish slightness, still some way from womanhood. Such sweet demureness.

I doubt we talked for more than five minutes. She said she'd never heard of asbestos, but that there was a greenish stone to be found on the island. Well, that could have been any number of common minerals. I never looked her out again. But now she's come back into my thoughts. Following the herds. A woman nurtured down the generations 'on the milk of deer beneath the ridge of storms'. Roaming through wild gardens up the back-tracks of my mind. And there's something here, in all of this, that's gone but not gone out: and these words come to me –

> For she was the girl from off the moor
> She was the last of the sheiling line
> She the *cianalas* that pierces the soul
> yet her father kept a light

I could camp here at Kinlochresort for the night, maybe try the estuary for a sea trout. But the evening sky is showing signs of colder weather. It's settling in rarefied shades of astronaut blue. Instead, I think I'll use these last three hours of waning light to make up some lost time. I'll cut inland, directly east across the Morsgail Moor. That will bring me to the head of

Glen Shandaig, and down to pitch camp halfway up the west bank of Loch Langabhat. From there, I'll be perfectly placed tomorrow morning to skirt the eastern slopes of a hill called Ascleit. Seumas Crawford had told me there are some great sheilings along its sides. Further north, he said, at Loch a' Sguair, there's a both that's in spectacular condition. After that, I'll promenade along the high Mothal Ridge. This, he'd added in his genial way, 'would give you a stunning walk on a fine day'.

Whether to go over or around the summit of Beinn Mothal is something I can decide at the time. Either way, it will bring me out at the Grimersta river. He'd told me where to ford it, a spot that's passable in most water conditions just by wading. Once on the other side, I'll walk another mile north-east, winding in and out around the little lochs until, if all is well, I see a bright green grassy bluff. This will be the Rubha Leathann – the 'Broad Promontory' – and by its side, Saint Bridgit's Sheiling. That's where I'd love to spend tomorrow night.

There's a conical little cnoc beside me called Tom Leatha. From its top, I manage to pick up just sufficient of a fleeting mobile signal to text my position to Vérène, and to say that all is well. I also take a compass bearing on a cleft between the hills that lead into Glen Shandaig. That will be vital if I lose my line of sight as I traverse this broad expanse of moor. I've packed up, and as I set off, the sun behind is slipping low across the sea. Scarp is now receding in a sparkling silver haze that shines from off the water. Overhead, I can't help but notice wisps of rippled cloud. Hmm. 'Mackerel sky/ mackerel sky/ never long wet/ never long dry.'

Out here, the year has hardly started. The heather is still stiff and brown and shows no yearnings for new growth. The *slèibh,* the fiery red bent deergrass of the bygone autumn, sways languid in tired tufts. All around are drifting curls of last year's moor grass. Here, in eddied swirls of drained-out golden locks. There, in lines combed out by the prevailing wind, aligned enough to chart a rough and ready compass course. Everywhere is vast and empty stillness. These parts, wrote W.M. Mackenzie, a local antiquarian, who had come to make a study of the bothan more than a century ago, are 'the scene of pastoral richness, quiet, and beauty, over which the shy deer boldly move among what were once the habitations of men'.[10] I see no deer, I see no habitations, but they're present in the place names. On my left, the rounded slopes of Sèilibridh or Shéilabridh are probably suggestive of the deer hunt. On my right, Beinn a' Bhoth, the Hill of the Both, is a nod to human habitations that predate the baptism of the land.

I'm turning over in my mind an epigram from Sorley Maclean.[11]

> *Tha tìm, am fiadh, an Coille Hallaig*
> Time, the deer, is in the Wood of Hallaig

Time is the deer, the wild, that moves in timelessness. The poet visits the clearance ruins at Hallaig, a Norse name that possibly means 'holy bay', on his native Raasay. While there, the people of the past – 'the Sabbath of the dead' – come back to life as woodland trees.

> And my love is at the Burn of Hallaig,
> a birch tree, and she has always been . . .
> a birch, a hazel, a straight slender young rowan.

The bard depicts a class of experience that just happens, sometimes, to the people of these liminal parts. What do I mean: *just happens*? Just that. You hear reports in private. I know of one, an eminent professor, a man grown from the rootstock, who told me of his visit to just such an abandoned village. While he wandered around amongst the stones, the voices of the dead awoke. 'What do you mean, *awoke?*' I asked. 'Just that,' he said, and he ran – terrified, he told me – back up to the present-day settlement, where a normal sense of time outwith the fiadh resumed its steadying hold upon his consciousness.

A breeze is getting up. What little warmth there was has left. I am nearing the cleft that has served as my landmark. The valley sides appear between the hills that head the glen. I can see them steepening to the stricture of the pass. Here, the ground is banked with hurdle after hurdle of suppurating peat hags. I clamber and I skid my way across each one. It's only my imagination, but they whisper to my footsteps' sucking sough.

'Alastair! Alastair! Step into your solitariness. *Within . . . within . . . within.*'

The sky above has dimmed from astronaut to cobalt grey. From behind me, the afterglow still squeezes through from under the horizon. Ahead, the east horizon has turned black. Night is almost on me, and a grim wind now hones its lonely edge upon a stone that runs too low and slow as yet to reach my hearing.

An hour ago, I'd warmed up enough to stop and take my fleece off. I had stood awhile, gazing back from whence I'd come, my mind awash with eddies and cross-currents from the day. The light had not yet faltered, and I had run my eye along the sharp relief of hills against the skyline that lay stretched out to the south. Distance had restored the smoky blue that mystifies such heights. I'd marvelled at Sròn Uladail, an enormous prow of overhanging rock that breaches to the surface like a whale, with its belly full of legends. Eastwards, to its left, lay the valley of the quaking bog, and there, the chasm of the river that comes rushing from Loch Voshimid with the island that likes to be visited.

Sir Walter Langdon-Brown's perception of the psychological importance of J.M. Barrie's play was shared by Sir Alfred Hitchcock. In later life, the Master of Suspense was asked by an interviewer if there was any film that he regretted never having made. He replied:[12]

Mary Rose, which I really wanted to do, but they didn't want to let me. Do you know, it's written specifically into my present contract that I cannot do *Mary Rose*?

Hitchcock had been deeply taken by the play when, at the age of twenty-one, he saw a 1920 performance in the Haymarket. By 1964, he had got as far as commissioning a screenplay and had gone with his wife to the Isle of Skye to look for a suitable island-in-a-loch location. He desired to call the movie *The Island That Wants to Be Visited*, and *The Times* reported that his sponsors would want concrete evidence of where the island was, so as to appraise its tourist potential. His critics say that the script was dull, and that no further explanation is required for the no-no that was meted out by Universal Pictures. The Master, however, believed that their veto came from fear. The public lacked exposure, as he put it, 'to these twilight-zone stories'. The movie would have been 'too irrational'. This was what had made it too high a risk to pitch to the pragmatic spirit of the age.[13]

Hitchcock would have loved the Gaelic term, *àit uaigneach*. It means a solitary place – remote, forlorn, unsettling. To which cue, I have gone into the cleft between the hills, and have come up to the prow of the watershed. An icy blast strikes in from east-southeast. I had not realised how much shelter I was getting in the lee of the pass. Those peat hags, for all their slippery awkwardness, were doing me a kindness.

The dusk is well advanced. Here, a twilight star comes flickering out. There, obscured by clouds. I wander on along this fissure in the land. Down below, just coming into view, is the leaden face of Langabhat. The wind is coming straight from off its water. It's sweeping up Glen Shandaig, I feel it dragging at my body heat, and my inner voice is warning *don't get cold*.

There seems to be the semblance of a track heading down the way. A sheep or deer path? I carry on, and on a little further, but something in the gloom feels queer. The patterns of the ground are unfamiliar. Then I see a mound, and then, another,

similar in size to what I'd found at Clàr Beag. And so they are!
Beinn a' Bhoth still has its *clachan* – a tiny village – depending
on what to count in this near-darkness, of some four, five, or
six bothan.

I climb on top of one, and yes: it is undoubtedly a beehive
structure, sealed with a cap stone that crowns the corbel. There
is no way inside because the peat has grown up around the
entrance and sealed it off. Whoever may have once lived here
has not been home, not for a very long time indeed.

I wish that Seumas Crawford were with me at this very
moment. To me, he is the Keeper of the Bothan. Why? Because
he cares so much about them.

'These bothan are not being taken seriously,' he once told
me, fretfully. 'It's a disgrace! They've hardly been recognised
since the days of Captain Thomas, Mitchell and Mackenzie.'

'How far back do you reckon they go?' I'd asked.

Some, to the days of the early Celtic Church. That's hinted
at by place names suggestive of priests, blessing houses or
tiny monastic settlements. Others, well, who knows? Tradition
holds as far back as the Druids. 'I would have no hesitation of
putting an age of two thousand years plus to some of them –
no hesitation at all,' he concluded, telling me that one
structure on which he was working was seated on a Bronze
Age site.

'They go back a long, long way, some of them do, Alastair.
Back into the mists of time.'

I move on, and through a world now dimmed to silhouettes.
They huddle by the valley sides, completely drained of colour,
sometimes rearing up to etch their darker outlines against the
sky. Loch Langabhat lies sunken in a brooding cauldron far
below. The wind has backed a few degrees. It now blows
straight from out the east. Cold, still low, but rising with a
mordant grindstone growl.

'Yes. I feared that might be the case,' had said the gentle
English brigadier, in his words of encouragement back at the

staff college; his astute awareness of the dilemmas of his profession. 'Such a pity.'

Such a pity, 'and he knows he shouldn't kill/ and he knows he always will'. And when the Cree First Nations activist and singer, Buffy Sainte-Marie, wrote 'Universal Soldier', popularised by Donovan, she said that it was 'about individual responsibility for war and how the old feudal thinking kills us all'.[14] *Dieu et mon Droit* perpetuates itself precisely because violence cauterises the soul. It relies on trauma – psychic injury that cuts off empathy – to sustain an unjust social order. That is why many of the relatively powerful, as Hitchcock intuited, shun the 'irrational' twilight zones of the unconscious. To the Mr and Mrs Morlands of this world – 'more-land' – and the Simon Sobersides, these zones disrupt the rigid ego structures of their own controlled and controlling universe. They don't even see the limits of their own carefully schooled worldview. As is often said by locals about a certain kind of incomer, who comes in to the island with unseemly avaricious attitudes – 'they can't help it'. The Universal Soldier, and his counterpart in the proxy warring worlds of finance, property and speculation, 'never sees the writing on the walls'.

Revealing the emotional impacts of a culture that cultivates the stiff upper lip of emotional blockage is part of what Barrie achieved with *Mary Rose*. More importantly, he opened out fresh insights into why war represents a failure of the imagination, marooning the imaginal world. This sheds crucial light on avenues of cultural healing for the future.

Writing *Mary Rose* when he did, it is likely that Barrie would have been familiar with the work that Captain A.J. Brock and Captain W.H.R. Rivers were pioneering at the Craiglockhart War Hospital in Edinburgh with such war poets as Wilfred Owen and Siegfried Sassoon. Around 1917, Brock corresponded with Sigmund Freud about their mutual interest in 'battle neurosis' or shellshock. Today, it is better known as post traumatic stress disorder (PTSD). Brock told the psychoanalyst that the condition's most characteristic symptom was a 'lack of solidarity' brought about by a 'segregation of the parts' within the mind. Elsewhere, he explained that such patients become 'like the fragments of their minds, isolated units, *unrelated in space and time*'. This state of splitting and dissociation manifests as a 'childishness' by which 'the ordinary progress of the individual's life appeared to halt; he ceased to grow up . . . or he might partly fall back into childhood'.[15] In a nutshell, Captain Brock described the syndrome demonstrated by Mary Rose.

In 1919, the same year as Barrie was writing his play, Sigmund Freud published an influential essay, *Das Unheimliche*, The Uncanny. He noted that the German term, *das unheimliche*, means 'the opposite of that which is familiar'. Also, that its etymology is *heimlich*, 'home', which links to *heimisch* ,'native'. As such, 'the unheimlich' (as the term is usually rendered into English) is literally the sense of uncanniness that results from a profound 'un-homing', or overturning of a person's native sense of place. It represents a disembedding, or eviction from reality; quite literally, an unhinging of the mind from its environment. The German concept has a close parallel with the Gaelic, àit uaigneach, 'a forlorn place', derived from *uaigneachd* – meaning 'loneliness', 'remoteness' or 'moroseness'. That, in turn, is rooted in *uaigh*, which is a grave, tomb, or home of the dead. The experience of nostalgia derives from this unhomed experience.

Strikingly, in the biblical gospels, the Gadarene or Gerasene demoniac or madman lived amongst the tombs of the dead. He self-harmed, using sharp stones, and named his demons 'Legion'. Jesus cast this legion out into a herd of pigs, which ran down the hill and drowned themselves in the Sea of Galilee. Liberation theology asks questions like: who ate pigs in that society? Not the Jews, but the Roman legionaries. How did the empire exert control? By getting around in ships. Scholars think it likely that Mark's gospel, which has the earliest version of the story, was written just after Vespasian's troops had slaughtered the youth of the demoniac's region in reprisals for the Jewish Revolt.[16] One can read the story literally, or as a parable. It names and unmasks a demonic spirit: the spirit of colonisation, that drives an unhomed people into tombs of living death. It engages that spirit. It casts it out and back from whence it came.

Around the same time as Freud was developing his thought on *das unheimliche,* he was also working on the 'death instinct', or Thanatos. This too, in response to what he had seen of psychological suffering from the terrors of the Great War. He came to view Thanatos as the counterpoint of Eros, his sense of the life instinct, and he concluded: 'We came to recognize sadism as its representative.'[17]

Back home, I have a collection of papers in a book from Cambridge University Press, called *Cultures under Siege.* Several chapters explore the unheimlich from contexts in which wars have rent the fabric of normality, and ripped the psyche open. The cover picture was taken in 1948 at a Polish residence for traumatised children. Its US Army war photographer was David Seymour, whose own Jewish parents had been slaughtered by the Nazis six years earlier. His image shows a little girl, Tereska, who had grown up in a concentration camp. Maybe eight years old, she stands beside a blackboard covered with a white chaotic scrawl, after being asked to draw the meaning of 'home'. Tereska wears a velvety black dress. Ash blonde hair sweeps back in wisps around her emotionally pummelled brow. Her eyes gaze out, uncannily wide, with the 'frozen awareness' of a child who has seen it all, but can respond very little. As Mrs Morland said, 'It has sometimes seemed to me as if a cold finger had once touched my Mary Rose.'

A key chapter is by Professor Yolanda Gampel of the University of Tel Aviv. Her life's work has been with children born in death camps, looking at how unresolved psychic injury knocks on to the children and the grandchildren. She speaks about the 'radioactive identification' of 'transgenerational indigestible trauma'. She explains that, 'when one experiences the uncanny or *unheimlich,* what has been hidden becomes visible, what is familiar becomes strange and frightening'. This takes the sufferer into 'the zone of the unthinkable and the unspeakable'. Here is a world where 'they can no longer fully believe what they see with their own eyes; they have difficulty in distinguishing between the unreal reality they have survived and the fears that spring from their own imagination'. It induces 'a break, a cleavage between the "me" and the "not-me", which can become an unstoppable wellspring of uncanniness'. Such a world now pivots on the cusp of anxiety and terror. The psyche invokes defence mechanisms, in particular 'psychic numbing'. It inhabits 'a world of estrangement', where the central characteristic is a blockage 'to the *articulation between internal and external worlds*'.[18]

Like Mary Rose, Bonnie Kilmeny attempted to come back into 'normality'.[19] She attempted to articulate or connect again between the worlds –

> But all the land were in fear and dread,
> For they kendna whether she was living or dead.
> It wasna her hame, and she couldna remain;
> She left this world of sorrow and pain,
> And return'd to the land of thought again.

Disarticulation between the inner and the outer life invites two possibilities. One, as we've just seen, is to withdraw from outer life into the sìthean of the inner life. To go back 'to the land of thought again'. This was the response of the Biblical demoniac, or 'the bleeding hearts and the artists' of Pink Floyd's *The Wall*. It is what happened to the alcoholic man who failed to place a needle in the sìthean door. Lost in the Mythos, unsorted in the Logos practicality of the outer life, he became emaciated. The cost of this response is self-harm.

The opposite possibility, one that equally hinges on psychic numbing, is to withdraw from the inner life and put all of one's expression into the outer life, into the world of ego. This is the response of the bullies who have been bullied, the hyper-competitive, the hard-line authoritarians and sociopaths. It is what happens to the one who never ventures into the sìthean in the first place. Validating only the things of Logos, the Mythos is kept at arm's length and she or he becomes brazen. The cost of this response is harming others.

Our wars in Afghanistan, Iraq, and elsewhere, argues the American philosopher and playwright, Professor Walter Davis, must be understood in their psychological depth if we are to have a hope of exiting the spiral of violence. These recent wars expose an 'underlying psychosis' of national narcissism, a doggedly rigid collective egotism, where the psychological function of George W. Bush was 'to cover the void at the centre of American society'.[20] Gampel said that if trauma carries on, undigested and not understood, we will find proxy 'chosen' traumas in a desperate bid to reach assimilation and closure. At both individual and collective levels, trauma can be likened 'to indigestible stones, that rattle around the belly of the world'. What's not dealt with in our history will literally stay on to haunt us, harming or self-harming, or both.

That is why we need the magic of the sìthean, but with the grounding of the iron needle from our plaid. The type of person who is qualified to heal the violence of our times is the one who can mediate between the inner and outer worlds, able to unblock the wellsprings of life's energies. It was in helping to fulfil that role that J.M. Barrie's shamanistic genius lay. His work is pooh-poohed – of course – by the sophisticates. These dismiss him as the king of 'kailyard' – writing of the populist and rural cabbage patch. But in his time, people sensed his consequence. From 1930, until his death in 1937, he was the chancellor of Edinburgh University. In the same year as he completed *Mary Rose*, the students of St Andrew's University elected him to be their rector.

His Rectorial Address, delivered in May 1922, showed the difficulties of carrying such a calling. The speech got off to an uncomfortable start. He shuffled, tongue-tied, at the podium, and when he finally broke the long, embarrassing silence and got going – his voice inaudible, fingers fidgeting with a paper knife – he was heckled from the floor. At that, a transformation came about the man. He struck out in a bardic register. He spoke about his prophecy, alluded to in *Mary Rose,* about the likelihood of a second world war.[21]

'You must excuse me,' he told the students, 'if I talk a good deal about courage to you today . . . the rib of Himself that God sent down to His children':

> [The] youth have for too long left exclusively in our hands the decisions in national matters that are more vital to them than to us. Things about the next war, for instance, and why the last one ever had a beginning . . . Do not be too sure that we have learned our lesson, and are not at this very moment doddering down some brimstone path.
>
> The war has . . . taken spring out of the year . . . The spring of the year lies buried in the fields of France and elsewhere. By the time the next eruption comes it may be you who are responsible for it and your sons who are in the lava. All, perhaps, because this year you let things slide . . . Courage is the thing. All goes if courage goes.

He illustrated courage with a letter that Captain Scott had written to him as he and his companions lay dying in the Antarctic. 'We are in a desperate state – feet frozen,' Scott had said, 'but it would do your heart good to be in our tent, to hear our songs and our cheery conversation.'

Barrie then turned to Nansen, the Norwegian explorer, who was awarded the Nobel Peace Prize that same year for having, as the citation put it, saved 'the remnants of the Armenian people from extinction', setting up a system to re-home refugees. With a lurch to unexpected psychological depth, allowing the rhetorical question suddenly to descend, the playwright asked – '*What is beauty?*'

'Sometimes,' he answered: 'beauty boils over.' Sometimes, the sheer trip-you-out epiphany of it all just blows the circuits of the mind, and shifts you from the organising frames of Logos to the poetic quicksilver of Mythos. And, at this point in the speech, he shared a legend that he'd heard from Nansen. It was about a monk, who'd wandered into fields and heard the lark begin to sing – and to sing and sing until its song had joined the heavens. On returning to the monastery, he found that he no longer recognised the doorkeeper. The other monks asked who he was. He said that he was Father Anselm. Eventually, they delved into a book. They realised there'd been a Father Anselm there a hundred years or more before.

Barrie took from Nansen's tale that time itself 'had been blotted out' in listening to the lark. The inner life had been restored from some unfathomed depth of being. 'That,' he told the students, 'was a case of beauty boiling over, or a soul boiling over; perhaps the same thing.

'Then spirits walk.'

The clachan of Beinn a' Bhoth has been left far behind me. Although my eyes are straining, I see the going's easier now. This path is more than just a deer track. It must be a footpath, made perhaps in olden times by people of the bothan plying to and fro from Langabhat.

The ground is levelling out. I am down onto a grassy plain with little ox-bow lakes. A burn, whose banks the path had followed, weaves in broad meanders on its way towards a sandy bay, from which Glen Shandaig takes its name. It must be getting to eleven. Were the skies clear, there'd be sufficient starlight to see reasonably. But the wind has come up strong and bitter. What specks of light had peeked out earlier have lost themselves behind thick clouds. I'm losing body heat and I need to pitch my tent soon – but where? Where to find sufficient shelter on a night like this is brewing up to be?

I'm afraid that when I bought my tent, I traded weight for flimsiness too far. I'm just not seeing any place that's suitable to make a pitch. The plain is much too windswept. The ox-bow hollows are tempting, but flood-prone. Short of struggling back into the hills, or lying very low with just the flysheet wrapped around me, I can't see where to go. My pack is dragging heavily, and I'm weary, weary; oh, my weary mantras from the afternoon are teasing me again. I feel so very much alone, yearning for refuge from this closing in of night.

Ahead I see a mound emerging from the murk. Another of those Ice Age dumps of sand and gravel. It's maybe ten foot high, I guess, grassed over. I've already skirted several, none of which afforded any shelter equal to the slicing of this wind. I just feel cold and yearning to lie down. A voice of low alarm is exhorting caution. I'm well aware that this can be the way you start to lose the plot. I'm shuffling slowly on towards the mound – when something stirs, and I stand rigid in my tracks.

Is that . . . *movement?*

My eyes scry out the last few photons of the dusk. Standing there, just near the hillock's base, are two red deer, a pair of hinds. I've walked head on into the wind. They've neither heard me nor picked up my scent. The poor things, startled, stare bewildered.

They hold motionless for maybe ten or twenty seconds, toss their heads, and without so much as a warning bark, gird their haunches into pounding piston strokes. I watch them glide across the turf, the elegance of wild things, lost in seconds to the folds of darkness.

I'm standing here before their mound, a pang of guilt at having stirred these gentle creatures from their rest.

'What will the sìth be making of all this?' I'm musing to myself, so far from Aberdeen, from cold remorseless Reason. Pulled now as on a long cast into Cameron's native world.

Then the pieces drop together to a pattern in my mind.

The brushstrokes rippled round the loch side yesterday.

The trail that led me through the bog this afternoon.

Where they had sought their shelter, no better quarters shall I find.

I struggle with the gusts, and manage to erect some semblance of a tent. At last, and staying fully clothed, I slip down inside the sleeping bag.

My unease at my transgression has calmed down, overtaken by a drowsy sea of gratitude. For ever since that stop for lunch at Loch a' Sgàil just yesterday, I've herded with the deer, the fiadh, the shy and fleeting cattle of the wild.

13

SMOKING OUT THE DEVIL

It was a night of wild and fretful sleep. The tent walls billowed out as if to burst, and then snapped back to give a ghostly pummelling. I pulled Osprey close in beside me as a bed mate, sheltering behind the bulk to fend off the worst of the battering, dozing, and then being shaken back awake again until, at last, exhaustion claimed the night and seemed to quell the tempest's force.

It was the dawn light that woke me on day five, Friday. People who study wilderness experience say that civilisation is only four days deep. The trappings fall away and we open to a world more primal.

I draw back the zipper and peer east. It looks Baltic out there. The sky's a hodden grey. Is it earlier than I'm thinking, and this, just the first glimmerings of dawn? I fire up the phone. The clock shows seven. Thankfully, there's no signal and so no beep-beep of messages. John Muir said that we don't go out to nature, we go in, but on a day like this I'd rather just be staying in. Deep ecology sounds fun until you're in the thick.

I clamber out into a porridge of low mist that cuts off the hilltops. The wind has backed north-east, and I can smell the freshening sharpness that signifies impending rain. Better get packed up while everything's still dry. I light my stove for a quick brew-up of tea. What little heat there is gets blown away before it hits the bottom of the pan. I make do with a lukewarm cup, and then the spits come on, and soon the splats. For the first time, I put on my waterproofs and pull up Osprey's red protective hood to keep my stuff dry. Thankfully I'm warm, and don't need to wear the fleece. It's comforting to know there's something in reserve.

The mist is creeping lower. I'd better take a route that hugs the lochs and streams. That way, you've always got a thread to follow if it drops right down. I'm going to walk along this sandy bay and then go up the next glen, heading west a while to skirt the shores of Loch Lomhain. From there, I'll curve around the eastern flank of Ascleit. I'll keep a lookout for the sheilings Seumas mentioned, then dip down towards Loch Coire Geurad, a coiled offshoot of Langabhat. From there, the map hints at a footpath running north to Loch a' Sguair. I'll go and try to find the both he said was nestled in the rocks above its north-west corner. Then after that, depending on the visibility, either over or around the Mothal Ridge, and from there, to the Grimersta.

I make a ceremonial little bow to thank the lodgings of the deer – very good Mythos; very dodgy Logos – and off I lumber. In contrast to the stalker's path of yesterday, the ground round here is heavy-going – spongy underfoot, from hummocked clumps of last year's ungrazed growth that have yet to settle down and rot. It forces me to stomp a lumpy heather loup, and as I reach Loch Lomhain, the heavens fully open. I stop and watch the smothering force of raindrops quell the waves, muffling down their agitation to a sullen surge that slaps against the rocky shore. The mist is sinking lower on the Harris Hills behind, and as I round onto the eastern face of Ascleit, the rain beats drum rolls on my hood. It forces me to pull the drawstrings tight, leaving – like one of those narrow church windows – just a leper's squint for vision under siege.

I know I must keep moving, keep the effort going, and take care. If the wet gets in, the balmy fug will soon become a clammy hand of cold, lifeless and life-draining. If there are sheilings here, they're not on this trajectory. I'm probably down too low. The mist has robbed me of a sense of altitude. The wind has now wound up to gale force. At times I have to lean so sharply forwards that I'd keel right over if it suddenly dropped off. The rain comes hurtling down in banded sheets. They lash across my shoulders, and any higher up, their icy flecks would turn to stinging hail. Probably it's snowing right up top.

I've been battling for an hour now, my pace has slowed, and my body temperature dropped. The low alarm is going off inside again. Nothing serious. It's just the 'getting cold' of the peripheral circulation closing down. The grip of chill in hands and feet that is, they say, stage one, mild hypothermia. It's at stage two, 'moderate', that the brain gets addled. 'Blue with cold' you'll notice first the coordination going. Before that happens, you need to heed the full alarm, put up the tent while still you can. Stage three is when the body's temperature has dropped by four degrees or more. Then – as I've heard them say – it's like a nice warm bath. You want to fall asleep, a nice long sleep, but no awakening seven years later from such a hill as that.

As youths, when we'd be bailing out the boats or pulling up the lobster pots, we'd sometimes touch the boundary of two and three. Our speech would slur like drunks. We'd wobble, dizzy, on our feet. We'd give each other knowing nods for home that, in their very understatement, warned 'we'd better pull like hell, boys!' In such effort, hauling on the oars, we'd be warmed up by the time we'd get back to the mooring. But that was in our youth. We had the energy reserves and stamina to prevail.

The worst thing would be the crushing pain that comes on as the circulation kicks back in. I've inquired of doctors, but never had its causes satisfactorily explained. It's just 'what happens when'. The pain comes on from out of nowhere, endures for several minutes, and feels as if your hands and feet are clamped into the screws of some medieval inquisition dungeon. You wouldn't want to go there. Yet, somehow, I pity those whose only chance to live an exercised outdoors life these days, is tugging on an outboard motor's starter cord.

A man-sized boulder looms ahead. I take the shelter of its lee, quickly yank my jacket off and put the fleece on underneath. Now I'm fully armed against the elements, wearing everything I've got. A chocolate bar completes the pit stop, and it's strange how quickly it revives my energy. I've noticed that quite often. As if before it's even melted in my stomach, the Numskulls in my Metabolic Department are shouting to each other: 'Ah! He's paying us attention now. Relax!'

Down below, the folds of Ascleit spread their stubby toes into the twists of Loch Coire Geurad. There's a gentle rise down by the water's edge that the map names as the Sìthean Mòr na Liana – the Big Faerie Hill of the Meadow. A couple of miles north-east are the dark cliffs of Sìthean Mòr Beinn a' Chuailein. Probably it means the Great Faerie Hill of the Mountain of the Cattle. Alternatively, of the Hair-ringlet or possibly the Hunting Hound. Even the experts find it hard to figure out many of these names. Most of them were first shifted from the oral to the written tradition by Irish sappers – military engineers – who made the first Ordnance Survey maps to a generous six-inch scale in the early 1850s. They would have spoken Irish Gaelic, but in transcribing from local Hebridean informants, all manner of strange spellings slipped in.

From where I hope to cross the Grimersta, the sapper map shows, within just half a mile of one another, no fewer than five sìthean place names. Names like the magnificently daunting Sìthean Dubh Gheàrraidh Dhubh Bheag – the Black Faerie Hill of the Little Black Garden of the Grazings. If the Eskimos have umpteen names for snow, the Arabs similarly for sand, then in Dwelly's Gaelic dictionary alone I've counted seventy-nine words or phrases pertaining to the sìth. There's one that says it all – *Sìth-bhrughach*; 'Abounding in fairy hills'. Reflecting on the double meaning of sìth as both 'peace' and 'faerie', Ronald Black points to the word's likely etymology as cognate with the concept of being 'settled' in a place, or, one might say, 'homed'. As such, the sìth were 'the peace people'. The are the gentry of the land who 'enjoyed peace when the main activity of the Celtic tribes was war'. Black cites the work of Tomás Ó Cathasaig, professor of Irish Studies at Harvard University, who conjectures that the homely sense of sìd or sìth refined over time to 'abode of the gods' and to 'hollow hill', because, 'for an unsettled, or migrant people, the notion of abode or settlement might readily be linked with that of peace'. To wit, in early Gaelic tradition, 'the concept of peace was closely linked to the otherworld'.[1] To set the unheimlich of *Mary Rose* into faerie as the psyche's refuge from war, is to sit very comfortably in this tradition.

When Torcuil MacRath, the bard of Grimshader in North Lochs was still alive, I asked if he thought that sìthean always means a *faerie* hill. He answered by telling me of a bodach in the village, an old man by then deceased, who'd peer out when the sun was rising on a dewy summer's day, and as every hillock steamed in the warmth, he'd solemnly announce: 'They've lit their fires early this morning.' 'Mind you,' Torcuil quickly added, drawing back from being tossed too high in the horns of elfland, 'he wasn't quite right in the head.' And yet, my friend's poetic sensibility was picking up something. The ecology of the imagination, the realm of faerie as the spirit of nature personified, comes alive through living in the stories; and this is what it means to be connected to the Mythos.

Whatever happened to the island's faeries? One explanation is that a strain of evangelical clergy, brought in from the mainland in the nineteenth century, introduced a different disposition. A herds boy on the Lochs road was asked by a passing gentleman if there were still faeries in the parish. 'No,' said the boy, 'they all left when Mr Finlayson came.' Ironically, prior to that, their Lewis nickname had been 'Finlay's people'. Thus the Gaelic saying, 'As numerous as Finlay's people.'[2] But to blame it all upon the clergy is to take an easy swipe. It's mainly through the writings of the clergy that the tradition was conserved. And then, there's living testimonies connected with the second sight. Not that I'd be wanting, in this age of Aberdeen, to be persuading anybody about anything wacky. Just that I'm intrigued by Nora Bateson's comment, about what we might be inside of.

Invigorated by my bar of chocolate, I'm off again – and coming up now to a sharp slope that leads down to the western tip of Loch Coire Geurad – the Loch of the Sharp-edged Cauldron. With such limited visibility, this hellish weather unrelenting, my mind finds little stimulation from 'outside'. Right now, it's like I'm banged up 'inside', away in the land of thought: and if from here you soared as like a bird across Loch Langabhat, six miles directly east to Eishken, you'd come to a haggard spike of mountain crag called Sidhean an Airgid – the Silver Faerie Hill.[3]

If you come down that mountain, past the Crag of the Ravens to the head of Loch Seaforth – the Faerie Port, or Port of Peace, if we venture to go by *Sithphort* as the sappers called it on their 1854 map[4] – you'll come to a hill marked as Sìdeabhal. At its foot, right beside the sea, there lies a soft spread of emerald turf, and on it, a substantial dry-stone ruin. Uniquely, as far as I'm aware, the walls incorporate part of a prehistoric stone circle. This was probably a residential quarter belonging to the nearby first stronghold of the Mackenzies of Kintail when they seized Lewis under the Crown's Commission of Fire and Sword in 1610. The circle's incorporation to such a utilitarian purpose has led it to be said that Mackenzie 'could not have been very reverent or superstitious', or he'd never have usurped a 'Druid' place of worship.[5]

These fertile south-facing slopes run riddled through with feannagan. They remained hand-worked for potatoes, turnips, oats and barley well into my lifetime. The last person to tend them in the old ways was Mary Kate Maclennan – *Ceiteag*, to most people. However, in the anglicised formality with which she'd address me as the son of her doctor, 'Katie' was the name by which, in a letter that I treasure, she explicitly invited me to call her.

As the night closes in I sit in her kitchen at Seaforth Head by an oil lamp burning from a wick of braided cotton. Being off-grid in such a remote part of the island, she does have a diesel generator, but disdains its hammering racket. In any case, why waste drums of diesel when a little cup of paraffin gives quite enough flame by which to read a book, or a visitor's face?

Were she living in the East, Katie would be treated as a God-intoxicated holy woman. There'd be a queue of western pilgrims knocking at her door, hoping that by sitting at her feet they might 'get the *cùram*' – as the Gaelic calls sudden spiritual enlightenment. However, because she's a fully paid-up member of the Free Church of Scotland, prone to handing out sutras from the Westminster Shorter Catechism of 1647 – well – let's just say that I'm the lucky one. I get to sit at her feet all by myself.

'How is it for you these days, Katie?' I ask. 'How is it being the last person, left all alone in the village? Don't you get lonely?'

'Oh a ghràidh!' she exclaims – literally 'oh my love' – with a radiance that breaks through an intense hawk-like intelligence. She's in her late eighties, her ashen hair drawn back in the old Presbyterian manner. She's sitting there in a working pinafore over a long dark skirt, and now and then her spectacle rims catch an amber fire from the lamplight.

'Oh a ghràidh,' she repeats: '*How can I be lonely* . . . when I'm with God?

I protest that she's living at the end of this long dark sea loch, several miles from the next nearest neighbours, surrounded by bleak mountains. Since her husband died, she's continued to run the croft pretty much single-handed.

'Don't you ever get frightened?'

'Oh a ghràidh, *how can I be frightened* . . . when I'm with God?

And she laughs, with a most infectious giggle, enjoying the sight of my wavering incredulity, then adding: 'Mind you, the Devil was in here recently.'

'The Devil.' I repeat. Deadpan. Eyebrows no doubt rising.

'Oh yes! You see, a ghràidh, the Devil is always on your back. But God is in your heart. So you have to fix your eyes upon your heart to stop the Devil getting in.'

We all have a stone in our hearts, she said. If we don't let God take it out, the Devil finds his way inside, then all we're left with is a stony heart.[6]

As for the Devil's visitation, she'd been hearing him in the house for some time, going *chirp-chirp* like a bird. Jane MacAulay, John's wife from Harris, had dropped in on a nursing visit. She'd heard the chirping too, and neither could figure out where it was coming from. After she had left, Katie scoured everywhere. Eventually she found where he was hiding. 'In the smoke alarm!'

She removed the device and threw it outside. 'I wasn't going to be giving house space to the Devil!' The next night, she opened the door and there were seven faeries dancing in a circle on the grass.

'You saw . . . seven faeries?'

'Oh yes my dear – and they were horrible.'

'Like, how?'

'Oh, they were about this high' – she holds her hand at chair height off the ground – 'and they had little short pleated skirts, and horrible skinny legs; oh, *horrible* legs. They were dark. Repulsive!'

'So the faeries are not . . . pretty?'

'Oh no, a ghràidh,' and she leans in closer. 'You see, the faeries are in league with *himself*.'

'All of them?'

One of the traditions is that the sìth were angels who were discontent with God's way of running Heaven. God said that they could leave, but as they were not wicked enough to join Lucifer in Hell, they settled the middle regions of the Earth.

For three days and nights they fell like snow, until God got worried that he'd have a labour shortage. As an old woman from the Uists told John MacInnes, 'With the voice of a sergeant major of the English army, he shouted *Halt!*' – slamming shut the trapdoor, and establishing the cosmic order.[7]

'You see them all as demonic?'

'The whole lot of them!' she insisted. 'You see, they are not of this world. They are in – how would you say it? – another sphere. An invisible world.'

And that was Katie's very straight Protestant take on the sìth. Such was what had led Yeats to write 'A Remonstrance with Scotsmen for Having Soured the Disposition of Their Ghosts and Faeries' because, he opined, 'In Scotland you are too theological, too gloomy.'[8] Katie wouldn't have seen it like that. She'd have seen her focus as being on the higher realms.

At one level, one could dismiss her story of the Devil's visitation as the confusion of an elderly person, not attuned to the wizmo-gizmo of electrical gadgets, living too much in a place of isolation. While true up to a point, it would miss the inner richness of her worldview. She had no television, no soap operas or adverts to generate a spurious sense of meaning. Instead, reality for her was elemental, based on raw experience, and self-evidently God-ordained. The fleeting changes in the weather, the weaving in and out of rainbows in the sky, even the vexed question of the rabbit population on her croft were all part of the give and take, the ebb and flow, of divine providence. When I'd sit in her company I'd encounter, carried through into the twenty-first century, a woman who held Thomas Boston's sense of 'every pile of grass . . . a preacher' of God's loving-kindness. Like with Barrie's Cameron, you could think that you had encountered a simple soul, and in some ways you maybe had, 'until you question him about the universe'.

She adhered, of course, to the Calvinist doctrine of predestination with the Damned and the Elect. But when I protested; when I asked how a God of love could damn anyone – and suggested that, in the very end, all might be 'saved' – she conceded through pursed lips: 'You might be right, but that would be *His* business.'

I asked how she had arrived at her spirituality. Was it something that had always been there? I was particularly curious as to why her emphasis was not just on God, but on the Devil, and why such belief in, and yet disdain for, the sìth. She told me a very personal story, a sequence of events that had entailed profound trauma in her life. Suffice to say, she'd lost her only son when he was five days old. That and its consequences broke her in both heart and mind. She'd had a vision that had warned her of upheaval. One night, well before going into labour, she had seen a 'blue man' standing on the stairs. In Gaelic lore, the 'blue men', the *fir gorm,* are the faeries of the sea. The Sruth nam Fear Gorma, the Straits of the Blue Men, lie out from the mouth of Loch Seaforth towards the Shiants. He had pointed to a pile of money that was in the house, and told her: 'Keep that . . . you will need it for the funeral.' In the agonising grief that followed, compounded by a further medical cause for suffering, her mind was stretched beyond the normal limits of endurance. It was then God opened to her.

The rational question would be: 'Does the Otherworld, the spiritual world in whatever its culturally-coloured permutations, exist?' But the mythic question is very different. That would ask: What *function* do these experiences and beliefs fulfil in the ecosystem of the mind? What *meaning* attaches to this sense of God and the Devil, or the angels and the sìth. What is the meaning that gives meaning to meaning? What, for that matter, gives meaning to anything? If we're all Mythos, we get lost in a dream world. If all Logos, we lose the symbolic world of meaning. Then the distinction between the angels and the faeries would reduce down to a single word: altitude.

As for the smoke alarm, neither Jane nor I had the heart to ask if she'd thought to change the battery. But in one of those funny ways of things, it got me thinking. I thought: that's actually the trouble with the Devil, if we might talk metaphorically.

There he goes. As the opening of the Book of Job tells us, 'up and down upon the face of the Earth', like the long straight lines upon a map that signifies a lawyer's pen – the claim of 'property', and evictions.

And he's always going *chirp-chirp*, always trying to draw attention to himself, because he only runs on battery power. Can't get no satisfaction – though he tries, and he tries, and he tries. Too proud to get wired in, to the mains supply of God, 'whose name is *Holy*'.

Forgive my treading on such ground, but I know that's where Katie would like me to rest her memory.[9]

I must for sure have been too low to find the Ascleit sheilings, but on the cauldron's rim at Loch Coire Geurad I'd tried for signal on my mobile phone, and managed to get through to Vérène. Hearing her, set loose a burst of joyousness in me. I took off, skipping and whooping down the ludicrously sharp gradient, braked by the up-blast of the gale that sustained me like a parachute. I called my mother too. She could hardly hear my voice against the storm, but such are island micro-climates that Stornoway, she said, was bright and sunny, with only a stiff breeze.

The hint of a footpath that I'd seen on the map turned out to be an old turf boundary dyke. However, the ground around it was so choppy that, for a while, I walked along the top like on a tightrope. The mist had closed right in. One by one I'd watched the landmarks fail. I hugged close to the dyke until, from out of the mists, the little Loch a' Sguair emerged, huddled up against a wall of rocks. The both, a single dome, was even better preserved than what I'd found at Clàr Beag, and I'm sitting now inside a nearby sheiling ring of stones. Another lunch of cheese and oatcakes. Musing on what happy times this sheltered corner must have seen. The days spent with the cattle. Evenings fishing on the loch. The smoke-cured tales around the hearth at dusk. No doubt there'd be a share of tears as well, and yet, as an island doctor friend who had been born in a blackhouse told me: 'We never needed therapists because we had each other.'[10]

It's out of the question in this visibility to traverse the Mothal Ridge across a line of three summits. I'll have to skirt Beinn Mothal's flanks instead. Ideally, I'd have gone the southern route, above Gleann Marstaig. There, within a two-mile stretch, the old sapper map shows ten places marked as *àirigh* – sheiling, or *geàrraidh* – the grazings that were germane to sheiling life. That way, however, would have brought me to the foot of Sìthean Mòr Beinn a' Chuailein, which was not the place to cross the Grimersta that Seumas had recommended. With this rain, I can't be taking chances. I'll therefore take the northern course, ford a small river, then the Grimersta, and come at last to the 'crag and tail' formation of the Rubha Leathann. There, I hope, I'll find Saint Bridgit's Sheiling, and there I'll spend my fourth and final night out on the moors, before re-entering village sociability.

The rain is picking up again. I pack up lunch and quickly take a compass bearing. Already, from this morning's use, the map is slightly damp. The hi-tech inkjet colours are at risk of smudging. Vérène had said to buy a plastic map holder – the kind you loop around your neck. For some stupid reason, I'd not done so. Too bad. Prophetic confirmation of the scripture written on our fridge magnet: 'If at first you don't succeed, try it your wife's way.'

The bearing that I've taken points me on a wayline, a line of sight, that runs twenty degrees east. I've set my eyes on a rock some several hundred yards in that direction. Once there, I'll take another bearing on another waypoint, and so on, landmark by little landmark through the mist. However, very quickly, the steepness of the climb proves greater than I'd reckoned from the contours on the map. This can't be right. I'll change course, just slightly. Head directly north a while, up a slope that feels more like my expectations.

On, and on and on. Plodding through the wind and rain. Pretty miserable. Just meandering along. Drifting in a moistish

sort of meditative mope. Can't expect to have it good every day.
Hit so lucky with the sunshine earlier. But what's that funny
noise?

At first I'm thinking it's a plane, but then a break comes in
the mist. A mile away, a tiny speck, a van is speeding on a road
that shouldn't be there. Civilisation cuts in with a thump. I pull
the map back out, align it north-south with the compass, and
face my error. Elementary! Never trust the naked eye in mist.
What I had thought to be Beinn Mothal in my veer to north,
was just the puny foothill of Cleit Mothal Mòr. I've gone and
put myself an hour off course. 'If at first you don't succeed . . .'

I change tack and climb, recovering position. Gradually, I
work my way along the flank and then down onto lower
ground. Here the small river I'd noticed on the map straddles
the moor. I cross it without difficulty, yet I'm troubled by its
vigour after just one morning of rain. I'm now into a flat land,
a zone that flows with bogs in all directions. The Grimersta is
a mile away, but the mist has dropped back down again with
vengeance. I can't see any hills at all. Even the lochs are dipped
right down into the hollows, remaining out of sight until you're
standing on their rims.

The land is quite devoid of any texture. It creates that
slightly weird feeling of mild sensory deprivation. I'm having
to micro-navigate, sometimes only seeing seventy or a hundred
yards ahead and stopping all the time to take another bearing.
The map is squelching to a Jackson Pollock quagmire. I inch
along, seeking boulders, knolls, even big tufts of heather that
stand out as waypoints. What can't be predicted are the tenta-
cles of branching pools. These lead me in and trap me in their
maze. It's like *The Lord of the Rings,* the Mere of Dead Faces
in the middle of the Dead Marshes. Tolkien said it was an old
battlefield, 'dreary and wearisome', where 'rotting reeds
loomed up in the mists like ragged shadows of long forgotten
summers'. That heaviness has settled onto me again. The same
cianalas feeling that I had last night at Kinlochresort. A gnaw-
ing burden of . . . unspecified emotion.

I come upon a little rise, a tiny cnoc a few feet higher than the swamps that fester all around. Perched on top are two or three haphazard rings of bygone bothan sites. There are no sheilings left intact around the Grimersta. I've heard it said they were destroyed when the estate was set up, to stop them from harbouring poachers.

I perch to rest, and from this misty cnoc the whole world goes drifting by. And I know what has brought the *nostos-algos* back. These moors – these *are* old battlefields. These sheiling ruins – these *are* the ragged shadows, of long forgotten summers.

In January 1815, Deaf Mackenzie – Colonel Francis Humberston Mackenzie of Kintail, Seaforth and Barbados – passed away. His four sons had predeceased him and the whole of Lewis fell to his eldest daughter, Mary Elizabeth Frederica Mackenzie, whose mother had been the daughter of the Very Reverend Baptist Proby, Dean of Lichfield. Lady Mary had been married to an elderly admiral, Sir Samuel Hood, who had commanded the British fleet out of Madras. He had died just three weeks prior to her father's passing. It was as a doubly bereaved young widow that she returned to Scotland.

A doyenne of the Raj, Mary had led a dashing life in India. She claimed she was the first British woman to have shot a tiger. However, tales of her intrigues with diplomats, the literati and native princes set the tongues of polite society wagging. Remarks were made about her 'roving propensities'. She was dubbed a 'Tom boy', and even her paternity was questioned with her sultry 'Gypsy' beauty. When she remarried, only two years after losing her husband, the Whig politician, T.B. Macaulay, described her to his sister as a 'wicked woman'.[11]

In contrast to such disapproval, Sir Walter Scott eulogised her in his heroic poem, 'Farewell to Mackenzie, High Chief of Kintail'. Here was a 'gentle dame', to be addressed in reverential terms. Elsewhere, he hailed her 'warm heart and lively fancy', with 'the spirit of the chieftainess in every drop of her blood'. I think of her as something of a feminist ahead of her time, a woman whose sense of liberty and, it seems, sometimes of taking liberties, curled the upper lips of stiff patriarchs. I can't help warming to Lord Teignmouth's story that, on her way back home from India, a strange sail was sighted. As the crew leapt to battle stations, the passengers were ushered below deck. However, the captain noticed what he took to be a skulking sailor hiding underneath a sailcloth. In ejecting the miscreant, he revealed Herself, hoping for a bit of the action.

Her second husband was a minor Galloway landowner, James Alexander Stewart of Glasserton, later to become the governor of Ceylon. Chronically short of cash, he ran an advertisement in the Inverness Courier in 1830 offering '. . . very extensive Sheep Grazings, of the best quality'. These would 'be arranged by removing to other parts of the Island all the smaller Tenants at present dwelling thereon'. This venture, the text continued, was 'well worthy of the attention of Capitalists'. It was, he wrote elsewhere, a 'grand improvement . . . the introduction of mutton in lieu of man'. For the people of Uig in south-west Lewis, it meant families being crowded together on insufficient remaining land. As a village elder told the Napier Commission half a century later: 'The rest were hounded away to Australia and America, and I think I hear the cry of the children till this day.'[12]

As her husband got on with being the Capitalist with a capital C – attempting such ventures as printing his own banknotes, and setting up a whisky distillery in Stornoway – Lady Mary seems to have become absorbed with religion. For reasons not so far researched, she became an ardent advocate of Puritan evangelicalism. She used her powers of patronage as the landlady to hand-pick evangelical clergy from the mainland, and appoint them over Church of Scotland island parishes. So began the hardline Calvinist strand of island religion. As the Uig historian, Donald Macdonald, puts the matter, albeit in simplified terms: 'One must remember the Calvinist type of religion did not start in Lewis till 1824.'[13]

The significance of 1824 was the arrival of the first, and most influential, of Lady Mary's hand-picked appointees, the Rev. Alexander Macleod. He was posted to Uig, a parish that had earlier been decimated by her father's press gangs, and where her husband's clearances were to include evictions from some of the best land to create the minster's glebe – his larder.[14] It was, says an Uig historian, Donald J. Macleod, a creed of 'hellfire in the pulpit, sheep on the glebe, and Seaforth's lucre in his back pocket'.[15] Macleod was horrified to find a parish where, as a biographer puts it, he 'witnessed with his own eyes their homage morning and evening to the sun and moon'. His sermons generated 'a sense of fear, amounting to well-nigh terror', and he never failed to raise 'his silvery voice against all those pleasures and practices that seemed to him to impair the spiritual life . . . dancing, cup-reading, ceilidhs, gay clothing' – even – 'galloping on broomsticks'. Such abominations 'opened the vials of his wrath', and he 'denounced them in unmeasured speech'.[16]

Macleod's own diaries describe his conscious use of the pulpit to warn that 'fears and terrors, terrors unspeakable, would never terminate through the rounds of eternal ages, if the offers of salvation were rejected'. He petitioned Lady Mary for funding to circulate Thomas Boston's works in Gaelic translation, as well as seeking grants from the Royal Bounty. This was the missionary fund of the British state, started by George I in 1725 to convert the Highlands to Protestantism, thereby hoping to quell rebellions. When Macleod saw – in his own words – that 'every heart was pierced, and general distress spread through the whole congregation' as a result of his preaching and refusal to baptise the children of waverers, he concluded, with utmost satisfaction: 'May it bear forth fruit!'

Macleod was far from alone in celebrating the achievements of authoritarian religion. As Dr John Kennedy of Dingwall – the town next door to the Mackenzies' mainland seat of power at Brahan – proudly summed up the achievements of such Ross-shire preachers in 1861: 'The power of the pulpit was

paramount in Ross-shire and the people became, to a great
extent, plastic to its influence.'[17]

The Mackenzies had already mastered fear as a mechanism
for colonising social control long before Lady Mary's time and
her evangelicalism. Between 1577 and 1706 twenty-three
members of the dynasty had been commissioners in prosecut-
ing witchcraft. While the records are scanty, it is established
that two women were burnt as witches in Stornoway in 1631 by
authority of the Privy Council, led by the Mackenzie gentry.
One historian of the era remarks that the 'religiously orthodox' would certainly have had plenty to bother themselves
about, given superstitions as trivial as 'practices connected to
holy wells and the pouring of milk on fairy knolls'.[18]

The same religious tactics that the British Empire deployed
in its colonies abroad had been pioneered at home as part of
the 'internal colonisation' or consolidation of the British Isles.
Sustained colonisation of the land requires colonisation of the
soul, what I call inner colonisation, where religion is structured
to control the spiritual life. As Deaf Mackenzie had said in his
1793 regimental recruitment poster, the name of the game was
'the defence of his Glorious Majesty . . . and the preservation
of our happy constitution in Church and State'. In his era, the
north-west frontier lay in the string of forts that straddled the
Highlands to keep the clans in good behaviour. There was, and
continues to be as an army base, Fort George, in the east near
Inverness. Fort Augustus was in the middle and Fort William in
the west, as well as lesser wild west garrisons. What the sword
had achieved at the Massacre of Glencoe in 1692 and again at
the Battle of Culloden in 1746, a Protestant reading of the
Bible would help to sustain, with its focus on personal salvation. As many an African freedom fighter would say: 'They
gave us the Bible, and we closed our eyes to pray. We opened
them, and they'd taken the land.'

Paulo Freire of Brazil called such tactics 'cultural invasion'.
Here, 'it is essential that those who are invaded come to see
their reality with the outlook of the invaders rather than their

own; for the more they mimic the invaders, the more stable the position of the latter becomes.'[19] Stigmatised and inferiorised, the colonised are thrust into a double-bind. They're damned to internalise their own oppression if they go along with the coloniser's norms. Or they're damned to the sword, hellfire, or just the privations of being a subordinate social class, if they don't.

Religions that make binary distinctions between people – whether as Elect or Damned, Mu'min or Kafir – are wide open to such political usage. A type of Stockholm Syndrome sets in, where a hostage group can enter into 'traumatic bonding' with their captors. As Alice Walker put it in *The Color Purple*: 'Some colored people [are] so scared of whitefolks they claim to love the cotton gin.'[20] Likewise, some folks are so scared of God that they buy into the notion of all hell to pay and play for others. Augustine even taught that those in Heaven will be well aware of the eternal sufferings of those in Hell. How else might they count their blessings, and 'for ever sing the mercies of God'?[21]

The only trouble is, the theology of fear discredits any god of love. It shrivels up the wells of spiritual life. It leaves the wounded neurotically seeking salvation from their wounds. No wonder growing numbers feel that atheism is a purer creed.

Such is the world that drifts past me, sitting on this cnoc amongst these fallen sheiling stones, surrounded by dead faces in these meres that morph amongst the mists of the Grimersta's headwaters.

A skylark rises straight up from the heather. I love to watch the way they sing, and slowly drop, and then rise on high to sing all over again. *Fosgag-Mhoire* they're called in Gaelic – Our Lady's Lark – or as Alexander Carmichael had it, the Songster of the Virgin Mary. In Luke's gospel, the Song or Magnificat of Mary proclaims a very different god; one who stands in solidarity with the poor, who 'has brought down the powerful from their thrones, and lifted up the lowly; he has filled the hungry with good things, and sent the rich away empty'.[22] The Buddha was a prince who found enlightenment while contemplating suffering underneath a tree. Krishna was a god who spent his spare time chasing after the gopi cowherd girls at their Himalayan sheilings. All of these are eminently worthy pursuits. What for me distinguishes Jesus is that he was born in the most humble of circumstances, in a country under military occupation, and spent his life amongst and suffering with the poor. That alone is too great a gift to neglect, just because it has been twisted, and to fail to bring it to the table of world faiths.

Such are the qualities that distinguish liberation theology – theology that liberates theology itself from the boxes into which it has been shut. Not all of the clergy sided with landed power. One who did not, the Rev. Donald MacCallum, preached a liberation theology on Lewis and elsewhere. The Church of Scotland censured him. His denunciation of 'the vices of the rich', his likening of the crofters' plight to the Israelites under Pharaoh, and his urging them to 'resist the Devil and he will flee from you' were deemed to be a part and parcel of 'inciting violence and class hatred'. In 1886 on Skye, the Royal Navy sent in two gunboats to suppress a rent strike. MacCallum was arrested, albeit later released. He is remembered by the people as *Caraid an Duine Bhochd* – the Friend of the Poor.[23] As the proverb says, it's the kail that tests the creed.

But now I must get moving. I ease myself up and trudge on again – more and more of the same enervating territory – steering only by the map and compass, hoping that I haven't goofed the route again. At last, a breakthrough. The mist starts rapidly to clear. Where there had been only drifting drapes of whiteness, a pitch black rectangle looms. As I move in closer, I see it is a boathouse, made watertight with lashings of Archangel tar. A wind vane, shaped as a salmon, gutters from a pole above the roof. What's more, the wind has dropped down to a gentle breeze.

A gravel path leads on ahead and puts the spring back into my step. My mood has lifted with the mists. To wit, I feel a tightening of the vice of *sin* within my entrails. I've got everything I need to fish – except permission – but some words assemble as a poacher's proverb in my mind:

> A sin not enjoyed is a sin wasted,
> and a sin wasted is a double sin.

The dainty little footpath traipses round some knolls. It glides towards a whisper, that murmurs to a roar.

And there it is, a wildly foaming torrent. The Grimersta, that bellows from the island's heaving heart and surges to the sea.

14

SAINT BRIDGIT'S SHEILING

After such dry weather, I'd have thought the chain of lochs that are up above would have taken longer than a day to fill up. But that's the trouble when the moor has gone so crisp. It takes several days to restore its absorbency. Initial rainfall runs straight off. What's before me now is startling. Seumas had clearly lacked the second sight when he'd suggested this should be an easy place to ford.

I'm standing at a short stretch of broad stream that links two lochs. At the upper end, it issues through a weir, built to hold back water for the fishing. At the lower end it comes out beside a boathouse. The darkness of the surface there tells me that the channel must be deep.

I'm walking up and down the bank, checking out my options, and nowhere offers easy passage. What's more, the temperature's not helped by molten hail that's drained down from the heights. Right now, my body's warm enough, but I'm mindful that this is not the day to chance it with heroics.

There seem to be three options. Plan C would be to accept defeat, walk a mile down the side of Loch Faoghail Charrasan, and then join a footpath that eventually meets the B8011, the road where I saw the van go speeding across to the coastal villages of Uig.

Plan B would be to ford at the widest part, with the slackest water. The problem is, the river runs lopsided. The far side would be easy. There the force is broken by a line of stones that stretch out from the bank. The challenge would be on this side. Here the torrent's raging at thigh depth, and at a speed that could easily sweep me off my feet.

Plan A – the one I'm going to try for – is to wade into the top loch, and walk a broad arc round above the weir. Whether that can work depends on whether I can get out far enough to escape the suction as the water gathers in a V-formation, to funnel through the weir.

It's worth a try, plus I've got a bright idea with which to circumvent the icy cold. Osprey is fitted with removable elastic straps for tying on loose tackle. I fit a couple of these over my waterproofs, tightly around the ankles, and thereby improvise a dry suit. At the same time, I unhitch the rucksack's waist belt, lest I'm forced to ditch him in a hurry – poor thing.

The water's freezing, sure enough, but as I wade in deeper, the dry suit takes effect. I can feel the pressure pressing round my legs, but with no icy leaks. My fishing rod doubles up as a walking stick. Yet it's hard going. A mushy peat bottom is strewn with large angular rocks. Their sharp edges suggest a relatively recent date of quarrying. I'd guess they've been dumped there to create a salmon lie, and to snag poachers' nets. The truth is that Grimersta has suffered poaching on a truly reprehensible industrial scale. No wonder they protect their stock. As for the poachers – 'string 'em up like grouse . . .'!

As I move towards mid-flow, the water's lapping up my thighs and the suction from the weir is getting stronger by the footstep. What I hadn't reckoned on is that the deeper in I go, the more buoyed up I become. That makes me lighter on my feet, with less and less traction to the bottom the more and more I need it. I'm caught in a devil's calculus. Either, I can wade out even deeper, to reduce the suction. Or, I stay in the speeding shallows, and try to keep a grip. Time to switch off Mythos, turn on Logos. A cubic metre of water weighs a ton. Where it crosses the weir, it's easily a metre deep and the weir's about a metre-and-a-half wide. It's pounding through at, very roughly, five metres a second, so that's a giddy eight tons of water every second, nearly five hundred tons, half a million litres, a minute. If I lose control, I'll be catapulted through in flailing helplessness which, for a pilgrim, would be very bad karma.

Well, it's been an honourable effort. I beat a retreat back to the bank.

Over to Plan B, but with diminished gumption. I munch a Mars bar to summon up fresh energy, and select the stretch where the river is most wide and shallow, choosing a spot that's just above a deep pool. If I lose my footing, I'd rather be swept to where I can swim out, than to be bounced about the rocks amongst the rapids.

I take some time to read the water – looking for where surface smoothness hints at hidden depth, where swirls and boils suggest a lurking rock with fast water flowing round the sides, and observing from their colour which stones might offer a decent grip, and which are maybe treacherous with slime.

I step in, initially just over ankle deep, but immediately the force of flow surges to my knees. Turning to face upstream, I lean with both hands on my fishing rod, creating a tripod effect like Highlanders would do with their staffs back in the days before the bridges were built. I bend near-double, spreading my legs wide, partly squatting to keep the centre of gravity low, and forcing each foot down against the bulwark of a stone to block it from being thrust downstream.

Shuffling sideways like a crab, I move on outwards. The water surges almost to my waistline. It's not the depth, it's more the force that counts; yet I'm managing to hold ground. There's no returning now. I'm inching closer to the line of boulders, and as I come in beneath their welcoming lee, the torrent drops right off.

From this point on, it's just a dander to the bank. And this is Bridgit's country.

*   *   *

From the west, an unexpected burst of evening sunshine slants through a brief parting of the clouds. Be that as it may, the mist still lingers on the hills, and the wind has veered defiantly back east – where 'the fishing is least'. But to poach the Grimersta is a ritual, a patriotic duty. Like John Buchan's character making a similar point, this is my John Macnab moment. Were there even a remote chance of catching anything, I'd tie something serious. In this heavy water it would be a Muddler, a bushy Hairy Mary or a Stoat's Tail. If the sun came back, a Blue Zulu on a dropper for the sea trout; otherwise a Bloody Butcher, or even a spidery Black Pennell if the light got worse. It's the way that a fly moves in the water as much as what it looks like that matters. But these conditions are a joke – so, just for the fun of it, I'll choose a fly with poaching *attitude*. A solitary Jock Scott – the tartan soldier of the fly box – rarely one we used in my day, though no doubt some would swear by it.

I tie it on with eight-pound nylon – rather light. On the Eishken lochs, Christopher would say, 'always double figures'. But this is just a wee trout rod, and with a trumpet fanfare running through my head, I cast it out upon the glorious Grimersta. I'm a dab hand now from yesterday's practice, and with a few flicks of the wrist, I'm reaching to the other side. The line arcs to a graceful curve as I draw it back across the current. Beautiful! You could argue that fly fishing is perfected spiritual practice. The one-pointed awareness, as you attend a rise. The vigilance of kundalini, coiled to strike. And every cast, a mantra. Yes, here I am! Standing on these banks that the very Masters of the Universe, the men who built the Empire, have dreamt of as their earthly compensation – albeit prior to karmic retribution kicking in. And the solitary burden on the conscience of yours faithfully – a mere half hour of *poaching* – is one that the island's foremost men of the cloth have assured us is no sin.

We used to get them coming to the house, the shooting and fishing set. Dad specialised at drawing hooks from out of thumbs and ears. The trick is to press down and depress the barb, before you tweak. Anaesthesia is handy too – both for patient and, especially, doctor – at seventy per cent proof. We had a couple of guests drop in every year from Grimersta. 'Drinks-before-dinner', as they'd say. The Farlow-Joneses, they were called, and I think that Claude was 'in the Stock Exchange', as they'd say, like we'd say we were 'at the peats'. I remember Virginia's description of the old Grimersta Lodge – its rusty bedsteads, fusty counterpanes, peeling wallpaper and clanking lavatories – never 'toilets' – flushed by chains with swinging truncheon handles, and ball-cocks that would hiss and splutter from on high, all night long.

My mother was incredulous. These were the richest people in the land. Why such affections of impecuniousness?

'But that's what they love about it!' said Virginia. 'It reminds them of their days at boarding school.' It reminded them of all that many of them ever had as a home.

Apparently, the place was riddled through with petty rules. A particular chair was reserved for some old buffer, with hell to pay for trespass. Meal times were strictly regimented, and after dinner, the ladies would withdraw while the 'boys' settled down to port, cigars and telling 'damned good stories'.

'You see, Jean, they like being told what to do. They want to know exactly where they stand.'

There were tiny shibboleths, codes of conduct that communicated in-group norms and status, in the most understated ways. You'd have to be in the know, to know; and those who don't know, simply don't know any better. Never do up the bottom button of your waistcoat, especially not Etonians. One never tips one's soup bowl towards one; and if one dribbles, one dabs it with a napkin, never a serviette. Some gentlemen came faithfully each year, with their fishing wife. Others, it would be quietly noticed, brought their fish wife.

I cast my way down the best stretch of the river. Not a rise to Jock Scott. Half an hour is quite sufficient. The dastardly deed is done. That's me good enough initiated. I'll now await my summons from Grimersta Lodge. Mind you, there's a sporting charm I rather like about these folks. As like as not, 'Drinks-before-dinner?'

My adrenalin surge has lost its oomph and the weariness is creeping back. Although the lower ground has cleared of mist, the weather's showing signs of closing in again. The wind is rising, tugging at my jacket in that lonesome manner. I guess it must be mid-evening. The sky is darkening, and I sense another stormy night ahead. With only Seumas' brief description to go by, it might be challenging out here to find the Rubha Leathann.

I dismantle the rod, and wander on. The semblance of a path leads me past the boathouse that is on the opposite bank, and, from there, I veer off on a compass bearing north-east. The lochs and land round here are aligned in troughs and wrinkles that mostly run north-west to south-east. I cut across them at right angles, up and down, making for Loch an Earbaill as the next main landmark.

Walking, walking, and inwardly I'm wrestling with this island. The heavy tangle of religion that takes its accent from imperialism. That violent religion, again, of violent men of violent times. How can any supposed Christian preach fear, I'm wondering, when Jesus said so often: 'Fear not'? Or when John, the beloved apostle, said that 'Perfect love drives out fear, because fear has to do with punishment. The one who fears is not made perfect in love'?[1]

Oh yes, there are countervailing texts in the Old Testament, but Jesus – if one wants to give him any credence in the matter – made an explicit point of sidestepping these. Early on in Luke's gospel, he reads his mission statement from Isaiah.[2] It's all about the liberation of the oppressed and those who life has bruised. What's rarely noticed is that he stops, dead, halfway through Isaiah's second verse. Had he carried on, the very next line would have proclaimed 'the day of vengeance of our God'. But he didn't carry on. Luke records: 'And he closed the book . . . and sat down.'

How, then, could Calvin have portrayed a God 'armed for vengeance'? How, then, could Alexander Macleod have taken such delight in kindling the fear of divine retribution amongst his Uig parishioners? How, then, under the *Dieu et Mon Droit* that every British citizen carries on their passport cover, can the United Kingdom justify a fleet of Trident nuclear submarines with names like HMS *Vengeance*? One wonders, sometimes, if angry men project onto the world an angry god; and if so, at what price to love?

The poet Derick Thomson, like so many Hebrideans of the twentieth century, wrestled with this legacy of a wrathful representation of god. His short poem, 'Although Calvin Came', testifies to an underlying island spirituality; to a love that maybe still runs deeper than the injuries.[3]

> Although Calvin came
> he did not steal the love out of your heart:
> you loved
> the tawny moor, and suffered pain
> when that land and the flower were taken from you,
> and a coffinful of songs was laid in the earth.

But now the Grimersta has dropped far out of earshot. I shuffle on amongst the heather, over hillocks and down through little hollows. An old tune known as *French* comes humming through my head. And with it, words from a Scots paraphrase of the Psalms that was written down in 1615 – ironically, straight from the tradition of John Calvin and John Knox.[4]

> I to the hills will lift mine eyes,
> From whence doth come mine aid.

From whence, indeed. And there's the question: *How, today, might we sustain the love not stolen from the heart?* How, given the traumatic scarring that we carry, and that they in their time also carried, even more so? How, when often it would feel so very much more *satisfying*, just to go down to the market, buy that AK47, and *shoot the bastards to Hell?*

*   *   *

Sometimes only stories, preferably real-life stories, can point a way to hope beyond dehumanisation. Around 1911, the Rev. Kenneth Macleod of Eigg wrote 'An Clachan a bh' ann' – 'There Was a Village'. To the best of my knowledge, it has never been published in English, but my dear friend and Gaelic cultural mentor, Catherine MacKinven, made me a partial translation.[5] It starts with a reference to the Act of Proscription, the so-called 'Disarming Act'.

> After the defeat at Culloden in 1746, the Clachan, the village, was like the rest of Gaelic-speaking Scotland, 'in a stir and troubled.' The 'wise men of London' decreed to strip the Highlanders of their traditional kilted attire, saying: 'We'll put trousers on the Gael, we'll take every sword and musket from them . . . so these wild men will become as meek as lambs.'
>
> Troops of English redcoats were sent to implement the new laws. A contingent was posted to the Clachan, the village, about which this tale is told, 'and by their way of it, because of their love for the people . . . they were in no hurry to leave.'

> However, in the course of his duties, the second in command fell down a cliff while searching for hidden treasure. His commander knew that there was a custom in the clachan to sing *tuireadh*, elegiac laments, over the dead. He called for those who performed such ceremonies.

> The three women came, politely, seemingly respectfully, and with tears in their eyes. But the song they sang in Gaelic had the words:

> > The Englishman has gone.
> > He's covered in fire that will never be quenched.
> > We'd be happy if the rest went the same way.

This pleased the commander, for he could not understand their language. He could only understand their tears, and gave them each a silver coin.

But as the women left, conscience struck them. Their position had been terribly conflicted. They had loved the Englishman, but deplored what he represented. 'God forgive us,' said the first woman. 'This is no night for mockery and our beloved man in deadly danger.'

'Hurry,' said the second. 'It would hurt me all my life if our beloved man (*fear ar gaoil*) should go without a *tàladh* (a death lullaby) in his ears or heart. It would be our loss, not his – the blessings of the poor are a *tàladh* and a pillow for him.'

They hastened back up the hill to the big house where the body was laid out. '*Gu Shealladh an àigh!*' said the third woman, who had the double sight. 'The door is closed – the soul is still within the body!'

They went in softly, sat by the bed, and began to sing:

You are going home tonight to the everlasting home,
to the house of autumn, spring and summer.
You are going home tonight on the sounds of the chant,
white angels awaiting you on the banks of the river -
God the father at your sleeping,
Jesus Christ at your sleeping,
God the Spirit at your sleeping.
Sleep softly. Sleep softly. Sleep softly.

His eyes were closed, the door of the soul was opened, his spirit took the road of the fathers to the sea and to the other side of the horizon.

'I will go,' said the first woman, 'and in the name of the Trinity I will bake a *bonnach* that will keep him right on this journey.'

'I'll do the same,' said the second. 'I'll prepare a lantern that will brighten his steps.'

'And I will take the three coins that we were given to the *Gobha*,' said the third, 'and he will make of them a key that will open the door of Paradise for our beloved man – *och nan och èire* – I grieve that he is no longer with us.'

The women took the contradictions of their lives, melded them to the contradictions of their oppressors' lives, and through redemptive sympathy, fashioned them to food, and light and to the Gobha's holy key.

Here is the triune weave of smithcraft, poetry and healing – the qualities of Brìghde – she who 'turned back the streams of war'. Alexander Carmichael wrote:[6]

Bride with her white wand is said to breathe life into the mouth of the dead Winter and to bring him to open his eyes to the tears and the smiles, the sights and the laughter of Spring.

So beauty boils over. So spirits walk. So articulation is restored between the inner and outer worlds; and the spiral of violence, thrust into reverse.

I must press on. Her sheiling should be close by in these moors.

Because the land is corrugated in long ridges, it forms a row of dipping bays along the shores of Loch an Earbaill. I pick a listless way across their sand and stony beaches. The wind is gaining force again. Rain clouds closing in. Dusk begins to settle. I want to get the tent up while it's still dry. Getting cold and weary – weary, weary. Come to think of it, not had a drink since Loch a' Sguair. I kneel down, cup hands to sup, and feel the run of water through my fingers, its cold trickle down the backs of my wrists. Such a very basic thing to do. Such animal survival.

I'm musing how I've morphed the meaning of this place; how I've assumed it to be Saint Bridgit's Sheiling. But Seumas never mentioned any saints. All he'd said, was *Bridgit's Sheiling*. I asked him how he knew. He said the sappers' map showed the ground beside the ruin as Gearraidh Ghill Bhride – the 'garden' pastures of the sheiling of her *ghillie*, her servant. This area is littered through with hints of sanctity. It's not just all the sìthean place names. There's also a small hill where I crossed the Grimersta – Airde Gille Mhicheil – the Heights of the Servant of Michael. There's a loch of the same name. Gille Mhìcheil is Carmichael in English – as with that latter-day saint by popular acclamation, the collector of the *Carmina Gadelica*.[7] In the Celtic Church, Michael was important as the patron of protection. Here he is next door to Bridgit. What's more, the flooded stream that I encountered before the Grimersta flows out from Loch an Fhir Mhaoil – the 'tonsured man' – which is to say, the Loch of the Monk.

I count along to Earbaill's fifth bay, then cut up directly north into the moor. I'm trying to figure out which of several grassy bluffs might be the Rubha Leathann. These little cnocs are special places. To me, they're stupas of the moors. The dung of cattle seeking breeze has built into the soil a deep fertility. In the high summer, they're spangled through with sky blue flecks of speedwell, wild pansy or 'heartsease', and tiny eyebright with its flares of seashell-white that burst from out of a golden yellow nucleus.

I make my choice of crag, and start to climb. There is a kind of ladder, made of bedrock rungs, that ripple through the tight-set sward and give me a sound footing. On Iona, Saint Columba saw the angels going up and down between the Earth and heavens from a little hill like this. Unusually, it has two names that bridge between traditions: Cnoc an Aingeal, the Hill of Angels, and plain simple Sìthean.[8] Adomnán, the seventh-century biographer of the saint, said that, 'One should take notice of this story', for the angels 'generally came to him as he remained awake on winter nights or as he prayed in isolated places while others rested'.

Such gems show why it was that Celtic anchorites – the anchors of the soul between the worlds – would place their sheiling hermitages in lonely spots like this. Places of just God and Nature. They say that Brìghde would awaken on spring's laughter, and spread her flowery mantle out across the Earth. The cattle yielded milk, the maiden filled to motherhood, and after harvesting the fields, perhaps the *cailleach*, the last head of standing corn, would be left alone as if a kind of offering back. There was, too, the corn dolly – the *maighdean bhuana* or Maiden of the Stubble. Her virtue, on being fed to the animals, was passed on to the following year's crop. Then there'd be the weaving of the Bridgit's Cross, the ears of which would sometimes go into the next year's seedcorn. These traditions varied with locality, most of them are overlapping. Through them we glimpse the triune principles of life, death and rebirth; of the Maiden, Mother and the Holy Crone – the turning, through the ages, of the feminine face of God.[9]

A decade or so into the twenty-first century, an old Catholic priest from one of the southern isles said quietly to me:

> I don't have to go to a church as a Hebridean. I only have to go down to the shore, pick up a piece of the tangle, listening to the birds and talking to the sea. Brìghde was at the heart of our religion. The tide coming in was bringing her gifts. She is in charge of all that. We don't worship her – we wouldn't use the words 'to worship' for Brìghde – but we go pretty near it.

And I'm scanning everywhere for ruins. Walking, sunwise, around the top of the ridge, wondering if I've got the right one.

In 1883, when Carmichael told the Napier Commission about the 'joyous life' once lived around the sheilings, he lamented that 'the smoke of the whole people, nuns and all, now ascends through the chimney of a single shepherd'. He added: 'Should not these places be marked and held sacred for all time coming?'[10]

There's nothing to the south, or west, or north. East?

I peer over the edge, and – ohhh! ohhh! – *there you are, my beauty.*

I have found the ring of fallen stones. Saint Bridgit's Sheiling.

From here, the land slopes gently down towards the misted hills of Eishken that loup across the bottom of the horizon. I have clambered down the cliff, and crouch beside the formless blocks. These have lain here, undisturbed, for a very long time. Their once-sharp edges have now rounded down to softness, and mottled white and grey with lichen shrouds.

I am gazing at the lintel stone, so long and flat and very thin. This would have carried all the weight above the door. It rests, reclining in the grass, retired amongst the other rocks, unharmed by any force of human hand.[11]

And God said unto Moses: *If you use stones to build my altar, use only natural, uncut stones. Do not shape the stones with a tool, for that would make the altar unfit for holy use.*

Once, all but the little children would have bowed their heads on crossing underneath. Visitors would have paused, to call a blessing on the house.

I likewise bow my head, ask blessing, step inside the ring and kneel.

Such sweetness. Tenderness. Holy, holy, holy.

And then I notice. A fresh-sprung fern is pressing through a cleft against the lintel. Not bracken, but a flush of verdure such as I have not seen elsewhere in all my walking.

A line from a John Martyn song comes willowing across my mind.

You curl around me, like a fern in the spring.

And in George Bernard Shaw's *Joan of Arc,* the inquisitor puts it to the lass that God's voice sounds only in her imagination.[12]

'Of course,' she answers. 'That is how the messages of God come to us.'

The rain is coming on. I pull my hood in tight.

'I'm with you always,' says the voice in my imagination.

'Do what you have to do with people, but try to keep your heart open.

'Go easy on rocky old Calvinism.

'Don't use hard tools on rocks that need their time to smooth.

'Never forget . . .

'*I curl around you, like a fern in the spring.*'

And it's just me, Alastair, alone out here. At Saint Bridgit's Sheiling as the night sets in. Absorbed in skeins of textured mist that drift in folds across the far south-east.

Only the rain, a rising tide that whelms the quilted lichens.

I watch it trickle down in dribs and drabs through tiny written runnels.

Kneeling at the lintel in this ring of unhewn stones.

PART 3

HARE

The Hare Trail: Days 7–12, North Lewis

15

THE BAPTISM OF THE GODS

I am lying in a bed. Nights in white satin sheets that smell so freshly laundered. The walls too, ever so white. I am looking at an Artex-coated ceiling, mind floating in and out amongst its swirling scallop shells; drifting from one to the next, seeing shapes and patterns in the gaps that fall between.

I become aware that my fingertips are pulsing. They're puffy and ragged round the damaged nails. That wrangle with the Bog Monster was only five days back but seems so very far away.

My legs feel set in plaster, but slowly sleep is lifting from their deep fatigue. I become aware of flu-like aches, and then the fireworks show begins – racking my whole body with shooting pains that race up and down the veins like piranhas tearing clumps of jellied muscle.

'This is how it would be to wake up in hospital,' I think. 'How do I know I'm not?'

I stand up, and sway from side to side. It's like I'm drunk, or in a minor earthquake, or when you're back on land from days and days at sea, and think the boat's still moving underneath your feet. But it's only waves of bouncing bogs that I've been sailing on, albeit with a similar effect.

I lie back down, let the world steady, and as my mind more fully comes to, take stock by counting on my fingers. Days one and two were threading through the azure bays of Harris. Days three to six were over mountain trails that brought me into Lewis. Now it's the seventh day, Sunday, and my totem mountain hare is about to take off on its final lap, darting north amongst the people, wells and near-forgotten temples of the villages of what we call the West Side.

On Friday night, at Bridgit's Sheiling, I'd camped beneath the lee of the Rubha Leathann, close to the Sìthean of Murdo's Loch. The rain and wind came hammering in with a refreshed vengeance. It blew in under the flysheet, and soaked the line of dirty clothes that I'd laid out as a defensive bund to protect my sleeping bag.

I'd been swithering about the weekend, about the Sunday. The question had come up when back at Café Spirituel. Somebody had asked how I planned to spend the famous Hebridean Sabbath, when everything 'grinds' to a halt. 'No,' I'd suggested. 'That's the wrong idiom. It is *rested* to a halt.'

It put me on the spot. I didn't want to seem peculiar, afflicted by a rigid touch of fundamentalism, and yet, I had to tell them that I'd not feel comfortable to spend a Sunday marching with a rucksack through the villages of home. The good people of Falkland looked politely quizzical. David Lorimer rallied to my rescue. He said, in his sprightly way, 'That's interesting. It's because he's in the island's mental field.'

Both in the sense of organised religion, and in its sense of what it means to be a community, this island is a religious community. In one of his commentaries on Gaelic poetry, Ronald Black makes an observation, very true for Lewis and Harris, that, 'Throughout the twentieth century respect for the Sabbath, rather than for the language, remained the principal marker of Gaelic identity.' Professor Macleod of the Free Church put it this way in a newspaper column: [1]

It's not Sunday ferries that will eventually undermine us. It's the loss of Sunday itself, the one day in the week when we might have time to reflect on where we came from and what we ought to be. Such a Sunday made metaphysicians of crofters and fishermen. Today's Sundays turn lawyers and accountants into football hooligans.

You have to grant this to Lady Mary of the Seaforth Mackenzies. The strict observance that her evangelicals brought in was felt by some of the more lowly as a liberation. It was their employment protection policy. No longer could labourers and domestic servants be made to work seven days a week. Today, the native islanders accept that many tourists either don't care, or don't know any better. But for me, being from here, it's different. Folks would feel it kind of wrong if I went clamouring past their doors, regaled with all my clobber. The more devout would feel it cut across their sanctuary, as if I'd tramped through their gardens. At its worst, the island's Sabbath can be obsessive legalism, like stories of the cock being covered with a basket on the Saturday night to stop him getting at the hens until the Monday. At its best, however, it creates a sense of collective retreat. It punctuates the week by setting aside time for fallowness of mind and family togetherness. It shields against the pressures and bland sameness of a 24/7 world. What's more, some incomers and tourists are its staunch defenders too. These days, there's even a growing creed of militant atheist Sabbatarians.

For me? I try to mark some rhythm to the week. I don't fuss overmuch when away in 'Aberdeen'. But here? Well, I've not come back to bust the island's code.

Yesterday, Saturday, I had walked out from Bridgit's Sheiling. I'd laid the compass on the map and found my wayline slotted perfectly along the wrinkles in the land. All I had to do was follow in their folds.

After an hour, I came to undulating swathes of feannagan, densely overgrown with heather. They laced both sides of a little glen as V-lined wheals, just east from where the Grimersta had joined the sea. Once, there was a village there on Cnoc an

Ruagain, the hill directly overlooking Grimersta Lodge. Today's map marks it as a sheep pen. The people had been cleared when Sir James Matheson set up his sporting estate. The baronet had made his fortune in the Chinese Opium Wars. He purchased Lewis following the death of James Stewart-Mackenzie in 1843. Disraeli launched a scarce-disguised broadside at him in *Sybil*: 'A dreadful man! A Scotchman, richer than Croesus, one McDruggy, fresh from Canton, with a million of opium in each pocket, denouncing corruption, and bellowing free trade.'[2] One can imagine the type.

It had felt weird, when the time came, to step from the moor back onto a tarmac road. I had crossed another threshold. A rumbling lorry bounced past, with clanking chains that dangled off the back like a portcullis. A car whistled by, too fast to make eye contact with the occupants. Then another, and another. *A-zippp . . . a-zippp . . . a-zippp* they went, like fleeing blobs of colour launched from a firework. It felt like all the world was out of kilter, but it was only me.

I felt unsettled, slightly vulnerable, and I did up Osprey's scarlet rain hood to be more visible. I hadn't fully realised at the time, but on the moor, every step had been a dance of shifting balances. In contrast, every step along the road plodded off a Henry Ford production line. On the moor, it was a rhythmic world; my movements contoured to the shape of space around me. Time slipped by in no time, which was why I'd felt that on the winding path, no stretch was ever long. On the road, however, especially on the long straight stretches of a Roman ilk, the monotony of sameness put the brakes on half an hour to drag like half the morning.

Where a finger of the sea pokes in at Loch Ceann Hulabhig, I'd dropped my bag beside a gate and climbed a short, unsurfaced track, that leads up to Cnoc Dubh – the Little Black Hill. From there, two miles away on the horizon, the naked eye can just make out the Callanish Stones, like a brooding field of chessmen. Although these were set in place some three thousand years before Christ, they take the sun-wheel pattern of a Celtic cross. Close by, immediately back across the road, there's another ring of stones with only five remaining menhirs, transfixed as if in never-ending prayer. These are off the tourist route and clad in thickly bearded tufts of a creamy lichen. They're encrusted, too, with lightly hammered silver flakes of *crotal* – the symbiosis of a lichen and a fungus that was used to dye the Harris Tweed.

I sat down and faced the huddled congregation. There must be about a dozen of these outliers from Callanish. They keep discovering more beneath the peat. Perhaps the people then were like us now, with breakaways of breakaways from the established kirk. Being out, alone, upon the moors had been a time to stand apart. But by this time, I could feel the welcome pull of people coming back into my mental field.

Running through the exposed crags of Cnoc Dubh is a massive vein of snowy quartz. Seumas Crawford, who lives nearby at Garynahine, had shown me the evidence that it had been quarried thousands of years ago. You can clearly see the stepped ledges, pitted with opaque impact scars on an otherwise translucent rock. They look like whitened rings, the size of peas or lentils, where people from the age of stone and bronze had chipped away to get their knives and arrow heads.

My friend's pride and joy at this site is a both, on which he's worked for several years. The original had fallen prey to vandalism. A man who'd feared its reputation as a 'Druid's house' had linked it to the Devil, and wrecked it with a crowbar. Seumas had carried out the restoration. He'd used archaeological photographs to identify and number each stone, and return it with precision to its rightful resting place.

One afternoon, in the summer of 2003, I'd dropped by to offer a hand. There he was with his archaeologist's trowel, built like a shotgun cartridge and ministering to the stones with hands of wrestled leather. He has that gnome-like demeanour that is often seen in men who work mostly on their own, with elemental forces. I had come to see him as an elder figure; one whose qualities of presence speak as deeply as their purely technical skills.

He set me working, digging out the matted turf that concealed a stone pavement leading up to the dome. We'd laboured together for several hours, mostly in silence. At the end, he said he'd been surprised by how much I'd achieved, and at my deftness with the spade.

'I never thought you'd be up to it!' he said, in the voice of overdone flattery and the wry smile by which such outdoors men will often pass backhanded compliments.

'Me neither,' I conceded. 'Thought I'd been too long on the computer.'

I was struck by how much I'd felt that this was *wonted* work – work that is our 'wont' – deeply fitting to our nature. I'd hardly thought that the skill to wield a foot-spade like a hand-trowel – that delicate matching up of brain with brawn – remains ingrained from years and years of early experience. I had felt forgotten muscle patterns sliding back to harmony. It was my body, itself, in homecoming.

A funny thing happened as I dug, and pulled, and cut the twisted roots from out amongst the cobbles. Gaelic words and phrases, even images of people from the past, came flooding through my mind. It felt like a reversal of the long ebb tide of childhood. Returning on the flow were echoes of the Old Folks, still here and all-accepting. The feeling carried on into the evening. It was like when you've seen an epic movie, and it keeps on running in your mind, long after you've left the cinema.

There's a passage in the *Tao Te Ching*, the teachings of Lao Tzu, in which the sage observes:

The myriad creatures all rise together and I watch their return. Returning to one's roots is known as stillness. This is what is meant by returning to one's destiny.

That was what it felt like. Roots and stillness, back to destiny. And when we downed our tools that day, it was an ancient path that stood revealed, the stones still tightly interlocked.

Some years later, I mentioned it to Seumas – the way I'd felt a sense of voices of the Old Folks awakening in my imagination. All he said was, 'I know what you mean' – and that was quite sufficient. I haven't asked him, but I think he too would share in Nora Bateson's observation that *we don't know what we're inside of.*

On that morning of day three, when I'd walked up the 'Lost Glen' on the way to where I'd seen the mayflies dance, I'd briefly stopped to sit down on a mound. Some twenty minutes later, I realised that I'd left my sunglasses behind. I considered retracing my steps, but as my eyes by then were two full days habituated, and the sunshine was falling mostly on my back, I reckoned – rightly as it proved to be – that I could manage without. But it set me on a path of thought. It seems to me that the eyes, like the skin, become accustomed to strong light. It's as if they too take on a tan, though whether that has any medical basis, I cannot say. The loss had put me on alert for photokeratitis – a painful night-time scratchiness, that is caused by ultraviolet damage to the cornea – and in so doing, it set me thinking of how the Inuit made goggles to prevent snow blindness. They'd craft the shoulder bones of reindeer, the thin flat scapulae, incising them with narrow slits to limit the low and reflected sun's intensity.

It's hardly an original thought. Just one that's shaped from such experiences. But could it be, I'd wondered, that we limit down reality in much the same way?

Could it be that memory – the means by which we hold our place in time – resides in more than just the electro-chemical networks of the brain? That the deeper realms of memory and meaning are not so much like data on a hard drive, as accessed by the server of the brain from a web beyond constraints of space and time? That even notions from neuroscience and the new physics – such as the quantum brain, quantum mind or quantum consciousness – are perhaps just early inklings of a whole new flight of understanding, that joins up to theology?

Time, said Plato, is 'a moving image of eternity'. Could it be that memory is a peering in on what's already there?[3] And the second sight, a widening of the slits in mental reindeer bone; and that this is why the seers will say it's like 'remembering the future', and that it can go both forwards and backwards?

In short, could it be that everything that ever was, or waits to be, *just is*? Is that what we're inside of; we who, perhaps, also 'inhabiteth eternity'?

Just as E.F. Schumacher only used the term 'small is beautiful' twice within his book of the same name, so Gregory Bateson's *Steps to an Ecology of Mind* hinges on its title and that single line: 'Mind is immanent in the larger system – man plus environment.'

When I asked Nora that night in Glasgow why she thought that her father had not developed the concept further, she said she thought that he had been discouraged. He was in his last decade of life when his book was published. She thought perhaps his friends and colleagues had wanted to protect his memory. To have gone further down a mystic road would have challenged the dominant scientific view of what it meant to be a human being. This was based on the mechanistic biology of 'value free' science. Indeed, it had been none less than Gregory's own father, William, who had both founded and named the modern science of genetics.[4] One can imagine, too, that the implications of interconnection might have been unsettling for some of Gregory's upper class social circle, for whom empathy might not have been at top rank in the comfort zone. Einstein had shown that space and time are fluid. If the human mind was to be entertained as somehow 'immanent' – inner or intrinsic – to such a universe of relativity, then what might be the implications for prevailing mechanistic and materialistic theories of reality? The very notion of an ecology of mind would have lifted the lid on a sìthean into which few, with reputations worth not losing, would have wanted to take a tumble.

Just as Bateson's studies of schizophrenia and addiction explored dissociation from the world under the pressure of trauma, so traditions of the sìthichean do much the same.[5] However, the tradition does not stay stuck only at the level of mental illness. If we might take *Mary Rose* as standing in its carrying stream, the 'call' that she heard whispering from the holes of the ground on her island had two elements. On the one hand, there were sounds of tempestuous fury, 'horrible' and 'unholy'. On the other hand, vying with them was 'music of an unearthly sweetness' that sought 'to put a girdle of safety round her' and which, at the end of the play, carried her 'into the empyrean'.[6] She reaches, at last, the healing depth from which, as John MacInnes commented, 'comes the creative power of mankind'.

The function of the sìth and sìthean, says Michael Newton in a study of the bardic process, is 'a way of speaking about the creative process [that] can take our consciousness into a realm beyond the mundane constraints of time and space'.[7] In Celtic myth, this empyrean is variously the green world, Tìr-fo-thuinn (the land-under-the-waves), or Tìr nan Òg (the land beyond the setting sun). Across the great water, such realms belong to the ever-young, a cosmic homecoming, the end of all our *nostos-algos*. Here life's full bloom, its fullness of potential, its beauty, is reconstituted.

A good example from the early Gaelic literature is the *Immram Brain*, the Voyage of Bran. It was first written down in Ireland in the late seventh or early eighth century. A woman 'in strange raiment' mysteriously appears inside Bran's locked-down fortress. She brings a silver bough, a sure sign of her Otherworld provenance, and sings of mythic isles across the western wave.[8]

> A branch of the apple-tree from Emain
> I bring, like those that are familiar;
> Twigs of white silver on it,
> And crystal-fringed with flowers.

> There is an island far away,
> Around which sea-horses glisten;
> Pillars of white bronze are under it,
> Shining through aeons of beauty.
>
> Without sorrow, without grief, without death
> Without any sickness, without weakness;
> But sweet music striking on the ear,
> That is the character of Emain.

A quality of many of these early texts is their articulation between the 'pagan' worldview of the Elder Faith, and Christianity. The 'old' Testament is bridged to the new. In the *Immram Brain* the sìth are a heavenly host whose 'colours glisten with pure glory'. They minister from out of timelessness to a human world decayed 'by greed and lust'. Far from being in competition with Christ, they anticipate a Christian redemption of the world. The *Immram Brain* continues:

> We are from the beginning of creation
> Without old age, without consummation of earth;
> It is a law of pride in this world,
> To believe in creatures, to forget God.
>
> A noble salvation will come
> From the King who has created us;
> A white law will come over seas,
> Besides being God, He will be man.
>
> He will delight in the company of every fairy-knoll
> He will be the darling of every goodly land;
> He will be a stag with horns of silver,
> A speckled salmon in a full pool.

Professor John Carey, an Irish-American who is a leading Irish-Welsh medievalist, holds that such texts achieved a remarkable 'imaginative reconciliation' between the traditions. Here the sìth and all their pantheon reflect 'not devilish trickery and evil magic, but the perfection of human nature as God had first created it'. As far as he is aware, this defence of the old religion is unique in the literature of medieval Christendom: 'an idea of brilliant originality, startling boldness, and beautiful simplicity'.[9]

Carey calls it 'the Baptism of the Gods'. Here, 'eternity is always present at the heart of time – or, to express the same thought in other language, Eden is always present at the heart of the fallen world'. The literature puns consciously on the double meaning of *sìth* and *sìthean*. It points towards 'the peace that passes understanding'.[10]

Why, in the greater scheme of things, does any of this matter? It matters, because the imaginal realm *is* the greater scheme of things. The pagan Celts were, as one of the early texts puts it, 'faithful to the truth of nature'.[11] Only too much narrowing of the slits in reindeer bone; only an excess of separation, of disarticulation from the inner life, or of 'sin' in traditional vocabulary, has closed the eyes of mortals and closed us to the underlying truth of Eden – thereby perpetuating violence in the world.

Human beings and the cosmos, the tradition tries to show, 'are portions and versions of one another'. That is what becomes visible as the slits open, the light gets in, and time starts to fall away in the course of 'the world's passage into eternity'. As such, Carey concludes, the ecology of the planet and the soul of humankind cannot be separated. 'If we hope to escape from spiritual death, this hope must be indissolubly bound to the survival of the world of which we are a part.'[12]

And that is where I left it at, as I came back down the track from the restored 'Druid's house' at Cnoc Dubh. Ecology emanates from the cosmic imagination. Imagination leads back to ecology. That's the ecology of the imagination, and it differs from what Gregory Bateson had tried to say about mind only in the reach, and the cultural antecedents, of its conception. Perhaps, too, in its implicit sense that the imagination is the counterpoint of materialism. Imagination is much more than neural pathways in the brain. It works with them, channels through them, but is ultimately born of soul.

I climbed back over the gate, heaved Osprey into harness, and carried on along the main road towards the first of the West Side villages. I had only gone a little way when I came across a wondrous sight – a *sgiobadh* – a communal work crew, cutting peats for the next winter's fuel. Half a dozen men and women were on the moor, chattering and laughing as many hands made light. As one would slice a square of tar-black ooze with the *tairsgear* – an L-shaped peat iron – another would hurl it up from the trench onto the heather bank to dry.

I thought of going over for a blether. Very likely, around here, they'd be some of Agnus' cousins. But I felt a shyness on me. I wasn't ready yet for social immersion. I carried on, over the Blackwater bridge and up to the white expanse of Garynahine Lodge. As I went, so many things were clicking hyperlinks of familiarity within my brain. My mother told me the story that when the Stornoway contractor, Willie 'Bucach', had completed our new surgery in the early 1960s, the work had been to a very high standard. Dad therefore recommended his firm to Captain Neil and Betty Perrins of the lodge, and of the family that made Lea & Perrins Sauce.

When the work was finished, the Captain said: 'Look, Willie. I know that you're a poacher. But to thank you for all you've done, I'm going to send you to the hill with a keeper and let you bag a legal stag.'

So, off went Willie with the stalker; and when he came back with a stag in the bag, the Captain said: 'So how did it feel, not to have to be a poacher for once?'

'Ach!' said Willie, 'To be honest, Captain, it wasnae the same at all.

'You see, if when you're going out, every rock doesn't look like a stag; and if when you're coming back, every rock doesn't look like the keeper – then there's just nae the same fun in it.'

Two miles on from the lodge, I reached the Callanish Stones. Been there, done that, so many times before, so I made a beeline for a hot meal in the Visitor Centre. I went into the gents, glanced in the mirror, and, *Oh my, oh my! That is some weirdo!*

My hair that hadn't seen a comb for days was whipped to a storm of curls, and my beard gnarled like lichen. My face had lost the muscle tone that social interactions normally compose. I looked as if I'd just been pulled from out of the Hill. When I went back out and nobody was looking, I quickly snapped a selfie so I'd not forget.

I headed on, up through the Stones, and there in the central circle was a woman from America, who asked if I would take her photograph. She wanted to be lying down, inside the burial crypt, pretending to be dead.

I took the camera and she lay down in her slacks and red shell jacket, grinning in the way that archetypal American tourists are archetypally meant to do.

'Stop smiling!' I chastised. 'You don't look dead enough.'

She grimaced. I snapped. We laughed at our tomfoolery. It was just ships passing in the night, but pleasing in its fleeting human warmth.

I walked on, through Callanish, towards Breasclete; and by now my legs were seizing up with gravity of lassitude. A dreary ache was in my bones as if a bout of flu was coming on. At Zimmer speed, I passed some modern buildings by a war memorial. There was a belfry with no bell – common in the Hebrides, an architectural throwback to when the Calvinists threw them down in Geneva to melt into weapons[13] – and a sign outside, that said: 'Callanish Free Church'. Further on along the road, beside a children's swing park that has no lock on the gate, there's another sign:

Welcome to Breasclete
Play area
Open: Mon. to Sat.

At the Stones, I'd finally made up my mind to take the Sabbath as a day of rest. Conveniently so, given how my body's giving up the ghost: but as they say, 'The Sabbath was made for man; not man made for the Sabbath.' The Visitor Centre staff had been very kind, and had helped me to track down the one and only remaining bed and breakfast room in the area for the weekend.

I turned off, right, at the foot of a hill. It seemed to take forever, grinding up the brae in bottom gear. My attention flagged, I went into a daze, and only when I neared the top did I realise that I'd walked right past the gate when halfway up.

A welcoming local woman showed me to my room. And that was how I came to wake up here this Hebridean Sabbath morning – with these satin sheets, these snowy walls, and the pilgrim scallop shells that swirl across the ceiling of the Loch Roag Guest House.

16

THE GREAT COSMIC POACHER

I'm just lying here in this comfortable bed, having a long lie on this, day seven, and watching how the Artex patterns shimmer into one another. I've come nearly two-thirds up the island since setting off from Saint Clement's. As for Saint James of the scallops, what providence it was that, after being martyred at Herod's sword, his scallop-encrusted body washed up on the shores of Galicia in north-west Spain. What beauty that they call his pilgrim paths, the *Camino de Santiago de Compostela* – the Pilgrim Path of Saint James of the Field of Stars. Where else, but in the Celtic world, might a suitably qualified sgiobadh of bards have been found to weave such a story together? And to think that it all starts off in Harris, with the emblematic shell to prove it, carved into the hunchback warrior's tomb.

I care little if these stories are embellished, as might be so for so much of religious tradition, including parts of the scriptures themselves. Unless we're in an academic mode, we miss the mythic point if we try to drive too sharp a wedge between fact and fable. I care mainly that they speak truths of the heart. There are at least four Jameses in the gospels and the distinctions tend to blur. Our scalloped friend is James the Greater, patron saint of pilgrims. However, in my state of reverie he jogs me on to James the Just, brother of Jesus. Tradition holds that he authored the *Epistle of James* that appears near the end of the New Testament. I love that little book, and the Dalai

Lama loves it too. In a rousing commentary, the Tibetan leader writes:[1]

> As I read the lines of this *Epistle of James,* I am struck by the similarities between this beautiful letter in the Bible and some of the texts in my own Buddhist tradition . . . It teaches us how to bring our spiritual vision to life at the highest level . . . It reminds us to relate to fellow human beings at a level of basic humanity . . . What matters most is basic warm-heartedness.

Strangely, for one who otherwise promoted the unerring authority of the Bible, Luther wrote James off as 'an epistle of straw'. He said that it has 'nothing of the nature of the gospel about it'.[2] The epistle is all about spirituality, the life of the soul. Luther, like Paul before him, was trying to structure a religion, a collective and even a politicised expression of faith. For Luther, 'justification' (or being made good in the eyes of God) is *sola fide*, by faith alone. This he held to be 'the article with and by which the church stands'. However, possibly to rein in some of Paul's slight excesses, Saint James tweaked a spanner in those works. 'Show me thy faith without thy works, and I will show thee my faith by my works,' he said, adding for good measure, to put it in the vernacular, 'Faith without the kail is dead.'

Neither did James teach eternal suffering for the Damned. Instead, he said, with crisp compassion: 'Anyone who has committed sins will be forgiven.' That didn't mean he let the selfish off the hook. Mean-mindedness attenuates the soul by self-destruction. It follows that, 'As the sun rises with its scorching heat and withers the flowers of the field, so the rich, in the midst of a busy life, will wither away.'[3] As for conflict, James the Just gave no quarter to 'just war' theory. He went directly to the roots of violence, asking: 'These wars and fightings among you, where do they come from? Do they not come from your cravings that are at war within you?'[4]

And I'm lazing in this Sabbath morning's easy peace. I'm musing – *do they not, indeed* – while far away, war in God's name is waging all around.

'It's very simple to explain the idea of Blair the Warrior,' said John Burton, the author of *We Don't Do God: Blair's Religious Belief and Its Consequences*.[5]

'It was part of Tony living out his faith.'

Burton had been Tony Blair's local political agent for more than two decades. He knew him very well, and saw the Prime Minister's motivation in leading the country to war as disarmingly self-evident. 'Tony's Christian faith is part of him, down to his cotton socks. How can you understand his thinking on any front if you don't understand his core beliefs?'

Blair 'believed strongly,' continued Burton, 'although he couldn't say it at the time, that intervention in Kosovo, Sierra Leone – Iraq too – was all part of the Christian battle; good should triumph over evil.'

It is as if Blair, for all the avuncular exterior, shares what the historian, Richard Hofstadter, called 'the paranoid style in American politics', a trait of 'heated exaggeration, suspiciousness, and conspiratorial fantasy'. In contrast to the clinical paranoia of an individual, a leader's political paranoia is 'directed against a nation, a culture, a way of life whose fate affects not himself alone but millions of others'. In America, it has been argued that it goes back to the siege politics of the early Puritan settlers – battling with the Indians, with the witches at Salem, or with Catholics, Communists and all manner of un-American activities. It is as if, suggests Richard Parker of the John F. Kennedy School of Government, the violent religious politics of late seventeenth-century Britain continued to play out on in the amphitheatre of the New World. Donald Trump is a case in point.[6] Sometimes, you have to wonder – like the picket-fenced obsession with property rights, and the need to carry guns – if unresolved anxiety lurks at the heart of it all.

Be that as it may, on 15 February 2003, one million of us marched in protest at the war on Iraq. The police described it as the UK's 'biggest ever demonstration'.[7] It failed to have any impact on the launch of Operation Iraqi Freedom, with US and British forces spearheading the invasion. One month into the war, I happened to be invited to a dinner with two serving generals of the British Army. I'd known both for a number of years. There could have been no other topic of conversation; but what riveted me was how the more senior man shared, with complete candour, his feelings that had come about once the political decision had been made to substitute diplomacy with war. It had torn at his conscience as he had set about ordering massive assaults, inflicting heavy enemy casualties.

'I have not seen the intelligence that Blair claims to have seen,' he told us. 'If it turns out that Saddam has no weapons of mass destruction, then Blair will have led us up the garden path.'

Out on the battle front, even as we were finishing our dinner, his men were killing and being killed. But this was no callous calling 'Forward!' from the rear, 'as the front rank died'. This was just one human being living out the Mythos of his time; caught up in the Myth of Redemptive Violence – the idea, perpetuated by any 'domination system', that violence can redeem violence. That petrol can put out the fire.[8]

'*Up the garden path*,' I whistled. 'But would that not make you – a war criminal?'

Our poor hostess visibly flinched. Chatham House Rule, for sure, but I'd stepped on the edges of decorum.

'That is something I take very seriously,' the general said, in a premeditated tone that put the table back at ease. It was as if he welcomed an opportunity for shared reflection. This man was of a military vintage that had a deep respect for the Nuremberg Principles; a generation that had been born into the world of a time when German officers were being hanged by allied forces under Nuremberg's provisions.

Principle I: Any person who commits an act which consti-
tutes a crime under international law is responsible
therefore and liable to punishment.

Principle IV: The fact that a person acted pursuant to
order of his Government or of a superior does not relieve
him from responsibility under international law, provided
a moral choice was in fact possible to him.

He had therefore gone in person to see the Attorney General to
seek assurance that the orders handed down from Number 10
were legal. Neither was he alone, at his level of command, in
having knocked on Lord Goldsmith's door.

'But you still felt ill at ease,' I said. 'So *why* did you issue the
orders? Why did you not . . . resign your commission?'

'Because . . .' said this dear man, wrestling with an enormity
of events that left him humbled, 'I was placed in a position
where I had to make a moral decision. Did I obey my own gut
feelings? Or did I obey orders from my own democratically
elected Prime Minister?'

In my experience, the military's use of 'just war' theory is more
than merely a mechanism to justify war. The military strategist
Carl von Clausewitz famously gave the definition that 'war is
thus an act of force to compel our enemy to do our will'.[9]
Without constraints, war would become 'absolute war'. Such is
the ever-so-logical endgame that Saint James understood to be
the outcome of unrestrained 'cravings that are at war within
you'. The military are acutely conscious of the need to limit
war. They hold nuclear keys. Time and again when I've spoken
at defence institutions, I've been told afterwards: 'You remind
us of the limits.'

I'm happy to play along with that, but I also suggest that
there is a spectrum of power's expression. Spiritually speaking,
the name of the game is to shift along that spectrum. It starts
with hard force, or as the military would say, the 'kinetic'

expression of power by weaponry. It moves to the soft force of persuasion by sub-lethal measures such as sanctions. From there, it moves to the psychology of convincement – the process of 'winning hearts and minds' (and even being open to being won). Lastly, and what I seek to point towards, the spectrum gets to the spirituality of transformation. That is where the full power of nonviolence comes into play. But the process has a ratchet. You can't just say, 'We'll try nonviolence, but if it doesn't work, we'll slip back to pulling a gun.' It has to work from an inner place of integrity, if need be to the point of sacrifice. Such is the mystery of the cross.

Here, at the end of the spectrum, the aim 'to compel our enemy to do our will' dissolves into a two-way process. The endgame becomes one of building relationships based on respect, fairness and helping one another to satisfy, not cravings, but fundamental human needs. This can only happen in a spirit of cultivating empathy. Power shifts from 'power over' to 'power with' to the deep 'empowerment' of spiritually-resourced power from within. Here is where the teachings of Jesus become such a rich contribution to the table of world faiths. 'Love your enemies, do good to them which hate you.' When Peter swiped his sword at the high priest's servant's ear, Jesus stuck it on again, symbolically restoring the enemy's capacity to hear.[10] There is transformative method, not just incredulous magic, in the seeming spiritual madness.

What about the few passages where Jesus appears to countenance violence?[11] When he said that he came to bring 'not peace, but the sword', he is warning, using metaphor, that his teachings will unsettle the Roman peace of those who guard the status quo, especially within families. When he turned over the money-changers' tables and fashioned a whip to drive 'them' out, the Greek is ambiguous, but modern translations point towards it having been the animals lined up for sacrifice that were driven out (thereby saving them). Their owners would have naturally followed. When he told the disciples to go out and buy swords, telling them that it was sufficient when they produced two, the passage that he quoted from the Hebrew Bible reveals it was explicitly to fulfil the prophecy that he would be perceived as a common brigand, the lowest of the low.[12]

All of these passages show that Jesus was challenging power, to the point of direct action in civil disobedience. None suggest that he endorsed violence against the person, not even framed as 'just war'. The nonviolent witness of early Christians became central to how the faith was spread through the Roman Empire. Even while in prison awaiting their tortured executions, the martyrs looked for every opportunity to forgive and convert their captors. In their willingness to follow Jesus in bearing but not reciprocating violence, they taught the way of transformative love. Like my friend who suffered in Papua New Guinea, they confronted their assailants in a way that sought to 'touch their hearts'. The hope was to catalyse *metanoia*, a Greek word that is usually translated as 'repentance', but actually means the radical transformation of the mind from within.

The co-option of Christianity into 'just war' theory rests on later interpretations of what the cross was all about. Was the God of Christ violent, or nonviolent; and if the former, in what ways does that legitimise our use of violence? Here the crucial question is – *Why did Jesus die?* The pivotal gospel text in answering this, is Mark 10:45 – 'For the Son of Man came not to be served but to serve, and give his life *a ransom* for many,' or as a text from Paul had it, 'as a ransom for all'.[13] This is called the Ransom Saying. In Christian theology, the million dollar question has been this. If human souls are *ransomed* – and if Christ died to pay the *ransom price* as 'an offering for sin' as Isaiah had prophesied – then precisely who might be the Ransomer of Souls?[14]

The question might seem arcane, but for its importance in understanding the religious dogmas (or teachings) that came out of trying to make sense of Jesus' death, and from there, to questions of how we should live, including 'just war' theory. Over each of the past two millennia, mainstream western

Christian thought has come up with a different line of answering the Ransom Question.

The first millennium's answer was the 'Classic' or *Christus Victor* view. The Devil is the Ransomer of Souls, and Christ, the ransom on the cross. Saint Gregory the Great likened it to a fishing trip. When Jesus died, the Devil, like a great sea monster, seized the tasty morsel thinking it an ordinary human soul, and plunged into the depths. As the Apostles' Creed has it, Christ 'descended into Hell'. At that moment, the Great Cosmic Fisherman struck. Only when it was too late did the Devil feel concealed within the barbed and burnished hook of God. In Gregory's own words: 'The bait tempts in order that the hook may wound. Our Lord therefore, when coming for the redemption of humanity, made a kind of hook of himself for the death of the Devil.'[15] The Devil, though not yet destroyed, is thereafter played out on a long cast. His power, though twisting and leaping, is at least held in check until the final showdown of end-times.

As for Gregory the Great, in my book that makes him the *Patron Saint of Poachers*. Which, joking apart, was precisely the problem. Come the second millennium, the *Christus Victor* theory of *why did Jesus die?* was facing two criticisms. To God, it attributed deception. To the Devil, too much power. Where might be found an alternative theory of 'the atonement' – the idea that Christ, in offering himself as the ransom payment, had 'atoned' or paid the price for human sin?

Enter Anselm, a monk from a noble family in Lombardy who, in 1093, was appointed Archbishop of Canterbury by William II, the brutal son of William the Conqueror. If the Devil was no longer to be Ransomer of Souls, who else was qualified to take the vacancy? There was only one other candidate in town. It had to be . . . old *Dieu* himself.

Anselm was a deeply pious man, but his framing of reality was profoundly feudal. To sin, he wrote, is 'to fail to render to God what God is entitled to'. God is entitled to our 'righteousness, or rectitude of will'. Our failure, since Adam, to deliver such fealty 'robs God of that which belongs to God, and thus dishonours God'. Without an honour code, the authority of the feudal hierarchy would collapse. Without fealty to God, the cosmic order would collapse. The only way to hold the show together, is that 'punishment should be inflicted'. However, God being a loving god, says: 'Receive my only Son, and offer him for yourselves.'[16] Through the sacrifice of Christ, human-kind was thereby spared eternal torment, and God's honour duly 'satisfied'.

This is therefore called the Satisfaction Theory of the atone-ment. If one goes into a church, and asks why a cross is on the wall, that would be the most doctrinally correct answer that most doctrinally correct western Christians would give. It is why many hymns contain lines such as these, which were sung in 1947 at the wedding service of the future Queen Elizabeth II:

> Praise, my soul, the King of Heaven
> To His feet thy tribute bring
> Ransomed, healed, restored, forgiven
> Evermore His praises sing.

Anselm's theory was pushed to its logical conclusion in the sixteenth century by the legally trained mind of John Calvin. 'We are all,' he said, 'offensive to God, guilty in his sight, and by nature the children of Hell.' Not one of us can examine ourselves 'without feeling that God is angry and at enmity with him', thus the context of God's being 'armed for venge-ance'. For the benefit of the Elect alone, however, Christ was sent to 'the bar of God as a criminal in our stead'. He 'inter-posed, took the punishment upon himself and bore what by the just judgment of God was impending over sinners.'

This, concluded the reformer, is 'what is meant and implied by *ransoming* us from the justice of God.' In this way, Christ's sacrifice 'satisfied and duly propitiated God the Father . . . appeased his anger . . . and by this tie secured the Divine benevolence.'[17]

Calvin's ramping up of Anselm's Satisfaction Theory is known as the Penal Substitutionary Atonement Theory. Such blood atonement theories remain at the core of most Catholic and Protestant dogma. They let God off the *Christus Victor* hook. God is exonerated from the charge of being the Great Cosmic Poacher. Unfortunately, especially in modern eyes and in the light of modern criminal cases, it puts God foursquare back into the dock, as the Great Cosmic Child Abuser. It normalises violence. Whether as crusader, jihadist or other holy warrior, such a psychology gives the political classes a sense of legitimacy in using violence to sort out a rotten world. Such a god must be a patriarchal hierarchy or else maternal wires might short-circuit the system. You'd only get some Brighde somewhere, turning back the streams of war. As for Mary – keep her as the patron saint of silent servitude, but not of no full-on Magnificat.

Is this what Jesus tried to teach? The theology of penal substitutionary atonement only adds up if the carriage of Christianity is drawn by an Old Testament warhorse.[18] However, Christianity is still a very young religion. There might be mileage further down the road, by which 'then spirits walk'.

At which point, it's time for me to walk. I rise, and with my land legs still awash, sway down the stairs and into the Loch Roag's dining room. Soon there's a rack of toast and two huge Stornoway kippers staring at me bug-eyed from a plate. I dig into one, and ask the waiter if he would be so kind as to wrap the other in foil for later. He obliges, with a 'Who would eat a cold kipper?' sort of courtly smile.

I'm wrestling with how to spend the day. It's one thing to respect the local Sabbath, to choose to take a welcome day of rest. But the done thing in these parts would be to go to church. I'm not sure I'd fancy the menu. There's no Quaker Meeting round here. The only option in the village is the Free Church – marked by the empty belfry.

Mind you, for all its conservativism these days, I can't help but feel a soft spot for the Free Church. It was the home of my Highland ancestors and the main denomination of the island folks who raised me. I cannot help but admire its origins. Donald 'Sligo' MacKenzie – the husband of Mary, on whose quinsy Great Uncle Jim had operated in Callanish in the 1920s – describes it in this way:[19]

> Until 1843, there was only the Church of Scotland. Unfortunately, the Church of Scotland in those days was governed and controlled by the landowners and ministers were appointed by them. Ministers said from the pulpit what the landowners wanted them to say – the very landowners who were driving the people off the land. That, of course, was the era of the Clearances, a time of great hardship for the people of the Highlands and Islands. Our oppressed people at that time decided to form their own church – the *Free Church of Scotland*.

And yet, they're called the Wee Frees, because of their insistence on Westminster Calvinism with its limiting sense of the Elect. Do I really want to spend the morning immersed in that?

Maybe it's just fall-out from the kipper – red herrings and all that – but wafting through my mind appears a red-robed Buddhist nun. We'd met when seated beside one another on an interfaith discussion panel that the Bishop of Edinburgh had chaired. Her name was Sister Candasiri. Her affiliation, the Amaravati Buddhist Monastery.

'I'm sorry,' I had to say, 'I've never heard of the Amaravati order.'

'Theravada tradition,' she said, and realising the trigger, said it with a twinkle in her eye.

'Theravada!' I said. 'You mean . . . the Wee Frees of Thailand?'

'I know!' she laughed, 'I know.

'But you see, when I first met them – ahhh – they were just such lovely people. I've been with them now for twenty years.'

She had grown up in Edinburgh. Like the bishop, she'd been a Scottish Episcopalian, a part of the Anglican family. However, Theravada had come to be her calling.

'You Buddhists!' I said, teasingly. 'You have this sense that everything's joined up. That we're all one, all part of the Buddha Nature. But tell me: where does that leave your prior belief in *God?*'

'*God?*' she asked, in feigned puzzlement, as if the answer wasn't blindingly obvious.

'It leaves me in . . . *total immersion.*'

O come on! I'm saying to myself, as I polish off the toast. *This walk is meant to be a holy pilgrimage. How about a bit of . . . total immersion?*

Better get a move on, then. The service starts in twenty minutes flat. I run upstairs, grab my coat, rush out the front door and almost bump into a dark-suited elderly man. He is, I think, of the family of the Loch Roag's owners. Evidently heading off to church, he looks me up and down. His demeanour tells me that he's wondering whether he should offer a lift to his near-assailant.

I'm too embarrassed to ask. Don't want to seem all 'holy' like. He doesn't want to cause embarrassment by asking. These days, you can talk about sex more comfortably than religion. In any case, I'm dressed more like a walker. He nods a little smile, gets into his little car, and trundles off down the hill at a suitably Sabbathly *vitesse.*

I've now got fifteen minutes, and near enough a mile to go. Off sets the hare, coursing at a suitably un-Sabbathly *vitesse.*

Pity. He'd have just loved it if I'd asked. Acceptance of, and acceptance by, the community and its ways. Had my plan been to go walking, then as likes as not he'd have gone out of his way to drop me off. 'Ah well, you see: you're in the islands now.'

Full speed, full stomach. A lift just lost to pride. And the kipper burps the way that kippers on the trot are prone to do. Up comes a sutra from Saint James' epistle.

Verse 4:10: 'Humble yourselves in the sight of the Lord, and he shall lift you up.'

Ouch!

It's such a lovely morning. The hills are veiled in rising wisps of vapour. The sun is almost breaking through.

Burp!

Verse 4:14: 'What is your life? For you are a mist that appears for a little while and then vanishes.'

And I'm vanishing as I go, full scarper down the road, kipper vapour in my train.

What had been a little flurry of slow-moving cars has passed me by and parked. The road's gone quiet and everyone's inside. The church that's by the war memorial, the church that has the belfry with no bell, now looms just several hundred yards away. And in a crazy flight of kippered fancy, Sister Candasiri's at my side. Her red robes hitched up high above her knees, she's hirpling along at quite some giddy rate.

She wants to know the story on the bell-less belfry. But part of me's not wanting to let down the side. Not wanting to push old friends into a corner, to leave no quarter for redemption from bygone violence, or ongoing reformation – even for rocky old Calvinism.

'Well you see, Sister, it's just where the past has left us stranded. I suppose the trick is to find new light by which to see new meanings.

'Perhaps to look up through the empty space, and see the sky, the moon, the sun and other stars.'

'Ah, so!' she says, quite breathlessly. 'I hear what you are saying.

'I have heard about this Hebridean Zen.

'I see you have . . . an architectural *kōan*.'

She means those gnarly riddles that the Roshis ask beginners. Questions that set up a clash between realities, supposed to trip the rigid mind out into deeper frames of knowing.

'Oh yes, Sister! Very nice way of putting it.

'Like – *what is the sound of one hand clapping?*'

'Ah, so!' she says. 'Applause! Applause!

'So now I think I understand, this Free Church *kōan* of yours . . .

'*What is the sound of an empty belfry chiming?*'

'Well maybe, Sister, maybe. Perhaps you'd better go and ask the minister . . .'

'Ah, so!' she says. 'But I like it very much.

'What church should need to have a bell, an empty bucket rattled?

'When God sounds from the Belfry of Creation.'

The doorman peers from out the porch. He takes a little walk around the car park, then takes a second look more pointedly in my direction. He's wondering if I'm walking to them, or past them. I raise an arm as if half-heartedly to hail a taxi. He returns a little wave, and draws back halfway out of sight in doorman's dignified decorum.

I stride in through the gates, shake the doorman's hand, and fast decelerate to seem at ease, if not a little odd, amidst the thirty or forty parishioners lined out on varnished wooden pews.

Oh dear, it's really not my scene. The Bible is carried in by a cohort of elders, all men in dark suits. The minister follows and takes up his place, not in a pulpit but at a lectern. But then Psalm 103 is first-off. I know it from the version that is sung by the Iona Community, derived from Taizé.

> Bless the Lord my soul,
> and bless his holy name.
> Bless the Lord my soul,
> he rescues me from pain.

The minister moves into an extemporary prayer. Not a script or note in sight. I have to admit, he has a fresh and cheerful manner. His words are simple, deep, and speak directly to the heart.

Next, Psalm 104. Verses eight to fourteen. Here is a God of Katie's world of immanence in all creation, the life force that unfolds into the grass that feeds the birds, the people and their beasts. A God of village wells, of Morag's world who 'sendeth the springs into the valleys, which run among the hills' and 'watereth the hills from his chambers'. And I'm starting to think – wait a minute – give me more such *total immersion!*

Then comes the sermon. Spotting that the congregation has a stranger in their midst, the minister explains that he's been working, week by week, through the Book of Job. It just so happens that they've got to chapter twelve – and I'm nearly jumping out of my seat. This is pretty much the most ecological, the most pantheistical – I beg your pardon – *panentheistical* chapter in the Bible. 'The tabernacles of robbers prosper' and those that mock God get rich. That's Job's sorry observation of the world that he was living in.

> . . . but ask now the beasts,
> and they shall teach thee;
> and the fowls of the air,
> and they shall tell thee.
> Or speak to the Earth,
> and it shall teach thee . . .

. . . because 'the soul of every living thing, and the breath of all mankind' is held in God's hands. The minister laments the fact that Job's full power of Hebrew poetry is lost in the translation. The prophets often turned into poets when doing their most full-on stuff. Here, he explains, is a book that explores unwarranted suffering at poetic depth. Prosperity, he tells his congregation – what the robbers store up in their tabernacles – is not to be equated with virtue. Neither is suffering to be equated with sin.

It's just too good to lose. This might be conservative evangelicalism, Hebridean-style, but it's certainly no American-type 'prosperity Gospel'. With probably a vain hope that I'll not be noticed, I whip out my pen and scribble down some notes – kind of a literary pinching of oneself.

'You must not judge a man's piety by his plenty, by what is in his hand, but by what is in his heart.' God is not a watchmaker who winds up the universe and leaves it to run down. Job shows that God is utterly involved in the unfolding of the Creation. 'By him all things consist.'[20]

Global warming, the financial crash of the past year, the scandal of the fraudulent expense claims of British politicians – *oh yes* – the tabernacles of robbers may prosper for a season; but in the end, God pours forth 'contempt upon princes, and weakeneth the strength of the mighty'.

We have neglected compassion for the orphan, the widow, the alien and the poor. The environmental crisis is a self-inflicted 'judgement' on our hubris. It is time that we faced up to spiritual bankruptcy. The God of love is *ravenous* for justice. God who, concluded Job, 'discovereth deep things from out of darkness'.

The service ended with Psalm ninety-two.

> How great are your works, O Lord!
> Your thoughts are very deep!
> The dullard cannot know,
> The stupid cannot understand this.

And I'm left pondering – who might have been the dullard? Who? Had I judged them only by their dogmas, only by the head and not the heart; and by my absence, missed such a sermon.

And I'd have missed lunch too! It had been Margaret, the wife of the Rev. Calum Macdonald of Callanish Free Church, who had welcomed me at the Loch Roag last night. She works there part-time as a waitress. After the service, they invited me with three of the elders back to their manse. We feasted on heaped plates of roasted island lamb, followed by a trifle, and sat around a peat fire and talked theology.

I'd raise a point. As often as not Calum would put the question to one of the elders, so everybody was kept on their toes. Atheism is a hot topic on the island, but we hit some rocky ground over the 'gay' issue. It was in the air because the Church of Scotland were debating it at their general assembly in Edinburgh that week. I said that we who are heterosexual should acknowledge difference, and in any case, Jesus had never said a single word about the issue. They said that Paul had carried the injunction over from the Old Testament to the New. I said that if we followed Paul's grounds for so doing, then we should also ban the island delicacy, the *marag dhubh* or Stornoway black pudding. The same Council of Jerusalem that had decided, after the death of Jesus, that Christians should uphold the sexual prohibitions of the Law of Moses had also carried forward the ban on eating products made from blood.

We could have gone on and on. We could have built it up into the *Marag Dhubh Controversy*. But it was a lovely fire that was blazing in the grate. I was mindful that the Law of Moses had also forbidden gathering sticks and the kindling of a fire on the Sabbath day. The penalty was death. However, Rabbi Abraham Heschel, one of the great modern Jewish liberation theologians, said that this means that, once a week, we should refrain from stirring up the fires of controversy. Just give each other a break. Listen for the voice of a deeper calling. Failure to do so leads to slow spiritual death. Good teaching, I thought, very good teaching. I drew back, from the head into the heart.[21]

There's something about spiritual energence that I call the First Love syndrome. Just like they say you never forget your first love, so it can be with how we first encounter religious doorways. For me, it's having a soft spot for the Hindu scriptures and the writings of Carl Jung, even though I've probably got blind spots to their foibles because of what they've otherwise given me. I suppose it's no different for Presbyterians with their Reformed faith. Calum would probably defend Calvin to the hilt. He'd probably think that I just get a little over-obsessed with sticking points like the Westminster Confession, or the Free Church's all-male ministry. For him, what led to convincement might have been some of Calvin's more sublime writings. For example, where the Genevan reformer said: 'Mankind is knit together with a holy knot . . . we must not live for ourselves, but for our neighbours.'[22] Raw spirituality may be God-given, but religions, at least in part, are fashioned through apprentice human hands.

'The old people of the island,' Calum told me, 'often say that there is only one quality in the human heart that the Devil cannot counterfeit.'

'The Devil?' I said, raising a liberal eyebrow.

'Yes. I've heard it several times. The old people in this community would say that there's only one thing he cannot fake.'

'And what's that?'

'We call it in the Gaelic, the *miann*. M-i-a-n-n.'

'Mee-an,' I echoed back. 'And what might that mean?'

I feel like I'm now cast as the stiff and starched George MacLeod, and that he's the Reverend Kenneth, on the brink of coming up with venison and honey.

'You could translate it as *ardent desire*,' he said. 'The ardent desire for God.

'The one thing in the human heart that the Devil cannot counterfeit, *is the ardent desire for God*.'

When the time came to leave, he asked where I was bound for in the morning.

'Up to Shawbost,' I said. 'To have a blether with . . . Doctor Finlay.'

To name the Atheist in Chief felt almost like a raising of the local demon.

'Well, he's been very busy recently, right enough!' smiled Calum. 'He's been on the radio this past week, arguing in favour of Sunday ferry sailings.'

'But I'll tell you something about Finlay,' he said, lowering his voice. 'There's more to Finlay than meets the eye.'

He explained that when he had got the call to the ministry, he'd been working in the Harris Tweed mill at the spinning machines. He'd lacked an academic background and didn't have the entry qualifications for the Free Church College. He tried to fill the gap, but failed some of the exams. He'd asked around for help, but needed lots of tutoring, and no-one had the time.

'But it was Doctor Finlay . . . and he didn't really have the time either . . . who came to my aid.

'If it hadn't been for Dr Finlay MacLeod, I wouldn't be the minister in Callanish today.'

17

SAGES OF SHAWBOST

Monday morning, day eight. It is dry outside with bright cloud and patches of sunshine. The wind is cold, having gone back into the south-east, but perfect for the twelve-mile hike north to Shawbost.

I've spent half the morning writing up my journal at the Loch Roag. Now, back on the road again, the cars are zipping past and Osprey's hood is blazing red for visibility. It takes me half an hour to get beyond the houses of Breasclete, then out onto a stretch of moorland that is etched with bygone peat workings. As I come up to the junction with the Tolsta Chaolais road a flood of lovely memories come in. This village was the birthplace of my old friend John MacGregor. He used to be the warden at the Gearrannan hostel when I'd bring my human ecology students there. He'd take us round, show us the ruins of the blackhouse where he was born, and explain the ways the village worked, the intricacies of interconnection. We'd drive on in the minibus to a lay-by. There, he'd impose a reverential silence, and with a chortle that was half in jest, half deadly serious, proclaim, 'How now, brown cow?' – and tell us of the dear old family friend that he'd buried there on the spot where she'd died.

People would be so attached to their cows. They were essential for the dairy economy, a gift of providence. A Scalpay seaman, Kenny Macleod, told me, 'I remember coming across a neighbour, who was an elder in the church, praying in his byre a couple of hours after we had buried their cow which had died in the field.' He added that people would have 'praying points' in the moor to which they'd go regularly, and that people of the generation to which John had belonged, those born in the early decades of the twentieth century, were immersed in a sense of 'total dependence on God and prayer to help with everyday things like food, safety and general activities'.[1] With some, this would play out in a very 'strict' way. Theirs could seem to be a joyless faith, thrawn with anxieties about salvation and devoid of 'worldly' song or dance. However, John was one who took things deep but with a joyous touch. The roadside shed in which he wove his Harris Tweed had a sign up outside: 'MacGregor's Boutique'. Inside, the walls were lined with whisky miniatures, and a placard that read:

Be not forgetful to entertain strangers: for thereby some have entertained angels unawares – Hebrews 13:2.

One day, in the early 1990s, the stranger who came unawares was Kenneth Clarke, the Chancellor of the Exchequer in the Conservative government of John Major. He chose his length of tweed for a suit, but only after John had cut it from the roll did the politician hit that endearing hazard of Hebridean holidays: he'd left behind his wallet.

John later said to me: 'Every time I see him on the telly wearing my tweed, I turn to Pat and say: *There's the man who balances the nation's books, but comes to my Boutique for credit.*'

I miss his cheery cherry-red face, his love of stories and of passing on traditions. And I miss his generous sharings of an Islay whisky called *As We Get It* – straight 'as we get it' out of the cask, undiluted. Such was his means of bootstrapping strangers unawares into angelic orbit, and that at 103° proof.

'How now, John MacGregor?' I utter, as a toast beneath my breath, and lay down Osprey by the road end: for this was where I had my very own uranium mine.

I was sixteen at the time, doing Higher physics at school in Stornoway. One day a geology PhD student came into the lab and asked to use the Geiger counter. He'd found a chunk of extremely dense black rock, with a dull metallic sheen and some yellow encrustation. The teacher, Donald MacKay, called us all round. He held the Geiger tube above the specimen. Sure enough, the radiation meter went three-quarters up the scale. It was pitchblende. Uranium ore. And as geology was my passion, I arranged to meet up with the impending PhD the following Saturday, and took the bus to exactly where I'm standing now.

The lode lay in an exposure of coarsely crystalline quartz and feldspar pegmatite. Near on forty years have passed, but I wonder if – just for old time's sake – I can still find the spot? I jump the fence, head up to one of several bare white outcrops on the hill, and there it is! The very spot. A neatly chiselled cubic hole, some several inches square. Material evidence for what had otherwise long since taken mythical flight in my fancy. I'd not left any of the pitchblende behind, but there are still some distinctive yellow traces of gummite, a secondary mineral of uranium. Here would hardly be the spot on which to sit for over long and rest the family jewels.

These days, an ethical geologist would never countenance such vandalism of 'a find'. But that was those days, and I have to say, what fun it gave me! At least, before the day it met its end in a municipal landfill site. I made my very own nuclear safe storage facility from a sheet of lead that I'd pulled off a disused sheep dip in Keose, and melted down in one of my mother's saucepans when she was out shopping. I made a mould out of two tin cans, one inside the other. Between these, I poured the mercurial liquid; and when it hardened and I'd stripped the cans away, I was left with a cylindrical encasement that proved thick enough to block even the release of gamma rays. It worked, just pure dead brilliant.

I proudly took it with me when I went off to study geology at Aberdeen in 1973. Barrie's Cameron never had such likes to supplement his Aberdonian studies. By then, to prove the claims of my very own Manhattan Project – the making of the Hebridean bomb – I'd bought my own ex-army Geiger counter. I'd bring 'the specimen' out at parties to liven things up. I kept it in the only storage drawer we had in our tiny hall of residence bedrooms at Hillhead. We'd sit up half the night listening to music – Mike Oldfield, Moody Blues, Pink Floyd and Barclay James Harvest – the latter with those lines to 'please lay down your pistols and your rifles' and to 'concentrate on what you ought to be'. And yet, for some reason, I was being very slow at finding any girlfriends.

One day, the lass I'd spent the best part of a year trying to coax, made a solemn announcement. 'I am never coming back into your room again.

'Not until you empty the drawer beneath your bed – of that *THING*.'

A little further on, I reach a loch with a herd of Highland cattle grazing by its side, and fish farm cages floating in the middle. There's a pickup by the roadside and I recognise the number plate – *TO 1 STA* – as in Tolsta Chaolais. Sure enough, from over the brow of a hill above a hatchery shed, appears an old school acquaintance, Alastair Fraser and his son Ranald.

Their weather-beaten faces convey the seasoned character that a life spent out of doors can impart. The youth must be in his twenties, and I can sense from his bearing that he doesn't suffer from confusion as to what it means to be a man, or just a human being, and to be finding his place in the world. Their business is to raise salmon fry in fresh water, then have them lifted out by helicopter for bringing on at sea.

'How are you surviving against the multinationals?' I ask.

'No problem,' Alastair replies. His father was 'Doc Fraser' – one of the best science teachers I'd ever had.

'We don't use chemicals. Never used them. Chemicals always let you down in the end. Good water flow and moderate stocking levels is the answer.'

The big companies, he explains, are greedy. That's why they get trouble. As far as possible his operation is organic. That gives a niche cost structure that makes it pay.

The two of them get back to work, I move on, but I'm struck by how the young man, who'd hardly said a word, had been so attentive to every nuance that had passed between us. I hear the old folks lament that the spirit of the past is dying out. Even we of my generation, after every village funeral we'll say to one another: 'There'll soon be no more of them left.' And we're right. There won't be. Not unless we pick up the baton and pass the spirit on, pass on the touch of blessing.

'How now, brown cow?' Don't forget what ground you're standing on. The game's not up quite yet.

I pass through Carloway, and up a long slow hill towards the Dalmore junction. Once the village in the glen down there hosted Teampall Dail Mòr. Its stones were robbed to build a house, sometime after the start of the Great War. Doctor Finlay's guidebook says: 'Between the two wars visitors came to seek it out, but the man next door told them, *Gone . . . Gone . . .*'

'Gone indeed,' adds Finlay, laconically.

Aye, Teampall Dail Mòr. Sacred to the memory of what was.

Onwards, and I'm coming in to Finlay's village, *Siabost* or Shawbost. A quick check on the phone, and its only half past four. There's time enough to drop in on my old friend, Kenny 'Leather'. He's an artisan, by his original trade, in all things made from hide.

It's always such a joy to visit Kenny, that I half skip down the brae and into the dip beside the bridge where he lives. His croft is a patchwork of feannagan. The West Side has a better micro-climate than where I've come from. Everywhere is planted out with cabbage drills, potato plots, flower beds and native tree nurseries. Threaded through them all is an eat-your-heart-out-Donald-Trump nine-hole golf course. On Google Earth it's even visible from space.

I knock three times upon the cottage door. There's some slow shufflings, the latch lifts, and a sleepy Kenny squints out through a narrow chink into the daylight. The poor man's been working the milk run on early morning shift, and I've woken him up.

'Alastair!' he roars, his beard wagging ivy trails. 'It'll be yourself! Wait till I get some clothes on. You go in and sit down by the stove.'

Soon the Raeburn is stoked up with peats and a whistling kettle set to boil. By many standards, Kenny lives in semi-poverty, surrounded by his tools and a few sturdy handbags and satchels for sale to passing tourists. But the leather-man doesn't do poverty. He does dignified frugality. Sufficiency without the need for surplus.

He offers me his best reclining seat. It's an antique dentist's chair with all the wheels and levers working. You have to mind out what he presses, especially – as I know from experience – when you're raising a tumbler of the amber liquid to your lips.

'And your pack?' he asks. 'You're hitch-hiking?'

'No. Walking. The sheilings, the temples, and the holy wells. You see, Kenny, I'm on a *holy pilgrimage!* Immersed in *God*, *war* and the *faeries*, the way one does, as you'll so eminently understand.'

Kenny wouldn't have much time for the Manhattan Project, but all the time of day for a mad hatter. 'I'm on my way to Doctor Finlay's, then this evening, up to Bragar to meet Catriona Campbell at the temple of Saint John.'

He lowers his voice to ceremonial register and sagely strokes the ivy. 'Ah . . . Teampall Eòin . . . or Cill Sgàire they also call it, from the Norse. You've not been there? I think that you will find it a very special place.

'And the wells, Alastair? You have been visiting the healing wells?'

'Only one so far,' and I tell him of the tussle with the Bog Monster.

'A rare privilege. A rare privilege, indeed! But it does not surprise me. You see, we have reached a time in history for the old wells to reopen. And they will be reopened. And some of them are *already* being reopened.'

The kettle starts to coo. He makes the tea, draws his chair more closely in, and shares experience.

In the 1970s, more than thirty years ago, he'd been an auxiliary nurse in the Lewis Hospital. In those days a special fridge of industrial proportions was kept in the duty room. It stored all manner of local delicacies: *Marag dhubh* – black pudding made from oatmeal and sheep's blood; *ceann cropaig* – from oatmeal and a cod's liver, stuffed inside its head; salted *guga* – from when the Ness boys would come back ashore with their haul from the annual gannet hunt. Most of the in-patients had come in from the country. Their convalescence happened quicker when they could have their own kind of food. But the fridge was also full of lemonade bottles. Each was labelled with the patient's name, and filled with water from their favourite spring or well.

'These days, they'd have rules and regulations, and we'd never get away with it,' he says. 'But the country people wanted what they thought of as the *beneficial qualities* of the water. That was always their expression. The 'beneficial qualities' for 'the health'.

It had taken just a single decade – from the late 1970s to the late 1980s – for the most recent wave of modernity to sweep the island. Television, that came in the decade before, would have had a lot to do with it. You'd see people chopping up beautiful old furniture for firewood. In the place of bespoke pieces that had been handed down through the family for generations, they'd buy a three-piece suite from a catalogue.

'It all happened so very quickly,' he says. 'As if they just flicked off one switch, and turned on another.'

I mention the island proverb: *A lot went out with the horse*.

'Absolutely, Alastair! People thought they'd just exchange the horse for the tractor. They never realised all the linkages they'd lose.

'They'd get a loan to buy the tractor. Then a job to pay the loan. And now we're wondering why we've no longer got the same time for each other.'

Nobody, he's careful to say, would want to go back to the hard old ways again. 'But we all know that something isn't right. We see it in the kids. A change has come about that we hardly understood before it was too late. You'll still find plenty here that's lost elsewhere, but there's not the same connections any more. People think it hasn't hit them: until one day, they might find they're standing very much alone.'

It's time now for me to leave Kenny alone, to move on up to Finlay's.

'But, the wells,' I ask. 'You said they're coming back?'

'It's a remarkable thing,' he replies, 'but in this last five years, as I've gone from door to door on my milk round, meeting a complete cross-section of the island, I've heard more people talk about old wells than in the whole of the rest of my life.

'You see, people are yearning for a connection with the past. Wanting to bring back control into their lives.

'So, yes. There's been people opening up their wells again and drawing water. Some want it for making their tea without all the treatment chemicals. And I'll tell you something else. I'm noticing, these days, that whenever people hear about a neighbour reopening a well, they get excited.

'Very excited indeed.'

Leaving Kenny's cottage, I cross the bridge and make my way uphill past hayfields edged by dry-stone walls. Twenty minutes further on, I turn up to the left, and a familiar stout figure strides out from a bungalow to greet me in the middle of the road.

'Welcome, pilgrim traveller!' hollers a beaming Doctor Finlay.

'A little *dance*, perhaps?' And then, dropping his voice to a wickedly conspiratorial tone: 'Let us dance *deiseil* around one another . . . and make sure that everybody in the village . . . is watching!'

We perform a little sunwise jig, just to show that paganism is alive and well. And we're laughing at our own ridiculousness. In my mind, at least, we're imagining the twitching of net curtains. For while God sees everything, the neighbours miss nothing.

Finlay's eyes play impishly behind the glasses of his full and rounded face. Recently retired from a career pioneering Gaelic television – helping the community to swing with change, but not to lose its footing – his much-feted atheism is expressed in a sticker on his car. The fish symbol of early Christianity is sprouting legs. It sports the caption: *Darwin*.

'Come on inside for something to eat,' he says, 'then we'll go and walk the land.'

The kitchen table is set with a ham salad and a bottle of red wine. His wife, Norma, is heading over to Callanish for a community gathering. I eat ravenously, and without lingering for a second glass, we step back out and into the softly settling mood of an early summer's evening.

The wind has fallen to a whisper. Children's voices jingle through the village and mingle with the lowing of cattle and the yakking of a sheep dog. Now and then we hear a mother's call, or the dying phut-phut-phut of a tractor being rested for the night. You feel that everybody's either here, or coming home. A sense that the village is complete, like the stillness when the flood tide reaches its high water mark.

We wander slowly through a flower-filled maze of pocket handkerchief pastures. These have supported human life for nigh on nine thousand years, yet still retain their soil in best of heart.

All around us are the markings out of time. The wire-mesh fences that go back for up to fifty years, and a thrush singing from the strand of twisted barbs that run along on top. The easygoing dry-stone walls, long sagged into the contours of the land. Rabbits have their warrens there and starlings tend their nests. Everywhere are heaps of rock and ruins tracing outlines under turf. These rest anonymous, except to those who carry their keys of meaning.

We wander over wobbling stiles and through ramshackle creaking gates. Finlay doesn't say a lot. He shows, and knows he's opened quite sufficient doors for me to walk through in this passing hour.

After a while, I tell him about the rediscovery of Tobar a' Ghobha at Leac a Lì. He's intrigued by the ambiguity of the map reference. It might be an error on his behalf, but it could also be cross-currents of tradition. His informant had been an old man in the village. Whatever the historical truth of the matter, he delights at the thought that the confusion had led to my encounter with the 'three wise women', as Jessie, Anne and Morag have become to me.

'You see,' he says, 'these wells grow over and close up so very quickly if they're not kept clean. The decade that Kenny Leather spoke to you about – the seventies through into the eighties – that alone was enough for many to have been lost. And yet, they mean such a lot to people.'

'How come?' I ask. 'If they mean something, people let them fall into neglect?'

'Because they'd not have wanted to take on the maintenance themselves,' he says.

The fashions of this day and age would have made them feel self-conscious. They'd be afraid of people wondering why they were digging around on somebody else's croft. In the past, people weren't so proprietorial. It would have been quite normal.

'But today?'

'It would be thought of as a strange obsession.' And he looked down to the ground, and shook his head.

'The women who you spoke to, they'd have felt a need within themselves, but they'd have lacked the justification of necessity to do what you could do.'

'So . . . you're saying that they were able to hide behind me?'

'Quite so – because you're a stranger to the village, but not a total stranger since you have island connections. When you turned up, you could be the key to unlock something that was already in the background of their minds.

'And just you watch . . . they'll probably be over that fence when nobody's looking . . . with a cup in hand to take a *deoch*.'

I'm curious as to why Finlay has it in for religion. He seems to me bestowed with such spiritual acuity.

It's not so much religion in itself, he says. 'It's more the psychology by which, on this island, it was used to manipulate the people's minds and maintain social control.'

In the past, his people would have considered the characters in the Bible to have been completely historical. They had no concept that large parts of the story might best be understood as metaphor. They heard the stories, and made sense of them in ways that they could interpret through their own lives.

'For them, the fear of Hell that Lady Mary's hand-picked evangelicals played on was very real indeed.' It had trampled over the simple sensitivity of what had been before.

We come up onto the brow of a hill. Here the evening light slings our shadows far across the grass, like men with standing stones attached. This is the eighteenth day of May, a mere five weeks from solstice. The sun is setting almost due northwest. At night it dips for just seven hours beneath the sea, and only when it's due full north is total darkness fleetingly achieved.

He raises up his arm, and points across the bay. Above the boulder beach, I see the walls around a vast village cemetery. I'm due to meet Catriona Campbell by its gates in half an hour.

The thin light catches face-on to the lichen-whitened headstones. Even from this distance, they shine like ruddy navigation beacons.

'There it is,' Finlay whispers, as we focus on a huddle of illuminated walls and gable ends that have survived against the winter gales.

'There is Cill Sgàire or Teampall Eòin. Some say Saint John the Evangelist, but in Ronald Black's view, the dedication is probably to Saint John the Baptist.'

The archaeologists, he says, reckon that it's fifteenth century. However, there is so much work still waiting to be done. What we can see today will rest on layers and layers of what was there before. 'Layers and layers of meaning and interpretation, that say different things to many different people.

'Layers and layers and layers,' he muses.

'Sometimes in these places, all that's left are the places themselves.' The history has otherwise all gone. 'We'll never get to the bottom of it all. Never at all.'

What matters, he suggests to me, is what comes into the mind. The imaginative possibilities. 'The layers of stories that weave through time, and how these speak to us today.'

The wind has dropped away completely. It leaves only residues of ripples, fading on the ocean's surface.

'*Teampall Eòin.*' He rolls the Gaelic sounds beneath his breath. '*Teampall Eòin,*' he repeats, so tenderly.

I'm thinking of that wild man of the desert, John the Baptist.[2]

If you have two coats, give one to whosoever has got none.

And John the Evangelist.

God is love.

A flock of oystercatchers rise and cut across our line of vision.

Red bills, white crosses flashing on their backs when veered in flight.

The servant bird of Bridgit – *gille-brìghde* in the Gaelic.

They're shifting over from the shore to evening fields.

U-vil, u-vil – I hear their winnowing call.

U-vil, u-vil – a blessing on the wing.

U-vil – u-vil – u-vil.

18

FLÉCHETTES IN THE SOUL

The island's pre-Reformation *teampaill* or 'temples' probably had much the same purpose as similar tiny chapels across Europe. They would be repositories for chalices, perhaps an icon, the cross or a statue of the Blessed Virgin. In France, Vérène and I have seen them used by peasant folk who might drop in for solitude and prayer. On the feast day of the patron saint, or at times of regional pilgrimages, mass might be celebrated on the grass outside as there would rarely be sufficient room to fit everyone under the roof.

Teampall Eòin is only some ten paces in length. Martin Martin, writing around 1695, confirms that such Hebridean sites were, indeed, the focus of pilgrimages and special festivals. These continued until the Presbyterian clergy were able to introduce a more instructional basis of religious observance. This had the sermon as its focal point, being of the preaching rather than the contemplative tradition. However, the old ways were deep rooted. Even as late as 1630, an English naval captain who had been sent to map Lewis and Harris was able to report to the Privy Council of Charles I:[1]

In theire religion they are very ignorant and have been given to the idolatrous worship of divers saints as doth appeare by theire Chappells which are yet to bee seene.

In other words, he had yet to see these saintly apparitions, and didn't harbour any great expectations. But I'm in luck. Catriona Campbell with her daughter, Peigi Ann, were to be seen appearing as I'd trudged across the beach and onto the *machair* – the sandy coastal pasture that is characteristic of the West Side.

I first met Catriona in association with Doctor Finlay, through their opposition to the proposed wind farm in north Lewis. The issue had split green groups down the middle. It had divided me within myself. On the one hand, our society desperately needs to decarbonise its energy supply. Think of Bangladesh. Think of parts of the Hebrides, so vulnerable to the sea level and storm surges. On the other hand, Great Britain is an energy-profligate country. We're bloated by consumerism and entertained by wars. Do we have to wreck the very beauty that can inspire a little care for the world?

In the midst of all this hand-wringing, Catriona put a powerful letter in the *Stornoway Gazette*. It spoke about indigenous identity and belonging. About the people and their place. Their *dualchas,* or cultural heritage, and how that rests upon their *dùthchas* as heritage in the land. I was very moved. I sent her a copy of *Soil and Soul*. She wrote back and said, 'Come and let me show you why the moor means so much to us.'

Last summer, with Anne, her artist and archaeologist sister, and little Peigi Ann, Vérène and I had hiked for several hours into the heart of the Barvas moor. We'd been taken to see their family sheiling. It was a small stone hut on a piece of raised and drier ground. Where the turf and rafter roof had partly collapsed, an incongruous blue tarpaulin could be temporarily pulled over improvised bare rafters. We made a peat fire in the middle of the floor, brewed tea in a chipped enamel kettle, and were enraptured listening to the sisters share their memories.

By their childhoods, around the 1970s, the family no longer had to go there for their cattle's summer grazings. Instead, and in the era before flying off to the sun, they went purely for the love of it. Catriona showed us a picture of their father, Kenneth, crouched outside the door, taken when the roof was still intact. His face was weathered with the rills of kindness. His whole bearing, of one substance with the stones.

Peigi Ann made Vérène and me lie down on the ground beside the door jamb, and examine its foundation stone. Chiselled on its surface was a deer with antlers, simple, like cave art. They knew not its story nor its age. Catriona just smiled, and said: 'We've been here for hundreds if not thousands of years.'

We talk very little as we walk, the three of us, amongst the ruins of Teampall Eòin. It sits within a partly walled enclosure. There is a nave, where the people would have stood, and a chancel for the altar. If you didn't know otherwise, you'd think it just another blackhouse ruin, although some of the stonework is superb. To Catriona and Peigi Ann, it evokes mystery and contemplation, a sacred place; and that, for all that their Free Church backgrounds might query such a notion.

The child leads me to the headstone of her twice-great-grandmother. Cut to an arched shape, it reflects what was by then the emerging modern mode. She describes it to me, coyly but observantly, as a 'rich one'. It stands out, but not sufficiently to be out of place, amongst its neighbouring uncut and unmarked stones. Many dozens of these poke above the grass, mostly less than knee height. Row upon humble row, they huddle round the temple, like figures warming round a hearth. The first time I ever saw such abject simplicity was at a famine cemetery in a field in County Mayo. To myself, I call them 'plainsong' headstones. Each speaks with such a rawness that they rend the heart. They're like notes dropped out of nowhere in those monophonic chants that the Gregorians revitalised, but which have Galician connections from the Celtic world of Santiago de Compostela. Links back to the underlying undivided church.

Set further back, and slightly higher up the slope, stands another wave of stones. These, too, are heartrending, but this time crisply cut from silver granite. These are the war graves that leave their footnotes in so many island cemeteries. Those with an Admiralty anchor mark a seaman's loss. To islanders, the symbol brings to mind a text from Hebrews: 'There is a hope both strong and steadfast which is the anchor of my soul.'

One bears the inscription:

> A sailor of the
> 1939–1945 War
> Known Unto God

It brings a tear into my eye. When you stop and think about it, what life is any life, if not so known in some way?

Most have laconic epigraphs, chosen by their families and inscribed along the bottom. Often these are lines of scripture, but Catriona calls to me – 'Come over and see this one.'

It is the resting place of Private Colin MacDonald of the 28th Seaforth Highlanders. Deaf Mackenzie's regiment. Killed in action – 1916 – in God-only-knows what hell-hole of that European tribal war. The inscription?

> To the memory
> Of my beloved son
> Whose death I deeply deplore

And all Catriona says is: 'How's that, for a statement about war?'

The island author, Calum Ferguson, who was born midway between the world wars, has written: 'From a very early age, I was conscious of having entered a world grief-stricken and still reeling from the war's seemingly never-ending punishment.'[2]

That world continued into my childhood. It was normal for us to see village women, and not particularly elderly, clad constantly in black. The wars, the sinking of the *Iolaire* and the departure of the *Metagama*, had left behind a generation of widows or spinsters. The world had, indeed, as J.M. Barrie warned in 1922, doddered down the brimstone path. Their sons or lovers in the lava had had the spring ripped from their year. It is salutary to remember that, even to this day, some of the eldest in this community turn out their lights each night with thoughts of how it might have been. How it might have been to have lived their lives with those whose lights went out forever. Lest we forget.

When the time came for my friends to leave, Peigi Ann handed me a brown paper bag with two freshly laid eggs. 'They're for your breakfast, from our own hens,' she said, and said so ever so brightly. 'We'd have brought you more, but thought you wouldn't want to carry much.'

They left me there, refreshed of spirit, at the Temple of Saint John. They left as soft at foot as they had come. I stood awhile, and watched them go. Meandering up the track beside a field fresh sown in sandy soil with barley. I stared, until they dipped below the brow, these people of the sheiling of the deer. A doe that sauntered between worlds, her calf following.

I turned, leaned on the cemetery wall, and watched the dying of the day. The sun dropped down across the bay and melted to a blazing Celtic cross. It stretched a golden shaft towards me at the temple, then slowly slipped between the covers of the sea.

I pitched my tent outside the cemetery walls. Soon I was fast asleep. Every other night had been completely dreamless. This night was different. I dreamt a dream that strangely had no images. Just words, and those, a single phrase that echoed on and on, like waves that flopped and lapped around the caverns of my mind.

There is a lot of love in this community.

Tuesday, day nine, and my next destination is Teampall Mhoire – the Temple of the Blessed Virgin Mary. I am making breakfast, sheltering snugly in the lee of Teampall Eòin. I'm boiling the Campbells' eggs in water that I'll then use for the tea, when, who should pop his head around the wall, but Doctor Finlay.

'I thought you'd like some sandwiches for the day,' he beams, so happy to have found me, and holding out a package wrapped in greaseproof paper. 'Also, if you've time before you go, I thought you might like to see the site of Fuaran Buaile Dhòmhnaill.'

We wander up the side of a stream, really more of a ditch, until we come to a spring line. It shows as a boggy zone with reddish-yellow staining where iron-rich water has seeped to the surface.

'Here was the Yellow Spring of Donald,' he said. It would probably have served the temple, and was said to cure tooth-ache, but around 1980 somebody unwittingly ran a digger through the site.

'And now it's gone, Alastair. Gone, gone . . . just like so many of them.'

We wander down to the seashore. He stoops beside a boul-der, and pulls aside the seaweed. It's partly hollowed, scooped out like the bowl of a lute.

'And what do you make of this?'

It was a Stone Age quern for hand-grinding corn, washed out from the soil by the encroaching sea in a storm a few years back. 'You see, Alastair,' he says, bringing back Catriona's words, 'people have been living here for a very long time.'

I ask him about Teampall Mhoire. He says, 'It's wonderful!' But I shouldn't expect to see anything. Remarkably, for such a remote edge of the western world, on 27 May 1403 the Pope in Rome addressed a letter 'to all the Christian faithful'. It was for 'granting an indulgence to visitors of the church of Saint Mary in Barvas in the Isle of Lewis, diocese of Sodor, on certain feast days and those who contribute to its reparation'.[3]

The walls and the baptismal font were still visible when visited in 1803 by the sheep farmer, James Hogg – the 'Ettrick Shepherd', or as Wordsworth had eulogised him, 'the mighty Minstrel'. He, whose *Bonnie Kilmeny* pulled together and preserved such a rich mélange of the old faerie lore, and to whom the temple was 'an ancient place of Popish worship'. By the time that T.S. Muir arrived in 1861, everything had disappeared beneath the sands of drifting dunes.

'And do you think, one day, the sands might *un-drift* themselves?' I asked, ever hopeful.

'They might,' Finlay said, with a prankish twinkle to his eye.

'You know, it would make a *great project* for an *archaeological dig.*

'Yes, that would bring it back.'

It's half an hour off noon, and only now am I heading up across the hill, towards the phantom of Saint Mary's Temple. Last night, Catriona had advised me to follow a line of posts that the community had put in to mark the coastal way. Eventually, you come to a little river. It cuts deep through the sand. The bed is always changing shape and the sides, sharp and slimy. 'Be careful,' she had warned. Looking at the map, I couldn't say which of several possible candidates she'd meant, but in my mind it had become Slime River.

I'd loved it, that intense flurry of human company, but now it's good to be alone and out in nature once again. Today's a day of sparkling seas and puffy white clouds. It's a wee bit darker on the far horizon. The weather is warmer here, by the ocean, than it was in the hills. The machair is bright green from the lime-rich shell sand that's carried on the wind. Everywhere is carpeted with yellow buttons of 'spring messenger' – the lesser celandine. There's even clumps of primrose breaking into flower on some of the more cloistered banks.

More than anything, today I've moved into a world of birds. The air's alive with eider, mallard, cormorant, guillemot and fulmar. The wind, that has returned since last night's calm, is singing with the mew of curlews and the long drawn-out pee-wit of lapwings. Below the cliffs, on sandy beaches spread between jutting rock outcrops, I see flocks of waders – redshanks, sandpipers and goodness knows what else – running up and down at every wave. They teeter, trill and pipe, excited as they dash to grab their fill of tiny crabs and sprats.

Far out to sea, the saffron-throated gannets climb, and plane, and plunge as headlong thunderbolts that spear into the shoals of fish beneath the great Atlantic's ceaseless swell. And everywhere, those wheeling gulls. So many different seagulls. These are, said Kenneth Macleod, 'the carrier between the Land-under-Waves and the Land-of-the-Living.' That explains the white gull on his stained glass window in the Gigha church. The fishermen of Barra call the Western Ocean, *Cuile Mhoire*, the Virgin Mary's Treasury.[4] He deeply loved that sense of feminine divinity, not sentimentalised, but as the tradition saw it, a living truth of nature.

Some of these cliffs are maybe sixty foot. I'm feeling blissfully happy as I almost bounce along their tops. It was the same on the road yesterday. It came upon me several times, fleeting but distinctively. I'd find myself, as it were, looking at myself with a transcendent clarity. It was as if the me was watching me, but from a place of more than me. Neil Gunn, the Highland writer, described the same when shelling hazelnuts as a boy. He was sitting on a river boulder and, 'I came upon myself sitting there.'[5] His experience was 'transitory, evanescent'. Mine too. I'd feel an expansive warmth come on, reach out to clutch for more, and in so doing snapped the ego self back stolidly in place.

I drop down towards a brackish lagoon, Loch Arnol, and crunch along the narrow bank of pebbles that are all that separates it from the sea. A rapid change has come into the air. Those earlier hints of darkness on the horizon have thickened up to heavy cloud, fast closing in. Looks like it's going to be a squally patch. Up I climb again, on to the next headland and over rows and rows of old feannagan. The strips of crofts of Arnol stretch inland to my right. These days, the village's conserved blackhouse is a honey pot for tourists and historians. I stop and watch four camper vans nosing around each other. They're all trying to get parked, or unparked, on the

single-track road, like over-fed dodgems in a fairground. As
I'm smiling to myself, a man comes out of the museum. He
strides down to the road's end and strikes out across the headland in front of me. He's got the heather loup – not walking
like a tourist – and his cap's more flat than woolly.

The first drop of rain splats my cheek. Out come the waterproofs and up goes Osprey's hood. Half an hour further on, I
meet the man returning. By now, it's bucketing. He doesn't
have a hood, but seems not at all put out. We stop to make
acquaintance. He works as a guide in the visitor centre. Slightly
built, silvering hair, this is Donald Morrison. Come rain or
shine, he always likes to take a lunchtime stroll.

Where am I going? Teampall Mhoire, I reply – as if such a
destination is just the done thing – and then, another three
miles on to camp for the night at the foot of his own village,
Siadar or Shader in the English. There I want to visit Teampall
Pheadair, Saint Peter's Temple. According to Finlay, some of
the old people knew it as Teampall Phàdraig after Saint Patrick.
He said that Peter and Patrick are equivalents in Gaelic. I'm
going to follow the old folks with Phàdraig. Not least, that will
help to differentiate it in my mind from another Teampall
Pheadair that I hope to visit further north, at Swainbost.

Oblivious to the downpour, evidently genetically programmed
to withstand 'total immersion', Donald settles in and starts telling me all about this ancient sacred site on the edge of his village.
You must have water at places where people will gather, and
Phàdraig once had three sources. There was Fuaran an Dèididh,
right down by the shore. 'That one was the cure for the tooth-
ache,' he says, 'and you would not drink from that well unless
you really needed to go there for *the treatment*. It was only used
for that purpose.' Unfortunately, it has now collapsed into the
sea. Thank God, I think wryly to myself, for dentistry.

Then there was Tobar Anndrais – Saint Andrew's Well.
That's also, sadly, past tense. It was on a croft just north of the
temple, and was believed to have the power to predict whether
a sick person would live or die. If a wooden dish was floated on

the surface and rotated sunwise – rejoice, rejoice! If, however, it spun in the opposite direction – alas, alas. But that's all gone now. Andrew's watering place was lost when somebody – he'd rather not say who – used it for a fencepost socket, and filled it in with stones.

The last surviving of the three is Tobar Mhoire, Saint Mary's Well. That's immediately across the road, just where it comes down from the village and bends sharply, passing closest to the temple.

'A little while ago,' he says, 'we restored it for the village. It was for the *historical* interest.'

I nod, in understanding at the rationale. They made a stone tablet to display its name, 'for the visitors'. Some of the village men go down from time to time to keep it clear of weeds.

'And how are these wells thought of in the village today?' I ask.

'The present generation . . .' he says, making a careful choice of his words, '. . . would mostly view them . . . *as superstitions*.'

'And the generation before the present?'

'Oh, that was very different! My father's generation held them . . . *in reverence*.'

I've now moved on, and come upon another beach, just before you get to Barvas. I'm hungry, looking for a nice spot to enjoy Finlay's sandwiches as the weather starts to lift. I'd dropped his name, of course, to Donald. That led us on to *atheism*. It kind of fitted with the pouring rain, and I was amused by his parting words: 'Finlay's more a Christian than he's pretending not to be.'

Well, I'm not quibbling. As far as I'm concerned, with his ham sandwich in hand, Finlay's just about to feed one of the five thousand. The only trouble is, after all these days of abstinence, I'm starting to crave greens. Sometimes when your body needs it, you yearn for the kail in ways that aren't just metaphorical. He and Norma can't have had any lettuce in the house.

But oh my, oh my! – I just can't believe what I've just stumbled on. Here I am. Walking through a bed of sea-tossed pebbles, the size of cricket balls. Each is varnished by the drizzle. With the light now perking up, it's bringing out their mottled whirls of quartz on grey and black, their little flecks of pink and green. And there. Right there, before my very eyes – sprung like Brìghde's fern back at the sheiling, from out amongst the stones no less – is *manna* from the heavens. The elongated heart-shaped leaves, the succulent fresh shoots, of a wild-grown clump of sorrel.

Wow! Give it just a thousand years, and see how they'll tell that one of Saint Finlay.

The 'cuckoo's meat' it's called in some parts – an early sign that summer's come. Before doing anything else, I take out the camera and snap a picture. If I didn't have the evidence, but was asked to give another talk in Falkland, then woe betide! Earth Mother would not otherwise believe that stones had turned to veg.

Leaf by leaf I pluck a bunch, layer it in amongst the ham, and munch upon the crispy lemon tang. Blessed be! The saint of Mary's Temple would appreciate that grace. Then off again – on across another narrow shingle fringe that leads to Barvas beach and Loch Mòr Bharabhais. The rain's gone off, the wind's swung round south-west, and the cemetery that marks the temple site is coming into view. I see its wall above the grassy plain, about a mile away. There's a sand quarry in the dunes, and two lorries trundle lazily to take their fill. A solitary digger nods its brainless head.

The machair here is absolutely flat. It doubles as a part-time army firing range. At school, the West Side boys impressed the rest of us by turning up with live rounds that they'd scavenged. They'd tell of lurid practical jokes that typically resulted in some poor victim's peat fire going bang.

The firing points step back, a line of mounds across my path. Each is exactly a hundred yards apart, extending for about a third of a mile. The cadets would aim at cardboard human cut-outs on the target butt. Red flags when firing signify a two-mile marine exclusion zone. If nothing else, the lobsters get a break from being potted.

In our day, the firing would be all with open sights. You had to have a steady hand to hit a human engine room from full six hundred yards. We were raised to consider telescopic sights unsporting. These days, however, they're all the rage – and not least so, for seeing God.

No kidding! In America, the ABC news channel has had under investigation precisely such a capability in standard issue rifle sights. *Trijicon*, a Michigan arms manufacturer, was founded by a devout Christian from South Africa. The catch line of the company is *Brilliant Aiming Solutions*™. 'That's mine!' They supply the Pentagon alone with 800,000 sights a year for the troops in Iraq and Afghanistan. Somewhat to the horror of the military, once it was found out, each is engraved with a Bible verse coded into its model number.[6] Number ACOG6X48PSA27:1 is currently on issue to the British infantry. Those last seven characters, refer to Psalm 27:1.

'The Lord is my light and my salvation. Whom shall I fear?' And whom, indeed? *Chirp-chirp.*

I'm now right in the range's line of fire. It's late afternoon, the rumbling lorries and the weary digger are calling it a day. I go up to inspect the butt. It's burrowed through with rabbits, and looks as if it might be now disused. I, too, do a little burrowing in the sand. Half wondering if I might unearth a spent bullet, or a brass cartridge case for a souvenir, for old time's sake – and then – for goodness sake!

Why should I even think of wanting such a souvenir?

War worms its way so readily into the minds of boys and men. A while ago, I was speaking at a military base and my host, let's call him Tom, was a half-colonel who'd just come back from duty in Iraq. He had some family connections to Lewis. We'd chewed the cud the night before and, while waiting to give my lecture, we had a bit of time to kill. He asked me if I'd like to see the museum of munitions.

He got the clearance, got it unlocked, and inside was every manner of warhead and projectile. Each was – in the engineering sense of the term – 'exploded', so as to show the brilliant logic of their ballistics, their vehemence of kinetics. Many of the lighter units of ammunition – not least, the cluster bombs – were filled with tiny barbed arrows, the size of fountain pen nibs, called *fléchettes*. These lacerate soft tissue in every way that cruelty could imagine.

One type of shell, the 'beehive round', contains hundreds of fluted fléchettes that emit a spooky drone when zipping through the air. The idea is that those it doesn't kill are left instilled with shell-shock. Another, the 'pyrophoric' fléchette, is coated with phosphorus to ignite in flight by atmospheric friction. Then the DIACBA: Direct Injection Antipersonnel Chemical Biological Agents. This was developed by the US Army in the 1950s, grooved to carry such pathogens as anthrax spores or Botulinum toxin into a soldier's shredded flesh.[7] The US has unilaterally ended its biological weapons programme, but the Taliban have cottoned on. They lace the shrapnel for their roadside bombs with dog shit, or pus squeezed from septic wounds, to spread infection to the maimed.

The museum had a table where a cocktail of fléchettes were displayed in little bowls, like nibbles at a party. I ran my fingers through them. They felt like fish hooks, but with an Orc-like aura. Lustrous alloys – black, bronze, and where rich in titanium for super-penetrative hardness, Payne's grey.

I drew out a pinch between my thumb and index finger. I felt their skewer points, their skiver edges, their jagged little daggers. 'This is the reality of war,' I thought. But what struck me most disturbingly, was their quasi-pornographic vice. They held a grip of fascination, even on my so-called pacifist mind.

I released my fingers. Let them drop. They plinked back into the bowl.

It was Tom who broke the silence.

'I thought you were going to ask if you could take some as a souvenir.'

'I nearly did,' I admitted, 'but then I thought, a souvenir of what?'

I knew he understood. We'd struck a common chord.

'Actually, Tom, I've been wondering if there's something I might ask. 'Did you ever kill when in Iraq?'

It had been in the Euphrates marshes. Clearing out remaining pockets of Saddam's men. He'd not done so directly, but had administered commands to guys who pulled the triggers and pressed the lethal buttons.

'Same difference, really.'

'And, can I ask? How does it leave you, now?'

In my mind I had the soldier who has come back home, and everyone at the party is grooving to Echo and the Bunnymen, but his mind's back into the firefight. Back to what was oh so very *real*. And nobody else quite understands. And his children know he's different: where's Daddy?[8]

'I notice three things . . .' began Tom. And God knows – I can't help but feel an admiration, indeed, affection for these men. Their sense of community. Their ethic of looking out for one another. The research that shows that most don't want to kill, they want to protect, and that's a form of love. Even young Harrier. Maybe, especially, Harrier.

There's something happens when a man comes face to face with Hell. It burns away the bullshit. It betrays the plastic world that passes for normality in all its crass vacuity.

'I notice,' repeated Tom, 'that I don't sleep so well. I get irritable more quickly. And I *feel the cold* more easily than I used to.'

Dante had described Hell's inner circle not as hot, but frozen.

I asked him what had been his proudest moment.

A pocket of the enemy was dug into a foxhole, hiding in the reed beds. The lads had itchy fingers and wanted the green light to blast them out. But the reconnaissance had suggested that such a lethal course of action might be avoidable.

Tom stopped them from opening fire. He said that he was glad to have that memory. It left him with a souvenir of those whose lives he could have taken, but chose otherwise.

We all take up positions on a long front. None of us can quite see how it looks from the next person's post. That's how I reconcile my differences with the military. Rarely does a human being get to glimpse full compass of the battlefield of life.

'Sounds to me, Tom,' I said that day as we parted, 'like you opted for the God's-eye view.'

I've left the rifle range and am edging towards the end of the plain. A stream meanders sluggishly to the sea along the base of the sand dunes. I can see some dried-out ox-bow arcs where it must have changed its course from time to time. And I know where I've got to. Slime River.

I'm not feeling great. Hope it's not a bug coming on. I'd felt a touch of something much the same this morning when coming up to Loch Arnol. A changing not just of the outer weather, but of the inner too. A kind of icky rawness, as if my stomach's being lightly sucked at by a pump.

When crossing the river that came out of Loch Barvas, I'd stopped and had a few casts, since the wind had changed. Hooked a salmon parr straight through the eye. Killed it, rather than to throw it back like that, and then there was another that I wrongly kept, just to help make up a meal – quite forgetting that I already had my cold kipper. On Voshimid, Cameron had told Simon that the trout landed in his boat had 'given themselves'. Mine didn't feel that way. 'It was as though some crime lay on my soul,' wrote Dostoevsky.[9] So much for the poacher! Left me musing that, in a way, we're all poachers in the flow of life. None of us, or very few at any rate, complete the cycles of gratitude and right relationships that open up to greater depths of being. That's what Jung was getting at when he said we've all got a shadow side. But the problem, said this visionary son of a Swiss Calvinist preacher, isn't that the shadow's there. The problem's when we deny it. When we fail to understand it as our psychological compost, our karmic burden, 'sin' as work-in-progress, and so we trip up on the bucket.

Set in this light, 'The fire of Hell,' says one of the many awesome Russian Orthodox thinkers, 'is the fire of love that gives remorse a terrible clarity.'[10] It only burns off encrustations of the ego, only strips away what's not most truly us.

That's the paradox that I see in many of the military too. They've been there, seen and even done terrible things, but mostly don't deny complicity. It can open up a truthfulness, a forgiveness, even, a re-articulation to the inner life.

In *The Brothers Karamazov*, Dostoevsky's saintly Father Zosima says we're all responsible for one another's crimes. 'No man on this earth can sit in judgement over other men until he realises that he too is just such a criminal.' We can't just carry on projecting shadow onto others – good state or bad state; with us or against us; the Elect or the Damned. The truth of interconnection is that we're all bound in with one another, with everything. 'However mad this may appear, it is the truth,' insists the Russian monk. 'Believe this, believe this implicitly, because therein is contained all the hope and all the faith of the saints.'[11]

I had taken out the stove, cooked and ate the two little fish, just to close the circle. Truly, all this walking, walking, walking. The fishes were just the coin that edges up the lid on things one hardly knows are there. Old fléchettes, long buried in the soul, that now and then turn in their cocoons, and leak a little toxin from their grooves.

And I'm standing by Slime River now. The green is just the algae that attaches to its white sand sides. It's just another little river, doing what a little river does when pushing to the sea. The digger has scooped out the dunes across the other side. The wind has finished off the job and left them flayed, like winding sheets that drape across the machair's edge. I climb up to the top, beyond the excavations, and walk towards the temple's cemetery. This ground was used for burials until perhaps a century ago. The grass is speckled through with plainsong headstones.

A young man from the village is out walking with his dog.

'Where is Teampall Mhoire?' I ask.

He has the softest energy. 'Probably, it's right beneath your feet.'

I wait until he's left, and sit down beside two headstones. Both are oblong, flat and have an eye the thickness of a finger through the top. Finlay had said he thinks they may be roof slabs, recycled from the temple. If so, they're all that still remains of it in sight. From here, I have an open view, north towards my final destination. I'm moving to the pilgrimage's end. I'm thinking of a man I once met in Sami land, up beyond the Arctic Circle of Finland. He told me that he came from Archangelsk, where they make the tar that caulked our boats. He told me that, in Russia, the further north you go the holier it gets.

The heavy clouds that brought the rain have nearly lifted. What few are left are drifting by in widening shrouds of blessed blue. In the Eastern church of Russia and Greece, the title that they often use for Mary is *Theotokos*. It means God-bearer, hence why she's also called the Mother of God. It nods towards a love that's very incarnate, the spirit one with matter, the re-articulation of the inner and the outer.

I used to fret about the song and dance around the literal 'virginity' of Mary. That may be how it's meaningful for some to understand. For me, however, a living myth speaks in kaleidoscopic ways to deep reality. I've come to see such 'virginity' as the archetype of transformation. As 'Our Lady' of perpetual renewal. That, of social justice as is shown by the Magnificat. That, too, in John Carey's sense of Eden ever-present in a fallen world. Like the first morning. 'Like a virgin . . .'

Mary transformed the terrible predicament of being pregnant, out of wedlock, in a harshly patriarchal and judgemental society. She gave expression to the truth that the Psalms had proclaimed. The truth that Jesus later underscored – that all of us are 'gods', all are 'children of the Most High'.[12] So her son was also, regardless of paternity. 'Be it unto me,' she told the angel. Let go into the life of God. 'Let it be, let it be.' Let it come to pass. 'There will be an answer.' Let go into the answer.

And I'm just sitting here as evening falls, at Saint Mary's in the forgotten diocese of Sodor, where once, it's said, indulgences were granted. Where people found conviction that the baggage that they carried was laid down, forgiven.

The cemetery is overhead the temple, as if the dead are lifted up on high. Transformation comes from somewhere hidden deep within. That's a symbol that can speak to me, and to many of the most broken people I know.

19

THE TEMPLE OF CRÒ NAOMH

Wednesday, day ten. I have just come up from viewing – and from underneath – the huge foundation slabs that are a part of the Teampall Phàdraig complex. They jut out from the cliff that overlooks a pebble beach, Mol Èire, at the foot of Siadar village. Nearby is Rubha na h-Annaid – the Headland of the Mother Church – and several other local names also point to what must once have been a major spiritual centre.[1]

One by one, as the coast gets gnawed away by storms, the masonry that was set in place by saintly hands crashes down onto the shore. I had raked around amongst the debris at the water's edge. I'd wondered if there might be anything to find. But apart from remnants of the temple walls – a low rectangle, settled in the grass above – there isn't very much remaining for the novice eye to see. There is, however, on the west face of a little inlet, a crack down through a sheet of rock that spouts a spring that's fast enough to drink from. It has a sulphurous metallic taste, musty and mephitic. Could that, I wonder, be what's left of the erstwhile Fuaran an Dèididh – the Fountain of Toothache? Is that medicinal savor why it was only used for toothache? If so, I'll tell Earth Mother that it granted me an indulgence – for the Cadburys and Mars bars.

Yesterday evening, after leaving Teampall Mhoire, I'd crossed a headland thick with old peat workings. There was what seemed to be a ruined village, and a solitary menhir – Clach An Truiseil. At nearly nineteen feet tall, about six metres, it is said to be the tallest standing stone in Scotland. It leans, like a human figure, at an angle. Some have interpreted the name to mean The Stone of Compassion, though Doctor Finlay thinks it might more likely be a person's name from long ago. I'd sat there for half an hour, dined like a king on my cold kipper that had, by a miracle of incorruptibility, not gone off, and then crunched across the pebbles to Saint Patrick's. I got my tent erected just as the rain was coming back for yet another stormy night. Now, dreich and rainy morning that it is, I'm sitting by the temple's well. I've drawn a cup of water, but take just a token sip, as it's somewhat green with algae fed by surface water runoff. As Donald Morrison had described, its capstone is of pinkish-grey Lewisian gneiss. Perched on top, a small arched block of sandstone, like a bookend, that proclaims in flowing Celtic script: Tobair Mhoire.

All around, the luscious meadow grass is set with wildflower herbs. Close to the rim, marsh marigolds are blooming – 'Mary's gold', the 'winking Marybuds' of Shakespeare's *Cymbeline*. 'Hark, hark! the lark at heaven's gate,' the bard sang out, 'my lady sweet, arise, arise, arise.' And so must I. My mission for the morning is heartened with an ulterior motive – the smell of coffee beans.

Back at Café Spirituel, what seems like so very long ago, a 'lady sweet', the renowned artist, Marianna Lines, had pressed one of her acclaimed spells into my hand. It was an original drawing – something I must frame for posterity – a map inked onto a paper napkin.

'Take this,' she'd said, like all the best faerie godmothers, 'and go and have a cup of coffee with Sue and Alex Blair at the Borve Pottery.'

I set off along the old unsurfaced road. It runs beside a row of blackhouse ruins that used to be the village. Once the A857 was constructed, the settlement moved inland – pragmatic if less elegant.

As I reach the main road the rain goes off and, having warmed up, I stop to take some clobber off. A vehicle pulls up in front of me. Guess what? The sticker on the back is sprouting legs.

'Good morning!' beams the ever-cheerful Doctor Finlay. 'I was hoping I might catch you before you disappeared across the moors again. I was wondering whether, to start the day, you might like some *coffee,* and some *freshly-baked* scones?'

Wow! The Great White Witch of Collessie had never promised scones as well.

'I knew that you'd be looking out for Bridgit's place, the well and temple. But they're both so hard to find. How about I take you there and drop you back here afterwards?'

You betcha! We motor off, down to the turning circle at the road end in Melbost Borve, and stop there beside a bungalow called Sundown. Through a gate we go into an undistinguished field.

'See anything?' Finlay asks.

'Err – grass?'

'Clear it away from around those,' he says, pointing to several little hummocks at our feet. I do so, and there are the stumps of plainsong headstones. We're in an unmarked cemetery.

'Can you see anything more?'

'Nothing. Just that wee ridge.'

'Take a closer look.'

Gradually, I pick out an oblong shape under the grass, about the size of a crofter's cowshed.

'That's Teampall Brìghde for you,' he says, with a flourish.

'Now, see if you can find the well.'

I look around, but absolutely nothing. The only visible feature is a heap of old posts, up by the fence that's north-east of the temple.

'Take a look under those fenceposts.'

They had been placed for dryness on top of a small concrete mound. It turns out to be the capstone of the well, and bears the imprint of a horseshoe, a mark of smithcraft.[2] The cap gives shelter to an exquisite grotto of lichen-mottled stones, one of which can be lifted in and out as a little entrance door.

Ever so gently, as if he is a priest officiating at a ceremony, Finlay moves it sideways. The daylight struggles to reach all the way inside, but there it is. We gaze into a casket formed of interlocking blocks of unhewn stone. An emerald jewel. The algae-fringed but crystal waters of the Tobar Brìghde.

A large white slug has found its heaven, sleeping underneath the lintel. We sit down upon the grass and settle into wordless contemplation.

A cup is lying to one side. After several minutes, Finlay nods towards it. He gives a little smile, and whispers: 'Be careful of the spider's web.'

We each sip several mouthfuls of the icy water. He sets back the stone and, slowly, we retrace our footsteps to the car. There we share his coffee and home baking.

'My *atheism*,' he told me, 'can be put very simply: compassion for all living beings and for the Earth on which they move. Everything else flows from this.'

And that would be the last that I would see of him on this pilgrimage. He dropped me back to where he'd picked me up from. I stood and watched him drive away, off back down the road to Shawbost. And I was thinking, almost saying to myself, with a twinge of sadness as he disappeared: Farewell and adieu, my Darwinian Druid guide. *Le gach beannachd.*

I venture into an Aladdin's cave of the Borve Pottery's hand-made mugs and lamp stands. Alex noses out from behind the firing kiln, wearing an apron and an umber smock that's reinforced with heavy elbow pads. He's a gentle giant of a man, probably around sixty, a bushy moustache with soft black curly hair, and muscled arms of such hirsute splendour that they must have spared the need for a few winter shirts in his lifetime. He's in the middle of preparing a firing, hands clarted with clay, but he yells to Sue, who's making lunch. In no time,

I'm sitting in their kitchen with a flock of happy hens clucking at the window.

They'd come from Lancashire to Lewis with two other families in 1973, attracted by the Highlands and Islands Development Board.

'I was always the sceptical one,' she concedes. 'We were back-to-the-landers, you know, grow your own vegetables and all that.'

She'd been the one who'd kept on saying that it wouldn't work out. The island doesn't even have a Marks & Sparks! But in the end, probably because they had the lowest expectations, they're the ones who lasted out the winters. Now the hopes for which they came are far surpassed.

'And the culture? Did you find that very different when you came here?'

'Oh completely!' and she laughs and laughs in reminiscence. 'The thing is, that when you first arrive you just can't understand how much at odds it is. People would tell you things like not to hang your washing out on a Sunday. Back then, most of them wouldn't watch TV on the Sabbath either. But no advice could have prepared you for just how great the difference really was.'

'And how would you describe that difference?'

'Well, it's the depth of what is found here. Their culture . . . it's like a deep, deep geological seam. It's there in the language . . . the music . . . the religion. You've no idea! Simply no idea until you've really lived in it. Until people start to open up and accept you.'

'Do you feel accepted now, thirty, forty years down the line?'

'Oh yes! I would never say that we're the same as them. But they make us feel very welcome. Lots of our business these days is from locals buying gifts. It's not just the tourist trade. That's very touching, very heart-warming.'

Lunch is on the table, and she gives a shout to Alex. 'The truth is, I've never come across a community anywhere with such a generous spirit. It's not the Scots who are mean here. We're the mean ones in comparison.'

'And the religion? How do you sit with the Free Church and all that?'

'Well . . . it's so hard to fathom. But underneath there's something very, very profound, something very lovely and connected, that's always been here. It's as if – whether they think of themselves as Calvinists or whatever – they're all drinking from a source so deep and so ingrained, they hardly know they've got it.'

I leave the pottery, heartily stuffed with cheese on toast and a clutch of four freshly-laid eggs to top up Osprey's larder. All I'm left with is a little flour, a single pack of oatcakes, some drips of honey and dregs of the muesli. I'd only meant my food to last a week. Now I'm almost out and it's a slightly funny feeling, but I don't want to have to go and find a shop.

The Abhainn Bhuirgh passes underneath the road on its way to the sea. There's a track that runs alongside. I saunter down a flight of dry-stone raceways that had once fed a string of Norse mills. They continued to be used into the nineteenth century. The stream flowed through the lower part of each mill hut. A wooden paddle – 'undershot' in that the water goes beneath rather than over it – turned one millstone against another by means of a shaft to the upper chamber. So the crofters ground their corn. Finlay told me that he'd just sent off a book about their history and locations to a Stornoway publisher. The illustration on the inside cover is by Seonaid Crawford, Seumas' daughter. It'll even include classical paintings of similar mills from Persia, Kashmir and the Punjab, not to mention classic Doctor Finlay sutras on such both-like stone huts: 'And they stand and ask themselves: *Where from, and when, and who, and why – and what now?*'[3]

I reach the sea near Bridgit's church and wander up the brae, past *Sundown*. A hundred yards ahead, an old man emerges from a working croft, strewn with agricultural implements. He dawdles over the road and seems to tinker with his rubbish bin. I can tell from his deportment that he's local, and think I guess his game. I'm right. In no time, it's back around a kitchen table, kettle on the boil, a huge plate of biscuits, cheese and baking, in the home of James and Peggy Morrison.

'I saw you walking down the burn, and thought I'd just come over,' James confesses, stretching back into an armchair that commands the corner by the window. He'd spotted me, like a stray sheep in the village, and was curious to enquire as to my earmarkings. Where am I from? Who are my people? Where am I going?

'Leurbost – Dr McIntosh's son – poaching.'

'Isobel's brother!' he shouts in delight. She once managed the catering at the oil rig fabrication yard near Stornoway. He was a welder with BP. Before that, weaving the tweeds and now, retired, he runs a few sheep.

They gave me such a happy hour, a constant stream of stories, leg-pulling and laughter. Why no poultry on the croft? 'The hen has not been born that didn't die in debt.'

As in the old ways, Peggy asked if I would say a grace before she poured the tea. Here, the pilgrim was caught slightly short. Quakers do it quietly. I said a few brief words – could have done much better – to which she said, 'Well – if *that* will be your grace.'

As for traditions of the local saint, well, James said he didn't know of any. But poaching, that's a different matter. The stream I'd just come down used to run with salmon when he was a boy, back before the factory ships sucked clean the sea.

'Now, you see, the salmon is a very clever fish. The wisest in the water. When you're at him in a pool, you'll feel him bump into your Wellington boots, trying to escape. But if once he feels your net, he'll never touch it again.

'What you do, is lay two nets in a V shape. Drive him up the pool and trap him in the cleft. And *that's the way we did it*, my boy. Oh yes, *a bhalaich*! That's the way it was done when we were young.'

'You'll be very welcome back here anytime,' he hollers, as I set off on my way.

'Always very welcome – unless I'm *on the watch below*.'

'The what?' I stop, and turn to catch his words again.

'That was in the merchant navy. You'd either be on watch on the deck above, or sleeping on the watch below.

'You'll always find me here, *a bhalaich*,' and he's chuckling to his parting shot. 'Always here. Until the day they lay me six feet under – *on the watch below*.'

My next destination, Teampall nan Crò Naomh, is usually translated, rather squarely, as Holy Cross Church. But this misses out on Doctor Finlay's 'layers and layers of meaning and interpretation'. *Naomh* means sacred, consecrated, or held in sanctuary, so 'holy' is good enough. Normally, however, the Gaelic for cross is *crois*. But *crò* has in fact a much wider semantic range. It suggests an enclosure. A circle, a needle's eye, a cattle fold, a hut-like cell and even, the heart and the blood that circulates.

Moreover, Ronald Black points out that 'the differences between *cnò* "nut" and *crò* "blood" are of gender and nasalisation only'. The night that succeeds *Féill Ròid* – Roodmass, the Feast of the Exaltation of the Cross – was in the old ways called *oidhche na cnò, na Cnò Naomh* – 'the night of the nut, the Holy Nut'. On this day, according to the Rev. J.G. Campbell of Tiree, people went out collecting hazelnuts. Even 'the devil goes a nutting'. The feast also marked the start of the rutting season for the stags. Campbell notes that 'the belling of red deer among the hills on this night is magnificent'.[4] *Crò,* or *Cnò,* therefore suggests a sense of the cross in a way that brings to mind, for me, the circled Celtic cross. It also suggests a sanctuary, the kernel or essence, and the heart with all its pulsing of the life force. Crò Naomh is thus both holy cross and temple of the sacred heart.

Out on the open moor again, another kind of *crò* was on my path. Dun Bhuirgh or Dun Borve is a prominent stone ring, a prehistoric *broch* or fort some thirty feet across. Its walls are some eleven feet in thickness at the base, and once they held within them seven beehive cells. Down the centuries, most of the smaller stones were carried away, quarried for walls and houses, thus robbing it of what would once have been a most impressive stature. When Captain Thomas documented the site in 1890, he quoted at length from an antiquarian, the Rev. Malcolm Macphail of Shawbost. Happily for posterity, the minister had placed on the written record the following facts:[5]

> Though neither history nor tradition are associated with Dun Bhuirgh, the fairies have long made it their residence. They used to be seen with their big black dogs, with large iron chains round their necks, going about like ordinary men in their *Bruithean*. They were of great assistance to the Borvians, often helping them out of their difficulties, and even performing apparent impossibilities.

At the pottery, Alex had warned me that the forecast threatened heavy rain. Sure enough, within a short time of having left the Morrisons' house, the clouds had thickened. Thinking that I'd better plan for another stormy night, but lacking the sun to tell the time by my compass, I'd reluctantly turned on my phone. All I'd wanted was to see the clock, but with capricious forces hanging round the bruithean, it grabbed a signal too – and *chirp-chirp*.

Normally, I only use this phone when travelling and don't give out the number. It was a text from Gehan Macleod. She had founded the GalGael Trust in Govan with her late husband, Colin, building boats to reconnect the hand, head and heart. My involvement on the board is why Vérène and I live there. The text was terribly apologetic, but could I call her urgently? Some trouble with *The Sun*.

I sat down on a stone inside the broch's enclosure. My call was answered by Helen, the office manager. It will suffice to say that, before we managed to recruit her, she was the king-pin in the running of a Glasgow demolition company.

'Alastair! How's it going? Still out on the moors *finding yourself?*'

Gehan rallied to the rescue. Turned out that one of Rupert Murdoch's hacks had slapped three hundred quid on the table of one of our volunteers – a man whose daily life battles with the bottle. He wanted him to help concoct a story about one of our young female heroin addicts. The commission was to write a piece about 'sex, drugs and the charities that mug the taxpayer'.

'It's horrible,' said Gehan. 'They're making up lies out of people's misery just to sell newspapers.'

The volunteer – who had served fourteen years in jail back in his gangster days – threw the money back, and came in to tip us off. Gehan had only needed reassurance that she'd handled things in the best way. But for a while, it drew me back into another world; that of those whose forebears had been uprooted from the land, the end-products of such inter-generational poverty. And yet, as Colin used to say, 'You can hold a person down for long enough, but sooner or later, they'll resurface. It's the buoyancy of the human soul.' We simply try to hold a space where folks can seek to re-articulate between their inner and their outer lives.

The full uncanniness of unheimlich, of deep un-homing caused by such structural violence, is an everyday reality for many of our people. Joseph Jones was born in Wine Alley, a now-demolished Govan slum. An exquisite musician, he'd seen hostels, prisons, hospitals, the lot. One night, he told me that his problem was he had the Devil in him.

I'd suggested maybe not taking 'the Devil' too literally. A useful metaphor, perhaps?

But Joe held me in his big soft puppy eyes. He said he wouldn't want to disagree: 'Not with yourself, Alastair.

'It's just that, you see . . . I can only make sense of my life with the Devil and God.'

It was just one of those funny little encounters. One that left me feeling, 'Who am I to argue?' That was all. But the following week, I was seated beside a naval chaplain at a luncheon function. He'd just returned from active combat in Afghanistan.

'You said, *active* combat?' I asked. 'A chaplain?'

He explained that it's not widely known, but in some of the special forces units the chaplains don't just go along to say the prayers. They don't fire guns, but they're an integral part of the fighting unit. He wondered: could he use Joe's story for a forthcoming sermon?

'I'll just need to check back with him,' I said, 'but there's not a lot to go on, is there?'

'I'll tell you why it speaks to me,' he said. 'In my branch of the services, I helped to run the course that trains the boys what happens if they're tortured.

'I'd tell them that if captured by the enemy, you may have everything stripped away. Your uniform, your health, your identity. Not even the family bonds of those you love may be enough to help you hold together.

'You may find yourself broken – quite beyond imagination – by the demonic forces brought to bear upon you. You may find yourself stripped down to where the only thing that's left . . . is God.'

Out here, north beyond the broch, I come to swathes of thick dark heather sweeping down towards the sea. Like back at Cnoc an Ruagain, it's growing over rows and rows of long-forgotten feannagan. They reach the edges of storm-bitten cliffs then drop, truncated, off the end.

Joe too dropped, truncated, from this world before his time. It's said the proud will ask: *If there's a God, how could this happen?* The humble say, and Joe would have said: *This has happened, God is with us.*

These coastal trails play hide and seek. The evangelicals could call them 'faith trails'. You have to keep on going in the hope they'll reappear. I'm just walking, walking, walking. On and on and on. Another step, another and another. Walking, to the Teampall nan Crò Naomh. Making for the Holy Cross. There used to be a ridiculous saying, 'It's X that marks the spot.' In my mind's eye, the temple up ahead exudes a golden glow, as if it is a gently flaming Celtic cross. I think I know why. It's probably a memory, or after-image, from that night at Teampall Eòin. The way I'd watched the sun drop down into the land-under-the-waves. Its refraction and reflection on the water. And how, in that low light, I'd watched devoid of sunglasses, not even slits in reindeer shoulder bone. That's the burning image that I'm seeing, where X marks the spot. The *cnò*, the kernel, and echoes of *sùil-chruthaich*, Creation's Eye, that sets the very Earth a-quake.

What is the cross? I'm saying to myself.

First millennium – *Christus Victor Theory* – ransomed to the Devil.

Second millennium – *Satisfaction-cum-Penal Substitutionary Theory* – ransomed to God.

What now – I'm wondering – *if anything?* Anything, that wouldn't be ridiculous, incredulous, to see us into this, the third millennium? If Jesus hadn't been such an activist for loving justice in the world – if he'd not been like one of us strung out to dry – I'd hardly even bother asking. I even know a church where they've taken down the cross, such was the creeping Christian cringe it caused.

So – *what is the cross?* 'What do you say to that, Alastair?' echoes Harrier, coming in upon another gyre, some higher mission drawing me when under fire to clarity.

'What does *pacifism* have to say to that?'

What, indeed?

I'd say, *nonviolence is the cross.*

Abbé Pierre was a radical French priest who, when the poor were dying on the Paris streets in the bitter winter of 1954, led

L'insurrection de la Bonté – the Uprising of Kindness – and awoke the conscience of a secular nation.

All his life, the Abbé had struggled with the Ransom Saying. It was through hard-pressed folks like Joe, that a whole new vista opened to him:[6]

> It has been while living for a long time amongst drug addicts that another explanation came to me. The addict is, in effect, at the same time his own executioner and the victim. He is both the ransomer and the hostage. Based on this observation, I realised that it is the same with all human beings. Because we are disconnected from our authentic divine source, we have become our own executioners. We are slaves to our disordered desires, to our egotism.

The Greek for 'ransom' in the gospels is *lútron*. It means 'to loose', as in the freeing of a captive's bonds. It means, as Walter Wink points out, to *liberate*.[7] Jesus was saying – and in ways that need not exclude other faiths based on love – that he came to give his life *as liberation* for humankind. That puts a slightly different angle on the cross. Therefore:

> Third millennium – *Liberation Theory* – ransomed to ourselves.

'Only forgiveness breaks the law of karma,' said the great Hindu-Christian scholar, Raimon Panikkar, in *Nine Sutras on Peace*.[8] Only *for-give-ness* – the power of love that melts the power of violence in its golden fire. A love to which resurrection is intrinsic, for this is love that cannot die, its greater part never having been born into the confines of space and time.

'Now, move on, *and live the rest of your life*.'

That, to me, is why the cross shines out, a supreme transformative symbol of nonviolence. Far from being past its sell-by date, the wrapping paper's hardly off the gift. We're still in the early days of what might be thought of as three eras of emergent Christian understanding.

'I have even heard people say,' said Gorky, 'that the Earth itself is a pilgrim in the heavens.'[9] All of us are walking on the pilgrimage of life. We're moved and beckoned by an inner light, the fire within the *crò*, the power that turns the stars around, the very 'atom of delight' – as Neil Gunn called his 'hazelnut experience'.[10]

That's what I sense an opening of upon this pilgrim pathway to the Teampall nan Crò Naomh. 'I have come to set fire to the world,' said Jesus, speaking both as a human being and as the archetypal principle of divinity incarnate. Not the fire of hell. Not in any sense of punishment. But as the fire of love. The cross absorbs the violence of the world.

I'd better take the greatest care. The moor has given way to fields. They're fenced down to the water's edge in narrow strips of in-bye crofting land. Some are fewer than a hundred yards across, and while the cliffs have dropped away to just some twelve-feet high, they're still enough to make a nasty fall.

Worldwide, the level of the sea is rising by an inch in every decade, and accelerating. Add storm surges and some natural subsidence, and that's the reason why this coast is getting undercut so rapidly. One moment I'll be on the path. The next, it drops away. Fences dangle off the end, giving crude measure of the loss of land. I cross from field to field by grabbing each last standing post with both my hands, and swinging round across the yawning chasm to the other side.

The temple is now coming into view. I see its outline, low upon a green cnoc, close against the sea. The council have put up a wall to stop it getting washed away.

In 1815, the artist William Daniell came and made an aquatint that now sits in the Tate. It's called *Remains of a Temple at Galston, Isle of Lewis*. Already, by his time, the roof was off and just the walls were standing proud. A shepherd sits bucolic by the plainsong headstones with his dog. A sailing ship is out at sea. That's what was, but all that still remains today are three deep-sunken walls. Only the upper third of a doorway pokes above the sand.

I enter, lie down in the long green sward, and press my face into the ground. I'm here, within the fold, the sacred heart of Holy Cross.

In a vision, Christ came to Julian of Norwich. He showed her something, round as a ball, the size of a hazelnut, and it nestled in the palm of her hand.[11] He said: 'It is all that is created.'

'What can this be?' she wondered. 'How could it last?' So fragile and so small.

'And the answer in my mind,' she wrote, was that 'it lasts, and will last forever, because God loves it.'

God is the primal atom of delight. Early evening, and the sky has darkened. Leaden, laden, and the sea has turned a heaving black. A cold wind rises once again, away up here, in holy north.

20

THE HEART OF THE SUN

Slowly, I draw away from the Teampall nan Crò Naomh. The wind has taken on a mean bite and flags me up a yellow card for body temperature. I set off again along the track. From here, it squeezes in between the sea and a robust stone wall that marks the boundary of Galson Farm.

Ahead, lies another lonely hillside. A series of long stone walls traverse its contours like a flight of ever-higher hurdles. There is a river at its foot, no wider than a road, but heavily in spate from last night's rain. Add to that an impending cloud-burst, and it looks grim, grim, grim.

I should maybe raise the tent right here and now, in the shelter of the wall while everything's still dry. It feels, however, like an awfully early hour to hunker down for nightfall. There's nothing worse than being banged up, sleepless for hours on end, in a sack of stormbound flysheet.

The farm wall meets the river at a right-angled bend. From round the corner comes a teenage girl. She must be of the village. She's heading in the direction of the temple, wandering in a pensive dream with a shock of golden hair that tosses on the wind. She seems not to have noticed me, but as the wall and coastline funnel us together, she lifts her head in a shyly murmured greeting.

'Excuse me,' I say, with a genial formality, to put her at her ease. 'Would you know the best way to cross those walls up there?'

She brightens, stopping short of smiling. 'Just climb over them.'

'There's no way through – by stiles or gates?'

'There aren't any. It's alright just to climb them.'

We pass, but the thought of climbing walls with Osprey seems a Herculean effort. There is an inn five miles away at Cross. Maybe, a hot pub meal? Even a bed for the night? I'm going to give myself a break from leaping hurdles. What's more, that swollen river's looking pretty deep. Don't fancy getting swept down to where it fans out on the shore.

I weave a weary way, up through the fields and to the steadings of the farm. As I come into a courtyard, I see a sign that says 'Galson Hostel'. A man and woman are sitting there inside a 4x4, just about to drive away. They'd seen me coming, thought that I might be a customer who'd booked, and waited to provide a welcome. Yes, they've got plenty of room at this time of year. There's just one guest at the moment, another's coming later. Yes, it's warm and quiet, and a bed can be mine for a tenner. Done deal!

With a surge of relief I scurry in the door. Literally, as I cross the threshold, the skies let loose their volley in a monsoon overture. After a few minutes it stops as quickly as it started, but with a violent grand finale, a whiplash tail of pea-sized hailstones. By the time I've got my clobber off, the ground outside has turned half-white.

Graham is an electrical engineer from Durham. As I enter, he sits stoically at the kitchen table with a bottle of wine beside him.

'I can offer you a glass of red,' he says, matter-of-factly, as his opening words, 'but no food. I've been cycling all day. There's no shops and I'm out of supplies.'

'I've got plenty of eggs,' I say, happy to find such company, 'and a little bread mix – though it's hardly enough for two.'

'There's some stuff left in there,' he suggests, pointing to a cupboard by the cooker.

Our luck is in. Somebody has remaindered half a bag of self-raising flour. I've never tried baking a loaf with a mix of yeasted flour and self-raising before, but needs must. I warm a little water, work it in with a smattering of salt, and a couple of teaspoons of sugar. If the yeast's going to go, that should set it off like a rocket. Tally ho.

Graham watches curiously, partly sceptical, partly intrigued, but willingly investing in the venture with a generously proportioned glass of wine. I knead the mix on the sideboard until the dough pulls out, all long and stringy. After half an hour, it's achieved a partial rise. Hopefully, the self-raising bicarbonate will do the rest. With biology and chemistry joining hands, into the oven it goes.

We've been chatting about electrical engineering in the way men do when flexing expertise, and checking out shared ground. In Papua New Guinea, a quarter of a century ago, I'd set up a couple of small village hydro schemes. I was an amateur and therefore find it fun to pick an expert's brains. Arcane stuff – like power factors, three phase voltage curves, and how induced currents with inadequate earthing can give an unexpected shock from the neutral wire.

'So, what brings you here?' he asks.

'Pilgrimage,' I say, slightly embarrassed, sensing that the poaching gambit isn't going to wash.

'Pilgrimage!' he guffaws. 'So you believe in Him-Up-There, do you?'

'Not like that! Not a *Him*. And not quite *Up There* either.'

'So, what *do* you believe in then?'

'It's not about belief. More, about experience. Ways of seeing. The ground of being from which our deepest selves emerge. The further reaches of consciousness – both as individuals, and cosmic consciousness – like the Hindu scriptures describe so well.'

He's landed a right one here, so I might well ramp up the voltage.

'You see, it's about the very *source* of life and underlying unity. Life as love made manifest. This whole spiritual . . .

shebang!' At which I clap both my hands together, just for a bit of fuse-blowing panache.

He laughs incredulously. My wine is kicking in very nicely on an empty stomach. We're both enjoying this stand-offish rapport.

'Look!' he says. 'I'm a Geordie. I'm from the north of England. Where I come from, if you talked like that, people would say: *Don't think about it, and drink plenty of beer.*'

'But that's the problem,' I retort. 'If they don't look, they won't see. They'll get all froth and no beer.'

Oh, he is enjoying this! Getting as good as he gives. What's more, emanating from the oven is an aroma that, back in the days of proper sacrificial offerings, would have been 'pleasing unto the nostrils of the Lord'.

Graham tops our glasses up again. Jürgen Moltmann, the German theologian, says he loves the company of atheists. By the second glass, all they want to talk about is God.

'So what's your *evidence*?' he asks. 'How are you going to *prove* to people that this *God* of yours is real?'

That's not, actually, the greatest of my worries. I'm more thinking to myself: *Better not let on about the faeries.*

'Spirituality!' he says, shaking his head. 'You know what? Where I come from, some people would get angry about *spirituality.*'

'Angry?'

'O-o-o, I don't know. I really don't know. But I'll tell you what they'd say. Some of them, they'd say: *Eee . . . ye'r doin' my head in!*'

There's a rattling at the outside door, and in comes Peter from the Isle of Barra.

He's been travelling the length and breadth of Lewis, knocking on doors for the Mori polling company, canvassing views about local government services. I kick off by asking what he thinks is his decisive skill in carrying out such work.

'Much of it,' he muses, 'is just getting people to converse.

The trouble is, people no longer know how to have a chat across the garden fence. They're all so caught up in their computers and TVs.'

'Even on the islands?'

'Even here.'

Turns out that he's the founder of a fledgling Isle of Barra distillery.

'Read about it just two weeks ago, in the *Stornoway Gazette,*' I tell him. 'Is it true that you've already sold the entire first year's production run?'

He gives a satisfied nod. 'Every single bottle.'

'Any samples in the car?' quips Graham, optimistically.

'Not yet. We've still to build the place.'

Graham's struggling to add this up.

'Hang on,' he says. 'If you've still to build the distillery, how come you've flogged the first year's output?'

'Cask sales! In advance. You see, there's a huge premium on the first batch from collectors. That's how you build the finance base for a new distillery.'

'If it's not too nosy,' I ask, 'how much to set one up?'

'About two million.'

'So, let me get this right,' I say. 'Your day job's doing door to door social research. At night, a backpackers' hostel. And you're trying to pull a couple of million for a . . .'

'That's the way you start a business!' he said, with a swish of entrepreneurial verve. 'What's more, you don't find wee communities that talk religion and philosophy in most hotel rooms.'

Graham's now getting his head done in from another direction.

'You're planning a distillery,' he coos, 'on the strength of *non-existent* whisky?'

'That's what the man said!' I chortle, as I swing the oven door open, with a swish of debonair élan.

'How's that for faith in spirits invisible.'

*   *   *

And if I have to give the dénouement myself – *Risen to perfection!* Crisp, golden, rounded – all astounded.

But now it's Thursday – day eleven of my twelve – and the rain is heavy, heavy, pounding on my back and shoulders. I've got my head huddled down, walking like the outer door is bolted fast and I'm going to stay inside. These last three miles of inland road, up to the Butt of Lewis, must be the bleakest stretch in Lewis. No houses. No vistas on the sea. Not even a decent river's saving grace. No wonder they say it's haunted. Just acre after acre of drab moorland, dripping peat hags, hardly even any traffic once the morning rush hour down to Stornoway is past.

I plan to head up to Teampall Pheadair, Saint Peter's Chapel, in the old cemetery at Swainbost. From there, on to Teampall Mholuidh and Tobar Rònain – Saint Ronan's Well – also known as Tobar an Teampaill, in the village of Eoropie at Ness. Tomorrow, my last day, I'll see if I can find Fuaran Stoth, a spring said to be good for the stomach and to confer feelings of wellbeing. Also, to visit the most northerly sacred site of them all – a little rise with what remains of Teampall Rònain. Finally, there will be the small matter of a closing ritual that's been shaping up in my mind. Then, the bus back to Stornoway, and from there, the ferry, train and Glasgow.

If I'd taken the route of the hurdled walls this morning, I'd be passing through North Dell by now. Somewhere there, in a field long since ploughed over, is the lost site of Teampall Chliamain. There's nothing any more to see. The very thought brings up a sutra, chiming like a messaged text from the Empty Belfry School of Hebridean Zen.

> The less there is to see
> the holier a place it be

Three sacred sites are consecrated to Saint Clement in the Outer Hebrides. The others are at Rodel, from where I started off, and Teampall Chliamain in the old graveyard at

Tigharry – Taigh a' Gheàrraidh – on North Uist. Clement is the patron saint of the Macleods of Harris and Dunvegan.[1] No-one can be sure which Clement it is, as there was more than one. Generally, he's assumed to be Clement of Rome, a first-century pope who was martyred in the Black Sea – tossed in with an anchor stone around his neck – the punishment for opening up a miraculous spring to relieve his thirsting fellow quarry slaves.[2] He thus became the patron saint of quarry workers. It was a nice thought in the Harris superquarry campaign.

That said, John MacAulay points out that the church in Rodel lacks his trademark symbol of the anchor. Could it be then, that the Clement in question is that of Alexandria, or both, in one of those classic saintly fusions? I'm thinking of the blazing heavenly sun that is carved into Macleod's tomb, and the old island practice of walking sun-wise round the church. The Alexandrian Clement loved solar imagery of the resurrection.[3]

> Hail, oh light for he who rides over all creation is the *Sun of Righteousness* who has changed sunset into sunrise, and crucified death into life.

There are other possible Clement candidates, including obscure Celtic saints who took the name. Maybe it's not the questions that matter. Musing on an English country chapel, T.S. Eliot said:[4]

> You are not here to verify,
> Instruct yourself, or inform curiosity
> Or carry report. You are here to kneel
> Where prayer has been valid. And prayer is more
> Than an order of words . . .

This, he said, is where we meet 'the intersection of the timeless moment'. For me, such timelessness unveils the deeper mysteries. 'Do this in *memory* of me,' said Jesus at the Last Supper. The bread, the body, as the fabric of the universe. The wine, the blood, its animating spirit. Here *anamnēsin* as 'memory' in the original Greek infers the calling back of real presence. And that, from outside of space and time, as the *apocatastasis* – the revelation of the true underlying nature of all things. That too, as the *parousia* – being 'alongside' the 'presence' or the 'essence' – the so-called 'second coming' of the Cosmic Christ that always is, always was, and always will be if we just *wake up*, which is 'enlightenment'.[5]

Hey! That mouthful would have been a cracker for Graham in our bread and wine party last night. They're just other ways to talk not just about the 'deep time' of geology and physics, but deepest time. The stilling point – 'be still and know' – at which, John Carey said of the early Celtic poetry, 'eternity is always present in the heart of time'. The world touched on in *Mary Rose,* by tradition's deepest realms of faerie, and Nansen's tale of Father Anselm's sojourn in the monastery garden. Therein the cosmic homecoming, the resolution and the healing of our deepest *nostos-algos.*

More peat. More moor. Just sufficient passing cars to keep the ghosts at bay. This weather's blotting out all sounds and has me muffled in white noise. There's nothing else to do but watch the rain in pitted craters boiling at my feet. Drops that splash and splash again with droplets from their splashes. The Celtic monks, like those across North Africa, sought out their places of retreat in deserts but *in oceano desertum* – in oceanic 'desert' hermitages.[6] This sea lane that I'm on is running as an endless shining stream. If I started on the Golden Road from Harris, I'm ending on the Silver Road to Ness. What's more, the verge round here is lined with bouquets of sea pinks. The soil is suited to them, thanks to ocean spray and added salt that the council spreads on winter ice.

Three churches jostle on the horizon as I come up to the village of Cross, the heart of Ness, both port and district. 'Eee . . . ye'r doin' my head in!' – I could imagine Graham saying if he saw them all. Mind you, it was a touching thing this morning. When we divided up the remainder of the bread and rinsed out the wine glasses, he'd asked me for the reference on William James – a classic piece of research on religious experience.

I can feel the hardness of the road taking its toll. Shooting pains are coursing through my knees. With little else for distraction, I watch each ache come on, linger, fade and then another takes its place.

That clarity of being, that sense of me observing me, is on me once again. Walking in that same vague sense of golden light as yesterday. Walking into Cross, the village, you could say that marks the spot. I'm glad I didn't take the headland route but chose instead this mono-toned monotony. Glad that it's still raining, and that I've spent the morning, as it were, inside. So glad about this *gladness* in my life that keeps on breaking through – as I keep on walking, walking, every next step.

'To what are you walking?'
Into the heart of the holy.
'Do you remember "Set the Controls for the Heart of the Sun"?'

The tune's been running in my head. Roger Waters borrowed lines from a book of Chinese poetry – Li Shangyin – Tang Dynasty, ninth century, same time as the Celtic saints. Yes, I remember the chant-like chords, the synthesiser glide.

'Watch little by little, the night turn around.'
The heart of the Sun. The heart of the Sun.
'Over the mountain, watching the watcher.'
The heart of the Sun. The heart of the Sun.
'Making the shape of, his questions to Heaven.'
The heart of the Sun. The heart of the Sun.
'Love is the shadow, that ripens the wine.'
The Heart of the Holy, the heart of the sun.

'The ancients considered the Sun to be a living entity, part of a divinely animated universe' – or so Rupert Sheldrake said to me, once upon a time.

*   *   *

And now, *Ladies and Gentlemen* – courtesy of Gerald Scarfe animations – we have the Satanic pleasure of presenting you with, *A DEMONIC VISITATION*.

Creeping towards me, cacophonously, at little more than a walking speed, and flaunting great revolving wings from out of the sides of its fat wasp-yellow carcase, crawls a council road-sweeping machine.

I step aside in abject disbelief. This road is haunted after all.

Here we are – in a world that's trying to reduce its carbon emissions – on an island that is closing schools because it can't afford to pay the teachers – and this *behemoth* comes sweeping rain from a surface clean enough to eat off.

'We don't draw our tea water out of wells anymore. We get it out of road sweepers.'

O woe, woe, bring on Saint Anthony the Great of Egypt.[7]

A time is coming when men will go mad, and when they see someone who is not mad, they will attack him saying, *You are mad, you are not like us.*

A side road leads me off down to the coast. I escape onto an unpaved path that comes out above Tràigh Chrois, the Beach of the Cross. The grass is luscious here, with banks of primrose breaking into flower. The rain goes off, I sit and picnic on the end-crust of bread, dipping it into the last drops of the lovely honey that had been given to me by a Muslim friend in Glasgow. That's what a place called Cross should be – a crossing place; and down on the beach, I cross another flooded stream, this time over wobbly stepping stones that only just permit my boots to stay dry. Fantastic boots they've been. Berghaus – *from the north of England, Graham!* Gratitude.

The headland on the other side is wimpled with feannagan. Further on, the land dips down into a stretch of wind-scourged machair. Here the grass again is white with drifting sands. Another river, this time with a footbridge, and just beyond, a hillside with a big hexagonal enclosure. In the bottom corner stands a single gable end. There is a long narrow window facing east. Somebody has cared. It has been temporarily reinforced with a simple wooden frame. This is Teampall Pheadair.

Carmichael tells that Peter is *us righ nan iasgair, Peadair treun* – 'the King of the Fishers, brave Peter'. The Christmas catch from boats on Uist was given to the poor, and known as *dèirce Pheadair* – Peter's tribute. The haddock, with black fingerprints behind its gills, is *iasg Pheadair rùnaich* – 'the fish of loving Peter'. And the petrel is described as *peadaireach* – Peter-like – because it flies so low above the waves it nearly seems to walk upon the water.[8]

The air is preternaturally clear, the way it goes when cleansed of dust just as the rain stops. There is no question. This whole place heaves with sanctity. Between it and the sea is Teampall Thòmais, and somewhere there's a hillock, Cnoc an Annaid. Serried rows of plainsong headstones face east with the gable window. None of them are more than kneeling height. Set further back, there are some larger monuments of more recent provenance. Lank lengths of last year's herbage lie flayed and tangled all around.

I push the gate and step inside. A freshly varnished plaque, mahogany I think, is set there on a plinth. An inscription reads: 'Over four hundred old Bibles were buried here on Friday 30th June 2006.' Most families didn't want to throw their careworn tattered pages out for dumping in the landfill. It's like rural Russians will often prefer to hang old icons in the forest, or float them down the river, and thus with veneration give what had been given back to providence. The plaque bears a passage from Isaiah: 'The word of our God will stand forever.' The kind of islander who'd visit here would mostly know the context. 'The grass withereth, the flower fadeth: but *the word of our God shall stand forever*.'

Down at the river, the wind has gusted hollows in the sand. As can happen in these ancient cemeteries, it has scattered out the bones. I kneel, and lift a human finger bone, its joints fused solid by arthritis. An old woman comes to mind, one of many from my childhood, their bodies racked with pain, their beings wrapped in prayer. John MacInnes tells about an old Skye woman who he knew when he was young. In her belief, the dead lie waiting in the village cemetery, 'longing until the last of the future generations should join them, whereupon their society would be complete'.[9]

I hold the finger for awhile, then gently put it back amongst the other relics of the saints. Here rest a humble people. Here, the consummation of the soul to soil. Ashes to ashes. Dust to dust. The ministry of laying down. And this is holy ground. 'Be still and know that I am God.'

'Be still and know . . .' the Psalmist urged; and thirty years ago, when I was travelling in the Himalayas, an old man from Sikkim knocked upon the door of where I stayed. He spun his prayer wheel, and when I asked him for the meaning of his utterance – *Om mani padme hum* – he gave to me the purest invocation: 'God come to my heart.'

I kneel again, this time within the walled confines of brave Saint Peter's temple.

Be still and know . . . come to my heart.

Be still and know . . . come to my heart.

That Psalm, that old man's wheel, they just keep spinning on.

'I'm with you always. Like a fern in the spring.'

And my eyes are on a level with the congregation of the plainsong headstones. The wind has settled down to calm. The smell of rain still lingers fresh upon the air, but the sun is now beginning to shine through. Before me is a quite remarkable sight. Hundreds of snails, with big striped shells, have risen from the tangles of dead foliage. They're clinging to the stones, and doing what God's creatures do when comes the merry month of May.

Love is living in the midst of death, and from my gut a song breaks out – a strange but old familiar song – and I can feel my eyes are filling.

Angus Smith, the minister of Cross Free Church, once told an interviewer:[10]

> You see, when you sing in Gaelic . . . you use so many grace notes and everybody can be slightly different but it all merges together into a kind of shimmer. And, to me, it's like the sounds of the sea, or the sound of the wind, or all the sounds of nature merging into one.

But stop! Ego cuts in and cuts me dead, in sheer embarrassment.

What if you are being heard?

I look around, but here is far from anywhere. The rain has kept folks shut indoors. There's just a herd of cows, lined up and watching from the hill. A rabbit pops out from a hole beneath a slab, noses around, and ducks back down again.

A voice fills my imagination.

THERE IS NOBODY HERE . . .

And freed from inhibition, I let the song resurge. I hurl myself upon its waves, dissolving into tides of tears that stream as holy unction down my face.

Everything is just . . . so beautiful.

And the voice – that is both of me and beyond me – says:

THERE IS NOBODY HERE, BUT EVERYBODY IS HERE.

There is a lot of love in this community.

At which the main switch trips. The fuses blow and melt the logic circuits of my mind. I throw away the reindeer shoulder bone and the sand is blown completely off the Hill.

'I will go down to Hallaig,' said Sorley Maclean. 'And when the sun goes down behind Dun Cana' – behind the sìthean of the bards – 'a bullet will come from the gun of Love.'

'And will strike the deer . . . sniffing at the grass-grown ruined homes.'

'Tha tìm, am fiadh, an Coille Hallaig.'

And time itself, in time will die, but die into the arms of Love.

. . . 's nuair theàrnas grian air cùl Dhùn Cana
thig peilear dian à gunna Ghaoil . . .
I will go down to Hallaig,
to the Sabbath of the dead,
where the people are frequenting,
every single generation gone.

They are still in Hallaig,
MacLeans and MacLeods,
all who were there in the time of Mac Gille Chaluim
the dead have been seen alive . . .
. . . and their beauty a film on my heart
. . . 's am bòidhche 'na sgleò air mo chrìdhe.

21

THE WOMAN AT THE WELL

I slowly pull away from Teampall Pheadair and climb the hill.
It overlooks a vast expanse of machair that, with the change of
weather, is blanketed with rabbits. Less than a mile away, the
last horizon starts to shrink before me as I walk. Here is the
Butt of Lewis and the tight-packed homes of Eoropie, each
with a narrow strip of croft land streaking up the back.

In the middle of the village, just above the line of houses,
stands Teampall Mholuidh – Saint Moluag's. The name probably means 'monk', or perhaps 'promontory' or 'patience'. This
contemporary of Saint Columba floated over from Ireland on a
rock (that is to say, sitting on the ship's ballast) and set up his
church on the Isle of Lismore, later the birthplace of Alexander
Carmichael. From there, he is said to have evangelised the Picts,
and to have had the power to cure insanity. I've heard that, even
into the present era, if somebody in Ness acts a bit daft people
might joke: 'Watch out, or we'll take you to the Temple.'

On picking it out from amongst the other buildings, I cere-
monially drop to my knees. That, according to Martin Martin,
is what peregrinating pilgrims did when first a temple entered
into view. 'They were in greater veneration in those days than
now,' and one of his informants in the late seventeenth century
could remember witnessing it at Saint Moluag's when he was a
boy. These days, the building is restored and cherished by the
Scottish Episcopal Church.

Martin also tells about the temple's jolly reputation. At Halloween and Candlemas – the latter equating with the feast day of Saint Bridgit at the start of February – the villagers engaged in what he felt obliged to call 'this ridiculous piece of superstition'. Pilgrims from all over the island would converge on the nearby beach. They brought a special ale, brewed with a peck of malt from every home. A cup was poured out on the waves in sacrifice to Shony, their sea god, with the hale and hearty incantation: 'Hoping that thou wilt be so good as to send us plenty of seaware for enriching our ground during the coming year.'

Afterwards, everyone would head off to the temple. They'd stand in reverential silence by a candle burning on the altar. As soon as it expired, 'all of them went to the fields, where they fell a-drinking their ale, and spent the remainder of the night in dancing and singing'. The historian W.C. Mackenzie has it that they all converged upon the church 'with lights in their hands' where 'they worshipped the saint all night long' in 'drunken orgies'. Although the people were nominally Protestant, 'the real religion of the people was simply saint-worship'. Instances of Shony veneration, he said, endured into the nineteenth century. The clergy, 'by means of argument, warning, and threats,' induced the people 'to give up their idolatrous practices'.[1] Thankfully so, of course.

I leap across a deep little stream, its width just inside the limits I could cope with, and, to my astonishment, find that I am standing at a ring of menhirs. There aren't supposed to be stone circles in Ness. It takes a minute or two of wandering about before I realise I've emerged inside a kiddies' theme park. I toss my head and mutter: *You're gone! gone! gone!* Snap, snap! It's time to pull the needle out and shut the sìthean door. Time to bring the Tardis back to earthbound orbit.

I amble up towards the houses. There is a tourist sign – 'Eoropie Tearoom – Not Open on Sunday'. But this is only Thursday, and I quickly find it does a tempting line in bacon butties. Oh well – 'A sin not enjoyed . . .'

Tobar Rònain should be somewhere by the roadside. I wander to and fro, peering through the long grass and the buttercups that line the verges. It's one of those sedately mellow evenings that often follows heavy rain. A woman with a little girl at heel comes idling up towards me. I notice there's no ring upon her finger. Perhaps a single mother.

'What are you looking for?' she asks.

'I am looking for Saint Ronan's well.'

She drops her voice, as if to make a personal apology. 'You won't find it any more.' She points down to an ugly concrete culvert. 'It used to be right there, but the digger knocked it in when they were widening the drain.'

I stutter in disbelief. Finlay had told me it was damaged, but not completely gone.

'Is this what has become of Ronan's Well?' I ask, indignantly. 'Holy water, running down the drain?'

'There are other wells,' she says, trying to console.

'What about Fuaran Stoth? Would that still be intact?'

'Oh, you should find it up the road. Look out for the streaks of iron coming from the spring. They say it used to be a cure for stomach ache.'

'And any others?'

'There's plenty. They used to be on nearly every croft. One had such good water that people kept on going to it until recently. But the man who owns the ground . . . he decided that he didn't want them walking on his land. And he . . . blocked it.'

'Blocked it?'

'Well . . . he put a dead sheep down. It was a bad thing to have done.'

We're both looking at each other wordlessly. The child is hugging tightly to her arm. I must seem to be a strange man.

'To poison a well . . .' I say, slowly. 'That is to destroy the flow of life that runs within a community.'

She nods, but refrains from commenting. The child is tugging at her dress, anxious to get moving.

'And Ronan's Well? Has there been any talk of restoring it?'

'A man from the village wanted to, but somebody from Health & Safety said he couldn't.'

Again, we look at one another in a shared sense of bewilderment.

I watch them wander slowly back along the road from where they came. I feel like I've been blessed by one whose inner well is always springing up.

A narrow path leads through the crofts, up to the staunch grey temple. There is a seagull sitting on a stubby stone finial. They punctuate the easternmost extremity of a mottled slate roof. There is a low-sunk doorway with an arch. Alongside, a high Celtic cross of silver granite, a memorial to those who fell in the Great War.

I sit down beneath its interwoven knotwork, and draw what little warmth I can from the thin evening sun. An epitaph is written on the plinth. To my surprise, it is a passage from the Apocalypse of Saint John, one that Tom Forsyth of Scoraig would often quote, stirring up our fledgling courage in the early days of the land reforming work on Eigg. He'd gone there with his wife, Djini, and camped for several days amongst the ruins of the cleared village of Grulin – the aptly named Stony Place. There, as a sign and portent, they had restored the Well of the Holy Women. The passage reads:

> To him that overcometh will I give to eat
> of the Tree of Life, which is in the midst
> of the paradise of God

'We have got to face the Angel with the flaming sword,' he'd often tell me. 'The fire of God that guards the Tree of Life in Eden.

'That's what it means to *overcome* – to overcome self-centredness that dims our eyes, and blinds us to eternity within a grain of sand.'

'What is the Tree of Life?' I'd ask.

'Been there all along. Concealed within this very world of brokenness. Its leaves are for the healing of the nations. That's what our deeper work is all about.'

Through the arched door, inside the church, the scene is set for services. There are pews and prayer books, children's artwork, and a Bible on the lectern. But it's getting on. I must take my leave. I want to pitch my tent above Stoth Bay, the local beach.

I take a last look back as I go out the door. There are a pair of candles standing by the altar, their holders garlanded in flowers. Apart from that, I see no hint of preparations for a bit of sea god revelry. What a pity. To think – I could have called up Doctor Finlay.

'A little dance, perhaps?'

Friday 22 May, and the year is 2009. It is, finally, day twelve. I wake up, and can scarce believe I've made it here. Once packed, I head back down the road and look, but to no avail, for Fuaran Stoth. I'll just have to draw my wellbeing from elsewhere today. When I get to the back end of the in-bye strips of crofting land, I break off to the east, and solemnly proceed towards a fence that corresponds to reference NB 524654 on the map. Up here should be the site of Teampall Rònain.

It takes some minutes searching, but there it is, for all that it is. A few foundation stones protrude from an eroded grassy ridge. Oh well – 'The less there is to see . . .'

I lie down on the turf beside them. It had rained in the night, but now the sun's come up and it's turning out to be a balmy island day. Candy clouds drift lazily through powdered tones of pastel blue, and I'm gazing southwards, back through all the horizons I've traversed. All those West Side villages, the Uig moors and Grimersta, the mountain passes of the Harris Hills, the whaling station and hotel at Tarbert, the Bays Café and John's boat shed – the whole array, like flights of locks all stepping down to meet the sea at Rodel.

The Butt of Lewis lighthouse stands behind me. A dozen leagues out north to sea lies the tiny island of North Rona, where Saint Ronan built his final temple. After bringing Christianity to Lewis in the seventh century, the monk decided that the people of Ness were too busy and too noisy for his prayer life. An angel sent the *cionaran-crò,* the leader of a pod of whales – with 'his great eyes shining like two stars of night' – and so the saint was spirited across the water.[2] On North Rona lived a people, of whom Martin Martin said, 'They take their surname from the colour of the sky, rainbow and clouds.'[3]

Some of the legends of the Hebrides go back, it is said, to the *Cailleach Bheag an Fhàsaich* – the Little Old Woman of the Wild. She, 'whose age even tradition failed to account'. Her maiden days were spent in Glen Corradale, South Uist. Her words described a kind of golden age, one where 'the little brown brindled lark of Mary bounded to the ear of heaven to herald the dawn', and where all the islands of the Hebrides were joined up into one.

Then came Culloden, followed by the Clearances, and in Carmichael's words, 'The whole of these faithful people of Corradale, and hundreds more, were evicted and driven to all ends of the earth – many of them to die moral and physical deaths in the slums of Glasgow and other cities.'

In 1869, a South Uist woman recited to him a poem of coming cataclysm. She prophesied a continuation of the 'overflowing of the Atlantic and the submerging of certain places'. In the end, there will come a time in which:[4]

The walls of the churches shall be the fishing rocks of the people, while the resting-place of the dead shall be a forest of tangles, among whose mazes the pale-faced mermaid, the marled seal and the brown otter shall race and run and leap and gambol – *Like the children of men at play.*

Flood legends don't need second sight in the era of climate change. The folk memories of many coastal peoples in the world look back to inundation after the Ice Age, when the global sea level rose by some 120 metres.[5] What intrigues me about the Hebridean legends is Otta Swire's account of three great floods. That of Creation, that of Noah, and that which has yet to come – but with the latter, 'Iona will rise on the waters and float there like a crown'. This, so that the dead 'will arise dry' to ease their recognition on the Last Day.[6]

To me, these places that I've visited, this spirit represented by Iona that rolls on into the present day, are a crown no inundation can wash away. This path to keep our feet dry – its old ways preserved by collectors like Carmichael, its new ways embedded in real-life communities – is nothing less than a heritage of world importance.[7] That crown is the *crò*, the heart or kernel of the places that I've visited, the people that I've met, and what it means to be a human being. Come what may, that might help us face what comes to pass.

We don't know what we're inside of. So far, the 'children of men' have only glimpsed at an ecology of the imagination, but the changes happening in our world are a basic call to consciousness.

But the walk is not quite over yet. The Stornoway bus isn't due until 11.40. I've one last duty. The closing ritual. The sacrifice.

I scramble down the rocks and onto Stoth beach. Kneel beside a stinking pile of rotting seaweed. Take from my pocket a strange cylindrical object. This, I shake with vim and vigour, in a manner that anybody watching would consider quite fanatical.

I don't have a copy of Martin's book with me. His version, anyway, was rather terse – too much on the 'short wave', to satisfy his metropolitan intended readership. So, needs must. With a furtive glance to make sure the tourists with their fancy camera phones aren't out yet, I raise my head unto the heavens, pull the silver popper from the sacred chalice – and as a golden fountain spurts across the famished waves I yell, in foghorn tones that send a flock of seagulls skirling from their nests –

Ho *Shony*! I invoke the tides of your benevolence!
May you send us your waves of providence
May we conduct ourselves in . . .
(Oh bugger, what else rhymes with *ence*?)
That this dear ocean be sustained:
And so I *sacrifice* to you –
This splendid can
Of *Irn-Bru*.

> P.S. The bacon butty teashop didn't have a licence, so I thought you'd like a shot of Scotland's other national drink.

> P.P.S. I gave you the literary version – on the long wave.

> P.P.P.S. Doctor Finlay says hello.

I cavort back to the village. An old man sees me coming, and sidles slowly over. He's in his late seventies, a thin Norse face, wry native intelligence, and he speaks hesitantly, double thinking from the Gaelic into English for my sake.

What has brought me here?

I talk about the poaching pilgrimage, about my failure to catch anything admissible. I leave unsaid the gift of landing everything.

'Did you spend the night in the village?'

He's looking for my earmarkings.

'No. I camped out at the bay. Was trying to find Fuaran Stoth, but couldn't see a spring or well of any kind.'

The surge of water turns some near-forgotten millstones in his mind.

'It was there when I was last that way,' he says. 'We used to go and clean it.'

'You did? And do you think it might get cleaned again?'

The mills of God are grinding very slow. For myself, I feel as if I'm dropping gently back to Earth inside a capsule. Little by little, I'm waking up from aeons of voyaging through space and time.

'I might . . .' he utters, falteringly. 'I might go up and have a look.'

The bus pulls in, and I sit down with Osprey by my side. The villages flit by as if a movie's running in reverse. The air's alive with Gaelic, but the further south we go, the more the balance shifts to English. I note the costly thoughtfulness, more costly than the norms out there can mostly understand.

By the time we draw up to the pier in Stornoway, they're chatting and they're laughing such a lot the driver has to shout to get them off. Within an hour I've crossed the world. Now, there will be shops and newspapers – and mountains not of stone, but of emails to catch up on.

I have arrived back at the Bay of Steering by the Stars. Back to this dear fishing port, whose motto – *God's providence is our inheritance* – runs as liquid sapphire through the veins. Like nectar from the honeybee, 'only kings and royal people get to taste that'.

Twelve days I've been away. Time now to get back on the ferry and to take the music home. I pull the needle from the sìthean door. I lay it down, and watch it settle back: the compass needle of the soul.

Acknowledgements

The walk just kept on walking in me for the seven years that it took for this book to find its final shape. There are so many people I could thank. Perhaps it will suffice to say to all those with whom I met on my journey: it was a blessing. Especially so, however, my thanks are due to the gatekeepers who so deeply structured my experience – John MacAulay of Flodabay, Seumas Crawford of Garynahine and Dr Finlay MacLeod of Shawbost.

My wife, Vérène Nicolas, may have had a break for twelve days in May 2009, but then endured a further seven years of living with an author. As I've slogged away at my computer, she's still not convinced about my fitness training. The other day at breakfast, the following formula came up:

$$\frac{7 \times 365}{12 \text{ days}}$$

I'm not sure what it means, but I'm told the answer comes out somewhere north of two hundred. Furthermore, 'Other great explorers achieved the reverse ratio.' Oh well. But thank you – for so much – my dear love.

Many friends and colleagues helped by reading over key portions of the text. These are in no way responsible for my errors. They include (in alphabetical order): Professor Timothy Gorringe of Exeter, John 'Rusty' Macdonald of Leurbost, Iain MacKinnon of Isle Ornsay on Skye, Jennifer McCarry of Glasgow, Maire McCormack of Linlithgow, Alex George Morrison of Leurbost, Andrew Morrison (Viscount Dunrossil of Vallaquie in North Uist) of Texas, Hilly Raphael of Oxford and David Thomson of Lossiemouth.

I also thank my literary agent, James Wills of Watson Little, for cajoling me to work complex material into a more accessible form, paring down the layers of paint to reveal the underlying picture on the canvas. Similarly so, Roger Smith, the indexer, my editors at Birlinn in Edinburgh, Andrew Simmons and Barbara Simmons, and its proprietor, Hugh Andrew, one of those rare surviving independent publishers with a flair for the Socratic arts of literary midwifery. For help in ways that that helped to keep my thinking, writing and hearing on track, special thanks to John and Fiona Sturrock of Edinburgh, and to Professor Michael Northcott of the School of Divinity at Edinburgh University. Michael involved me in his three-year Arts & Humanities Research Council Project, *Caring for the Future Through Ancestral Time*, which helped to deepen my thinking about time and climate change as I wove them softly into this book.

In using Gaelic, I had to live within my own limitations. My friend, Babs Nicgriogair of the Bay of Stars, gave the Gaelic a dusting off when Cath MacKinven could no longer continue with the task, and Iain 'Jock' Mackenzie of Keose helped me to sort out some of the Gaelic pronunciations in the glossary. Even then, there are difficulties, especially with place name spellings from maps, changing conventions and the vagaries of quoted texts.

Readers might notice my double dedication of this book. I hold a huge debt of gratitude to Catherine MacKinven. She was a Gaelic-speaking native, a widowed lady of the manse, who held a vast but quietly-stated cultural and theological knowledge. She took it on herself to become my cultural mentor as I wrote, most weeks sending letters filled with photocopied articles, or her own translations from Gaelic lore. She pressed me to press deeper into the tradition, and not to shy from expressing what was coming through. Old age took its toll just as we were due to run a week together – *The Pilgrimage of Life* – at Iona Abbey in 2014. Without her, this book would have been finished very much more quickly, and very much more poorly. At times, what will come through as my voice is really hers behind me. Such is the beauty and the braided richness of a living culture's carrying stream.

Now, one of the advantages of an 'acknowledgements' page, is that they're read by only the most dedicated. They can therefore be a hiding place to share things only for the most determined. The writing of this book was a very difficult process. It took me back into the Hill for seven years. I'd get lost down rabbit holes, and later have to delete most of my diggings in the sand. However, I was helped to bear the process by several major dreams along the way. The last will be enough to share, and that, by way of closure.

I was in an island church where I'd been asked to preach the Sabbath morning sermon. But I'd only brought a New Testament. The tiny huddled congregation, mostly dressed in heavy black coats, were expecting a lesson from Amos, but that's Old Testament. All that I could remember from the prophet off by heart, were the lines:

> Let justice roll on like a river
> And righteousness, like a never-failing stream

Somehow, magnificent though such sentiments are, they weren't quite sufficient for those I was charged to address. I stood before them, tongue-tied, cringing with embarrassment, and this spasm of anxiety went on and on for very near the full allotted hour.

With only minutes to the end, I stared in desperation at the wooden board on which the numbers of the Psalms were set out. As I gazed, the lettering began to fade. It never went away. The Psalms endured – my Presbyterian friends will be relieved to know – but it was like watching an old photographic plate developing. As if from out of a wash of silver nitrate in the dark room, the backdrop of an image slowly came to view.

And there she was again! Crouched, vigilant, amongst the rocks of Roineabhal.

The Blue Mountain Hare. My pilgrim guide along the way. Ancient, wild, eyes full of love.

And I have returned from out the Hill now, but never fully so.

Walking, walking, every next step.

Deeper, ever deeper.

Into the *Crò Naomh*.

Gaelic Glossary and Pronunciation Guide

This rough guide to some of the key terms used in the book is not definitive. The spellings and approximate pronunciations (in italics) vary with context, locality and the era out of which I might have quoted. As such, my usage is not always consistent.

Abhainn river or burn (a small fast-flowing river) – *a-vane*.

A bhalaich my boy, my lad, term of endearment from an older to a younger man – *a val-aich*.

A ghràidh my dear, literally 'my love', one of dozens of terms of endearment – *a-graii*.

Àirigh a 'sheiling' or hut made of wood or stone at the summer grazings in the moors – *ar-ai*.

Aisling dream or vision – *ashling*.

Àit uaigneach a solitary place – remote, forlorn, unsettling, grave-like – *ayt u-uayg-nech*.

Anaghnàthaichte the extension of the natural into the realms of the 'supernatural' – *ana-gra-eech-ah*.

An dà shealladh 'the two sights', second sight, ESP – *an da shall-ach*.

Baile, bal village – *bal-uh*.

Beannachadh blessing (**le gach beannachd** – with every blessing) – *bee-ann-ach*.

Brìghde one of many variations of Bride or Bridgit, Celtic goddess and Christian saint – *Bree-jah*. In the Gaelic, Bride should have a grave accent, thus Brìde. However, as most of my usage is either from the English or from Gaelic citations that lacked the accent, I have left it out, except where quoting material where it was included. See also endnote 14 to Chapter 2.

Bodach old man – *bod-ach*.

Both, bothan (plural) a hut or bothy, usually applied to the corbelled stone 'beehive' structures out on the moors – *bo-th, bo-th-an*.

Broch prehistoric circular stone fort – *broch* (rhymes with loch).

Brugh, bruithean interior of a faerie 'fort' or sìthean – *broo, broo-an*.

Bùrach a grand muddle – *boo-rach*.

Cailleach, caillich (possessive) old woman, holy old woman – *cal-ea-ach*.

Cianalas wistful longing, nostalgia, soul-felt weariness, sometimes translated as 'the terribleness' of being cut off from one's land and people – *key-an-a-lass*.

Cille small church or cell for spiritual retreat, anglicised as 'kil' as in Kilbride, the cell of Saint Bride – *keel-u*.

Clachan small, usually clustered, village settlement – *clach-an*.

Cnò nut, especially the hazelnut – *cn-ooh*.

Cnoc small hill – (a **cnocan** is even smaller) – *knock, knock-an*.

Crò sometimes translated as cross, but literally an enclosure, sheep or cattle fold, cell, centre, the heart or the blood – *kr-awe*.

Crodh-sìth the 'cattle of the faeries', the deer –*kr-owe-shee-h*.

Crotach hunchbacked – *crow-tach*.

Cùram sudden religious conversion, Gaelic equivalent to the Greek *metanoia*, also means 'care' – *coo-ram*.

Deiseil sunwise, as to process deiseil on entering a cemetery, also means 'ready' – *dee-sel*.

Deoch a drink (of water, etc.) – *joch* (rhymes with loch).

Drùdhadh pertaining to the Druids, the essence, that which is penetrating, also means a 'soaking' – *droo-ugh*.

Dualchas cultural heritage – *doh-ul-chas*.

Dubh black – *dooh*.

Dùthchas heritage in the land – *dooh-chas*.

Each-uisge mythical water horse (sometimes rendered 'kelpie') – *eh-ch uis-gah*.

Eòin name anglicised as Ian or Iain – *ee-in*.

Feannagan lazybeds (raised cultivation beds) – *fea-an-agan*.

Fiadh the wild, wilderness, the red deer – *fee-agh*.

Fir gorm the 'blue men', the sea faeries – *fir-gorm*.

Fuaran a spring, often used synonymously with a well – *foor-an*.

Gaoth nan sìth gust of wind stirred up by a passing faerie host (see also **Oiteag shluaigh**) – *Ga-oth nan shee-h*.

Geàrraidh the 'garden' or in-bye grazing area close to a sheiling – *gee-arr ay*.

Gearr-fiadh the 'short deer' or blue mountain hare – *gee-arr fee-agh*.

Ghillie a boy, a male servant, an oarsman at the boat or pony boy on the hill – *gilly*.

Ghlas (**Glas** feminine) hues of green, blue, silver and/or grey – *glass*.

Gobha, ghoba (possessive) blacksmith – *go-a*.

Gralloch to gut, to disembowel, the intestines – *gralloch*.

Iorram (Scots Gaelic) or **immram** (Irish Gaelic) – a rowing (of a boat), a long sea journey that may lead to the ocean of the soul – *yor-am* or *im-ram*.

Irn-Bru a post Bronze Age faerie fortification (see **Brugh**), an intoxicant recipe of which was stolen from the **Sìth** by a Glasgow soft drinks manufacturer – *the bru*.

Loch a Scottish lake – *logh* (with a deeply guttural *ch* like the Jewish name *Chaim*).

Machair alkaline soil formed from wind-blown shell sand along the coast, creating grassy flower-rich pastures – *machhh-ar* (there's that guttural *ch* again).

Marag dhubh black pudding, trademarked to Stornoway, made of blood and oatmeal – *marag dooh*.

Mhoire the name Mairi or Mary specifically as the Virgin Mary – *Vor-u*.

Mholuidh name anglicised as Moluag or variations thereon – *maol-u-aie*.

Miann ardent desire, used by the old folks for the ardent desire of God – *mee-an*.

Mile taing a thousand thanks – *meala-tang*.

Naomh holy, sacred, consecrated, sanctuary – *nuh-v*.

Oiteag shluaigh faerie wind (see also **Gaoth nan sìth**) – *oitag sl-ua*.

Phàdraig or **Pheadair** name anglicised as Patrick or Peter, equivalents to each other – *far-draig* or *fay-dar*.

Sgiobadh a communal work team – *skip-agh*.

Sìth, sì *or* **sìdh, sìd, sìdhe** the faeries, 'the gentry', the Otherworld inhabitants – *shee-h* or *shee-y-e*.

Sìth-bhrughach abounding in faerie hills – *shee-h vr-ooh-agh*.

Sìthean small hill or **Cnoc**, often inhabited by the faeries – *shee-han*.

Sìthichean faerie lore and belief systems – *shee-iu-han*.

Siubhal sìth 'faerie motion' of gliding eloquence in music – *soo-hal shee*.

Sùil-chruthaich literally, 'the Eye of Creation', a quaking bog – *sool kr-ooh-ich*.

Tàladh a death lullaby, to send the soul on its journey – *tahl-ugh*.

Teampall, teampaill (plural) the pre-Reformation 'temples' or chapels of the Outer Hebrides and a much smaller number of Inner Hebridean and West Highland sites – *tea-am-pall*, *tea-am-pill*.

Teine sìth faerie fire – *tina-shee-h*.

Tobar, tobraichean (plural) a well for drinking water – *tobar*, *tob-rach-an*.

Tuireadh elegiac laments sung over the dead – *tour-ugh*.

Bibliography

URLs are shortened, and valid as of first going to press.

ABC (2010) 'U.S. Military Weapons Inscribed with Secret "Jesus" Bible Codes', *ABC News*, 18 January, http://goo.gl/R4CzpM.

Adomnán of Iona (1995). *Life of St Columba* (ed. Richard Sharpe), Penguin Classics, London.

Ayres, Peter (2013) 'Wound dressing in World War I – The kindly Sphagnum Moss', *Field Bryology* 110, 27–34, http://goo.gl/V8QoHm.

Barrie, J.M. (1922) *Courage: The Rectorial Address Delivered At St. Andrews University May 3rd 1922*, Hodder & Stoughton, London, http://goo.gl/WOaCYX.

—(1925 (1920)). *Mary Rose*, Hodder & Stoughton, London, http://goo.gl/JTsMvK.

—(1928 (1904)). *Peter Pan, or The Boy Who Would Not Grow Up*, Project Gutenberg, http://goo.gl/YK83eb.

Barrowman, Rachel & Hooper, Janet (2006). *Lewis Coastal Chapel-Sites: Topographic Survey 2005*, University of Glasgow, Glasgow, http://goo.gl/j8DYD6.

Barrowman, Rachel (2008). *Lewis Coastal Chapel-Sites Survey 2007–8*, University of Glasgow, Glasgow, http://goo.gl/wnXVR6.

Bateson, Gregory (2000 (1972)). *Steps to an Ecology of Mind*, new edn, University of Chicago Press, Chicago.

Bateson, Nora (2011) DVD. *An Ecology of Mind*, Bullfrog Films, Oley, PA.

BBC (2001). 'Infinite Justice, out – Enduring Freedom, in', BBC News, 25 September, http://goo.gl/FJgkSg.

—(2003). '"Million" march against Iraq war', BBC News, 16 February, http://goo.gl/2a8Nko.

—(2016). 'Donald Trump and the politics of paranoia', BBC News Magazine, 24 January, http://goo.gl/n20YD9.

Bennett, Margaret (2009). 'Stories of the Supernatural: from Local Memorate to Scottish Legend'. In: Henderson 2009, pp. 167–84.

Birkin, Andrew (2003). *J.M. Barrie and the Lost Boys*, Yale University Press, New Haven.

Black, Ronald (2005). See Campbell 2005.

BMJ (1928). 'A Surgical Outpost in the Hebrides', *The British Medical Journal*, 2 June, pp. 954–5, http://goo.gl/VXSyj3.

Boettner, Loraine (1932). *The Reformed Doctrine of Predestination*, Christian Classics Ethereal Library, Grand Rapids, MI, http://goo.gl/EQTL64.

Boston, Thomas (1852). *The whole works of the late Reverend and learned Mr. Thomas Boston, Minister of the Gospel at Etherick*, George & Robert King, Aberdeen. Vol. I, https://goo.gl/MMEjLo; Vol. XI, https://goo.gl/RHXomh.

Bradley, Ian (2003). *The Celtic Way*, 2nd edn, DLT, London.

—(2009). *Pilgrimage: a Spiritual and Cultural Journey*, Lion Hudson, Oxford.

Brock, Rita Nakashima & Parker, Rebecca Ann (2008). *Saving Paradise: How Christianity Traded Love of This World for Crucifixion and Empire*, Beacon Press, Boston.

Burton, John & McCabe, Eileen (2009). *We Don't Do God: Blair's Religious Belief and its Consequences*, Continuum, London.

Bush, George W. (2000). 'Remarks at the Simon Wiesenthal Center in Los Angeles, March 6', *The American Presidency Project*, http://goo.gl/ootLjt.

Calvin, John (1553). *Commentary on John*, Christian Classics, Grand Rapids, MI, trans. William Pringle, http://goo.gl/TB7m6R.

—(1555). *Commentary on Acts* (Chapter 13), Biblehub, http://goo.gl/xoLo1z.

—(1559). *Institutes of the Christian Religion*, trans. Henry Beveridge, Christian Classics, Grand Rapids, MI, http://goo.gl/i66I92.

Câmara, Hélder (1971). *Spiral of Violence*, Sheed and Ward, London, http://goo.gl/7HwGXL.

Campbell, Angus Peter (2012). *An T-Eilean: Taking a Line for a Walk Through the Island of Skye*, Islands Book Trust, Kershader.

Campbell, Iain D. (2011). 'Viewpoint', *Stornoway Gazette,* June 23, p. 17.

—(2012). 'Viewpoint', *Stornoway Gazette*, February 16, p. 9.

Campbell, John Gregorson (2005), ed. Ronald Black. *The Gaelic Otherworld*, Birlinn, Edinburgh.

Campbell, John Lorne & Hall, Trevor (2006). *Strange Things: The Story of Fr Allan McDonald, Ada Goodrich Freer, and the Society for Psychical Research's Enquiry into Highland Second Sight*, Birlinn, Edinburgh.

Carey, John (1999). *A Single Ray of the Sun: Religious Speculation in Early Ireland*, Celtic Studies Publications, CSP-Cymru Cyf, Aberystwyth.

Carmichael, Alexander (1883). 'Statement by Mr Alexander Carmichael as to the Farming Customs in the Outer Hebrides' (pp. 213–16) and 'Grazing and Agrestic Customs of the Outer Hebrides' (pp. 451–82) in *The Napier Commission: Report with Appendices* (sometimes called Vol. 5), The Crown, Edinburgh, http://goo.gl/Uo2sbH.

—(1900). *Carmina Gadelica: Hymns and Incantations . . . orally collected in the Highlands and Islands of Scotland*, Vol. 1, T. & A. Constable, Edinburgh. These, vols. 1–3, can be found in PDF by searching www.archive.org.

—(1900b). *Carmina Gadelica*, Vol. 2, T. & A. Constable, Edinburgh.

—(1940). *Carmina Gadelica*, Vol. 3, (ed. James Carmichael Watson), Oliver & Boyd, Edinburgh.

Chamberlaine, John (1716). *Magnae Britanniae Notitia: Or, the Present State of Great-Britain*, (publisher unspecified), London, https://goo.gl/Kor56v.

Charlton, Noel (2008). *Understanding Gregory Bateson: Mind, Beauty, and the Sacred Earth*, SUNY, Albany.

Clausewitz, Carl von (2008). *On War*, Oxford University Press, Oxford.

Clément, Olivier (1993). *The Roots of Christian Mysticism: Texts from the Patristic Era with Commentary*, New City Press, New York.

Clough, Monica (1994). 'Early Fishery and Forestry Developments on the Cromartie Estate of Coigach: 1660–1746', in Baldwin, John R. ed. *Peoples & Settlement in North-West Ross*, Scottish Society for Northern Studies, Edinburgh, pp. 227–42.

Corbin, Henry (1969) trans. Ralph Manheim. *Creative Imagination in the Sufism of Ibn Arabi*, Bollingen Series XCI, Princeton University Press, Princeton.

Crossman, A.M. (2003). 'The Hydra, Captain A.J. Brock and the Treatment of Shell-Shock in Edinburgh', *Journal of the Royal College of Physicians of Edinburgh*, 33, pp. 119–23, http://goo.gl/ZgGkw4.

Davidson, Hilda Ellis (1998). *Roles of the Northern Goddess*, Routledge, London.

Davis, Walter A. (2006). *Death's Dream Kingdom: The American Psyche Since 9-11*, Pluto, London.

Disraeli, Benjamin (1845). *Sybil or The Two Nations*, Baudry's European Library, Paris.

Dostoevsky, Fyodor (1998). *The Karamazov Brothers*, Oxford Word's Classics, Oxford.

—(1991). *Crime and Punishment*, Penguin, London.

Draper, Robert (2009). 'And he shall be Judged', *GQ.COM*, June, pp. 84–94, http://goo.gl/lPH9Cv.

Dressler, Camille (2014). *Eigg: The Story of an Island*, Birlinn, Edinburgh.

Dunbar, Janet (1970). *J.M. Barrie: the Man Behind the Image*, Collins, London.

Duncan, Angus (1995). *Hebridean Island: Memories of Scarp*, Tuckwell Press, Phantassie.

Dunn, Douglas ed. (1992). *The Faber Book of Twentieth-Century Scottish Poetry*, Faber & Faber, London.

Dwelly (1911), *Scots Gaelic – English Dictionary*, online searchable version, http://goo.gl/3RENHU.

Dymes, Captain John (1630). *Description of Lewis by Captain Dymes*, State Papers published as Appendix F in Mackenzie 1903 (below), pp. 591–5.

Eagle, Raymond (2014). *Seton Gordon: the Life and Times of a Highland Gentleman*, Neil Wilson Publishing, Castle Douglas.

Eliot, T.S. (1959). *Four Quartets*, Faber and Faber, London.

Evans-Wentz, W.Y. (1994 (1911)). *The Fairy Faith in Celtic Countries*, Carol Publishing, NY.

Fanon, Frantz (1967). *The Wretched of the Earth*, Penguin, Harmondsworth.

Ferguson, Calum (2007). *Lewis in the Passing*, Birlinn, Edinburgh.

Follett, Westley (2006). *Céli Dé in Ireland: Monastic Writing and Identity in the Early Middle Ages*, Studies in Celtic History, Boydell & Brewer, Rochester, NY.

Fossard, Lee (2014). *La Vieille dans la toponymie du Royaume-Uni et de l'Irlande: trace d'un ancien culte voué à la Nature?* (The Old Woman in the toponomy of the United Kingdom and Ireland: traces of an ancient cult dedicated to Nature?), Linguistics, HAL Id: dumas-01080422, http://goo.gl/hmq6jV.

Freire, Paul (1972). *Pedagogy of the Oppressed*, Penguin, Harmondsworth.

Freud, Sigmund (1997 (1919)). 'The Uncanny', *Writings on Art and Literature*, Stanford University Press, Stanford, pp. 193–233.

—(1984 (1923)). 'The Ego and the Id', *On Metapsychology*, Vol. 11, Penguin Freud Library, London, pp. 339–407.

Fromm, Erich (2001). *The Fear of Freedom*, Routledge Classics, Abingdon.

Funk, Robert W., Roy W. Hoover & The Jesus Seminar (1993). *The Five Gospels: What Did Jesus Really Say?*, HarperCollins, NY.

Gampel, Yolanda (2000). 'Reflections on the prevalence of the uncanny in social violence', in Robben, Antonius C.G.M. & Suárez-Orozco, Marcela M., eds, *Cultures under Siege: Collective Violence and Trauma*, Cambridge University Press, Cambridge, pp. 48-69.

Gillies, Anne Lorne (2010). *Songs of Gaelic Scotland*, Birlinn, Edinburgh.

Glacken, Clarence J. (1973). *Traces on the Rhodian Shore*, University of California Press, Berkeley.

Goodenough, Kathryn & Merritt, Jon (2011). *The Outer Hebrides: a Landscape Fashioned by Geology*, Scottish Natural Heritage, Battleby, http://goo.gl/38XaNf.

Gordon, Bruce (2011). *Calvin*. Yale University Press, New Haven.

Gordon, Katherine ed. (2006). *Voices from their Ain Countrie: the poems of Marion Angus and Violet Jacob*, Association for Scottish Literary Studies, Glasgow.

Gottlieb, Sidney ed. (1995). *Hitchcock on Hitchcock: Selected Writings and Interviews*, University of California Press, Berkeley.

Gunn, Neil M. (1986). *The Atom of Delight*. Polygon, Edinburgh.

Hedges, Chris (2003). *War is a Force that gives us Meaning*, Anchor Books, USA.

Henderson, George (1896). *Dain Iain Ghobha: the Poems of John Morison (Collected and edited with a Memoir)*, Knox Press, Edinburgh.

Henderson, Lizanne, ed. (2009). *Fantastical Imaginations: The Supernatural in Scottish History and Culture*, John Donald, Edinburgh.

Hennessey, Patrick (2009). *The Junior Officers' Reading Club: Killing Time and Fighting Wars*, Allen Lane, London.

Heschel, Abraham (2011). *Abraham Joshua Heschel: Essential Writings*, Orbis, Maryknoll.

Hietala, Thomas R. (2003). *Manifest Design: American Exceptionalism and Empire*, revised edn. Cornell University Press, NY.

Hofstadter, Richard (1996). *The Paranoid Style in American Politics*, Harvard University Press, Cambridge, http://goo.gl/cqJ7cV.

Hogg, James (1919). 'Kilmeny', *The Oxford Book of English Verse*, No. 514, http://goo.gl/rPIa7R.

Hooper, Janet (ed.) (2008) (see also Barrowman 2006). *The Papar Project – Hebrides*, www.PaparProject.org.uk, http://goo.gl/cT255D.

Hunter, James (2014). *On the Other Side of Sorow: Nature and People in the Scottish Highlands*, Birlinn, Edinburgh.

ILC (International Law Commission of the UN) (1950). *Principles of International Law Recognized in the Charter of the Nuremberg Tribunal*, https://goo.gl/oozxSq.

Jack, Ian (2011). 'Will Rupert Murdoch end up like Citizen Kane?', *The Guardian*, 22 July, http://goo.gl/RKPxm9.

Jack, R. D. S. (1991). *The Road to the Never Land: A Re-assessment of J. M. Barrie's Dramatic Art,* Aberdeen University Press, Aberdeen.

James, Saint (the Just) (2000). *The Epistle of James, with an introduction by the Dalai Lama*, Canongate, Edinburgh.

Johnson, Samuel & Boswell, James (1984). *The Journey to the Western Islands of Scotland*, Penguin, Harmondsworth.

Johnston, Thomas (1909). *Our Scots Noble Families*, Forward Publishing, Glasgow.

—(1929) *The History of the Working Classes in Scotland,* Forward Publishing, Glasgow.

Jones, George (2005). 'Blair "relished" sending troops into Iraq', *Daily Telegraph*, 19 September, http://goo.gl/1O1fWy.

Jussie, Jeanne de (2006). *The Short Chronicle: A Poor Clare's Account of the Reformation of Geneva*, University of Chicago Press, Chicago.

Kennedy, John (1979). *The Days of the Fathers in Ross-Shire*, Christian Focus, Inverness, http://goo.gl/d9stA.

King, Martin Luther (2000). 'My Pilgrimage to Nonviolence', in Wink 2000, pp. 64–71.

Langdon-Brown, Walter (1938). 'Myth, Phantasy, and Mary Rose'. In his *Thus We Are Men*, Kegan Paul, London, pp. 123–51.

LaViolette, Patrick & McIntosh, Alastair (1997). 'Fairy Hills: Merging heritage and conservation', *ECOS* 18 (3/4), pp. 2–8, http://goo.gl/h9Li82.

Lawson, Bill (1991). *St Clement's Church at Rodel*, Bill Lawson Publications, Northton.

Livingstone, David (1870). *Missionary Travels*, Harper, New York.

Longley, Clifford (2002). *Chosen People: the big idea that shapes England and America*, Hodder & Stoughton, London.

Lugar, Richard (1999). 'President Bush's 75th Birthday', *Congressional Record – Senate,* 12 July, pp. 15497–502, https://goo.gl/9Cc1h5.

Luther, Martin (1520). *Address to the Nobility of the German Nation*, Modern History Sourcebook, Fordham University, https://goo.gl/bB5GD2.

—(1543). 'On the Jews and their Lies', in Lund, Eric ed. (2002). *Documents from the History of Lutheranism 1517–1750*, Fortress Press, Minneapolis, pp. 76–8.

—(1546). 'Prefaces to the New Testament', *Luther's Works*, Vol. 35, Fortress Press, Philadelphia, https://goo.gl/FkyqJ7.

MacAulay, John (1993). *Silent Tower*, Pentland Press, Edinburgh.

Macaulay, Rev. Murdo (1980). *Aspects of the Religious History of Lewis*, John G. Eccles, Inverness, http://goo.gl/qrOMYq.

MacCoinnich, Aonghas (2015). *Plantation and Civility in the North Atlantic World: The Case of the Northern Hebrides, 1570–1639*, Brill, Leiden.

MacColl, Allan W. (2006). *Land, Faith and the Crofting Community: Christianity and Social Criticism in the Highlands of Scotland, 1843–1893*, Edinburgh University Press, Edinburgh.

MacDiarmid, Hugh (1985). *The Complete Poems of Hugh MacDiarmid*, Vol. 1, Penguin, Harmondsworth.

Macdonald, Donald (of North Tolsta) (1990). *Lewis: a History of the Island*, Gordon Wright Publishing, Edinburgh.

Macdonald, Donald (of Gisla, 'the Dolly Doctor') (2004 reprint). *Tales and Traditions of the Lews*, Birlinn, Edinburgh.

Macdonald, Finlay J. (1984). *Crotal and White*, Futura, London.

—(2003). *Crowdie and Cream*, Time Warner, London.

MacDonald, Fiona (1994). *Island Voices*, Canongate, Edinburgh.

MacFarlane, Norman C. (1995). *Apostles of the North*, The Gazette Office, Stornoway.

MacInnes, John (2006) ed. Michael Newton. *Dùthchas Nan Gàidheal: Selected Essays of John MacInnes*, Birlinn, Edinburgh.

—(2009) 'The Church and Traditional Belief in Gaelic Society', in Henderson 2009, pp. 185–95.

Mackenzie, W.C. (1903). *History of the Outer Hebrides*, Simpkin, Marshall & Co., London.

Mackenzie, W.M. (1904). 'Notes on Certain Structures of Archaic Type in the Island of Lewis – Beehive Houses, Duns and Stone Circles', *Proceedings of the Society of Antiquaries of Scotland*, VOL. XXXVIII, pp. 174–204, http://goo.gl/xXknkk.

Maclean, Calum I. (1964). 'The Last Sheaf', *Scottish Studies*, Vol. 8, pp. 193–207.

Maclean, Magnus (1925). *The Literature of the Highlands*, Blackie & Son, Glasgow.

Maclennan, Malcolm (1979 (1925)). *Gaelic Dictionary*, Acair, Stornoway.

MacLennan, William Murdoch (1976) recorded by Emily Lyle. 'Childhood Memories of Lewis', *Tobar an Dualchais*, Edinburgh, http://goo.gl/zx2koA.

MacLeod, Alexander (of Uig) (1925). *Diary and Sermons of the Rev. Alexander Macleod*, Robert Carruthers Printers, Inverness, http://goo.gl/VI7ta8.

MacLeod, Donald J. of Bridge of Don (2015) ed. Alastair McIntosh. *The Highland Clearances on the Isles of Lewis and Harris*, web published, http://goo.gl/vQlRj5.

MacLeod, Finlay ('Doctor') (1997). *The Chapels in the Western Isles*, Acair, Stornoway.

—(2000). The *Healing Wells* of the Western Isles, Acair, Stornoway.

—(2009). *The Norse Mills of Lewis*, Acair, Stornoway. (All three listed here are also available in Gaelic editions from Acair).

MacLeod, John (2008). *Banner in the West: A Spiritual History of Lewis and Harris*, Birlinn, Edinburgh.

Macleod, Kenneth (Coinneach MacLeoid) (1908) 'Sea-Poems', *The Celtic Review*, Vol. V, pp. 146–8.

—(1911). 'An Clachan a Bha ann'. In: MacKay, David N. (ed.), *Leabhar a' Chlachain: Home Life of the Highlanders, 1400–1746*, Maclehose, Glasgow, pp. 135–45.

—(1927). *The Road to the Isles: Poetry, Lore & Tradition of the Hebrides*, A & C Black, London.

MacQueen, Angus (Canon) (2008). 'Under the Mantle of Holy Bride', in Domhnall Uilleam Stiùbhart (ed.), *The Life and Legacy of Alexander Carmichael*, Islands Book Trust, Port of Ness, p. 183.

Mansfield, Stephen (2004). *The Faith Of George W Bush*, Tarcher/Penguin, NY.

Marsden, John (1995). *Sea-Road of the Saints: Celtic Holy Men in the Hebrides*, Floris Books, Edinburgh.

Martin, Martin (1994 (c. 1695)). *A Description of the Western Islands of Scotland*, Birlinn, Edinburgh.

McGinty, J. Walter (2003). *Robert Burns and Religion*, Ashgate, Farnham.

McGrath, Alister E. (1995). *The Christian Theology Reader*, Blackwell, Oxford.

—(1997). *Christian Theology: an Introduction*, Blackwell, Oxford.

McIntosh, Alastair (2000). 'Saint Andrew: Non-violence & National Identity', *Theology in Scotland*, University of St Andrews, VII:1, pp. 55–70, http://goo.gl/648Umk.

—(2001). *Soil and Soul: People versus Corporate Power*, Aurum, London.

—(2008). *Hell and High Water: Climate Change, Hope and the Human Condition*, Birlinn, Edinburgh.

—(2011). 'A Nonviolent Challenge to Conflict', chapter 3 in Whetham, David (ed.), *Ethics, Law and Military Operations*, Palgrave Macmillan, Houndsmill, pp. 44–64, http://goo.gl/5Fd27C.

—(2012). 'O Donald Trump, Woe Donald Trump', *Earthlines,* Issue 1, May 2012, pp. 43-6, http://goo.gl/1CBcjv.

—(2013). *Island Spirituality: Spiritual Values of Lewis and Harris*, Islands Book Trust, Kershader, http://goo.gl/QNu759.

—(2014). 'Foreword' to the new edition of James Hunter, *On the Other Side of Sorrow: Nature and People in the Scottish Highlands*, Birlinn, Edinburgh, xv–xxxix, http://goo.gl/khtYKd (extract).

—(2014b). 'Lost lexicon of piety recovered', *The Herald*, 23 June, p. 16.

—(2015). *Canoe Pilgrimage to the Isle of Boreray*, http://goo.gl/bk8rpi.

—(2015b). *Spiritual Activism: Leadership as Service* (with Matt Carmichael), Green Books, Cambridge.

McKay, J.G. (1932). 'The Deer-Cult and the Deer-Goddess Cult of the Ancient Caledonians', *Folklore* 43:2, pp. 144–74.

Meek, Donald ed. (2003). *Caran an t-Saoghail: The Wiles of the World: Anthology of 19th Century Scottish Gaelic Verse*, Birlinn, Edinburgh.

Merton, Thomas ed. (1965). *Gandhi on Non-Violence*, New Directions, NY.

Meyer, Kuno (trans.) (2000). *The Voyage of Bran (Imran Brain)*, In Parentheses Publications, Medieval Irish Series, Ontario, http://goo.gl/sxHlp7.

Mitchell, Arthur (1880). *The Past in the Present: What is Civilisation?* David Doublas, Edinburgh.

Moral, Tony Lee (2013). *Hitchcock and the Making of Marnie*, revised edn. Scarecrow Press, Lanham, chapter 'Mary Rose', pp. 197–221, not in earlier edition.

Murchison, T.M., ed. (1988). *Sgrìobhaid Choinnich MhicLeòid. The Gaelic Prose of Kenneth MacLeod*, Scottish Gaelic Texts Society, No.16, Edinburgh.

Napier, Lord (1884). *Report of Her Majesty's Commissioners of Inquiry Into the Condition of the Crofters and Cottars in the Highlands and Islands of Scotland, in 1884*, The Crown, Edinburgh, https://goo.gl/OsnE4S.

Neat, Timothy (2013). 'Hamish Henderson – the Art and Politics of a Folklorist'. In: Chambers, Bob (ed.), *The Carrying Stream Flows On*, The Islands Book Trust, Kershader.

Newton, Michael ed. (2006). *Dùthchas Nan Gàidheal*, see MacInnes 2006.

—(2006b) *'Bha mi 's a' chnoc*: Creativity in Scottish Gaelic Tradition', *Proceedings of the Harvard Celtic Colloquium*, 18/19: 1998 and 1999, Harvard University, https://goo.gl/1gJ2dg.

OCA (2016). *Hieromartyr Clement the Pope of Rome*, Orthodox Church in America, http://goo.gl/vRheVC.

O'Cathain, Seamus (1995). *The Festival of Brigit: Celtic Goddess and Holy Woman*, DBA Publishing, Dublin.

Ó Crualaoich, Gearóid (2003). *The Book of The Cailleach*, Cork University Press, Cork.

Oppenheimer, Mark (2014). 'Evangelicals Find Themselves in the Midst of a Calvinist Revival', *New York Times*, 3 January, http://goo.gl/HStZfq.

Ormond, Leonee (1987). *J.M. Barrie*, Scottish Academic Press, Edinburgh.

Panikkar, Raimon (1991). 'Nine Sutras on Peace', Interculture XXIV:1, pp. 49–56, Montreal, http://goo.gl/eIawm.

Pierre, Abbé (2005). *Mon Dieu . . . Pourquoi?* Plon, Paris.

Roberts, John L. (1999). *Feuds, Forays and Rebellions: History of the Highland Clans, 1745–1625*, Edinburgh University Press, Edinburgh.

Rumsfeld, Donald (2011). *Known and Unknown: a Memoir*, Sentinel, NY.

Sainte-Marie, Buffy (1964). 'Universal Soldier', *It's My Way!*, album website http://goo.gl/FQz727.

Shaw, George B. (2001). *Saint Joan*, Penguin, London.

Smith, G. Gregory (1919). *Scottish Literature*, Macmillan, London.

Smith, Iain Crichton (1986). *Towards the Human: Selected Essays*, Macdonald Publishers, Loanhead, http://goo.gl/edwEWO.

Smith, Rupert (2006). *The Utility of Force: the Art of War in the Modern World,* Penguin, London.

Starmore (née Matheson), Alice (2008). *Mamba – the Exhibition* (exhibition catalogue), Windfall Press, Gress.

—(2012). 'Isabella's Crag: Language, landscape and life on the Lewis moor', *Earthlines*, Issue 1, 4–9.

Starr, Mirabai (trans.) (2014). *Julian of Norwich: The Showings*, Canterbury Press, London.

Steigmann-Gall, Richard (2004). *The Holy Reich: Nazi Conceptions of Christianity, 1919–1945*, Cambridge University Press, Cambridge.

Stewart, R.J. (1990). *Robert Kirk: Walker Between Worlds – A New Edition of The Secret Commonwealth of Elves, Fauns and Fairies,* Element, Longmead.

Surtees, Virginia (1984). *The Ludovisi Goddess*, Michael Russell Ltd, Salisbury.

Swire, Otta (1966). *The Outer Hebrides and their Legends*, Oliver & Boyd, London.

Sylvester, Rachel & Thomson, Alice (2007). 'Dr Bari: Government Stoking Muslim Tension', *Daily Telegraph*, 10 November, http://goo.gl/aTPQpD.

Thomas, F.W.L. (Captain RN) (1859). 'Notice of Beehive Houses in Harris and Lewis; with Traditions of the "Each-Uisge," or Water-Horse, Connected Therewith', *Proceedings of the Society of Antiquaries of Scotland*, Vol. III:1, pp. 127–44, https://goo.gl/bPoBf6.

—(1867). 'On the Primitive Dwellings and Hypogea of the Outer Hebrides', *Proc. Soc. Ant. Scot.*, Vol. VII:1, pp. 153–95, http://goo.gl/jMlqdL.

—(1890). On the Duns of the Outer Hebrides. *Archaeologica Scotica*, Vol. V, pp. 365–415, http://goo.gl/y3hX6D.

Thomas, R.S. (1996). *R.S. Thomas* (anthology of poetry), Everyman, London.

Thompson, Paul (2009). 'Donald Rumsfeld's holy war: How President Bush's Iraq briefings came with quotes from the Bible', *Daily Mail* / *Mail Online*, 20 May, http://goo.gl/H8u7wo.

Thompson, Paul & Drury, Ian (2010). 'Shot in the foot: Propaganda fear as our troops are given U.S. guns carrying secret Bible codes', *Daily Mail* / *Mail Online*, 20 January, http://goo.gl/8naCIk.

Thomson, Derick (1982). *Creachadh na Clàrsaich: Plundering the Harp*, Macdonald Publishers, Edinburgh.

Thomson, Iain R. (2001). *Isolation Shepherd*, Birlinn, Edinburgh.

Truffaut, François (1985). *Hitchcock: A Definitive Study of Alfred Hitchcock*, Simon and Schuster, New York.

Walker, Alice (1983). *The Color Purple*, The Women's Press, London.

Ward, Benedicta (trans.) (1984). *The Sayings of the Desert Fathers*, Liturgical Press, Collegeville.

Watt, Eilidh (1989). 'Some Personal Experiences of the Second Sight'. In: Davidson, Hilda Ellis, ed., *The Seer in Celtic and Other Traditions*, John Donald, Edinburgh, pp. 25–36.

WCF (1647 (1986 edition)). *Westminster Confession of Faith* (with introductory statement of the Church of Scotland's partial dissociation in 1986), http://goo.gl/ZCWQR.

—(1991). *The Shorter Catechism*, Knox Press, Edinburgh.

Weaver, J. Denny (2001). *The Nonviolent Atonement*, Eerdmans, Grand Rapids.

West Side Historical Society (undated). *List of emigrants from Arnol, Bragar and Shawbost on the Metagama*, http://goo.gl/qO4uWU.

WHFP – West Highland Free Press (2011). 'Donnie Foot – "the People's Theologian" – and the West Highland Free Press', 27 May 2011, p. 20.

—(2011b). 'Island men can expect to die earlier than most', *West Highland Free Press,* 28 October, 1.

—(2015). 'Survey shows youth attachment to the Isles', 13 November 2015, p. 7.

Wink, Walter (1992). *Engaging the Powers: Discernment and Resistance in a World of Domination*, Fortress Press, Philadelphia.

—(2000) ed. *Peace is the Way: Writings on Nonviolence from the Fellowship of Reconciliation*, Orbis, Maryknoll.

—(2002). *The Human Being*, Fortress Press, Minneapolis.

Winthrop, John (1630). *A Modell of Christian Charity*, Collections of the Massachusetts Historical Society, http://goo.gl/y5fA7f.

Wynne-Jones, Jonathan (2009). 'Tony Blair believed God wanted him to go to war to fight evil, claims his mentor', *Daily Telegraph*, 23 May, http://goo.gl/DSWsuh.

Yeats, W.B. (1990 (1893)). *The Celtic Twilight*, Prism Press, Bridport.

Endnotes

To minimise intrusion in the text, I often group nearby references into a single note. See www.AlastairMcIntosh.com/poachers pilgrimage/ for this book's web page with additional resources.

Beginnings

1. 'The Moon in Lleyn', Thomas 1996, 82.
2. McIntosh 2011.
3. Luther 1520.
4. WHFP 2011.

1 The Devil's Debut

1. BMJ 1928, for a swashbuckling account of the following story.

2 A Sacred Landscape

1. Goodenough & Merritt 2011.
2. Various sources, mainly Mackenzie 1903, xxxvi–xxxix. All of this is fairly speculative.
3. Pliny, first century, IV:30.
4. Bradley, 2003, 2009. Adomnán 1995, p. 127 (I:20). Sharpe's commentary to this passage (his endnotes 108 and 109) states that the pilgrim in question had a Pictish, not a Celtic name. Sharpe also discusses manuscript claims that, by the eighth century, Irish clerics wanting to live an eremitic life had reached as far as the Faeroes and Iceland, before being driven out by the 'heathen' mores of 'Northmen pirates'. Adomnán stresses that the mission from Iona stretched out across the known world. Columba's destiny, from before birth, was to 'become famous through all the provinces of the ocean's islands, and he will be a bright light in the last days of the world' (p. 105, Adomnán's 2nd preface). In this he was 'predestined to lead the nations to life' (p. 207, III:3).

Right at the end of the hagiography, Adomnán affirms that Columba had, indeed, 'earned a reputation that is famous not only in our own Ireland and in Britain, the largest of the ocean's islands, but has also reached the three corners of Spain and Gaul and Italy beyond the Alps, and even Rome itself, the chief of all cities' (p. 233, III:23). In the Celtic era the Hebrides and western seaboard of Scotland formed a Gaelic-speaking cultural continuum with Ireland, united (not divided) by the information superhighway of the Irish Sea and Sea of the Hebrides. Then the big dividing barrier was Druim Alban – the Ridge of Scotland – the name given to the mountain ranges running down the middle of the mainland, to the east of which were the Picts that Columba evangelised. It is to such geography that we might look for the earliest origins of Scotland's east–west divide.

5. Ordnance survey, Ross-shire (Island of Lewis), Sheet 27, 1851, http://goo.gl/zB8iTi. This shows the name as Airidh na'n Sagart, but Rusty, the blacksmith (John Macdonald, 31 Leurbost) considers that it should be Àirigh, consistent with the presence of the sheilings.

6. Discussion in *Soil and Soul*, McIntosh 2001, 18–19, citing John MacAulay of Flodabay.

7. Campbell 2005, 33–4. Campbell notes that this story is also localised in Ferintosh (Black Isle, Ross-shire), and he gives similar examples from Iona and Mull. In the latter instance, the faeries speak English, to which the narrator remarks: 'It is well known that Highland Fairies who speak English are the most dangerous of any.' Ronald Black's commentary (p. 319) suggests this is 'the steep slope negotiated by the Tarbert-Stornoway road where it descends to Scaladale in North Harris', or I think it may be a little higher on the same mountainside, above where *Lochan nan Clach-Mòra* is marked on the OS map by the roadside.

8. The Qur'an, XVIII:31, Yusuf Ali edn. ('The Cave').

9. Bateson 1972, 317, my italics. The chapter was first published in the journal, *Psychiatry*.

10. Bateson 2011. In this book I have sometimes used literary licence with the sequencing of time, projecting thoughts or incidents that happened later on back into my thoughts during the walk. While actually walking, my mind was empty for much of the time. I even came back and told Vérène that I wasn't sure if I had material for a book. Much of the conscious reflection took place later, interwoven with dreams, subsequent events and conversations that connected with the pilgrimage in a continuum in my mind that felt outside of strict time boundaries, as if the walking, reflecting and writing became a continuous process. The encounter with Nora is an example. The panel did not take place until 17 February 2012 by which time I was well into writing the book. Her event was fittingly called *Remembering the Future*. Her words that night helped me to constellate ideas I'd been working on from well before the walk. In particular,

I had been stimulated by a paper on creativity and the Celtic mind, delivered at Harvard University by my friend, the Gaelic scholar Michael Newton (Newton 2006).

Apart from such occasional loose playing with the sequencing of time when telling anecdotes, and apart from the need sometimes to protect sources by disguise and to reconstruct conversations from notes and memory, I have not assumed literary licence. Any magical realism is for real.

11. 'War is a force that gives us meaning' – Hedges 2003.

12. Martin 1994, 207. He gives it as *Tey-nin-druinich*, but as that is antiquated, I have used Captain Thomas's version in referring to Martin, as quoted later.

13. Maclennan 1979, 136.

14. The most scholarly study of Brìghde is O'Cathain 1995. Black (in Campbell 2005, 586) states: 'The saint's name is in the nominative *Brighid*, in the genitive Brìghde or, for short, Brìde.' I have gone for the simple but poetic for my mainly English-speaking readers.

15. MacLeod 1997. For archaeological surveys of the ecclesiastical sites see Barrowman 2006 & Barrowman & Hooper 2008. Also, the Papar Project compiled by Hooper 2008.

16. Eagle 2014, Chapter 7.

17. In MacLeod 2000, 75–7.

18. Shonny 'Mhòr' Macdonald of Berneray. Just don't ask him to tell the one about the wife of Pabbay climbing high onto a cliff in exchange for a shilling, to show the excise man her husband's *poit dubh*.

19. Alastair 'Alda' Ferguson gave me his source as the late Berneray tradition bearer, Roddy MacAskill. Hansen's biography of Armstrong leaves just enough genealogical wriggle room for the story possibly to have foundation, and Neil is a very island name, not otherwise in the Armstrong family. See discussion in McIntosh 2015. On the monks, Martin 1994, 138–9.

20. Follett 2006. A modern Scottish movement, that understands itself to be continuing the spirit of this tradition, is www.ceilede.co.uk

21. Johnston 1909. Tom Johnston, initially brought to prominence by Ramsay MacDonald, became the wartime Secretary of State for Scotland under Winston Churchill.

22. Statistical Account of 1792 quoted in Lawson 1991, 7.

23. MacLeod 1997, 9.

24. Calvin 1559, 1:11:1 (p. 95).

25. Jusse 2006, 122. See Gordon 2011 on Farel's iconoclasm and close friendship with Calvin.

26. See discussion in McIntosh 2013, 20–3; 100–1.

27. Translation as in MacAulay 1993, 10–12. I have added a comma after 'former times'.

3 Blue Mountain Hare

1. Job 38:8, 29. Another face of the Rodel tower has an equally sexualised male figure, said in tourist guides to be known locally as Suemas a'Bhuid, translating into the vernacular as 'Jimmy the Willy'.
2. Genesis 28:17.
3. This is what John MacAulay of Flodabay said. He also told me that her tomb was originally just to the right of the entrance door and raised above the floor. However, it was moved by Historic Scotland because of a recurrent problem with dampness. It now lies (out of sight and mind), 'underneath the floor of the church, and directly below the window in the south transept' (MacAulay 1993, p. 15).

    John also pointed out that the Sìol Thormoid are known as the Macleods 'of Harris and Dunvegan', the stress being on Harris, although Dunvegan Castle is located on Skye.
4. Gillies 2010, endnote to her Introduction.
5. MacInnes 2009, though he is not writing specifically about Màiri.
6. Macleod, Kenneth, 1927, 223.
7. I discuss such, including the satirical attacks of Hugh MacDiarmid, Sorley Maclean and the 'Celtosceptic' leanings of Donald Meek, in McIntosh 2014.
8. 'One Who Sang *The Cradle Spell of Dunvegan*', Macleod 1927, 169–78.
9. This high regard was expressed by both Professor Donald Mackinnon and Professor James Carmichael Watson – each of them pioneering holders of the chair in Celtic at Edinburgh 'There is only one man, Kenneth Macleod,' Mackinnon told Mrs Kennedy-Fraser in the 1920s. 'None now living can match his understanding,' wrote Carmichael Watson in his Editor's Note to Vol. 3 of the *Carmina Gadelica* in 1940. See McIntosh 2013, 146.
10. Dressler 2014 (1998). McIntosh 2001.
11. Thanks to the ethnomusicologist, John Purser, for this translation of what is a common Gaelic epitaph.
12. Neat 2013 states: '*The Carrying Stream* is an old "folk" phrase' that was given new meaning by Hamish Henderson of the School of Scottish Studies. I have recorded a similar palpable experience of being swept up in the stream at the height of the Eigg land reform campaign in McIntosh 2001, 185–6. (If we don't talk about such experiences, our silence becomes the voice of complicity in contributing to their delegitimisation by materialistic worldviews.)
13. Campbell & Hall 2006, 7.
14. Martin 1994 (1695), 105. Herman Moll's map of 1714, http://maps.nls. uk/view/74417584, see also my Chapter 7. Curiously, other English language maps do not reflect Moll's explicit association with sainthood. The 1850s OS six-inch series, like the present day version, shows it as Eilean Mhuire, which requires a Gaelic understanding to decode the spiritual import. John MacAulay tells me that early cartographers and writers often spelt Mary's name as 'Mhuire' (e.g. Rev. Macphail in

Thomas 1890, 366), but that most Lewis and Harris people today would render it as Mhoire. He adds that the isles: 'all have individual names, but are locally known collectively as "Na h-Eileanan Mor" which is generally accepted as meaning the Big Islands, which does not really make good sense. My own thoughts are that this was meant to be Eileanan Mhoire, or, Mhuire – the Virgin Mary's Islands, and the local name is a corrupt form of that. The north-easterly island in the group is called Eilean Mhuire' (pers. com. emails 2015).

Martin says of the Shiants, 'Island-More hath a chapel in it dedicated to the Virgin Mary . . .' (p. 105). This infers but does not directly state John's view. He then says of Eigg's kenning name (the name by which it is known by mariners when at sea): 'The natives dare not call this isle by its ordinary name of Egg when they are at sea, but island Nim-Ban-More, i.e., the isle of big women' (p. 304). However, I have heard a Roman Catholic opinion on Eigg that this is a Protestant misnomer, and that it should properly be translated as Island of the Holy Woman Mary, 'nim' being a corruption of *naomh* (holy, sacred).

John MacAulay's opinion of this (pers. com. 2015) is: 'I'm fairly certain that Martin Martin's *More* [in the Shiants] is the Virgin Mary's island. Likewise, Eilean na'm Ban *More* [for Eigg] is also the Virgin Mary's island. Had it been 'big women' it would be Eilean na'm Ban *Mor*. MM was supposedly a Gaelic speaker, but I'm often surprised at some of his writings.'

15. Eliot 1959, 42; MacDiarmid 1985, 422 ff.
16. 'Boy I was', Macdonald 2003, 10. Eilean na Caillich story, Macdonald 1984, 149–60
17. Unfortunately, the early Ordnance Survey maps for Harris lack the rich detail of those for Lewis, where the landowner (Matheson) helped finance the operation. However, the maps of both the 1843–82 and the 1888–1913 six-inch series show an island at the NW head of Langabhat with 'stepping stones' leading out to it, as well as a Dun (or fort) on a nearby island. John MacAulay has confirmed to me: 'I have always been led to believe that Eilean na Caillich was the one with the causeway.' Google Earth (which I had not used to look at the territory before going on the pilgrimage) shows markings that may be sheiling settlements and traces of feannagan (raised bed cultivation) near Eilean na Caillich, and what could be the ring of a collapsed both on the island. The OS maps also mark the remains of a dun (or fort) on a smaller island nearby. Half a mile to the north-west there's a loch in the hills called Loch na Caillich (Loch of the Old/Holy Woman), and just over a mile to the east, at Holasmul, the tiny Lochan Bhrighde (Little Loch of Brigit), with a long line of nearly a hundred small cairns, of evident spiritual significance, that Seumas Crawford (with John's local expertise) documented and surveyed in 2012.

In reviewing my manuscript, John wrote: 'Maybe you could add that about halfway along the eastern shore of Loch Langabhat there is a small bay inside a string of small islands. On an ancient map this area is called A Chomraich (the sanctuary, or, a place of sanctuary). There is also a cairn – Carnan a'Chomraich. It all adds to the spiritual signifi-cance of this place.' This raft of spiritual associations, as John has emphasised many times, is substantially feminine, in a way that he feels to be associated with the ancient traditions linking Brìghde to the Hebrides generally, and Harris in particular. The parish church at Scarista was originally consecrated to Saint Bride, and Harris itself was the pre-Reformation Parish of Kilbride (see note on Kilbride at the end of Chapter 5).

18. McIntosh 2000.

4 The Elder of Roineabhal

1. See material added to the 2004 edition of *Soil and Soul*, http://goo.gl/ WKFoJm.
2. Full details of this engagement are on my website at http://goo.gl/ hZZTbK. Lafarge has now merged with Holcim, and I came off the Sustainability Stakeholders Panel in 2013, after serving for ten years.
3. West Side Historical Society, undated.
4. WHFP 2011b – Island women have a life expectancy of 82, one of the best in Scotland; but on average men die at 74, ranked as the eighth worst in the UK, alongside deprived urban areas like Glasgow, Manchester and Belfast.
5. WHFP 2015. This youth survey suggests 40% want to be living on the island in five years' time, and 48% to be back by the age of 35.
6. Napier 1884, 1176. Professor Donald MacKinnon, a friend of the Rev. Kenneth Macleod, was one of the six Napier commissioners.

5 On the Golden Road

1. *The Acts of Andrew*, in McIntosh 2000. In the Orthodox tradition, Andrew is the *Prōtoklōtos*, meaning 'first-called'.
2. Augustine's *Letter 189 to Boniface*, http://goo.gl/1Z2eJF, using the translation in Aquinas' *Summa Theologica, Question 40: War*, http:// goo.gl/3fJGz2.
3. WCF 1647, 6:IV.
4. Calvin 1559, 2:16:1. For further discussion of these points, and in an island context, see McIntosh 2013.
5. McGinty 2003, 41–43. The poem naming Thomas Boston is Burns' 'Letter to James Tennant, Glenconner'.
6. This is from Boston's commentary on the Westminster Shorter Catechism, of which question eight answers: 'God executeth His decrees in the works of CREATION and PROVIDENCE.' Boston 1852, Vol. I, 129, 223.

7. From *A View of the Covenant of Works from the Sacred Records,* Boston 1852, Vol. XI, 317–320.

8. While writing this, I entered Crothairgearaidh into Google, and to my astonishment, the single reference that came up is to an academic thesis, in French, by one Lee Fossard (Fossard 2014). He describes having visited Lewis to be shown the shape of an old woman in this hill, his informant being 'Doney Martin'. (Wait till I get hold of that old milk-man and ask what tales he's been telling to the poor French tourists!) I'd never noticed this shape myself nor heard of it talked about, though when shown in Fossard's photographs (taken from the place beside John-Neil Montgomery's house, where we'd leave the road to get the mussels), it stands out sure enough.

9. Some scholars have argued that, during the era of the Penal Laws imposed by English colonisation, Irish Catholic priests were forced to seek training on continental Europe where some fell under the influence of the Dutch theologian Cornelius Jansen (1585–1638). Like the Calvinists, Jansen emphasised original sin and total depravity. Jansenism was subsequently declared heretical by the Catholic Church. Other scholars refute this as a major influence, suggesting that the 'strictness' of Irish-American Catholicism is better explained by the knock-on of Victorian English morality on its Irish subjects, as well as by asceticism from religious orders rubbing off on lay society. It should be noted that Presbyterians were also persecuted under the Penal Laws in that they sought to impose a very Anglican version of Protestantism and thus, in part, the explanation for Irish Presbyterian emigration to America.

10. Luke 7:36-50; Mark 14:6.

11. The ranking varies from year to year. In 2014, the most recent at my time of writing, the UK had slipped to 6th place, SIPRI, http://goo.gl/zBQOhI.

12. WCF 1647, 3:I. The theological parallels between some expressions of Calvinism and Wahabbism in Sunni Islam are striking, as is the histori-cal penchant of both towards authoritarian psychology and enforcement.

13. Ferguson 2007, 101–110.

14. Ferguson 2007, 50–61.

15. Peter 1:4, KJV. Other translations say 'participants', both being true to the Greek.

16. Carmichael 1900, 166. I have left the spellings in his original forms.

17. Carmichael 1900, 166; Carmichael 1900b, 114–5.

18. Carmichael 1900, xv. The present-day Church of Scotland at Scarista was consecrated to Brìghde, and in its vestry, John MacAulay (who is an elder there) has framed a *Record of Serving Ministers*, going back to 1542. This states: 'Originally, the Parish of St. Bride, which included Barra and St. Kilda; was later known as the Parish of Harris.'

The legal document to which I refer is one that I stumbled upon by chance, pertaining to the disposal of the estate of Alexander Hume in the *Edinburgh Gazette* of 24 February 1832, p. 64. This states: '. . . the following Subjects as included in the said Process of Ranking and sale, viz – The Patronage of the Churches and Chapels of the whole Lands of Harris, lying within the parish of Kilbride, commonly called Harris, and Sheriffdom of Inverness.' It is revealing that even church patronage – the right to confer a minister on the population – was, in those days, something to be bought and sold.

Another angle on Kilbride is from Otta Swire, who cites Miss Ada Goodrich Freer as maintaining that, during the first half of the eighteenth century (i.e. before the arrival of Protestant evangelicalism), Harris was not called Na Heradh or The Herries, but Kilbride (Swire 1966, 61). Freer was commissioned by the Society for Psychical Research in the 1890s to conduct a survey of the second sight in the Hebrides. Her work, published in *Folklore*, was later discredited as having been substantially plagiarised from Fr Allan MacDonald of Eriskay. How much of it was valid, nonetheless, would be difficult now to appraise, as she appears to have been a woman who played loose with the truth. Her biographer, Trevor Hall, explores the implications of her having lost both parents in childhood, and while I have not read his book, I suspect that she might be an example of Barrie's Mary Rose syndrome.

6 The Blacksmith's Well

1. Crichton Smith, 1986.
2. Calvin had his opponents summoned to the Consistory (Geneva's religious court) to answer charges of dancing at a wedding in defiance of his preaching – a matter that threw him into fury. In other inquisitions, it seems probable that he participated in torture by the rack of his opponents to procure confessions of heresy. He was also instrumental in the execution, by live burning at the stake, of Michael Servetus for heresies of which pantheism was prominent (Gordon 2011, 140–1, 215, 217–32). The suppression of dancing was, in places, undoubtedly carried into the Highlands and Islands (McIntosh 2013, 54, 100. Carmichael 1900, 4–5).
3. Henderson 1896, xliii.
4. Trans. Meek 2003, 281–7
5. MacLeod 2008, picture caption facing p. 174: There is a lovely energy to this picture, which includes Morag. It reminds me of traditional Mennonites or Amish, albeit with a different theology but probably no difference in the underlying piety.
6. Cited in Ayres 2013.
7. Henderson 1986 (biographical sketch), xlix–l. Henderson (p. xlv) describes him as 'An aristocrat of nature's creation.'
8. 2 Samuel 23:14–16.
9. This poetry is a reprise from Derick Thomson's 'An Tobar' / 'The Well', the first three verses of which are quoted at the start of this book, from

Thomson 1982, 48-9. The theme is continued as a separate poem, but of the same title, on pp. 240-5.

10. The late Norman Macleod of Bridge House, Leverburgh, crofter, lobster fisherman and retired policeman, pers. com. (letter) 21 November 2001.

11. John MacAulay says the well was on the sharp hill leading south out of Tarbert, but was lost when widening the road.

7 *My Own Lochs Now*

1. Kinlochresort – Ceann Loch Reasort – *ceann* = head; *ruadh* = red (Old Norse); *fjord* shortened to *ort* – thus, The Head of the Red Fjord (John MacAulay pers com., 2010; though an alternative etymology has it as the Boundary Fjord, bounding Lewis and Harris).

2. Sarah Scott (née Morrison) of the Harris Hotel says that at the time, both the hotel and the castle were under the same ownership, and that it was usual for visitors to stay at one while on the way to the other: a journey made in Barrie's era by pony trap. The dining room has now been double glazed, but the JMB pane has been conserved and is on display in the hallway.

3. Dunbar 1970, 246–50. The dedication was to the five orphaned Llewelyn Davies boys (Barrie 1928). Birkin 2003, 203–6, includes a photograph of the island (or rather, tiny island cluster) on Loch Voshimid. There was also Norwegian inspiration based on what was probably a true-life child abduction story, see Moral 2013 (new edn), 197–205. All quotes from *Mary Rose* that follow are from Barrie 1925.

   The expression about the island liking to be visited is close to a saying that Kenneth Macleod (1927, 54) renders as: *Dh' iarr a' mhuir a bhi 'ga tadhal*, 'The sea likes to be visited'.

   A local source on the Voshimid connection to *Mary Rose* was the Rev Angus Duncan of Scarp who died in 1971 (Duncan 1995, 151–3). In 1966, Nicolas Llewelyn Davies wrote to Duncan, saying that he had more or less ridiculed the idea of a Voshimid connection to the play until, in 1964, he returned to the lochside and sat down just opposite Mary Rose Island (the capitalisation of the name is his). He wrote: 'Strange as it may seem, I had the most vivid recollection' of sitting with Barrie by the waterside, looking across to the island, and Barrie recalling an old legend 'which I think first sprang from Scandinavia' (Duncan 1995, 151–3, 200–1). The Rev. Duncan's memoirs are compiled by his eponymous son, Angus Duncan, who added this correspondence in an appendix.

   As seems to befit Presbyterian clergy, Duncan observed in his writings that the Scarp of his childhood was full of sìthean, faerie hills. 'Island children had implicit faith in fairies.' The dog would pick their presence up and show alarm, even when humans couldn't see them. 'We did not

regard the fairies as either friendly or hostile. They were neutral, keeping to their own company and not likely to interfere with us unless taken
by surprise' (Duncan 1995, 115).

4. Moral 2013, 205.

5. Ormond 1987, 133–5.

6. Hogg 1919. James Hogg (1770–1835) compiled his version of Kilmeny
from what was already in the Borders ballad tradition. *Kil* = church of;
and *meny* is thought possibly to relate to Eithne, the visionary mother
of Saint Columba. This creates lovely resonances and interweaving of
traditions.

7. Langdon-Brown 1938.

8. MacLeod 1997, 51 & 71. MacLeod also cites the tradition, from Martin
Martin, that women were buried in St Tarran's and men at St Keith's. It
seems to be through Martin that the association between Keith and Chè
is presumed. However, in Twitter discussion (of all things) with the Irish
scholar, @VoxHib, *Vox Hiberionacum*, another possibility is invited. He
pointed out (24 Nov 2015) that there is also a standing stone of the same
designation on North Uist, Clach Mhor A'che. Menhirs often marked
burial. He suggests that Chè might be a corruption of the Old Irish *caí*,
meaning lamenting, weeping or keening (death song) – http://edil.qub.
ac.uk/9072. Thus, Teampall Chè would make sense as Teampall of the
Keening, this fitting with its male designation and therefore the place at
which the women would keen for their departed menfolk.

9. Martin Martin, John Chamberlayne and Daniel Defoe all recognised
the value of Hebridean fisheries to the newly fledged Union of England
and Scotland. Moll had been the maker of Martin's new map of the
Western Isles (Martin 1994, 2–3). Two years after the publication of
Moll's map of all Scotland, John Chamberlayne FRS, citing Martin as
his informant, wrote in *Magnæ Britanniæ Notitia* that, with English
investment, these fisheries which were the best in Europe would become
'one of the Blessings which this Island will reap by the late Happy
Union', and that, 'the Settling of a Fishery in those Parts, will raise a
Nursery of stout and able Seamen in a very short time, to serve the
Government on all Occasions' (Chamberlayne 1716, 384). In other
words, the fishing grounds would be good recruiting grounds for the
Royal Navy and building up the Empire. See also Clough 1994, and a
major new study of the colonisation of the Hebrides published as this
book was undergoing its final edit, MacCoinnich 2015.

10. Macdonald 2004, 220.

11. Johnson & Boswell 1984, 51.

12. The purchase of the land by the North Harris Trust involved a private
partner who bought the parts of the estate in which the community
were not interested, namely, Amhuinnsuidhe Castle and its associated
salmon fishing. The funds required for the land purchase were received
from a multitude of private donors, the John Muir Trust (JMT),
Comhairle nan Eilean (the Western Isles Council) and Scottish Natural

Heritage, plus local fundraising events and such statutory sources as the Scottish Government's land fund. David Cameron, the inaugural chair of the Trust, has asked me to mention that the JMT, which is dedicated to the conservation of wilderness areas, put no conditions on the community in making its contribution. The relationship with JMT operates by mutual respect, similar to the pattern established with the Scottish Wildlife Trust's community partnership on Eigg.

The Trust's board is elected by local residents, the area having a population of about seven hundred people. Its guiding goal is adapted from the definition of 'sustainable development' from the Brundtland Commission of the United Nations: namely, to further 'forms of progress that meet the needs of the present without compromising the ability of future generations to meet their needs'. Further information from http://www.north-harris.org.

13. The incident with the bucket might have been a separate occasion, I don't remember clearly. There was more than one such scare, as polecats also made an appearance in our part of the island at about the same time.

After the shooting, I skinned the poor beast, tanned its hide with a chromium product called Sheeptan, and proudly presented it like ermine to my mother. She was underwhelmed, pointing out that she'd need rather a lot to make as much as a stole. According to my sister's friends, I also had a penchant for presenting prospective girlfriends with tanned mice and rabbit skins. Apparently, the story of the uranium, told in Chapter 17, was not an isolated instance. Casanova never knew the likes!

14. See Dwelly's Gaelic dictionary entry for 'moon'. The old names for the moon are from the South Uist poet, Angus Peter Campbell, https://goo.gl/lzKDnN.

8 The Rising of the Sìth

1. Thomson 2001, 86.
2. Campbell & Hall 2006, 7 (Vikings), xiii (Jung).
3. Email from Iain Thornber, 25 November 2011.
4. Same Thornber email as above, with attached extract from his stalking journal, entitled: *Glengalmadale and the Oiteag Sluagh*.
5. See her elegiac account of this transhumance, Starmore 2012. Alice is best known for her books of knitting designs.
6. Starmore 2008, 60.
7. This is Cath MacKinven's view. For discussion of spelling variations and nuances between sìth and síd, and the relationship between faeries and peace, see Black's commentary in Campbell 2005, especially p. 293. I should emphasise that, as one who does not have the Gaelic other than a smattering of words, I should not be considered an authority on these matters.

8. Campbell 2005, xxxiii, 41; Yeats 1990, 38.
9. Evans-Wentz 1994, 8, xxxiv.
10. LaViolette & McIntosh 1997.
11. Corbin 1969, 248. *Le monde imaginal* = the imaginal world, or realm. See also (in French) www.amiscorbin.com.
12. Genesis 6:5, 11. Swire 1966, 63-65. Otta Swire was writing for a popular readership and usually fails to give her sources. They seem to be a mixture of existing writings such as Martin Martin, and personal experience. As a child, her family would be guests of the Mathesons at Lews Castle in Stornoway. While her writings do not attain the standards of modern folklore studies, the ethnographer Ronald Black, in his introduction to her book on Skye, warmly praises her achievement none the less.
13. John MacAulay pers. com. suggests, *lys* = light; *kyntyre* = headland. The sands of gold story is from Swire 1966, 74.
14. This quote is the context of the illustration on the cover of Glacken 1973.
15. Isaiah 28:16, KJV.
16. Carmichael 1900, 190–195, '*Laoidh an Triall* – Hymn of the Procession'. I have omitted two verses, and the last verse is specific to the version collected from the Barra fishermen.

9 *Two Airmen*

1. Mrs Cecil Frances Alexander, who wrote 'All Things Bright and Beautiful', was born in colonial Ireland but had a deep spiritual sensitivity and a concern for the poor. However, her politics in this verse may have been shaped by her English father having been the land agent (factor) for the Earl of Wicklow.
2. Paraphrased, partly in my own words, from 1 Samuel 8.
3. Luther's 'On the Jews and their Lies' (1543) reproduced in Lund 2002, 76–78. Steigmann-Gall (2004) quoting Goebbels (p. 21), Koch (p. 2), Himmler (p. 235), 'favoured nation' etc. (p. 15).
4. Fromm 2001, 77 & 32, my emphasis. Fromm explores both the Lutheran and Calvinist backdrops to Nazism in his chapter, 'Freedom in the Age of the Reformation' (pp. 33–88).
5. Smith 2006, 25 & 237.
6. McIntosh 2011.
7. King 2000, 70. For a more complete exposition of the case I put to the military for nonviolence, see my paper in the textbook edited by UK Defence Academy staff, McIntosh 2011.
8. Like many sayings attributed to Gandhi, this is loosely based on translations from the Hindi, but is consistent with material in such anthologies as Merton 1965.
9. John 18:11; Luke 22:51; John 18:36–37.

10. Câmara 1971.
11. Sylvester & Thomson 2007.

10 *Rule, Britannia!*

1. MacDiarmid 1985, 422 ff., 'On a Raised Beach'.
2. John 18:36–37. It may be objected that twice in the gospels, Christ appears to raise the sword – Matthew 10:34 and Luke 22:36. However, in the first case this is clearly as a metaphor, and in the second, it is symbolically to fulfil a prophesy of Isaiah's that he would be seen as a brigand.
3. Calvin 1553, commentary to John 10:35.
4. Longley 2002; Hietala 2003. In contrast to Calvin's interpretation of power in Romans, Walter Wink (1992) holds that, in human hands, power becomes fallen, can be redeemed, and must therefore be called constantly back to its higher, God-given vocation.
5. Boettner 1932, 275–281.
6. Oppenheimer 2014. Calvinistic Baptists are often known as 'strict' or 'particular' Baptists because of their sense of being a 'particular' or Elect people.
7. Lugar 1999.
8. Mansfield 2000, 68 (my emphasis), 109.
9. BBC 2001.
10. Jack 2011.
11. Rumsfeld 2011, 59.
12. Thompson 2009; Draper 2009.
13. John 18:11; Matthew 26:52.
14. Jones 2005.
15. Thomas 1859. I have corrected 'boths' to *bothan*. See also Thomas 1867 and Mackenzie 1904.
16. Mitchell 1880, 58–72.

11 *Venison and Honey*

1. My contemporary, Rusty (John Macdonald) of Leurbost, tells me that as children they'd be told not to go out to the loch alone, 'in case the each-uisgue gets you'.
2. My use of 'mythopoetic' is based on the more correct 'mythopoeic'; however, the latter is usually used to suggest a *fictional* narrative. I consider that there is nothing fictional about poetry. Poetry is primarily the heart's mode of direct perception of reality. It is engagement with *poesis* as 'the making' of reality. My usage overlaps with, but does not imply any necessary connection to, Robert Bly's use in the context of the Men's Movement, where the mythopoetic means the use of myth specifically to aid self-understanding. The sense of myth as being

something that is untrue, is a usage that dates only to the mid nineteenth century.

3. Yeats 1990, 120–1.

4. From a Biblical perspective, Jesus never promised us the letters of Paul, or Hebrews. If we go by Saint John's gospel (e.g. 14:16–18), he only promised us the Paraclete – the discerning power of the Spirit – and that is the standard to which all subsequent scriptural exegesis should be subordinate.

5. In Gordon 2006, 12, my emphasis.

6. Smith 1919, 19–20.

7. McKay 1932. See also Ó Crualaoich 2003, 124, about Ireland, and Ronnie Black's discussion in Campbell 2005, 306–8. The Gundestrup cauldron suggests a shamanic relationship with the deer.

8. MacInnes 2006, 500. This is from the abstract, prepared by Michael Newton, of John's paper, *Am Fàsach ann an Dùthchas nan Gàidheal*.

9. 'Looking at Legends of the Supernatural', MacInnes 2006, 459–76. John MacInnes draws explicitly on Jungian psychology in this essay. Although born in Uig in 1930, his family moved to Raasay, off Skye, before he was eight.

10. Black (in Campbell 2005, lxxx) alludes to this line of Loch Ness Monster interpretation, but his promised Note 151 turns out to be about something else. My memory of his thesis is from one of his columns in the *West Highland Free Press* in the 1990s. Black also draws attention to Campbell's view that, properly speaking, the each-uisge is of the loch and the kelpie of the river (p. 372).

11. MacInnes 2006, 500.

12. MacInnes 2006, 459–76, including remaining quotes, this section.

13. This was Norman's letter of 21 November 2001, five pages of typescript, written about two years before his death. It said: 'I thank you above all for the dogged perseverance with which you resisted the rape of fair maid Harris by corporate powers and the help you enlisted from such unlikely quarters as Chief Sulian Stone Eagle Herney. I like his conclusions: *If we fail to find the solution and cure for Mother Earth, Mother Earth will cleanse herself of the offending organism that is killing her.*' However, Norman took issue with some of my interfaith appreciation, saying: 'Your theology as far as I can follow it, leans too much towards the New Agery that is sweeping the world, a mish mash of all faiths and deities male and female stirred into one unholy *brochan* in the belief that it cannot do you any harm as there is no God anyway (Psalm 14).' So – that was me, fair told! It's a good example of how the island way of mentoring between an older and a younger man will proceed with praise in the one moment, and reprimand in the next.

14. For typical examples of the second sight from the records of Fr Allan McDonald of Eriskay, see material reproduced in Part 4 of Campbell & Hall 2006. The degree to which these stories continue to circulate in local culture is remarkable. Literally as I was final-editing this passage,

the '60 years ago' section of the *Stornoway Gazette* reproduced a report of 20 December 1955 about the 'Benbecula seer' who stopped his work, and announced: 'The minister's son has been drowned on Loch Langavate and they cannot find him; but I "see" the body.' The man went to join the search party, they dragged the loch at the place of his vision, and recovered the body. This story was at least third hand and could be considered indicative of a genre but not reliable – though were it untrue, locals would quickly say. Others come first or second hand. The case with my mother and the dog is written up in full in McIntosh 2008, 200–3.

15. Kirk in Stewart 1990, 39–45. Tarbett, also spelled Tarbat.
16. Bennett 2009. For an insight into the degree to which the second sight continues in modern times, see Watt 1989.
17. Clough 1994.
18. 'To be born . . .', from Barrie's introduction to the 1913 edition of my favourite childhood book, R.M. Ballantyne's *The Coral Island* (cited in Moral 2013, 201). 'To die . . .', from the end of Act III, Barrie 1928.
19. Livingstone 1870, 12.

12 *Catching Mary Rose*

1. Campbell 2011: 'Of course the past awakens a sense of nostalgia . . . *Cianalas* – that Gaelic sense of wistful longing – is a great word but a horrible feeling.'
2. Donald J. Macleod of Bridge of Don, see Macleod 2015, 15. I use his estimate (below) about the 700 souls. Most of the households would have been extended families with elderly maiden aunts etc. as part of the typical household.
3. The designation, Seaforth Highlanders, was used in Mackenzie's recruitment campaign of 1793 (see below), but it was not until 1881 that the Seaforth Highlanders were formally created within the British Army, following merger of the Ross-Shire Buffs with the Duke of Albany's Own Highlanders.
4. 'Very severe' – from Napier 1884 (Vol. 2), 859. Reports from *The Times* of 1839 in Macleod 2015, 31.
5. Roberts 1999, 142–147. Mackenzie 1903, 187–188.
6. Sources and discussion in McIntosh 2013.
7. Johnston 1929, 203.
8. Duncan 1995, 74. In contrast, the present proprietors of Scarp, the Bakewell family (hello Petra!), have always been welcome on Harris, the more so now that they have brought in investment to open up the Isle of Harris Distillery at Tarbert – the world's first commercial 'social distillery', as it proudly calls itself.

Kinlochresort itself continued to be sparsely occupied into relatively recent times, but clearances of the villages to the north and south meant that no road was ever put in, leading to the settlement's complete abandonment in 1963.

9. Pers. com. from Maureen Russell of Bridge of Weir, 4 May 2015. Her mother, the daughter of Peggy and William, was Morag MacKay of Ardnacille, of Scalpay.

    Commenting on this, Kenneth Macleod, a mariner of Scalpay, has said (pers. com. email 23 April 2015): 'People of that generation were very strong spiritually and would have regularly prayed outdoors . . . I remember coming across a neighbour, who was an elder in the church, praying in his byre a couple of hours after we had buried their cow which had died in the field. There are similar stories of people having praying points in the moor which they would go to regularly. Sometimes I think we have lost that total dependence on God and prayer to help with everyday things like food, safety and general activities.'

10. Mackenzie 1904.

11. Sorley Maclean's 'Hallaig', in Dunn 1992, 129–33. Web version http://goo.gl/hJoCDG. For commentary, see MacInnes 2006, 418–21. At the end of this book, where I return to Hallaig, my source for Dun Cana (or Dun Caan) as a sìthean of bards, into the present, is Newton 2006b, 329 (footnote). I did not want to place the footnote there as it would have disrupted the emotion.

12. Interview with John Russell Taylor, Gottlieb 1995, 59–63.

13. Moral 2013, 44, 209–18 (on *Times* and non-commercial prospects). Truffaut 1985, 307–9 (on irrationality). Moral's chapter, 'Mary Rose', became available in a later edition of his book only when I was at a late stage of editing. It offers a comprehensive overview of the scattered sources.

14. Sainte-Marie 1964.

15. Crossman 2003, my emphasis.

16. Mark 5:1–20; Luke 8:26–39. The account is in Josephus, Book 3:7.

17. Freud 1997. Freud 1984, 380–381. Freud did not use the term Thanatos (after the Greek god of death). Rather, it was later applied to his concept of the 'death instinct'.

18. Gampel 2000, my emphasis.

19. Hogg 1919.

20. Davis 2006, 13 & 35, xiii.

21. Barrie 1922. Dunbar 1970, 271–6. One critic who appreciates Barrie's dramatic importance and refuses to have him relegated to the kailyard, is Jack 1991, 21–4.

13 Smoking Out the Devil

1. Black in Campbell 2005, 293. These quotations are Black summarising Ó Cathasaigh's thoughts.

2. Herdsboy in Macaulay 1980, 97. Finlay's people, Maclean 1925, 151.

3. This peak is the reclined woman's nose of the so-called 'Sleeping Beauty' complex. There is an archival recording in the School of Scottish Studies of an old man of nearby Airighbhruthach telling how, when he was a child, it was pointed out to him as being 'the Silver of the Faeries' (MacLennan 1976).

4. Often, today, a purely Norse derivation is suggested – *sja-fjörör* – 'sea firth'. However, the sapper maps, surveyed in the early 1850s, used variant spellings. These included *shìthford* and *sheaford*. Their intention does seem to have been to convey *sìth*, but perhaps in the sense of *peace*, as this highly contorted loch was long renowned for providing safe anchorages in any direction of the wind.

5. Macdonald 2004, 85. There is some question as to the exact site at Seaforth Head. Macdonald (2004, 84–6, 89–90) holds that it was at the stone circle site on Croft 6, but Christopher Macrae (pers. com, telephone, 2 March 2016), the present Head Keeper and grandson of Macdonald's source, Duncan Macrae, tells me that he always understood it to be a few hundred yards to the east, at the point on the road below where the present-day memorial to the Seaforth Highlanders was erected by Mr Ian Mitchell of Stornoway. This view would be consistent with the presence there of a mound with substantial stone foundations. Seumas Crawford thinks that it was a on a nearby island in the sea loch.

6. Katie would, of course, have been thoroughly versed in passages like Ezekiel 11:19.

7. John MacInnes, Saint Bride's Day Lecture, University of Edinburgh, 1 February 1996, oral delivery.

8. Yeats 1990, 92–5. Margaret Bennett has remarked that, within her own island family and locality, traditional belief had no need for labels to separate one category of experience from another, as 'the entire system is simply taken for granted'. This can 'range over an extensive continuum of belief in God, the Holy Spirit, the Devil, angels, saints, fairies, ghosts, spirits of the dead . . . and so on' (Bennett 2009, 179).

9. Mary Kate Maclennan of Seaforth Head died on Sunday 13 May 2012. Although I mentioned her in *Soil and Soul* (p. 25), it was only in the last two years of her life that I had the opportunity to spend several evenings with her, and a subsequent wonderful visit with my son, Adam. I have back-written this aside into the pilgrimage story by way of a reflection on a rainy morning. I also used part of my story with her in *Island Spirituality*. In March 2015 I sent a copy of this to her sister, Mary Ann Mackenzie of Totescore, Skye, who I had chanced to meet on Harris as they were a Luskentyre family. She wrote back saying: 'The book will be a forever reminder of how dear Ceiteag was to the family and the people she met and held dear.' I mention that, because it would be easy, in today's world, to doubt the very existence of such a person; or to question how they might be esteemed within their own families and communities. For more on this theme, see McIntosh 2013, 81–2 and Watt 1989.

10. 'Never needed therapists' was the late Dr Donald Murray of Back, later-ally of Crossbost.

11. For referencing of these and following remarks, see Chapter 3 of McIntosh 2013 (now free online at the web link). Also, biography in Surtees 1984.

12. Again, references and more detail in McIntosh 2013.

13. Macdonald 2004, 99. Calvinism had been the religion 'by law estab-lished' in Scotland since 1560, but Macdonald is referring to its hard-line expression on Lewis, to which I have applied the loose term hyper-Cal-vinism. I use that term in its more traditional sense of holding a belief in 'limited atonement', though it could be argued that such is just plain *Calvinism*, and such is what Macdonald means.

    The paradox of most island Calvinist preachers, including Alexander Macleod, is that they adhere to the Westminster Confession's doctrine of limited atonement – 'Neither are any other redeemed by Christ . . . but the elect only' (WCF 1647, 3:VI) – but, at the same time, teach justifica-tion by faith through freely-offered grace, *as if* anyone so choosing 'to turn to Christ' can be 'saved'. Quite how this sits with the Arminian heresy that they otherwise repudiate, is complex to fathom.

14. Macleod was well aware that these clearances, two years after his arrival, reflected poorly on him. In one of his begging letters to Lady Mary, he requested that his sheep might graze land other than that which she was in the process of clearing for his benefit, 'as some of them are foolishly disposed to blame me for their removal'. He worried, lest 'this circumstance may render my gospel ministration unsuccessful' (Macaulay 1980, 182).

15. Macleod 2015.

16. MacFarlane 1995, detailed citations in McIntosh 2013.

17. Macleod 1925. His letters to Lady Mary in Macaulay 1980, 181–4. Kennedy 1979, 98. Again, see McIntosh 2013 for a more complete exploration of these themes.

18. MacCoinnich 2015, 243.

19. Fanon 1967. Freire 1972, 122.

20. Walker 1983, 225. The gin, a hand-cranked machine for teasing out cotton fibres on the plantations, epitomised forced labour.

21. Augustine, *City of God*, XX:22, http://goo.gl/FMEYd8, and XXII:30, http://goo.gl/1wBgWu.

22. Luke 1:51–3, NRSV.

23. MacColl 2006, 169–78.

14 *Saint Bridgit's Sheiling*

1. 2 John 4:18.

2. Luke 4:17–20, reading from Isaiah 61:1–2, KJV.

3. Thomson 1982, 172–3, used with the late poet's kind permission.

4. Scots Psalter of 1615, the paraphrase of Psalm 121.

5. Macleod 1911. With Cath's approval, I have abridged her translation, placing some of Kenneth's original turns of phrase in quotation marks to better catch their nuances. Cath died in October 2014.

   Macleod's story could be an account of the *bardo* journey of the dying process, straight from *The Tibetan Book of the Dead*. The women start off in what I would describe as the *shamanic function* that mediates between the worlds, there to perform 'keening' songs that ease a soul's transition through the watery veils of death. However, tempted by revenge for their sufferings, their gift of blessing turns to venom. They slide into the *malefic function* of becoming sorceresses of the dark arts. It is one thing to withhold blessing, but quite another to curse. Later, as their consciences awake, they rise to the *prophetic function*. Compassion leaves them as the handmaids of redemptive love.

6. Carmichael 1900, 172.

7. At an ecumenical service held in Griminish Church in 2006 as part of an academic conference, Canon Angus MacQueen of South Uist and Barra said of Alexander Carmichael: 'I realised that [as children] we were still living in the world of Carmichael, moving gently to the rhythm of the passing seasons, conscious of the hand of God guiding our path . . . I realise how sensitive his approach to our prayer life was, as if he were eavesdropping on the private life of those old folk who included their God in every passing moment of the day' (MacQueen 2008). What Carmichael saved in the six volumes of the *Carmina Gadelica* endures, in part, as a continuous living tradition and not merely as a burnished fossil.

8. Adomnán 1995, 200, 218, and Sharpe's commentary on the place names (p. 368).

9. Ó Crualaoich 2003, 139–40; 184–5. Davidson 1998, 67. Maclean 1964.

10. Carmichael 1883, 460.

11. Exodus 20:25, NLT. The Hebrew *chereb,* usually translated as 'tool', literally means a sword. As such, this passage metaphorically says that the altar of God should not be built on a foundation carved out by violence.

12. Shaw 2001, 59. The late Walter Wink alerted me to this in his discussion of imagination, Wink 2002.

15 The Baptism of the Gods

1. Black 1999, 719. The Macleod quote is from one of his 'Footnotes' columns in the *West Highland Free Press* from around 2009, but I have lost the original cutting.

2. Disraeli 1845, 43.

3. Plato's *Timaeus*, 37d, trans. Jowett. 'Wherefore he [the Father creator] resolved to have a moving image of eternity, and when he set in order the heaven, he made this image eternal but moving according to number, while eternity itself rests in unity; and this image we call time.'

4. Charlton 2008, 13.
5. Scholars of folklore have explored faerie as a set of 'retrieval codes' to talk about borderline issues, including mental illness, disability and child abuse. See Black 2005, li–lxvi.
6. Barrie 1925, 93, 139.
7. Newton 2006b. On Tìr-fo-thuinn (below) see Macleod 1927, 59–63.
8. Meyer 2000. This choice of verses are a medley of my own compilation. Emain Ablach is the land of apples, of which Avalon is another version, both overlapping with if not the same as Tìr nan Òg.
9. Carey 1999, 11–12, 32. This John Carey, the medievalist, is not to be confused with the Oxford literary critic.
10. Carey 1999, 34, 29.
11. Carey 1999, 38.
12. Carey 1999, 106, 91, 106. Blake: 'To the Eyes of the Man of Imagination, Nature is Imagination itself.'
13. See, for example, Jussie 2006, 122. Also www.re-soundings.com.

16 The Great Cosmic Poacher

1. James 2000, viii, xv.
2. Luther 1546. However, he dropped this dismissal, and other judgements on James, in the 1522 edition.
3. Epistle of James 2:18–26, 5:15, 1:10–11.
4. Epistle of James 4:1. I have used both the KJV and NRSV to combine both poetry and clarity.
5. Wynne-Jones 2009 quoting mostly from Burton & McCabe 2009.
6. Hofstadter 1996, 3–4. I hit on Parker, BBC 2016, just as this was going to press and in the same context of Donald Trump's psychology. The presidential runner self-identifies as Presbyterian and attributes his religious values to his mother, who was an émigré from the Isle of Lewis (at a time when it was mainly the men who emigrated). I have explored aspects of this relationship in a poetic work, McIntosh 2012; see also McIntosh 2013 on island religious psychohistory. Trump's narcissistic psychology fits the thesis of this book concerning disarticulation between the inner and the outer life. He appears to be a man for whom everything is on the outside, with little empathy and high narcissism. This might connect with any family trauma that he himself carries from both parents' separation from their home countries, but also, especially given the Hebridean Calvinist backdrop, with the trauma arguably carried by America's Protestant conservative evangelicals with their often binary world-view. An irony is that Hebridean evangelicals are mostly evangelical and socially conservative, but not politically conservative, because they have retained the strong and empathetic links to community that an émigré loses – see my discussion in Chapter 11. For my research on

the 1820s MacKenzie clearances of Trump's maternal ancestors, see https://goo.gl/zzCMB8.

7. BBC 2003.
8. Wink 1992.
9. Clausewitz 2008, 13.
10. Luke 6:27; Matthew 5:44. The ear – John 18:10-11; Luke 22:49–54.
11. Because, within my own community on the Isle of Lewis, there is little mileage to be had in arguing about the authenticity of what has been handed down in the Bible, I tend to argue from face value, and therefore metaphorically. However, there is now a vast literature on authenticity based mainly on textual analysis. An accessible synopsis of scholarly thought are the findings of the Jesus Seminar (Funk & Hoover 1993), though I think sometimes they miss the metaphorical possibilities in some of the texts that they consider improbably attributed to Jesus.
12. Matthew 10:34; John 2:12–22 where the ambiguity is mainly around the Greek, *te*, and which the NIV translates as: 'So he made a whip out of cords, and drove all from the temple courts, *both* sheep and cattle; he scattered the coins of the money changers and overturned their tables'. Luke 36:38, 'And he was reckoned among the transgressors' quotes Isaiah 53:12. In exploring such texts I roam between the multiple translations now available on sites like www.BibleHub.com, especially looking at the Greek and Hebrew originals and the semantic range of key translated words.
13. Also in Matthew 20:28. Paul (or attributed to him) in 1 Timothy 2:6.
14. Isaiah 53:10.
15. Saint Gregory in McGrath 1997, 397–8. The line in the Apostles' Creed probably hinges on 1 Peter 3:9 – Christ 'preached unto the spirits in prison.' Catholic and Protestant traditions differ in their interpretations. On atonement theories and nonviolence, see Weaver 2001.
16. Anselm in McGrath 1995, 182–3.
17. Calvin 1559, 2:16.1–2.
18. Like with predestination, penal substitution is pivotal to the Calvinist worldview. In his newspaper column, one moderator of the Free Church – a man for whose ministry I nevertheless have much respect – called for, 'a healthy emphasis on the central tenet of the Christian faith: the penal, substitutionary atonement of Christ' (Campbell 2012).
19. 'Sligo' in Ferguson 2007, 187.
20. Colossians 1:17.
21. Council of Jerusalem, Acts 15:20 (where Paul and Barnabas were the messengers). Numbers 15:32–36 (sticks) & Exodus 35:3 (fire). Heschel 2011, 150–4 (essay on 'The Sabbath').
22. Calvin 1555.

17 Sages of Shawbost

1. Kenneth Macleod, a seaman of Scalpay, email pers. com. 23 April 2015.
2. Quotes that follow – Luke 3:11; 1 John 4:16. *U-vil* is Kenneth Macleod's rendition of the oystercatcher's call, see 'St Bride's Bird' in Macleod 1927, 101–2. Also, for the bird in less plaintive mood he suggests *Fal liu o* (p. 48).

18 Fléchettes in the Soul

1. Dymes 1630. On Dymes and the English 'planters' (i.e. colonisers) of Stornoway, see MacCoinnich 2015, 321–5.
2. Ferguson 2007, 2. The Hebrews quotation, above, is 6:19.
3. MacLeod 1997, 18. The diocese of Sodor was formed in the Norse era and extended down the Hebrides and West Highlands to the Isle of Man, where the name is still retained. Kenneth Macleod mentions the 'Sodor Isles' in poetry (Macleod 1927, 49).
4. Macleod 1927, 101, 40.
5. Gunn 1986, 20.
6. ABC 2010. Thompson & Drury 2010. The Psalms verse is confirmed on a (transient) soldier web forum, 'British 3 Rifle Infantry MTP' at https://goo.gl/qF1xoy.
7. In my brief time in the museum I did not have chance to pick up on this detail. What is written here has been filled in by later research into fléchettes in general. Also, the ABC news story did not break until a year after my walk. I have back-written it in as the pilgrimage continued to take shape in my mind during the years that I wrote this book.
8. Inspired by a passage in Hennessey 2009, 252–3.
9. Dostoevsky, *Notes from Underground,* as in the editorial extract used by McDuff in Doestoevsky 1991, xvii.
10. Clément 1993, 303. Where Jesus said he came 'to bring fire to the earth' (Luke 12:49), this can be read as Hellfire, the fire of the Spirit, and/or the fire of love. What reading might the overall spirit of Jesus suggest?
11. Dostoevsky 1998, 402–4 (see also 206).
12. Psalm 82:6, quoted by Jesus to defend himself against blasphemy in John 10:34. 'Let it be' (below) – Luke 1:38 KJV – which other translations render as, 'Let it be . . .', including the famous version according to Saint Paul of Liverpool.

19 The Temple of Crò Naomh

1. See Barrowman 2008. Her work was not readily available until 2014, but it now adds rich context and factual information to the temple sites discussed here. For my purposes, I've held to a folk focus with Dr Finlay MacLeod's handbook, and not tried to be an archaeologist.

2. I didn't see the horseshoe because of the fenceposts. I was later given this information by Jill Smith, author and artist of Àird Uig, who regularly attends the well. In the early noughties, she was told by an old woman who lived in the nearby house that her brother-in-law had set the horseshoe imprint into the cement cap 'for luck'. She added that the lady – who had looked her in the eyes, grasped her by the arm, and taken her to see the well – 'told me how she and another lady cleaned the well, by filling it with stones, then taking them out and while the water was low, scouring it with heather. She said it never ran dry, and people came from miles around in times of drought (from Carloway) and would sit for an hour waiting for their pail to fill. Oh the pace of life then.' Pers. com. emails 12/13 November 2015.

3. MacLeod 2009, quote below from p. 47.

4. Campbell 2005, 558, with Black's commentary on p. 598. See also Dwelly's and Maclennan's dictionaries.

5. Thomas 1890, 374. Captain Thomas credits Sir James Matheson with stopping the destruction of island archaeological sites (p. 375). Many of these would be robbed for building stones once the old superstitions had worn off with the advent of modernity and evangelicalism. Doctor Finlay writes: 'An Old Norse word for fort is Borgh, and Bhuirgh is the genitive' (email 26 January 2016). In Ireland, sìthean are commonly referred to as 'faerie forts', these being to where the original mythological inhabitants of the land retreated when the Milesians (us) arrived, bearing weapons of iron, such as would have chopped down the forests and destroyed the primordial ecology.

6. Pierre 2005, 69–70. My thanks to Joëlle Nicolas, my mother-in-law, a theologian of French Huguenot (Calvinist) extraction, for drawing my attention to this passage and helping me to translate it.

   Orthodox theologians, and probably also J. Denny Weaver (Weaver 2001) with whom I have discussed this matter, would argue that Liberation Theory is only a new representation of *Christus Victor*, and that a liberationist praxis is what the Church Fathers were always trying to express with their imagery of the Devil. Perhaps, but such imagery needs dusting down and rendered fit for future purpose, which is what Walter Wink has done with his Jungian exegesis of the Powers that Be.

7. Wink 2002, 109–10. Walter Wink's critique of blood sacrifice atonement theories here are of huge future importance.

8. Panikkar 1991. I have tided up the quote into the version that my colleague Alastair Hulbert, myself and others used with Panikkar when we hosted an event with him in Govan, Scotland, in 1990 – http://goo.gl/Rnikab.

9. Maxim Gorky, *The Lower Depths*, 1903.

10. Gunn 1986. 'Inner light' is based on John 1:9, known as 'the Quaker text'. Consider also Luke 12:49.

11. Starr 2014, 13.

20 *The Heart of the Sun*

1. Macleod 1908, footnote.
2. OCA 2016.
3. In Brock & Parker 2008, 173. Clement of Alexandria came out with pithy statements, like: 'Everything belongs to the God of beauty; everything subsists in the God of beauty' (Ibid., 167). Although venerated as a saint in the Eastern church, the Western church (or Rome) bumped him off its list of saints during the sixteenth century purge of the aptly-named Cardinal Caesar Baronius. Just possibly, Clement was ahead of his time. In 'The Rich Man's Salvation', he insisted on the spiritual equality of women, and had a penchant for gender-bending statements, like: 'God . . . to us became feminine. In His ineffable essence He is Father; in His compassion to us He became Mother' (Chapter 37, http://goo.gl/DhyGuH).
4. Eliot 1959, 51.
5. Luke 22:19 (*anamnēsin*); Acts 3:21 (*apocatastasis*); 2 Peter 3:12, James 5:7, etc. (*parousia*). These mystical Greek words of the New Testament resonate with Plato's concept of time and eternity that was touched on in Chapter 15.
6. Marsden 1995.
7. Ward 1984, via *Orthodox Church Quotes*, http://goo.gl/kXmjON.
8. Carmichael 1900, 322–5.
9. MacInnes 2009, 186. Apparently she was Presbyterian too, but sometimes the old ways linger.
10. MacDonald 1994, 63–69. This remarkable interview includes: 'Gaelic has its own culture. How will I put it? It's bardic. Gaelic songs are full of love and feeling and passion and emotion. Take the word "dear" or "darling" . . . Gaelic has about 70 words for that.' Not bad for one of the most hard-line Calvinists of my childhood. Shows what richness can lie behind the stereotypes.

21 *The Woman at the Well*

1. Martin 1994, 106–8. Mackenzie 1903, 524–7.
2. Carmichael 1900, 126–7. The identification of the *cionaran-crò* with the pilot of a pod of whales comes from Professor Donald Meek.
3. Martin 1994, 100–104.
4. Carmichael 1900b, 270–2. 'Children of men' – the italics are Carmichael quoting within the quote, I'd guess, as a reference to the apocalyptic imagery of Psalms 90:3 and 115:16 KJV. Campbell 2012, 63–4, recounts a similar version of this legend from his own South Uist background, observing that it speaks to 'a very different ecological environment to the one we have today . . . it creates a wholly different aesthetic – indeed a wholly different cosmology.'

Dòmhnall Uilleam Stiùbhart, who headed the Carmichael Watson Project at Edinburgh University until recently, tells me that he thinks the poem Carmichael refers to will be the one archived at CW150/56 – 59 at http://goo.gl/YW6mNO (pers. com. 2015). The text appears to be fragmentary and mostly not (yet) translated into English. Its source was Mary MacMillan, a domestic servant from Lionacuith, South Uist.

5. See my chapter in McIntosh 2008, 107–39.

6. Swire 1966, 63–65.

7. In 2014, it was my great pleasure to be asked by Dr Domhnall Uilleam Stiùbhart to serve as a referee with his application to have the Carmichael Watson Collection at the University of Edinburgh granted *Memory of the World* recognition by UNESCO. See *The Herald*, Glasgow, 19 June 2014, and my subsequent Letter to the Editor, McIntosh 2014b. The application was a success. The world has recognised the deep spiritual heritage of the Hebrides. The rest is over to us.

Index

Note: Topographical names are generally given using the most common spelling. Where this is English, the Gaelic equivalent (if appropriate) is given in brackets. Entries such as 302n refer to the endnotes.